WITHDRAWN

Kenneth Woodbridge

Landscape and Antiquity

Aspects of English Culture at Stourhead 1718 to 1838

Kenneth Woodbridge

Landscape and Antiquity

Aspects of English Culture at Stourhead 1718 to 1838

CLARENDON PRESS · OXFORD · 1970

Oxford University Press   *Ely House, London W.1*

Glasgow	Bombay
New York	Calcutta
Toronto	Madras
Melbourne	Karachi
Wellington	Lahore
Cape Town	Dacca
Salisbury	Kuala Lumpur
Ibadan	Singapore
Nairobi	Hong Kong
Dar es Salaam	Tokyo
Lusaka	
Addis Ababa	

Made and printed in Great Britain by
William Clowes and Sons, Limited
London and Beccles

Preface

The hall at Stourhead in Wiltshire is dominated by two portraits; one of the second Henry Hoare (Pl. 22a); the other of his grandson, Sir Richard Colt Hoare (Pl. 24b). The first is of a young man on a rearing life-size horse, and conveys the idea of someone active and outward looking, although this may be just the energy and swagger of youth. The painting opposite shows a scholarly-looking man, standing before a landscape which might be Italian. He holds a drawing and a portfolio, and seems unaware of the fresh-faced boy who pulls at his arm and points beyond the picture. Both these men devoted much of their lives to giving shape among the Wiltshire Downs to their generation's conception of 'antiquity', with very different and in each case outstanding results. Their characteristic contributions to Stourhead are respectively the landscape and the library. But whereas Henry Hoare imposed a classical vision on the Wiltshire countryside, Colt Hoare, the contemporary of Constable and Wordsworth, recorded what he saw, most notably in the various volumes of his histories of *Ancient* and *Modern Wiltshire*.

This book originated in the study of an eighteenth-century landscape garden. Its scope, however, goes far beyond this, for it covers the lives of two men, and a period from 1700 to 1838 when, as Mr. Christopher Hussey has put it, 'the relation of all the arts to one another, through the pictorial appreciation of nature, was so close that poetry, painting, gardening, architecture and the art of travel may be said to have been fused into the single "art of landscape"'.[1] To that list the appreciation of antiquity can be added, particularly in the present context where it constitutes the bond between the two halves of this book.

Henry Hoare's Paradise was first published in *The Art Bulletin* and is here included in a revised and extended form.

The partners of Hoare's Bank have generously contributed towards the cost of the illustrations; and I am greatly indebted to Mr. H. P. R. Hoare not only for access to family papers, but for his interest and useful comment over a number of years. The Marquess of Ailesbury has been very kind in making available letters to his ancestor, the first Earl of Ailesbury, who was Henry Hoare's son-in-law. Without these we should lack the graphic picture of the man in his later years.

[1] Christopher Hussey, *The Picturesque* (1967 ed.), p. 4.

The National Trust, which now owns Stourhead, has extended me many courtesies besides permission to publish material from the Stourhead Archive in the Wiltshire County Record Office at Trowbridge. I would especially like to thank Commander Geoffrey Palmer and Mr. Thomas Sherwood.

Without the encouragement of Mr. Richard Sandell, Librarian of the Wiltshire Archaeological Society, I might never have embarked on the story of Sir Richard Colt Hoare. I am grateful to him in many ways; as well as to Mr. Maurice Rathbone, the Archivist for Wiltshire, and to Mr. K. H. Rogers and Miss P. Rundle for their expert advice and assistance.

My thanks are also due to the following: Lt. Col. J. L. B. Leicester-Warren for kindly allowing me to see the Tabley Records; Mr. R. M. D. Winder, Archivist to Messrs. Hoare and Company; Mr. T. Hopkins, Archivist to the Cardiff City Library; Mr. Brian Redwood, Cheshire County Archivist; Mr. Ivor Collis, Somerset County Archivist; the Librarian of the Society of Antiquaries; the Somerset Archaeological Society, and the staff of the Bath Reference Library.

I am indebted to Professor Stuart Piggott and Mr. L. V. Grinsell for their comments on *The Rape of the Barrows*; and I have to thank Mr. H. C. Bowen for information about Steeple Langford Cow Down and help with the illustrations concerning it. Mr. Evelyn Joll has given assistance over the Turner illustrations. I have also benefited from the stimulus and special knowledge of friends, particularly Mr. Eric Freeman, Mr. Laurie Fricker, Mr. Miles Hadfield, Mr. Edward Malins, and Dr. Peter Willis. Miss Sandra Raphael, formerly Librarian of the Linnean Society of London, has given me much assistance, not least in proof reading and with the index.

I am grateful for permission to quote passages from: Virgil, *The Aeneid*, W. F. Jackson Knight trans. (Harmondsworth, 1958); J. W. Goethe, *Italian Journey*, W. H. Auden and Elizabeth Collins trans. (1962); "The Memoirs of Thomas Jones", *The Walpole Society*, Vol. XXXII. My debt to other authors will be evident.

Freshford, 1970.   K.W.

Contents

List of Plates

Measurements to nearest quarter inch

1*

Abbreviations

Arch. Rev.	Architectural Review
FS	Documents at Hoare and Co.'s bank, 37 Fleet Street, London, E.C.4
Journal W.C.I.	Journal of the Warburg and Courtauld Institute
S.A.S.	Somerset Archaeological Society
S.R.O.	Somerset Record Office
ST	Documents at Stourhead, National Trust
TOT	Documents belonging to the Marquess of Ailesbury, Sturmy House, Savernake, Wiltshire
T(ST)	Documents at Wiltshire County Record Office, County Hall, Trowbridge: Stourhead Archive
T(TOT)	Tottenham House Archive (Savernake)
W.A.M.	The Wiltshire Archaeological and Natural History Magazine
W.A.S.	Wiltshire Archaeological Society

Introduction

Stourhead

Where Salisbury Plain ends, and Wiltshire, Somerset, and Dorset meet, a shelf of land extends for several miles before descending abruptly to the valley of the Frome and the plain of Glastonbury. The westernmost part of this area forms a triangular ridge, the watershed of the Brue, the Wylye, and the Stour, all of which rise within a short distance of one another and flow west, east and south respectively. The road from Frome skirts Longleat, climbs to Maiden Bradley and, some four miles further on, passes the small village of Stourton, where, from before the Conquest, stood the castle of the Stourtons, lords 'of the River Stouer from its fountains to the sea'.[1] This was represented on their arms, 'sable, a bend or, between six fountaines'. Their house, according to John Aubrey, was very large, very old and little considerable as to architecture. Henry Hoare, the banker, who bought the manor in the early eighteenth century, demolished it and built near the site a small Palladian mansion, later extended by two wings, which now stands in a park facing the chalk. He named it *Stourhead*.[2]

About three hundred yards to the west of the house, at a place traditionally known as *Paradise*,[3] the ground falls steeply to where two valleys converge; and here, in the 1750s, a dam was built to contain the headwaters of the Stour and form a lake-landscape famous in its day and now one of the most perfect survivors of its kind (Pl. 3).

The lake may also be approached by a road which descends dramatically from the bleak upper landscape into the almost subterranean atmosphere of Stourton; an effect which is increased, especially in summer, by the planting of the hillsides. Unlike some other villages which were removed from an idyllic scene, this one has been incorporated in it, its cottages and mediaeval church contrasting oddly with a classical temple, modelled on the Pantheon, across the water. There are, in fact, two scenes which merge: an English one with a Gothic flavour, symbolized by the cross (Pl. 8b),

[1] 383.255.
[2] Grid reference, Frome sheet of the one inch Ordnance Survey, ST 7735.
[3] An agreement dated 9 Jan. 1724, for Joseph Andrews to install an engine to pump water to the house at Stourhead, contains the phrase 'from Withy bed pond to Ye top of Parradice Coppice' T(ST) 383.57. See also 'Paradise Temple', 'Paradise Well', on modern Ordnance Survey Sheet ST 73 SE (1962).

moved from Bristol in 1765, which stands to the left of the entrance; and another recalling a pagan Italian past. To these subsequent generations have added an arboretum, a choice collection of trees and shrubs, particularly azalea and rhododendron. These later additions have, to some extent, blurred the classical image and the original intention to evoke the numinous. It is thus with some bewilderment that the modern visitor enters the little Temple of Flora (Pl. 1), shaded by beech and half buried in rhododendron and yew; the urn with a bacchanalian relief, the female busts in niches and those of two young men on pedestals, the wooden thrones and altars are like the properties of some forgotten play from which the actors have long departed. The inscription over the door reads *Procul, o procul este profani*.[4]

The path round the lake is designed to give a series of living pictures and calculated surprises. From Flora it is devious; the lake and the Pantheon are lost to sight in a coniferous plantation to the north, a dramatic change from light to dark, and an outward look up a desolate valley known as Six Wells Bottom. Turning back along the lake the winding path obscures the way ahead, until suddenly it plunges into the grotto, set at an angle to it. Here is the apotheosis of water. As the springs flow about the statue of the nymph[5] (Pl. 7a), something of the awe surrounding pagan sanctuaries survives, which makes her more than a garden ornament. Pope's verse, engraved on the rim of the basin, reminds us that this was a poet's conception; one which was not realised in his own grotto at Twickenham. 'It wants nothing to complete it', he wrote to his friend Edward Blount, 'but a good statue with an inscription, like that beautiful antique one which you know I am so fond of:

> Hujus Nympha Loci, sacri custodia fontis,
> Dormio, dum blandae sentio murmur aquae.
> Parce meum, quisquis tangis cava marmora somnum
> Rumpere, seu bibas, sive lavere, tace.
> Nymph of the grot, these sacred springs I keep,
> And to the murmur of these waters sleep;
> Ah, spare my slumbers, gently tread the cave!
> And drink in silence, or in silence lave.'[6]

By contrast, the English scene (Pl. 6a) through the opening is pure picturesque. Ahead, Cheere's River God[7] (Pl. 7b), in his cave, heaves himself up on his oar. Serpentine steps lead to a grassy platform before a rustic

---

[4] Virgil, *The Aeneid*, VI, 'Away, you who are unhallowed, Away'.
[5] For the origins of this statue and inscription see Otto Kurz, 'Huius Nympha loci', *Journal W.C.I.*, XVI (1953), p. 171.
[6] Alexander Pope, Letter to Edward Blount, 2 June 1725, *Correspondence*, G. Sherburn ed. (Oxford, 1956), II, p. 297.
[7] FS(Acc.) 7 Aug. 1751. Not to be confused with an earlier statue once below the Temple of Flora. For a long time the River God has held nothing. At the time of writing it is intended to restore the oar, which will give meaning to his gesture.

cottage, and all at once we are faced with the Pantheon at close quarters, a visual shock for which no intermediate image has prepared us (Pl. 6b). This building, which dominated the scene on entering the garden, now rewards us with the rich texture, yellow, grey, and red, of the fine-grained oolite. From the steps of the portico we look back at the scene we have left. Inside the rotunda Rysbrack's *Hercules* (Pl. 7c) faces the entrance, flanked by his *Flora* and an antique *Livia Augusta as Ceres*; four other casts and copies from the antique stand before the remaining niches. John Wesley, although he admired the scenery, could not 'reconcile statues with nudities either to common sense or common decency',[8] nor could he admire images of devils. He may, however, have climbed the rock-work bridge through the Hermitage (Pl. 13a) to the Temple of Apollo (Pl. 5), from where he would have looked down on what Horace Walpole had described as 'one of the most picturesque scenes in the world'.[9]

[8] John Wesley, *Journal*, ed. N. Curnock (1909), vol. VI (12 Sept. 1776).
[9] Horace Walpole, 'Visits to Country Seats', *Walpole Society*, XVI (1927–8).

The Cultural Background[1]

Stourhead has been claimed as a forerunner of the 'natural landscape' epitomized by 'Capability' Brown; but to regard it as original is to misinterpret its significance. Rather, it is the personal expression of a number of tendencies present in mid-eighteenth century, used in ways which make it unique.

The origins of English interest in landscape are bound up with a philosophical dilemma: how to reconcile empirical scientific discovery with the structure of the universe as described by the fathers of Christianity. The answer, put rather baldly, lay in God's works, and in the principle of plenitude which was, in Professor A. O. Lovejoy's words, 'the assumption that no genuine potentiality of being can remain unfulfilled, that the extent and abundance of the creation must be as great as the possibility of existence and commensurate with the productive capacity of a 'perfect' and inexhaustible Source, and that the world is the better, the more things it contains'.[2] A study of the phenomenal world would, it was believed, reveal a rational purpose; hence Nature and Reason, the twin foundations of eighteenth-century optimism.

In mediaeval philosophy the idea had prevailed that truth was to be found in the scriptures and the writings of the Fathers of the Church. Nature at the Fall had become the home of Satan and his devils, who included the gods and demi-gods of classical mythology; hence Wesley's outburst at Stourhead. The whole art of landscape and its mystique, culminating in Turner, Constable, and Wordsworth, depends on the belief that Nature is *good*. Nature includes Human Nature, which must also be good, i.e., *rational*. The art of landscape is but a projection of the human psyche.

For the purpose of this book it is unnecessary to go back further than John Locke and his disciple, the third Earl of Shaftesbury, to understand the political overtones which the concept of the Natural Order added to the English landscape movement. According to Locke, men if given free-

[1] I am particularly indebted in this section to Basil Willey, *The Seventeenth-century Background* and *The Eighteenth-century Background*, paperback editions (1962).
[2] Arthur O. Lovejoy, *The Great Chain of Being*, paperback ed. (New York, 1960), p. 52.

dom would seek the good because they were endowed with reason which enabled them to recognize what was in their own interest. 'Men living together according to reason', he wrote, 'without a common superior on earth, with authority to judge between them, is properly the state of nature.' 'To understand political power right, and derive it from its original, we must consider what state men are naturally in, and that is, a state of perfect freedom to order their actions and dispose of their possessions and persons, as they think fit, within the bounds of the law of nature, without asking leave, or depending upon the will of any other man.'[3] Locke's liberty was not what subsequent generations were to make of it. It was not licence to overthrow the existing social order, but the freedom to enjoy property without interference; and this applied particularly to those who had it, rather than to 'the vulgar' who had not yet heard of the Rights of Man.

But for a generation which had defeated the autocratic principle in kings and had suffered under religious intolerance, freedom had significance. Grounds laid out in geometric order were not quite the setting for natural man, or at any rate for discourses about him. The idea that natural surroundings, or the countryside, favoured the poetic or philosophic mood was not new, of course. Horace and his Sabine Farm found echoes in Rapin's *Hortorum* (1665), translated into English by John Evelyn the younger in 1673. In Lord Shaftesbury's *The Moralists* (1709), Theocles's apostrophe, introducing his meditation on the universal genius of Nature, almost paraphrases Rapin. 'Ye Fields and woods, my Refuge from the toilsome World of Business, receive me in your quiet Sanctuarys, and favour my Retreat and thoughtful Solitude',[4] says Theocles. Philocles's response is commonly assumed to have ushered in the *jardin anglais*.

> I shall no longer resist the Passion growing in me for Things of a *natural* kind; where neither *Art*, nor the *Conceit* or *Caprice* of man has spoil'd their *genuine Order*, by breaking in upon that *primitive State*. Even the rude *Rocks*, the mossy *Caverns*, the irregular unwrought *Grotto's*, and broken *Falls* of Waters, with all the horrid Graces of the *Wilderness* itself, as representing NATURE more, will be the more engaging, and appear with a Magnificence beyond the formal Mockery of princely Gardens.[5]

The literary elaboration of the theme by Addison and others has

[3] Bertrand Russell, *History of Western Philosophy* (1961), pp. 602 f.
[4] Anthony Ashley Cooper, 3rd Earl of Shaftesbury, *The Moralists: A Philosophical Rhapsody*, Part III (1709), p. 344. Cf. René Rapin, 'Of Gardens', trans. James Gardiner, 1706, p. 105.

> And happy he, who in a Countrey Seat,
> From Storms of Bus'ness finds a calm Retreat....
> Where all around delightful Landskips lie
> And pleasing Prospects entertain his Eye.

[5] Ibid., p. 393.

frequently and ably been indited.[6] Pope's influence was paramount; first, as a vehicle by which the philosophy of natural landscape was disseminated; second, as the friend of men like Bathurst, Burlington, Cobham, and Lyttelton; third, as a gardener himself. The *Essay on Man* described the Natural Order and man's place in it; it was also a justification of the *status quo*:

> Order is Heav'n's first law; and this confest,
> Some are, and must be, greater than the rest.

The thoughts in the famous *Epistle to Lord Burlington* were not original. D'Argenville's *The Theory and Practice of Gardening*, an English version published in 1712, contained the suggestion that each site for a garden required 'a new line of thought, and a compliance with nature'. And Sir William Temple had written in *Upon the Gardens of Epicurus* (1699) '. . . greater sums may be thrown away without effect or honour, if there want not sense in proportion to money, or if Nature be not followed; which I take to be the great rule in this, and perhaps in everything else. . . .' Nevertheless Pope's lines summed up the principles and evoke the essence of what was done at Stourhead.

> Consult the Genius of the Place in all;
> That tells the Waters or to rise or fall,
> Or helps th'ambitious Hill the heav'n to scale,
> Or scoops in circling theatres the vale,
> Calls in the Country, catches opening glades,
> Joins willing woods, and varies shades from shades,
> Now breaks or now directs, th'intending Lines;
> Paints as you plant, and, as you work, designs.

When these lines were written changes had already taken place in practice, in which Pope's own example and his close association with William Kent played an important part. Before discussing Kent's contribution, we must, however, distinguish two aspects of the landscape; the laying out of whole estates and the making of gardens. Economics were behind the former, for wood had many uses; 4000 grown trees were needed for one ship of the line. Apart from being deeply interested in Earl Bathurst's vast planting programme at Cirencester from 1716 onwards, Pope also invested money in it. On the other hand his own garden at Twickenham was but 200 yards long and half as broad, a place for philosophers (or dissident politicians), reflecting the taste he had outlined in his anonymous *Essay on Gardens* in 1713. 'There is certainly something in the

---

[6] Elizabeth Wheeler Manwaring, *Italian Landscape in Eighteenth Century England* (1925); Christopher Hussey, *The Picturesque* (1927), both republished by Cass, London, 1965 and 1967 respectively. Edward Malins, *English Landscaping and Literature, 1660–1840* (1966); Maren-Sofie Røstvig, *The Happy Man* (Oslo, 1954 and 1958).

amiable simplicity of unadorned Nature, that spreads over the Mind a more noble sort of Tranquillity, and a loftier Sensation of Pleasure, than can be raised from the nicer scenes of Art. This was the Taste of the Ancients in their Gardens, as we may discover from the Descriptions (that) are extant of them.'[7]

The first 'natural landscape' originated, it is suggested, at Castle Howard, when Charles Howard, Earl of Carlisle, preserved Wray Wood from being cut into a star. Stephen Switzer, writing in 1718, said that in Wray Wood 'Nature is truly imitated, if not excelled'. No plans exist, but an account written in 1732 suggests that, in addition to winding paths and openings to reveal scenes beyond its boundaries, there were ponds and fountains in the wood, including 'a statue of Diana in a basin designed as rocks, surrounded by spruce firs, well chosen as they hang in the same manner as the rocks'. 'It is clear', writes Mr. Christopher Hussey, 'that between 1718 (or earlier) and 1732 a prototype woodland and water garden had been made in Wray Wood ... perhaps 15 years before Kent's analogous treatment of the "River Styx" and the Elysian Fields at Stowe.'[8] How much John Vanbrugh had to do with this is not certain. The house and its siting were his conception; he was working on the Temple of the Four Winds when he died in 1726. He and Carlisle were fellow members of the Kit-Cat Club where, with Addison and others, new ideas of landscape must often have been discussed. This, and Vanbrugh's dramatic sense, would lead them to conceive architecture in relation to scenery. Vanbrugh, according to Mr. Hussey, must be credited with the invention of 'the approximation of the garden to painted landscape, with lakes, vistas, temples and woods worked into a composed whole'.[9]

Stowe was perhaps the most influential source of landscape innovation. Its owner, Sir Richard Temple (later Viscount Cobham), also a member of the Kit-Cat Club, employed Vanbrugh to design buildings between 1719 and the latter's death in 1726. During this time he worked with Charles Bridgeman,[10] a young man who was later to become the royal gardener. Few of those concerned with new ideas of landscape were gardeners in the technical sense. Vanbrugh always left such details to others; Bridgeman fulfilled the need not only for him, but subsequently for William Kent. Thus, although Bridgeman's own garden lay-outs retained the straight or radiating avenues and clipped hedges of an earlier style, he must yet be considered as an important figure in the movement.

Bridgeman was appointed at Stowe about 1713. Not long after, he collaborated with Pope in the lay-out of Lord Burlington's grounds at

7 Alexander Pope, 'On Gardens', *The Guardian*, no. 173, 29 Sep. 1713.
8 Christopher Hussey, *English Gardens and Landscapes 1700–1750* (1967), p. 125.
9 Hussey, *The Picturesque*, p. 128.
10 Dr. Peter Willis's monograph on Bridgeman is not published at the time of writing. For an authenticated list of places where Bridgeman worked see Willis, 'The Work of Charles Bridgeman', *The Amateur Historian*, vol. VI, no. 3 (Spring, 1964).

Chiswick. Richard Boyle, third Earl of Burlington,[11] is important to the story of Stourhead in a number of ways. He brought together Pope, Kent, Bridgeman, and ultimately Henry Flitcroft; together with Colen Campbell and William Benson, he was responsible for the Palladian revival; and incidentally, the Hoare family became related to the Boyles by marriage.[12] Burlington inherited titles and riches at the age of ten. At twenty-one, in 1714/15, he spent a year on the Continent, and from that time, although his strong Whig connections would have favoured a political career under George I, his whole interest was in the arts. In 1719 he made a second journey abroad, mainly to study the buildings of Palladio round Venice. He returned to England with William Kent, who remained with him as friend and collaborator for the rest of his life.

At this time Kent was solely concerned with painting which he had been studying in Italy, supported by some Yorkshire gentlemen who had faith in his genius. He turned to architecture after 1726, when he was appointed Master Carpenter at the Office of Works; later becoming Master Mason and Deputy Surveyor. Our immediate interest, however, is not in his work as an architect and interior designer but as an influence on gardening and landscape. It was generally agreed by his contemporaries that Kent provided the visual sensibility to link the ideas of the painters with those of poets and philosophers. Philip Southcote, originator of the garden farm or *ferme ornée*, told Pope's friend, Joseph Spence, that Burlington and Kent were the first introducers of the natural taste in gardening. Spence later noted that, 'Mr. Kent was the sole beginner of the natural taste. At Kensington (below Bayswater) and Chiswick—the latter, October 1733'.[13] This was an area south-west of Bridgeman's layout. According to Stephen Wright, who was with Kent at the Office of Works, 'the Serpentine river was the first thing done in it',[14] a feature he elaborated at Stowe, and used to perfection at Rousham where he had the Cherwell itself as a subject. This, however, would hardly justify Pope's 'All gardening is landscape-painting—just like a landscape hung up'.[15] Pope had studied painting and explained how features could be made to seem more distant than they were by darkening or perspective; and how lights and shades could be managed 'by disposing the thick grove-work, the thin and the opening in a proper manner, of which the eye is generally the properest judge'.[16] But where was the model for a landscape at the same time natural, picturesque and ancient? Kent, who had studied in Italy, would know; it could be found in the idealization of the classical Italian scene by Claude Lorrain and others.

[11] For Burlington and Allen, 1st Earl Bathurst, see J. Lees-Milne, *Earls of Creation* (1962).
[12] Lord Dungarvan, son of John Boyle, Earl of Cork and Orrery, married Susanna, elder daughter of Henry Hoare II, in 1753. See below p. 39.
[13] Spence's *Anecdotes*, ed. James M. Osborn (Oxford 1966), 1060.
[14] Ibid., 1064.   [15] Ibid., 606.   [16] Ibid., 611.

Kent was appointed architect at Stowe in 1730, following James Gibbs, who had succeeded on Vanbrugh's death in 1726. Bridgeman's heroic design was now to be blurred, his clipped vistas transformed, first by Kent and then by Lancelot (not yet 'Capability') Brown, into a series of Claude-like scenes. As Southcote is reported to have said, 'Lord Cobham began in the Bridgeman taste: 'tis the Elysian Fields that is the painting part of his gardens'.[17] These were pure Kent. The sides of a shallow valley were planted with trees; a stream flowed from a grotto into a series of serpentine pools, named the River Styx. Across the water the Temple of British Worthies looked symbolically to the Temple of Ancient Virtue, a political allegory not lost on people of his time.

Lord Cobham had withdrawn from active political life in 1733, ostensibly because of Sir Robert Walpole's excise policy. In fact it was part of a more general dissatisfaction with Walpole's influence at court and his intolerance of any criticism, an opposition which included near-Jacobites like Henry St. John, Viscount Bolingbroke, as well as disgruntled Whigs. The faction was identified with Frederick, Prince of Wales, who had quarrelled outright with his father, George II. Both George and Walpole were notoriously uninterested in the arts; Frederick not only patronized poets and writers, but had demonstrated his support for the new taste in gardening. Politics and poetry became associated with the landscape both at Stowe and Hagley, the seat of Cobham's cousin, George Lyttelton.[18] Lyttelton was the patron of James Thomson,[19] whose long poem recalled the changing aspects of the seasons and the philosophic moods which nature should evoke. *Autumn*, especially, was the time

> For those whom wisdom and whom nature charm
> To steal themselves from the degenerate crowd,
> And soar above this little scene of things—
> To tread low-thoughted vice beneath their feet,
> To soothe the throbbing passions into peace,
> And woo lone Quiet in her silent walks.[20]

With such 'Philosophic Melancholy',

> Ten thousand thousand fleet ideas, such
> As never mingled with the vulgar dream,
> Crowd fast into the mind's creative eye....
> The love of nature unconfined, and, chief,
> Of human race; the sigh for suffering worth
> Lost in obscurity; the noble scorn
> Of tyrant pride; the fearless great resolve;[21] etc.

[17] Ibid., 1122.
[18] Sir George Lyttelton, *d*. 1773. In 1783, Richard Colt Hoare married his niece Hester Lyttelton. See below p. 69.   [19] 1700–48.
[20] Thomson, *Poetical Works* (Oxford 1908), 'Autumn', lines 964 ff.   [21] Ibid., 1014 ff.

In a later edition of 1746 he inserted an apostrophe to William Pitt, the brightest hope of Cobham's 'Young Patriots', himself an enthusiastic recruit to landscape gardening.

> Oh! lead me to the wide extended walks,
> The fair majestic paradise of Stowe!
> .   .   .   .
> And there, O Pitt! thy country's early boast,
> There let me sit beneath the sheltered slopes,
> Or in that Temple where, in future times,
> Thou well shalt merit a distinguished name,
> And, with thy converse blest, catch the last smiles
> Of Autumn beaming o'er the yellow woods.
> While there with thee the enchanted round I walk,
> The regulated wild, gay fancy then
> Will tread in thought the groves of Attic land;
> Will from thy standard taste refine her own,
> Correct her pencil to the purest truth
> Of nature, or, the unimpassioned shades
> Forsaking, raise it to the human mind.[22]

Thus, Mr. Hussey suggests, Kent's aim in the Elysian Fields was 'to raise Nature to the human mind and by the same process raise the mind by exhibiting Nature's purest, i.e. ideal, truth, as manlike God intended her to be before man's Fall degraded her with him. Regarded thus the creation of 18th-century landscapes, so far from mere indulgence, constituted an act of faith in the fundamental excellence of humanity and the perfectibility of Nature.'[23]

Thomson continued, however, with a call to action.

> While thus we talk, and through Elysian vales
> Delighted rove, perhaps a sigh escapes—
> What pity, Cobham! thou thy verdant files
> Of ordered trees shouldst here inglorious range,
> Instead of squadrons flaming o'er the field
> .   .   .   when the proud foe,
> The faithless vain disturber of mankind,
> Insulting Gaul, has roused the world to war.[24]

Pitt, besides a gardener, was of course the prophet of imperial expansion; and Thomson the author of 'Rule Britannia'.

[22] Ibid., 1041 ff.
[23] Hussey, *English Gardens*, p. 100.
[24] Thomson, 'Autumn', lines 1070 ff.

The Patriarch

In the eighteenth century purchase of land was one of the few ways of investing surplus wealth; and those who did so thereby established themselves in the hierarchy of country squires. When the Hoares first came to Stourhead in 1718, they were mainly engaged in business. Between 1720 and 1785 they increased their holdings of land in Wiltshire, Somerset, and Dorset by some 10,000 acres, so that Sir Richard Colt Hoare, who died in 1838, lived very comfortably from his estates. The foundations of the prosperity which made this possible were laid in the seventeenth century by Richard Hoare (Pl. 21a),[1] son of a successful horse-dealer. At the age of seventeen, a year before the Fire of London, he was apprenticed to a goldsmith; and in 1672 he was in business at The Golden Bottle, Cheapside, later moving to Fleet Street, where the firm of Hoare has flourished ever since.

Throughout the seventeenth century the goldsmiths had been evolving a banking system. It was their practice to accept valuables and money in trust, which they lent out to necessitous merchants at high rates of interest. For money deposited they gave receipts, called 'Goldsmiths' notes'; and from this it was not a long step to issue promissory notes not necessarily backed by coin or bullion. Thus arose the earliest kind of bank-note in England.

By the time of Charles II two great obstacles to trade, distance and credit, had been surmounted. 'The Goldsmith banker was a reliable person for transmitting money overseas, and his notes were accepted as transferable instruments by traders of the day. When this stage was reached the private banking of the goldsmiths had become an integral part of the commercial life of Stuart England.'[2]

In the circumstances it is not surprising that goldsmith bankers had considerable power and influence. Edward Backwell,[3] who possibly originated the system, lent money to Cromwell, and was nevertheless employed

[1] Information about Richard Hoare and his business can be found in H. P. R. Hoare, *Hoare's Bank, a Record, 1672–1955*, (rev. ed. 1955).
[2] R. D. Richards, *The Early History of Banking* (1929), p. 225.
[3] d. 1683.

by Charles II to negotiate all his principal money transactions. Sir Robert Viner[4] was another goldsmith on intimate terms with the king. Both suffered, however, from being too heavily involved in Stuart finances. In order to meet the increasing demands of court extravagance and the Dutch war, Charles' government had hit on the device of anticipating part of the annual revenue by borrowing from the goldsmiths. By 1672 they were more than £2,000,000 in debt, over half of which was owed to the bankers. Such was the deficit that the government suspended payment of interest, thus precipitating many into bankruptcy. The Stop of the Exchequer, as this action was called, put an end to Viner's business; and Backwell took refuge in Holland to escape his creditors.

Some goldsmiths, such as Francis Child[5] and Charles Duncombe,[6] were not affected by this crisis, and may have indirectly benefited; others may have taken the opportunity to enter the banking business, and it is perhaps significant that Hoare and Company's first ledger is dated 1673. Richard Hoare joined with others in lending money to the exchequer from 1690 onwards.[7]

When the Bank of England was founded in 1694 it was unpopular with two groups of people who were politically opposed; the first saw the moneyed interest being pledged to support the revolution settlement; the second feared a monopoly which would strengthen the monarchy. Duncombe, Child and Hoare were closely associated in the attack on the Bank and were clearly more concerned with the threat to their business than with politics, for Child was a Whig and Hoare a Tory. They denied that they had organized a run; but Duncombe, the most virulent opponent, withdrew £80,000 in 1695 and retired from banking. He bought the Helmsley estate in Yorkshire for the unprecedented sum of £90,000. His successors built a new mansion and named the place 'Duncombe',[8] where, as did the Hoares at Stourhead, they made a landscape with temples which, later in the eighteenth century, was extended to include a prospect of the ruins of Rievaulx Abbey.

Richard Hoare's business prospered, and on Queen Anne's succession he was knighted. Of his eleven sons, only two became partners; Henry, who built Stourhead, and Benjamin, the youngest. His eldest, Richard, from whom most of the present partners are descended, was an import and export merchant; but his business was largely carried by his father, to whom at one time he owed £62,000.[9] His poor success may in some measure have been due to the war with France which, as Sir Richard wrote to his

[4] 1631–88.
[5] 1642–1713. Whig M.P. for Devizes, 1698–1708.
[6] *d.* 1711.
[7] H. P. R. Hoare, op. cit., p. 26.
[8] See Hussey, *English Gardens*.
[9] H. P. R. Hoare, op. cit., p. 6.

son John in Italy, 'makes trading very bad & daingerous (and) has tyed up your brother Richard's hands'.[10]

Letters[11] written to John, James and Tom Hoare, who at various times between 1700 and 1714 were resident abroad, show the kind of education they received under the guidance of Richard Hoare's strongly patriarchal hand. In him the puritan ethic of prudence and diligence is displayed, and the moral and economic virtues are intertwined. He regularly offered them the prescription for the kind of success he had himself achieved, although addressed in terms he felt appropriate to each; for John a tender concern; for James benevolent reproof; for Tom outraged despair with hardly room for hope. Characteristically he read their conduct from the accounts which he required them to send him. 'You did very well in sending me an account of your expenses, which is not perfect,' he wrote to John, who, for a consideration of £300 had been placed with Scudamore and Henshaw at Genoa to be educated in the Turkey trade. 'I would not have you want for anything that is fitting and convenient for you; and as I give you that liberty I do hope you will be a good husband and not spend your money in any way extravagantly.'[12]

James was at school in Amsterdam to qualify for a merchant's service, learning French and Dutch besides improving himself at writing and accounts. Younger and more irresponsible than John, his father could take his complaint of 'giddiness in the head' in more than one way.

> The doctor is of the opinion that your dizziness proceeded from drinking too much tea and coffee. Let me desire you to take a resolution not to drink above two dishes in one day of either or both. I know by my owne observation on myself that a quantity of 3 or 4 dishes does me harm. You may see how carefull I am of you in relation to your health, hopeing that you may live to be a comfort to myself and mother and in your well doing wee shall allways be pleased, and any account of your extravagancy or ill liveing will be very displeasing to us. The account of money that Mr. Hale has paid you and for you, in the year past, gives me reason to tell you that you have begun to be extravagant. (It is) far beyond what your brother Richard ever spent in one year. I would have you give the watch maker something to take the watch again; or if you cannot return it on some loss, I will have you give it to Mr. Hale to keep for you, as also your sword.... I caution you to be a better husband for the future and let me

[10] Richard Hoare to John Hoare, 23 Apr. 1702, ST.

[11] These are copies, mostly in other hands, bound in one volume at Stourhead, National Trust (ST). Tom Hoare's original letters to his father are with Hoare and Co., 37 Fleet Street, London (FS). The dates of the letters follow the practice of commencing the year on April the first. They precede the reform of the calendar in England. Sir Richard Hoare's letters have the old style date which is eleven days behind the continental date of Tom Hoare's.

[12] R.H. to John Hoare, 1 May 1701, ST.

have you please yourself in doing your master's business and
not in foolish vanities which I knowe will soone bring greater
inconveniences on you.[13]

When business allowed, travel for pleasure was permitted, although in
Italy there were dangers not present in Holland. Sir Richard frequently
warned John to preserve himself 'from the infection of the Religion of the
country', to keep steadfast to the Protestant faith, and avoid disputes with
those who held contrary views, which might, moreover, compromise him
with Jacobite sympathizers. As he said, many ill consequences had attended
such arguments. Rebellion, as 1715 and 1745 were to show, was a very real
menace; a man in Sir Richard's position had to be above suspicion. So he
hoped when John went to Rome he would travel in company with gentlemen of good reputation, not given to drinking or other vices; to be sure
at all times to keep away from women he might suspect of lewdness, and
generally to conduct himself prudently. Otherwise he was free to go where
he was inclined, with money to buy silks, fans, gloves and other things as
presents for his mother and sisters. And his father asked him for 'some
small pieces of painting of about 18 inches to 24 inches, but let them be
good of the sort for I doe not care for bad paintings'.[14] 'It will be for your
future satisfaction', concluded Sir Richard, 'if you write down every night
what observations you made in the precedent day, which I shall be pleased
to read when I am soe happy as to see you'.[15]

Sir Richard, indeed, must have had little leisure for cultural matters; but
he had taken a house in the country, at Hendon, where he had a garden.
He asked John for the prices of lemon or 'cittern' trees; but when he found
his tenure was uncertain and there was no greenhouse, he abandoned the
idea of anything which would not endure the uncertain English climate,
and asked for 'some roots or seeds of fine flowers or anything that keep
green all the year about'.[16] And Jimmy was required to send 'seeds or roots
of the best gilly flowers or any other good flower (excepting toolips)'.[17]
The ship by which they were sent was taken by French privateers, who by
1703 had started to interfere seriously with British shipping.

Tom Hoare, who arrived at the house of Mr. Henry Schuurmann in
Amsterdam early in October 1708, was also to be employed in learning
languages and methods of business. But his immediate dispatch from
England was due to drinking, whoring and swearing, sins which, if he continued to commit them, would undoubtedly be punished by 'the Torments
of Hell for Ever'. Such occupations were also attended by ill consequences
in this world, for one of Sir Richard's clerks, with whom Tom had been

[13] R.H. to James Hoare, 26 Jan. 1702, ST.
[14] R.H. to John Hoare, 1 Dec. 1704, ST.
[15] R.H. to John Hoare, 2 Feb. 1704, ST.
[16] R.H. to John Hoare, Jan. 1702, ST.
[17] R.H. to James Hoare, 5 Feb. 1702, ST.

intimate, had embezzled money and disappeared, it was suspected with a woman. Tom professed himself much troubled at the conduct of his former companion and the 'great inconveniences and hardship'[18] to which his father had been put. But, as he wrote to his brother Henry, he had himself made false entries in accounts. 'I did often think of acquainting you off all these Matters & Transactions that you might know how they were before I left England, but my Notice was soe short and the Terrors of them soe great wch. was the occasion as I could not doe it.'[19] Tom, indeed, promised to change his ways; and Sir Richard, with cautious optimism, entrusted him with the sale of valuable diamonds in Hamburg. Tom had little choice in the matter. 'I leave myself intirely to your disposall & what you think Proper I shall think very Agreeable...for you understand the affaires of the world, and knows what is for our Good Better then we ourselves which have not seen so much of it.'[20]

Predictably, Tom's accounts did not satisfy his father, who saw in them proof that he had not forsaken 'those Abominable Wickednesses, (for) which by most of your letters you have seemed to be very much grieved & afflicted'.[21] 'I find a great many Guilders lost att Cards & Lotterys & spent at Play Houses, if you do proceed in such Methods I doe not know what your expenses will amount to in a year.'[22]

Nor was Tom successful in the Hamburg assignment. We can sympathize with him; he had no established position in the community and no experience, yet the acumen required of him might well have taxed Sir Richard himself. He was to observe, compare, and report; to play off one astute and experienced dealer against another; to ask questions but not to answer any; and all this without a proper knowledge of the language. Having no regular employment he inevitably spent his time in coffee-houses and wine cellars. Business friends urged Sir Richard to have his son home, 'to preserve him from ruin and idle loose acquaintances'.[23] But Sir Richard was inexorable. He was convinced from reports that reached him that Tom was too far gone in 'hard drinking & other Debaucheries', the consequences of which he knew to be eternal damnation. Tom was only too aware of his predicament and, as he put it, his heart was full of 'expressions of uneasyness'. 'Time seems very long and tedious to me, and I now begin to grow forward in years, and haveing no Imployment or Business to doe, therefore I doe not know how or which way I may gaine my Bread for the future.'[24]

---

[18] Tom Hoare to R.H., 19 Oct. 1708, FS.
[19] Tom Hoare to Henry Hoare (Brother), 4 Jan. 1708, FS. An item in a balance sheet, apparently made by Henry Hoare after his father's death, reads 'supposed to be lost by servants as by my brother Thomas his account of £2000'.
[20] T.H. to R.H., 5 Feb. 1708, FS.
[21] R.H. to T.H., 3 May 1709, ST. There is a note to say this letter was not sent.
[22] R.H. to T.H., 27 May 1709, ST.
[23] Samuel Free to R.H., 12 Jan. 1711, FS.
[24] T.H. to R.H., 8 May 1711, FS.

In 1712 he moved to Lisbon, 'a place noe wayes pleasant nor agreable for it is the Nastiest Citty as ever I saw'.[25] Two years later Sir Richard's agents wrote to say 'By what we can hear from thence he lives after the same manner as he did here & that he has so abused his constitution that they doubt very much of his being able to hold out very much longer. He has a continual cough on him & wee believe in a deep consumption.'[26]

Sir Richard died not long after, in 1718. He had represented the City of London in Parliament from 1709 to 1713; and was Lord Mayor in 1712. Jimmy was already dead; Richard followed in 1721, and John was killed in the same year when he fell from a horse. Their brother Henry lived a little longer to carry on the business and vindicate Sir Richard's principles.

[25] T.H. to Lady Hoare (mother), 2 Sep. 1712, FS.
[26] Cudsden, Milner, and Danby to R.H., 5 Jan. 1714, FS.

Part I

Chapter 1

Henry Hoare's Paradise

The House

About the time of his father's death, Henry Hoare (Pl. 21b) bought the manor of Stourton in Wiltshire. Sir Richard, along with other goldsmith-bankers, had been a founder and director of the South Sea Company; and although he had resigned this position in 1715, the Hoares had substantial holdings. The Company's offer, in 1720, to incorporate a large proportion of the National Debt in its capital, in return for reciprocal advantages, was followed by heavy speculation, and during the summer the price of its stock rose to 1000;[1] only to be followed by panic selling, so that by the end of the year it had fallen to 132.[2] Henry and his brother Benjamin certainly made a profit, and it is possible that the purchase of Stourton was a means of investing this. Benjamin, not long after, acquired Boreham House[3] near Chelmsford. It is of passing interest that John Aislabie, who as Chancellor of the Exchequer was held responsible for the government's part in the South Sea deal, retired after his disgrace to his estate at Studley Royal[4] near Ripon, and there created a landscape which, in spite of the formality of its ponds and canals, anticipated Stourhead in some of its aspects.

Henry Hoare became known as 'Good' Henry, perhaps because of his business acumen, or in contrast to his brother Tom: certainly to distinguish him from his son, called 'the Magnificent', and from all the other Henry Hoares. He was one of the four founders of the Westminster Hospital; in other charitable causes he gave his support equally to relieving distress and the spread of Christian teaching. His memorial describes him as pious without being censorious, just, merciful, and blessed with a good understanding.

The Manor of Stourton, heavily encumbered with debt at the beginning of the century, had passed in 1714 from Edward, the thirteenth baron, to Sir Thomas Meres. In 1717 his son, Sir John Meres, conveyed it to Vigerus Edwards and John Mellor in trust for Henry Hoare, to whom it was finally

[1] H. P. R. Hoare, op. cit., p. 35.
[2] Ibid., p. 36.
[3] See C. Hussey, 'Boreham Hall', *Country Life*, XXXVI.
[4] See Hussey, *English Gardens*.

made over in 1720. The new lord of the manor acquired not only 'Houses Edifices Buildings Dovehouses Barns Stables Gardens Orchards Yards Backsides Closes Lands Meadows Pastures Feedings Commons Wasts Fold Courses Trees Woods Underwoods Hedges Ditches Furzes Heaths Moores Marshes Ways Passages Waters Watercourses Mills Springs Fishings Piscaries etc.',[5] but rights, among others, to goods and chattels of felons, fugitives, and outlaws; to parks, warrens, and fairs; to the fishing in and of the River Stour, and the patronage of the living of the parish church.

The house of the Stourtons, a rambling building with two courts, was without doubt inconvenient. It was decided to build a new one. How far 'Good' Henry was responsible for the innovations is uncertain. He was undoubtedly influenced by his cousin, William Benson, whose sister, Jane, he married. Benson is chiefly on record as the incompetent successor to Sir Christopher Wren in the post of Surveyor General. His appointment in 1718 was resented by Vanbrugh and Nicholas Hawksmoor, whose baroque taste in architecture he sought to displace. In spite of Hawksmoor's gibe that 'in extream need of employment [Benson] could find nothing at that time but the Office of Works to fall upon, so disguising himself under the pretence of an architect got himself made Surveyor General',[6] Benson had, in 1710, designed and built Wilbury House near Newton Tony in Wiltshire, 'in the stile of *Inigo Jones*'. The words are those of Colen Campbell in 1715, when he paid Benson the further tribute of having rediscovered Inigo Jones and showing at Wilbury 'a particular Regard to the noblest Manner of Architecture in this beautiful and regular Design'.[7]

Benson had bought the estate in 1709, when he was 27. It may have been to that place Sir Richard Hoare referred when he wrote to Tom in 1709, 'Brother Hoare and Brother Harry have gone to Cozen Benson's in Wiltshire & from thence to some other places'.[8] Wilbury is now thought to be the first building in the Palladian revival, the political overtones of which were implied by Lord Shaftesbury in his *Letter concerning Design* (1712) expressing the need for a building programme in a new 'national taste', to replace that of 'a single court architect with too much of the Gothick'.

It has been suggested that William Benson had German connections through his mother. Sir Richard Hoare wrote to John in May 1701, 'Your cousin Billy Benson is gone to Hamburgh, and from thence to Sweden'. Tom, from Hamburg in 1710, refers to cousin Henry Benson. Following George I's dissolution of Parliament in January 1715, Benson was elected as Whig member for Shaftesbury. In the same year appeared the first

5 Abstract of title, 383.716.
6 Quoted, Hussey, 'Wilbury Park', *Country Life*, CXXVI (Dec. 1959), p. 1014.
7 *Vitruvius Britannicus*, vol. I.
8 R.H. to T.H., 5 Aug. 1709, ST.

volume of Campbell's *Vitruvius Britannicus*; and the first part of a translation by Nicholas Dubois of Palladio's *I quattro libri dell' architetura* with plates by Giacomo Leoni. 'These two books have certain things in common,' writes Sir John Summerson. 'Both are dedicated to George I and thus stamped as Whiggish products. Further, both evince the same distinct architectural loyalties—namely to Palladio and Inigo Jones as the two modern masters to whom the British architect is to look for guidance, to the exclusion of all others.'[9]

The first great house designed by Campbell was Wanstead, for Sir Richard Child, son of Sir Josiah Child, chairman of the East India Company. Lord Burlington, the sponsor of the new movement and Campbell's most famous convert, employed him to remodel Burlington House, Piccadilly, shortly before making the second tour abroad referred to above. Meanwhile, when Benson was made Surveyor in 1718, Campbell was appointed his deputy and resigned with Benson the following year. By then Henry Hoare had already commissioned him to design a house in place of the old manor of Stourton. In this Benson had a hand, if we are to judge by an entry concerning sums paid to Farmer King of Stourton: 'By money he craveth to be allowed or pd by order of Mr. Benson to Mr. Johnson for pulling down the house.'[10] A further entry is more specific, 'By bill of pulling down ye old castle...£114. 12. 11d'.[11]

The work of building was done by Nathaniel Ireson, a master-builder of Wincanton, and was apparently in progress in July 1719 when an account book entry refers to 'a Messenger to find out Mr. Ireson to send him to Stourton'.[12] The designs for the house were included by Campbell in the third volume of *Vitruvius Britannicus*.[13] A map of 1722 (Pl. 9a) shows Stourhead with a formal forecourt to the east, and a walled garden to the south. Colt Hoare wrote that 'the immediate precinct of the mansion was surrounded with walls and decorated with fountains'.

Compared with Wanstead, Stourhead was a place of modest size; not a great house but a villa, as Summerson[14] points out, deriving both in plan and elevation from the one which Palladio designed for Leonardo Emo at Fanzolo. How 'Good' Henry regarded it is not known. Although one of

[9] Sir John Summerson, *Architecture in Britain 1530–1830* (Harmondsworth, 1955 ed.), p. 188.
[10] Account book, 1717–29, T(ST) 383.58.
[11] Ibid.
[12] Ibid.
[13] Campbell's design shows a portico, but the house was built without one. Cf. Francis Nicholson's painting of c. 1813 (Pl. 15a). This also shows the pediment and parapet crowned with urns. There are three decorative variations shown in Campbell's original drawings. (1) Urns over the pediment and at the corners of the parapet. (2) Male statues over the pediment and urns at the corners of the parapet. (3) Three female statues over the pediment and balls at the corners of the parapet. Campbell's intended portico was added in 1841. When the house was restored after the fire of 1902, three lead statues were removed from the Pantheon and Sun Temple to the portico. The entry in 'The Annals of Stourhead', 1903–4, which refers to this, says they were by Rysbrack, but there is no record of Rysbrack making lead statues for Stourhead and they are probably by John Cheere.
[14] *Architecture in Britain* (1963 ed.), p. 196.

the first patrons of the new style, he was no Whig, and it is unlikely that he was drawn to it for philosophic reasons. Fashion more probably influenced his choice, setting the seal on his newly acquired status. On the other hand an idealized Roman villa suitable for a gentleman philosopher honouring a contemplative life in rural surroundings would doubtless have appealed to Benson, who is known to have admired Virgil and Milton and to have encouraged Christopher Pitt's translation of *The Aeneid*.

Why the Palladian canon should have had a particular appeal in 1720 has been a subject for speculation. There were characteristics of the style which accorded with the temper of the times. In the first place, the outside of Stourhead is 'masculine and unaffected'.[15] Inside there is a greater degree of ornamentation, but behind the appearance is the rational measure harmonizing the parts of the building with one another. Indeed '...the systematic linking of one room to the other by harmonic proportions was the fundamental novelty of Palladio's architecture...',[16] especially for domestic buildings. The measurements given by Colt Hoare[17] are: hall, a thirty foot cube; music room, thirty by twenty feet; cabinet room, thirty by twenty feet; dining room, twenty-five by twenty feet; saloon, originally thirty by thirty feet. These proportions are similar to those used by Palladio in the Palazzo Porto-Colleoni[18] at Vicenza, a building whose design Campbell had recently used in remodelling Burlington House. The genesis of Palladio's ideas on proportions has been fully examined by Wittkower.[19] The doctrine of the mathematical universe was a recurring theme, but it was precisely the idea that beauty is related to mathematics which was attacked by Hogarth, Hume, and Burke, the spokesmen for Henry Hoare II's perhaps more secure generation. In the visual arts at any rate, the sensory qualities of objects played an increasing part in addressing the passions.

'Good' Henry had little time to enjoy his house for he died in 1725. Henry Hoare II (from now on referred to as Henry Hoare) was born on 7 July 1705. It is likely, though not recorded, that his early childhood was spent in Fleet Street, or at his grandfather's house at Hendon. But sometime, probably after the visit to Wiltshire in 1709, his father had acquired a house, at Quarley[20] in Hampshire, near his cousin Benson. It was here that Henry Hoare passed his early manhood, hunting and drinking with other fashionable young men until he found the 'gay and dissolute style of life' was affecting his health.

[15] Inigo Jones, quoted by Summerson, op. cit. (1955 ed.), p. 67.
[16] Rudolf Wittkower, *Architectural Principles in the Age of Humanism* (1952 ed.), p. 113.
[17] Sir Richard Colt Hoare, *History of Modern Wiltshire*, Hundred of Mere (1822), pp. 70 ff. The present house differs in detail from the plan shown in *Vitruvius Britannicus*. Much of the interior of the central block was rebuilt following a fire in 1902.
[18] Wittkower, op. cit., p. 115.
[19] Ibid., pp. 51 ff.
[20] Colt Hoare, small ms. book of memoirs, ST. A large Venetian window at the east end of Quarley church has the inscription, 'GULIELMUS BENSON ET HENRICUS HOARE F.A.D. 1723'.

On his father's death Henry succeeded to the business. He was then nineteen. The only partner was his uncle Benjamin, with whom he is shown by John Wootton in the hunting scene (Pl. 23a) in the small dining room at Stourhead. When he was twenty-one he married Ann, the elder daughter of Lord Masham.[21] The large equestrian portrait by Wootton and Dahl (Pl. 22a), which dominates the hall at Stourhead, dates from this time. If it is difficult to see the banker, the life style is there by which he became known as 'the Magnificent'. Ann died in childbirth the March following their marriage. Just over a year later Henry married Susan, daughter and heiress of Stephen Colt of Clapham.

They did not yet live at Stourhead, which had been left to his mother for her lifetime. It is nevertheless probable that Henry was often there and was actively concerned in completing the house. His private accounts[22] show that between 1726 and 1734 he spent about £10,000 on building and £3000 on furniture.

In 1734 (the year he became M.P. for Salisbury) he bought Wilbury from his uncle, William Benson, for £14,000.[23] It seems more than likely that Benson's cultural influence was decisive for Stourhead. As will be shown, the inspiration of Virgil (to say nothing of Milton) was an important one for the garden. Benson's interest in these authors is well known, and he probably introduced Henry to them, and to artists like Wootton, Rysbrack, and Flitcroft, whom Henry consistently employed up to their death. Wootton and Flitcroft banked at Hoare's. Rysbrack's earliest recorded commissions for Stourhead were for a 'bust of Inigo Jones in statuary marble' and 'two figures of Inigo Jones and Palladio in plaster'.[24] In 1738 Benson commemorated Milton by a commission to Rysbrack for a bust in Westminster Abbey;[25] at the same time he had from the sculptor busts of the young and old Milton which are now at Stourhead. The grounds of Wilbury were probably laid out by Benson in a semi-formal manner; but of greater interest is the proximity of Amesbury Abbey where Pope and Gay often visited the Duchess of Queensberry. In 1726 Henry Flitcroft made a series of estate maps for the Duke which show the disposition of the grounds round the house before Charles Bridgeman's modified plan of 1738. In this Bridgeman used existing features, particularly the iron age hill-fort and barrow on the wooded hill rising steeply above the River Avon. Henry Hoare, as a near neighbour, would certainly have been

[21] Abigail Masham brought the Privy Purse account to Hoare's Bank in 1710, when she supplanted Sarah, Duchess of Marlborough, as Queen Anne's favourite.
[22] At 37 Fleet Street, Hoare and Co. have ledgers with accounts of Henry Hoare's personal expenditure from 1726 to 1785; also personal account books 1752–78, 1778–83, 1770–85 (entries in the last two differ). These will be referred to as FS(Acc.). Henry Hoare kept other ledgers of which one, running from 1732 to 1749 and entitled 'Wilberry Accounts', is at Fleet Street, FS(Acc.)W; and another, running from 1749 to 1770 is in the Stourhead archive at Trowbridge, T(ST) 383.6. There are items which appear in the latter ledgers and not in the bank ledgers and vice versa. Some entries are duplicated.
[23] 21 May 1734, FS(Acc.).   [24] Receipt, 9 Apr. 1729, T(ST) 383.4.
[25] Rupert Gunnis, *Dictionary of British Sculptors, 1660–1851* (1953), p. 112.

3—L.A.

interested in these developments; and his subsequent employment of Flit-croft at Stourhead makes them doubly significant.

The first entry recording payment to a painter is to 'John Wootton in full', £53 14s. 0d. on 13 July 1725.[26] Wootton was then in his forties and known chiefly as a painter of horses. He had lately been in Rome and on his return, as Constable later said, 'painted country gentlemen in their wigs and jockey caps, and top boots, with packs of hounds, and placed them in Italian landscapes resembling those of Gaspar Poussin, except in truth and force'.[27] There is a receipt from Wootton dated 9 January 1728[28] for 'Pictures painted for Henry Hoare Esq.'.

A large landscape	£73	10	0
A sketch of the Bloody			
Shoulder'd Arabian Horse	£15	15	0
A small landscape at Sunsett	£10	10	0

Between 1725 and 1734 Henry paid Wootton six sums ranging from £63 to £21;[29] subsequently, up to the painter's death, there were more commissions, mainly, it appears, for landscapes. When Horace Walpole visited Stourhead in 1762 he noted eight paintings by Wootton and not more than two by any other artist. Altogether it is possible to name twelve paintings of his that were at one time there.[30] In 1728 Richard Wilson was fourteen and had not yet left Montgomeryshire. Wootton has therefore a claim to be the first English landscape painter. Was it he who aroused Henry Hoare's interest in the vision of Claude and Gaspar? The only other painter, apart from the portrait painters Hysing and Dahl, with whom Henry seems to have dealt in this early period is Arthur Pond, from whom in 1727 he bought 'two views of Venice', 'two views of Rome', a picture of 'the Cascade of Tivoli', and 'The Ruins of Rome' by Gio. Paolo Pannini. Pond at this time was only twenty-two. He had been a fellow student with Kent at Cheron and Vanderbank's Academy in St. Martins Lane. He became better known as a dealer, and the paintings Henry bought were probably the work of copyists whom Pond employed. Some years later Vertue, the engraver, referred to him sarcastically as 'Mr. Pond... the greatest or top virtuoso in London, followed, esteemed and cried up by all—Mr. Pond—all in all!'[31] Henry continued to patronize him until

26 FS(Acc.).
27 C. R. Leslie, *Memoirs of the Life of John Constable*, Phaidon ed. (1951), p. 320.
28 T(ST) 383.4.
29 FS(Acc.).
30 There are three main sources of this information: Horace Walpole, 'Visits to Country Seats', *Walpole Society*, XVI, 1927–8, pp. 41–2; *Schedule of pictures at Stourhead as left by Henry Hoare*, T(ST) 383.9; Colt Hoare's *History of Modern Wiltshire*. Not included in any of these lists but now at Stourhead are, *A Hunting Scene*, showing Henry and Benjamin Hoare on horseback near an obelisk, and the *Bloody Shoulder'd Arabian Horse* mentioned in the receipt above.
31 Quoted by W. T. Whitley, *Artists and their friends in England 1700–1799* (London and Boston, 1928), vol. I, p. 17.

his death in 1755. There is only one of his pictures now at Stourhead, an indifferent portrait of Henry's daughter Susanna (Lady Ailesbury).

Sometime, probably about 1737, Henry Hoare went abroad for a long period. In 1739 and 1740 he paid some £3750 to agents[32] through whom he bought works of art on a scale he never repeated and it may be assumed that much of this sum was spent on paintings. Customs charges were paid in 1739 for '2 pictures'[33] and in 1740 for 'figures etc. from Leghorn'[34] and for '2 cases of pictures from Mr. Smith of Venice'.[35] It is impossible to say for certain what the paintings were. Walpole[36] later mentioned pictures by Annibale Carracci, Domenichino, Dolci, and Maratta; two by Nicolas Poussin and one by Gaspar; one by Claude and two by Rembrandt; two by Sebastiano Ricci; Italian scenes by Marco Ricci, Pannini, Canaletto, and Anesi; and various other paintings by seventeenth- and early eighteenth-century masters. There were also in the saloon, originally intended as a chapel, copies of large mythological subjects after Reni and Guercino.

Meanwhile, as throughout his life, Henry Hoare attended to the business in Fleet Street. During the leisure hours which he spent in residence there, he acquired the habit 'of looking into books and the pursuit of that knowledge which distinguishes only the Gentleman from the Vulgar and teaches him to adorn the fortune he acquires or possesses and which, without the lessons in History (which is philosophy teaching by example) the most envied Height of Fortune will not be enjoyed'.[37] This was part of the advice he passed on, long after, to his nephew Richard. At first, until he had worked himself 'by habit into a love of reading', he used to 'murder (his) sweet precious time in looking at the insensible Vulgar who passed under the window'.[38]

Wealthy, with a growing family of two sons and two daughters, Henry, at the beginning of 1740, must have been at 'the height of fortune'. In that year, however, his younger son died at the age of seven. He had lost a daughter in 1735. It was the beginning of a series of bereavements which touched him deeply and which followed regularly through the remainder of his long life. After his mother's death in 1741 he took up residence more or less permanently at Stourhead. Hardly had he begun to look forward to living in that place when, in 1743, Susan died, leaving him with a son of thirteen and two small girls of eleven and six. He did not marry again and these are the circumstances in which he began to make the garden.

[32] Sir John Lambert; Vernet Whateley and Co., G. Beloni; Peter Meyer and Co. FS(Acc.).
[33] 6 Nov., FS(Acc.).
[34] 19 June, FS(Acc.).
[35] Presumably Consul Joseph Smith. 20 Jan., FS(Acc.).
[36] 'Visits to Country Seats', pp. 41, 42.
[37] Letter from Henry Hoare to his nephew and prospective son-in-law, Richard Hoare (father of Richard Colt Hoare), Dec. 1755, FS.
[38] H.H. to R.H., Dec. 1755, FS.

Chapter 2

The Genius of the Place

'The pleasures of the fancy are more conducive to health than those of the understanding', Addison, with pre-Freudian insight, had written in 1712. 'Delightful scenes, whether in nature, painting, or poetry, have a kindly influence on the body, as well as the mind, and not only serve to clear and brighten the imagination, but are able to disperse grief and melancholy, and to set the animal spirits in pleasing and agreeable motions.'[1] It is interesting to note that work on the contemporary landscape at Hagley also coincided with the loss of a wife, when Sir George Lyttelton's beloved Lucy died in childbirth. Lyttelton's friend and neighbour, William Shenstone, started the transformation of the Leasowes shortly after his mother's death in 1743. And Pope, whose thought and example perhaps provided leaven for the movement, terminated his garden with cypresses leading up to his 'mother's tomb'. Pope indeed was celebrated at Hagley; the urn to his memory is still there, though overturned and fast disappearing into the earth. At Stourhead the inspiration of his grotto is acknowledged, and the wish he expressed in connection with it fulfilled.

Kent's work at Chiswick, Stowe, and Rousham was complete before a start was made at Stourhead in 1743/4. Rousham, in Oxfordshire, which he was called upon to redesign about 1739 is largely unaltered; and although it is much smaller than Stourhead, and the site and plan are quite dissimilar, it must be considered a prototype. The circuit walk uses three levels of the steep ground along one bank of the Cherwell. The path turns sharply back on itself and the planting, in which effective use is made of contrasting deciduous forest trees with yew, is contrived to reveal different aspects of the few buildings that there are. But attention is more often directed outward toward the Oxfordshire landscape, and the intention seems entirely pictorial, without such literary and personal references as were made elsewhere. This probably means that General Dormer left more to Kent, whereas, as we shall see, Henry Hoare was personally involved, whatever professional help he may have called on.

Another innovation, the path 'with a continued series of new and delightful scenes at every step...', was begun in 1734[2] by Philip Southcote

[1] Joseph Addison, *The Spectator*, no. 411, 12 June 1712.   [2] Spence's *Anecdotes*, 1126.

at Woburn Farm, near Chertsey. This form, a belt of trees surrounding an estate, was adopted by Shenstone at The Leasowes which, even in its present forlorn state, illustrates how different were the images in its rambling progress from those in the compact circuit round the lake at Stourhead. The latter is nearer to Kent than to Shenstone for reasons which Hadfield makes clear. 'Kent strove to create an Elysium; a classical paradise seen through the eyes of Claude. Southcote's ambition was an arcady: the ideal countryside.'[3] Nevertheless, as at Stourhead, there was a right and a wrong way round The Leasowes; and what Shenstone wrote later might well apply to Henry's garden, especially the implied sense of movement. There is room for it 'to resemble an epick or dramatick poem', 'more striking scenes succeeding those which are less so'. The element of change is here introduced as a principle. It is 'not easy to account for fondness of former times...for every kind of straight line: where the foot is to travel over what the eye has done before'. 'Lose the object and draw nigh obliquely'[4] might describe the approach to the Pantheon at Stourhead. But any ideas that Shenstone expressed in his letters and elsewhere would not have been available to Henry Hoare in 1744. That was twelve years before Burke's essay *On the Sublime and the Beautiful*. Lancelot Brown was twenty-nine, still under Kent at Stowe. Shenstone was nine years younger than Henry; and although he frequently exchanged ideas on gardening with his neighbour at Hagley, the only reference to Stourhead in his considerable correspondence was in 1761 to a 'Piece of Writing which a Friend of mine sent me...partly written in Mr. Hoare's lovely grounds at *Stourton* in Wiltshire'.[5] Sir George Lyttelton, however, had an account at Hoare's Bank from 1751, the year he succeeded to the baronetcy, until his death in 1773, when Henry recorded, 'I grieve for the Loss of my amiable Friend, Lord Littleton, I feared something was the matter by His not coming here to his promise. His heart was broke.'[6]

When Lyttelton was secretary to Frederick, Prince of Wales, he had under him Charles Hamilton, whose improvements at Painshill are mentioned by Walpole in 1748.[7] Hamilton, who was a year older than Henry Hoare, opened an account at Hoare's Bank in 1747, and in later years, as we shall see, there was exchange of advice and a certain amount of rivalry between the two gardeners.[8] Painshill's Temple of Bacchus was a building somewhat similar to the Temple of Flora.[9] Both places had a grotto, a hermitage, a tower, and a Turkish tent. Eventually Hamilton

[3] Miles Hadfield, *Gardening in Britain* (1960), p. 200.
[4] William Shenstone, 'Unconnected thoughts on Gardening', *Works* (1773), pp. 114 ff.
[5] Shenstone, *Letters*, ed. M. Williams (1939). The inscription on the original entrance to the Grotto at Stourhead, *Intus aquae dulces* etc., was also on a stone seat at the Leasowes. See R. Dodsley, *Description of the Leasowes* (1764).
[6] Letter from Henry Hoare to Lord Bruce, 22 Aug. 1773, T(TOT).
[7] See Gordon Nares, 'Painshill', *Country Life*, CXXIII, 1958, p. 621.
[8] Letter from Henry Hoare to his daughter Susanna, 23 Oct. 1762, TOT.
[9] See illustration in O. Siren, *China and the Gardens of Europe in the 18th Century* (New York, 1950), plate 35.

over-reached himself and toward the end of his life had to sell his property to pay his debts. Part of these were certainly to Hoare's Bank from whom he borrowed £6000 on mortgage in 1766. Lyttelton had borrowed £10,000 the year before, so there is no doubt that Henry, as a banker, benefited from the master passion and was able to build better.

As a formative influence, however, Burlington's circle seems altogether more significant for Stourhead. Burlington had an account with Hoare's Bank from 1717 to 1736, and between 1721 and 1726 borrowed some £20,000 from it. It was Flitcroft, another Burlington protégé, whom Henry employed to design his buildings from 1744 onward. Henry Flitcroft was then forty-seven. He was the son of a gardener to William III, and was apprenticed to a joiner, being admitted to the freedom of the Joiner's Company in 1719. In 1720 he came to the notice of Lord Burlington, who employed him as a draftsman and architectural assistant, and through whom in 1726 he became Clerk of the Works at Whitehall. He was thus very closely associated with William Kent, whose drawings for *The Designs of Inigo Jones* he prepared for publication. When Kent died in 1748 Flitcroft succeeded him as Master Mason and Deputy Surveyor. According to Colt Hoare, Henry 'did not think seriously of improving his place by plantation till he had gained the age of forty years. When he began he proceeded *con spirito* upon a widely extended scale.'[10] This would certainly agree with the evidence which will now be given concerning the forming of the lake and the features around it. But we may question whether it was true of the area immediately adjoining the mansion. There are two clear pieces of evidence on the disposition of the grounds before and after Henry made his improvements. The first is an estate map of 1722[11] (Pl. 9a) which shows Campbell's house with a walled garden to the south and a formal forecourt to the east. In the valley where the lake now is there were two large pieces of water; a pool near the springs to the north-west, the site for the Grotto; and a tank,[12] probably serving the village of Stourton, near the site of the Temple of Flora.

A second estate map was made in 1785[13] (Pl. 9b), the year of Henry Hoare's death. The walled garden had by then disappeared, and a stretch of grass, with a path and trees on either side, extends over what was formerly shown as pasture, from the village to the house. At the end of this vista was the statue of Apollo, bought from John Cheere in 1745.[14] This area of pleasure ground extended west and then north-west into a wide terrace along the crest of the hill overlooking the valley. The trees border-

[10] Richard Colt Hoare, MS. memoirs, ST.
[11] T(ST) 383.316.
[12] A plan in the library of the Wiltshire Archaeological Society at Devizes, made when the lake was drained in 1792, shows this clearly.
[13] Wiltshire Record Office, 135/4.
[14] 2 May 1745, 'By Mr. Cheere for Apollo and Diana & his packing cases in full . . . £51. 5.' F.S.(Acc.)W.

ing this walk had been planted for twenty-four years in 1757.[15] It seems therefore that Henry had been improving this area some time before he took possession. He also altered the approach from the house to the village, abolishing the forecourt, sweeping the driveway in an arc before the house, and turning it through a gateway belonging to the old castle. This is probably the one which Colt Hoare moved to its present position in 1799.[16] About 1743, Henry started planning his grand project to form a landscape with a lake as its central feature. In August 1744, Flitcroft wrote to him concerning work at the house. He continued:

> I have sent the design of the Circular Open Temple of the Ionick Order, Antique, but before I send the construction of the stone-work must be certain of the dimention of the stone you can raise at your quarry and also must desire to know if it is weather proof, especially for the crown of the dome; this I shall be glad to know soon. I am glad you go on so well with the decoration of your salon and hope it will be executed to our wishes.[17]

Henry jotted down the measurements of his stone in the margin. A week later Flitcroft wrote again:

> I have inclosed. the section and construction for the entablature and dome of the Round Temple for which I find your stone will be too small; but it may be done with the Shaftesbury stone which you say will resist the weather and is as fine graind. as Portland, therefore I should recommend caution in using your stone and desire you will not think of having above three stones in each pillar besides the base and capital, wch. makes 5 pieces in each. I am sorry Ireson is so unreasonable in his demand about the raising and scapling your stone. I thought the acct. of it had been kept by your gardiner, and that the price was to be proportiond. to that Acct. This indeed is but labourer's work; but as to the masonry of the Round Temple if it be not excellently well done it will not answer your purpose in being both a beautiful and lasting piece of work; if he be not capable of doing it as it ought, some other person should be employd.; and I must particularly desire that the foundations of this temple may be done in a very different manner from the coarse and ordinary manner in which ha-ha walls are generally done, or it will not do justice to this monument I hope you will transmit to posterity, to be a credit to the time in which it was done. Tis too true that workmen of this age study only their too much profit, rather than

[15] See I, 3, p. 42 and note 29.
[16] Annals of Stourhead, ST.
[17] Henry Flitcroft to Henry Hoare, 18 Aug. 1744, T(ST) 383.907. Punctuation has been added and spelling amended where this assists reading without affecting the sense.

to be expert in geometry and mechanicks and the nature of materials, whereby they deserve encouragement and is the reason so few buildings are well performed.[18]

Then follows a passage which suggests that Flitcroft was doing more than carrying out designs for buildings at Henry's request. 'My next shall bring you sections of the proper moulding for this building, and after that the Temple of Ceres, with the Rocky Arch in which I propose to place the River God and a sketch of how I conceive the head of the lake should be formed. Twill make a most agreeable scene, with the solemn shade about it and the variety of other agreeable circumstances.'[19]

There is no trace or record of a 'circular open temple of the ionick order' at Stourhead. This was obviously an important building, and the circular form suggests the Pantheon. How Henry could have changed his mind about the building for this site will be discussed below. Dr. Richard Pococke, who visited Stourhead in 1754, wrote: 'To the south of the house is a lawn with a piece of water, and from that is a winding descent over the above mentioned valley; in the way is a Dorick open Temple, and below, over the water, is an Ionick temple, with a handsom room in it.'[20] In spite of its topographical inaccuracy,[21] a plan made by the Swedish artist, F. M. Piper, in 1779, gives an idea of the layout of the garden. The lawn to the south of the house is terminated by a statue of Apollo Belvedere on a rise. A path to the right leads to a terrace; and in the way is an open temple[22] (Pl. 13b). From another drawing it can be seen that this is not Doric but Ionick. Pococke probably inadvertently switched the orders. 'Over the water', read as 'overlooking the water', would describe the Tuscan Doric Temple of Flora (Ceres). The Ionick open temple, it can be seen, contained an urn and two busts, probably those now in the Temple of Flora. Flitcroft's third letter gives instructions for this building:

I have inclosd. to you the plan and elevation of the Temple of Ceres, with a scetch of the entablature showing how the try-

[18] H.F. to H.H., 25 Aug. 1744, T(ST) 383.907.
[19] Ibid. The 'rocky arch' was in the bank below the Temple of Ceres. It housed the spring known as Paradise Well, and a statue by Thos. Manning. This was bought 28 Jan. 1743, i.e. before the Temple of Flora was built. W. R. Gunnis, *Dictionary of British Sculptors*, mentions a Manning who provided figures for grottoes in 1743. He suggests this was John Manning the Elder, 'an ingenious statuary of Hyde Park Corner'.
    The arch with the statue is shown in a painting by C. W. Bampfylde, see I. A. Williams, *Early English Watercolours* (1952), Plate CLXXX, fig. 370. This is a reclining River God, in the classical manner, as in the antique *Nile* in the Vatican. Cf. also, Claude Lorrain, *Landscape with Parnassus*, Liber Veritatis, 126. The painting is at Edinburgh. The later River God by Cheere, which is now in the Grotto at Stourhead, is baroque. I have not been able to trace a model for it.
[20] Richard Pococke, *Travels through England*, ed. J. J. Cartwright (Camden Society, 1889), II, p. 43.
[21] Among other things the viewpoints indicated by dotted lines do not correspond with the actuality.
[22] The temple no longer exists and is probably the one removed by Colt Hoare (*Modern Wiltshire*, p. 66) and illustrated by Piper as *Loge wid Terrassen*. (Pl. 13b.)

glyphs and metop(e)s should be proportioned with the scul(l)s and be introduced therein; a great deal of the old entablature will come in (as stone) but I believe must be entirely new wrought, for I much doubt if any part be tolerably exact. I have also sent a plan and section for the manner of laying the foundations which must go down to the terra firma, or be pyled in a good manner to prevent the least settlement, which would be a very bad thing in these sort of buildings. But if the hill, in the place where this building is to stand, be natural firm earth, then following the pland. positions will be sufficient to make a very good building. The entablature at the ends will be plane as appears in the breaks at the ends of the portico. Pray let them take care to make the pediments true pitch, which in the present portico is too high. A section of the inside of this building shall be soon sent, with a particular drawing of the doorcase and pedestal moulding, but this will be sufficient to enable you to talk with the mason about the building. The entablature on the inside portico will be plane and the cornice to which may be stucco. The covering of this building I believe must be of slate. I shall be glad to hear how your other works go on.[23]

It is clear from this that Henry Hoare was supervising the work himself. The mason in this case was probably Nathaniel Ireson who built the house and was established at Wincanton where he had opened a quarry. From 1745 onwards his name does not appear in the ledgers possibly because of the difficulty mentioned by Flitcroft. Instead, Henry employed William Privett of Chilmark,[24] near Tisbury, where a fine sandy limestone, similar to Portland is quarried.

[23] H.F. to H.H., 1 Sep. 1744, T(ST) 383.907.
[24] Called 'Willm. Privet of Chillmark', in ledger entry of 30 Dec. 1745, FS(Acc.). According to Chilmark parish register there were a number of stonemasons called William Privett. One died in 1747, and another in 1772. A fine-grained limestone similar to Portland is quarried at Chilmark, and is probably that used in the Temple of Flora, the Pantheon and the pediments of the grotto. See also, estimate and bond of 'Wm. Privett, Robt. Moore Sen. and Robt. Moore Ju. for the true performance of the Obelisque', dated 1746, T(ST) 383.907:

> Whereas the above bounden William Privett Robert Moor the Older and Robert Moor the Younger have come to an Agreement with the above named Henry Hoare for the erecting and setting up of an Obelisk in or near the Garden of the said Henry Hoare at Stourhead aforesaid of the height of one hundred foot at the loest part of which said Obelisk is to be built with Stone to be raised brought and used from the Quarries of them the said William Privett Robert Moor the Older and Robert Moor the Younger at Chilmark aforesaid and some doubts arising to the said Henry Hoare whither the Stone to be brought from Chilmark and used as aforesaid will endure and stand all weather without receiving damage thereby the said . . . do hereby warrant the same stone to stand firm sound and good against all weather for the Space of Five Years from the finishing and compleating the said Obelisk without receiving any damage thereby either by shelling flaws or otherwise.

The Obelisk at present bears a dedication from Sir Richard Colt Hoare to his grandfather. 'To commemorate in some small degree the improvements which my predecessor and benefactor

The first phase of the garden seems to have been complete by the end of 1745, and we may assume by the entry in September, 'By Willm. Privet on Acct. of Temple',[25] that it included the Temple of Ceres (Flora) (Pl. 1). A visitor to Stourhead, writing in *The London Chronicle* in 1757, described the inside of this building as it then was. 'Here is the Figure of the Goddess, with her proper Emblems, standing in Front as you open the Door. On each Side are two commodious Seats, which are made in Imitation of the Pulvinaria, or little Beds which were placed near the Altar at the Time of Sacrifice, on which the Pagans were wont to lay the Images of their Gods in their Temples. Eight or ten Feet below, level with the Water, in a subterraneous Grotto, is another Figure of the River God.'

A ledger entry on 5 December 1746, reads, 'By Mr. Wootton for a Picture, a Compn. to my Claude Ln...£36. 15.'[26] This is the first record of Henry Hoare's interest in Claude. Up to this point there is no evidence that Henry Hoare had been particularly inspired by the landscapes of this painter. Before considering if this now became the case, we have to distinguish between literary and pictorial sources of inspiration. We have discussed the part which writers played in establishing the idea of 'natural landscape'. Henry Hoare knew by heart at least some of Pope's *Epistle to Lord Burlington*[27] and although the evidence for this comes after the event, it is probable he had *the genius of the place* in mind before 1744. He was familiar too with *Paradise Lost*. 'I hear you have been at Stourd. without the dame,' he wrote to his nephew Richard, 'so fear you *saw undelighted all delight*[28] tho'' you trod the enchanting paths of paradise.'[29] As Horace Walpole said, '(Milton's) description of Eden is a warmer and more just picture of the present style than Claude Lorrain could have painted from Hagley or Stourhead...where the river bursts from the urn of its god, and passes on its course through the cave.'[30] Just as Eve remembered it on the day of her creation when

> I first awak't, and found myself repos'd
> Under a shade on flours, much wondring where
> And what I was, whence thither brought, and how.
> Not distant far from thence a murmuring sound
> Of waters issu'd from a Cave and spread
> Into a liquid plain.[31]

completed on his beautiful demesne at Stourhead, I caused the following inscription to be sculptured on a tablet, and affixed to the base of an Obelisk which he had erected.' R.C.H., ms. memoirs, ST. It was rebuilt with Bath stone in 1839; and again restored after it had been struck by lightning in 1853. *Annals of Stourhead* (ST).

[25] Sep. 1745, FS(Acc.)W.   [26] 5 Dec. 1746, FS(Acc.)W.

[27] Cf. below, letter Henry Hoare to Richard Hoare (nephew), 30 Jan. 1755, FS. Also (p. 51 below) H.H. to Lord Bruce, undated, 1764. T(TOT).

[28] Cf. *Paradise Lost*, Book 4, lines 285 ff.

[29] H.H. to Richard Hoare, Jan. 1755, FS.

[30] Horace Walpole. 'On Modern Gardening', *Anecdotes of Painting*, IV (1786), p. 268.

[31] *Paradise Lost*, Book 4, lines 450 ff.

Indeed, this might almost describe the pagan scene[32] which Claude had painted a decade earlier; the engraving of which, by Vivares, was published in 1743.

Clearly in Henry Hoare's mind was the intention to evoke the numinous; and particularly in the celebration of water, as at Clitumnus[33] (Pl. 4b) which he could have visited when in Italy. Such places, in any case, were models for the classical temple in the landscape, quite apart from the painter's reinforcement of it. He would probably have read the younger Pliny's description:

> A dark and shady wood of old cypress trees stands upon a small hill, under which a spring makes a passage....Having issued forth in this manner, it forms itself into a large basin of water, so very clear and transparent, that you may number any pieces of money and any shining little pebbles, which are thrown in...Adjoining is an old and awful temple. The god Clitumnus appears standing, clothed and adorned with the *praetexta*.[34]

Henry Hoare also had conceptions of how to achieve visual effects in planting, similar to those which Pope had expressed. 'The greens should be ranged together in large masses as the shades are in painting: to contrast the *dark* masses with *light* ones, and to relieve each dark mass itself with little sprinklings of lighter greens here and there.'[35] The planting and the obvious expedient for making a lake, to dam the valley and let the contours determine the shape, resulted in qualities of irregularity having little to do with theories of the serpentine; although it did unconsciously accord with Hogarth's principle of *intricacy*, 'that peculiarity in the lines...that leads the eye a wanton kind of chace'.[36] The landscape at Stourhead thus came to have many of the qualities later associated with *the picturesque*; whereas, as Pope used the term, it simply meant 'like a picture'.

It could be argued that whereas the siting of the Temple of Flora and the Grotto can be explained by reasons other than pictorial necessity, the Pantheon is the most important visual component of the whole design at Stourhead. This temple appears in a number of Claude's paintings. Henry Hoare owned a version of the theme in a copy of *View of Delphi with a procession*, the original of which has never left the Doria-Pamphili Collection in Rome. *Coast view of Delos with Aeneas* (Pl. 2b), now in the National Gallery, has a Doric portico in the foreground with the Pantheon facing it, and a bridge to the left, in the same relative positions in which these

---

[32] Claude Lorrain, *Narcissus*, National Gallery, London. It shows a sleeping nymph based on the same classical original as the statue at Stourhead.

[33] The suggestion comes from Miss Georgina Masson. The theme is elaborated in 'The Sacred Landscape', *Apollo*, Sep. 1968.

[34] Quoted, Richard Colt Hoare, *Recollections Abroad*, II, p. 243.

[35] 'Mr. Hoare c. 1752.' Spence's *Anecdotes*, 1105.

[36] William Hogarth, *The Analysis of Beauty*, V (1753), p. 25.

features are seen on entering the gardens at Stourhead. The painting was one of six illustrating the story of Aeneas.[37] Originally made for an unknown patron, it was later in the collection of a M. de Viviers in Paris, and was said to have been in a sale in 1737, about the time Henry Hoare was travelling abroad. In *Landscape with Egeria mourning over Numa* (Pl. 2a), the Pantheon is seen across a lake (as from the terrace at Stourhead) which does in fact represent Lake Nemi.[38] It is here the nymph Egeria was said to have disturbed the worship of Diana by her lamentations for her husband Numa, until Diana out of pity 'turned her body into a cool spring, and dissolved her limbs into everlasting waters'.[39] Henry Hoare would have been familiar with Ovid's version of the story. The hillside past the Temple of Flora was known as the Mount of Diana. If, however, the analogy with Lake Nemi was at one time in Henry Hoare's mind, it seems likely that it was superseded by another.

The earliest reference to the Pantheon at Stourhead is in 1753 when William Privett was paid £300 on account for the 'Temple of Hercules'.[40] We may assume the building was fairly advanced when Pococke visited in July 1754 as he described it as having 'a grand portico of the Corinthian or Composite order'.[41] The lead for the roof was also bought that year.[42] Walpole said that the original design was altered.[43] Among the drawings at Stockholm[44] attributed to Piper there is a section of the Pantheon which differs in important details from its present form as to the construction of the dome and the interior treatment. Another section by Piper shows the dome and the treatment of the interior as it is now, with the bas-reliefs and the frieze from Balbec which was probably not earlier than 1757. The first section is probably one of Flitcroft's original designs, not only on account of its style, but also because Piper would not have drawn something which did not exist. It looks as though, whatever may have been added or altered, the building was ready to receive Rysbrack's *Hercules* (Pl. 7c) in 1757.[45] The statue had been commissioned ten years earlier.[46] It is also recorded that in 1744 the sculptor, 'finding himself somewhat at leisure, business not being so brisk...he therefore set himself about a

[37] See below.
[38] Henry Hoare bought a painting from Richard Wilson which he called 'The Lake of Avernus' 1760 FS(Acc.). This is later referred to as 'The Lake of Nemi' or 'Speculum Dianae'. See Woodbridge, 'The Sacred Landscape', *Apollo* (September 1968), p. 210.
[39] Ovid, *The Metamorphoses*, trans. M. M. Innes (1955).
[40] 16 June, 29 Sep., T(ST) 383.6.
[41] Pococke, *Travels through England*, p. 43.
[42] 10 Oct. 1754, 'To Henry Jordan of Blandford, His Bill to Geo. Cannick for lead for the Roof of the Pantheon, £223. 3.' FS(Acc.).
[43] 'Visits to Country Seats', p. 43.
[44] The originals are with the Royal Academy of Fine Arts, Stockholm. Negatives with R.I.B.A. Drawings Collection, 66 Portland Place, London.
[45] 18 Feb. 1757, 'a pedestal for Hercules', FS(Acc.).
16 July 1757, 'a Gratuity for the Hercules beyond the Contract', T(ST) 383.6.
[46] Agreement dated 1 July 1747, T(ST) 383.4.

model of Hercules'[47] in terra cotta (Pl. 37). It might immediately be assumed that the decision to call the Pantheon the Temple of Hercules followed from this. But it is possible that Henry already had a statue of Hercules in mind when he saw Rysbrack's model. This assumption becomes more plausible if we study the iconography of the garden.

The pictorial and literary clues point to *The Aeneid*. The painting in the National Gallery called *Coast View of Delos with Aeneas* (Pl. 2b), which bears more than a casual relation to the design of the garden, refers to an episode in Book III. According to Roethlisberger,[48] Claude took the subject from Ovid's version of the story in Metamorphoses 13. The painting shows Anius (king and priest of Delos), Anchises, Aeneas, and Ascanius standing on a terrace outside a Doric Portico overlooking the harbour at Delos. Beyond them is a temple like the Pantheon. The story in *The Aeneid* reads:

> To Delos I now sailed, and our tired band received a safe and kindly welcome in the harbour. We disembarked and paid reverence to Apollo's city. The king was Anius, who was priest of Apollo as well as king, and wore the holy bay-leaves and ribbons on his brow. He came to meet us and recognised Anchises as an old friend. He shook hands with us, treating us as his guests; and we walked up to the palace. Reverently I entered the temple built of ancient stone and prayed; 'Apollo, grant us a home of our own. We are weary. Give us a walled city which shall endure, and a lineage of our blood. Let there be some new citadel for us; henceforth preserve it as a remnant of Troy saved from the Greeks and from merciless Achilles. Who is to be our guide? Where do you bid us go, where settle our home? Be to us a father-god; tell us your will and speak direct to our hearts.' I had scarcely spoken when of a sudden everything seemed to quake, even the God's entrance-door and his bay-tree; the whole hill on which we stood appeared to move and the shrine seemed to open and the tripod within to speak with a roar. We bowed low and fell to the earth. A voice came to our ears: 'O much enduring Dardans, the land of your ancestors whence you are sprung shall receive you on your return to her generous bosom. Seek out your ancient mother. And from this land the House of Aeneas, the sons of his sons, and all their descendents shall bear rule over the earth's widest bounds.'[49]

The connection between this painting and the garden is admittedly conjecture. The inscription on the Temple of Flora is not. The quotation,

[47] M. I. Webb, *Michael Rysbrack*, (1954), p. 121.
[48] Marcel Roethlisberger, *Claude Lorrain*, I (1961), p. 420.
[49] Virgil, *The Aeneid*, W. F. Jackson Knight trans. (ed. 1958), p. 77.

Procul, o procul este profani, is from the sixth book. After leaving Carthage Aeneas came to 'Euboean Cumae's coast' where he 'made his way to the fastness where Apollo rules on high, and to the vast cavern beyond which is the awful Sibyl's own secluded place'.[50] Here the priestess of Apollo and Diana 'invited them into the temple on the height'[51] where the oracle told Aeneas of the future. Aeneas then asked, 'Since it is said that here is the Eternal Gate of the Infernal King and near here the marsh in the darkness where Acheron's stream bends round, may I be granted to come within sight of my dear father face to face....'[52] The story continues:

> There was a deep rugged cave, stupendous and yawning wide, protected by a lake of black water and over this lake no birds could wing a straight course without harm, so poisonous the breath which streamed up from those black jaws and rose to the vault of sky; and that is why the Greeks named this place 'Aornos, the Birdless'. Here the Priestess set in place four bullocks black of hide... and laid them, as the first taste of the offering, on the sacrificial fire; and as she did so she cried aloud to Hecate, the mighty in Heaven and mighty in Hell. Others applied the knife to the victims' throats and caught the warm blood in bowls. Aeneas took his sword and smote a lamb with fleece black as soot in offering to the Mother of the Eumenides and her Great Sister, and a barren cow for Proserpine herself. Now he began the nocturnal altar rite to the King of Styx. He

---

[50] Ibid., 6, p. 147. Sir John Clerk (1684–1755), the Scottish Antiquary, who made many improvements to his estate at Penicuik at the beginning of the eighteenth century, wrote in his journal for 1742,

> This year I made the antique Cave at Hurley where I made a large pond, and stocked it with Carp and Tench. ... I caused this pond to be inclosed, and the little hill in the middle got the name of Clermont. This is a Rural Scheme which, in my opinion, adds a good deal of Beauty to the Enclosures of Pennicuik house, as it resembles the Grotto of Pausilipo at Naples.

On a later occasion he wrote of this lake,

> Nor can I omit another fish-pond, or lesser lake, noteworthy for its position and solitude, which a poet only could describe. It is surrounded by hills and steep rocks, and no-one can get access to it but by the mouth of a frightful cave. To those who enter, therefore, first occurs the memory of the cave of the Cuman Sybil, for the ruinous aperture, blocked up with stones and briars, strikes the eye. Then there comes upon the wayfarers a shudder, as they stand in doubt whether they are among the living or the dead. As, indeed, certain discords set off and give finish to musical cadencies in such a way as to render the subsequent harmony more grateful to the ear, so does the form of this mournful cave, with its long and shady path, followed by the light and prospect, make the exit more delightful. For suddenly the darkness disappears, and as it were at the creation of a new world.

Memoirs of the Life of Sir John Clerk of Penicuik, Baronet ... extracted by himself from his own journals 1676–1775, ed. John M. Gray (Edinburgh, 1892).

[51] Ibid., p. 148.

[52] Ibid., p. 150.

laid whole carcasses of bulls on the flames and poured rich olive oil on the glowing entrails. And, behold, soon before the first gleam of the rising sun, the ground bellowed beneath their feet, the slopes of the forest-clad mountains began to move, and there appeared shapes like hounds howling and just visible through the shadows; the Goddess[53] was coming and was very near. '*Stand clear!*' cried the Priestess, '*All you who are unhallowed; stand clear!* Be gone from all the Grove. But you, Aeneas, whip blade from scabbard and step forth on your way. It is now that you need courage and a strong heart.' Saying no more she plunged frantically down into the opened cavern, and strode onwards. With dauntless pace Aeneas followed where she led.[54]

Is the path round the lake an allegory of Aeneas's journey? The imperceptible descent to the Grotto and the steep climb out of it evoke the sibyl's words, *Facilis descensus Averno*! 'Light is the descent to Avernus! Night and day the portals of gloomy Dis stand wide: but to recall thy step and issue to the upper air—there is the toil and there the task!'[55]

That something of the kind was in Henry Hoare's mind is confirmed in a letter he wrote some years later. 'I have made the passage up from the Sousterrain Serpentine & will make it easier of access facilis descensus Averno.'[56]

We have seen that the earliest recorded purchase of statuary for the garden was from Manning for a river god. In the Aeneid we read that Aeneas, faced with war against Latium and the need for allies, 'was tossed on a heaving tide of anxieties'.[57] He then 'sank on the river bank under heaven's chill height. . . . And there appeared to him the God of the place, old Tiber himself . . .' who told him, '. . . here is your home assured and here for the Gods of Home is their sure place'.[58] And Aeneas 'cried from

---

[53] Hecate, who was said to be accompanied by the sound of howling dogs.

[54] *The Aeneid*, p. 154.

[55] Ibid., p. 151.

[56] Henry Hoare to Lord Bruce, 23 Dec. 1765, T(TOT). There is an inscription on the original pedimented entrance to the grotto, *Intus Aquae dulces, vivoque sedilia saxo, Nympharum domus.* 'There is a cave directly in front at the foot of the cliffs. *Inside* it are stalectites and *fresh water, and there are seats there cut in the living rock, for nymphs have their home in the cave.' The Aeneid,* 1, p. 167, describing the place in Africa where Aeneas landed after his flight from Troy. See note 5 above.

[57] *The Aeneid*, 8, p. 201.

[58] Ibid., 8, p. 202. Horace Walpole ('Visits to Country Seats', p. 42) says there were lines of Virgil under the River God. Colt Hoare (*Modern Wiltshire*) gives lines from Ovid, *Metamorphoses*, I, 574 ff., describing the Vale of Tempe.

> Haec domus, haec sedes, haec sunt penetralia magni
> Amnis; in hoc residens facto de cantibus antro
> Undis jura dabat, nymphisque colentibus undas.

This was the home, the dwelling, the most secret haunt of the great river, Sitting here, in a cave hewn out of the cliffs, he was dispensing justice to the waves and to the nymphs who inhabited the stream. [Trans. M. M. Innes.]

his heart to the sky: "Nymphs...whose birth is of the rivers, and, Father Tiber, you, and your hallowed stream, receive me....Whatever spring may fill the pools which are your home, and wherever you yourself emerge in grandeur from the soil, always shall you be celebrated by me...".'[59]

Having followed the river god's instructions to seek out the Arcadians as allies, Aeneas found that 'on that very day the Arcadian king was paying anniversary honours to Amphitryon's mighty son Hercules'[60] who, on that spot, had killed the man-monster Cacus. Thereafter his rites had been observed, and an altar erected to him, "our 'Greatest Altar' we shall always call it, our 'Greatest' it shall always be".'[61]

All this suggests that Henry was celebrating the founding of Rome, just as he, like Aeneas, was establishing his family in a place. It is worth noting in passing that, according to the twelfth-century chronicle of Geoffrey of Monmouth, Aeneas, through his grandson Brutus the Trojan, was an ancestor of the British race. Although by mid-eighteenth century this myth was no longer taken seriously, it does make the subsequent jump at Stourhead, from classical iconography to King Alfred, seem rather less inconsequential. In 1748, the year the bill[62] for the Grotto (Pl. 18b) was presented, his only surviving son (yet another Henry) was growing to manhood. It seems there was a strong bond between them; not only did he represent his hopes of immortality, but he was able to share his interest in the arts. In 1750 he wrote from Aix where he was passing with his travelling tutor, Mr. John Rust. The letter contained an account of pictures in the Luxembourg and also said, 'The Claude you desire me to describe is remarkable for having a Jupiter and Europa in the foreground; it is a seaport with trees on the left hand & on the right a Castle on the Top of a Rock projecting into the sea, which you see through some Trees.[63] It is a pleasant picture but not a warm one & neither that nor any of the others are in good preservation enough for you to buy. I mentioned to you before the only one I thought worth anything, the Bourgognone.'[64] The writer died at Naples the following year, aged twenty-one.[65] For Henry it was the most

[59] *The Aeneid*, p. 203.   [60] *The Aeneid*, p. 204.   [61] Ibid., p. 209.

[62] Bill from Wm. Privett and Co. for work done 'about the Grotto at Stourhead', 1748. Items include 'coping round the cupulo', 'Ribbs', 'Pediments', '37 days at the quarry', '935 days work my men at 2s. 6d.', 'Labourer 110 days at 14d.', 'Myself 101 days at 3s.', T(ST) 383.4.

[63] Probably Roethlisberger, op.cit., I, p. 276, Liber Veritatis III; II, fig. 193. Location unknown. In the Collection of Sir Joshua Reynolds by 1771.

[64] Letter to Henry Hoare, 25 Dec. 1750. T(ST) 383.907.

[65] *The Gentlemen's Magazine* for 1789 mentioned that John Rust was 'the travelling tutor to Sir Richard Hoare's son, of Stourhead'. This must have been a mistake for Henry. The writer added, 'The young gentleman died upon his travels, and charges of neglect were attributed to Mr. Rust; notwithstanding which, Sir Richard settled an annuity of £400 upon him after his return to England.' This was a large amount, but it is confirmed in Sir Richard Colt Hoare's notes of annuities he took over on his father's death which include, 'J. Rust (decd) £400'. He also recorded, in the MS. memoirs at Stourhead, that in his grandfather's time Mr. Rust, a lively, pleasant, and witty companion, was a constant visitor at Stourhead. Rust was a relation by marriage, as Elizabeth Rust was the second wife of Henry's brother, Richard (1709–54).

bitter experience of all. Some months later he wrote to his brother Richard, 'I have been taught by our Holy Religion, by former Visitations, Tryals and Afflictions to submit myself before the Throne of God who (unworthy as I am of the least of His Divine favours) still supports me under a Grief I never expected or wish'd to have survived; but His will be done, His Mercys are infinite, His Judgments like the great Deep.'[66]

[66] Henry Hoare to Sir Richard Hoare (brother), 14 Mar. 1752, FS.

Chapter 3

Cleopatra

Left without an heir (for who could say what the future held for his two daughters) Henry Hoare might well have felt discouraged from immediate thoughts of adorning his inheritance. It is perhaps for this reason that there is only one entry for building in the accounts of 1752, 'By Mr. Privet being an extra Allowce. on Obelisk Acct.'[1] He had been about this since 1746[2] but it could hardly have taken so long to build and Privet had meanwhile been on other work.[3] It was also at this time that he began to think of a villa at Clapham Common, where in later life he would spend his winters and eventually die. Flitcroft again was the architect.[4] The house,[5] which was of Suffolk brick, faced the common with a centre block of three stories flanked by two narrow four-storey wings; these in turn were linked by ornamental walls to coach houses and stables on either side, whose treatment echoes the Palladian motif of the temple on the terrace at Stourhead. No trace remains today of the pleasure grounds which Henry Hoare made at Clapham, and on which he looked from the bow windows of his drawing room there, down towards the Thames and Chelsea Hospital in the distance. This room was painted with subjects from mythology, but what these were and who painted them is not recorded.[6] Doubtless there was a movement of pictures and furniture between Stourhead and Clapham, although there is no reason to suppose that the Surrey home remotely rivalled the Wiltshire one.

In 1752 Henry was forty-seven. It is clear that he regarded himself primarily as a banker; but the shrewd and rational qualities demanded by

---

[1] 29 Nov., T(ST) 383.6.

[2] See I, 2, note 24.

[3] Sep. 1745, 'Temple'. FS(Acc.)W. 4 Dec. 1749, 'Bridge and other work', T(ST) 383.6, and the Grotto.

[4] 24 Nov. 1753, 'By Mr. Flitcroft for his trouble at Clapham House in full . . . £200.' T(ST) 383.6.

[5] I am indebted to Mr. E. E. Smith, Hon. Sec. of the Clapham Antiquarian Society, for a photograph of a lithograph of the house and for his notes on its history, *The Hoare Family in Clapham* (Clapham Antiquarian Society, March 1959).

[6] E. E. Smith ('John Brogden', Clapham Antiquarian Society, February 1964), quotes an auctioneer's catalogue saying these were by 'an Italian artist'. There is no evidence of any such in Henry Hoare's accounts, but a large sum was paid to Arthur Pond, 5 July 1753 and 8 March 1754, T(ST) 383.6. See below.

this calling overlaid an emotional nature which found expression in his garden and later in letters about it to his daughter and granddaughter. But besides being the language of feeling and intuitive thought, the arts are instruments of self-assertion. Henry still needed to elevate himself in the social hierarchy and, above all, he still needed an heir. The year in which he started the Pantheon was also that in which he allied himself with the Boyle family and in which Richard, 3rd Earl of Burlington, died. The latter's Irish titles devolved on his cousin, John Boyle, Earl of Orrery, whose son, Lord Dungarvan, married Henry's daughter Susanna on 11 May 1753.

Lord Cork, or Orrery as he was before Burlington's death, had literary pretensions. He was a friend of Pope; and his *Remarks on Swift*, whose dislike of Walpole's government he shared, were published in 1751. He showed little appreciation of Swift's genius; and it had been said of him that he would have been a man of genius himself 'if he had known how to set about it'. His house at Marston, near Frome, was not far from Stourhead; but having acquired, by marriage, Caledon in County Tyrone, he went to live there in 1739, and to compensate for being 'buried to the World', found amusement in embellishing this landscape.[7]

Lord Cork readily complied with his son's inclination to marry into the family of a wealthy banker, for although, as Lady Cork put it, Susanna 'was of Birth far inferior to the Ladys of those Noble Houses from whom both my Lord and his son were descended', he was badly in need of financial support. Henry, for his part, 'expressed himself highly sensible of the Honour done to his Family'.[8] He settled on his daughter, '£25,000 in money; £1,000 for clothes, jewels estimated at £3,000 and his house in Lincolns Inn Fields for her life, which with the Furniture and Pictures left in it cost him £10,000'.[9] The pair settled at Marston where Lord Cork had made many alterations to the house, inside and out, and 'brought water which was a very Expensive Article as the Springs are far from the house and conveyd hither in Leden pipes'.[10] He also 'Enlarged and Beautified the Gardens (and) in all this the Plans were approved of or Designed by Lord Dungarvan whose Genius is very much inclined towards architecture'.[11] Dungarvan thus had interests in common with his father-in-law, who perhaps found in him some compensation for the son he had lost. Dungarvan's name is associated in the ledger of 1757 with the purchase of Robert Wood's *Ruins of Balbec*; and later that year there is an entry 'To Mr. Wilson[12] Lord D.'s Friend painter for Romeo and Juliett'.[13]

---

[7] See Desmond Fitz-Gerald, 'Irish Gardens of the Eighteenth Century', *Apollo* (September 1968), 204 ff.
[8] Account written by Margaret, Countess of Cork and Orrery, of an estrangement between the Earl and Henry Hoare, annotated by the latter. T(ST) 383.909.
[9] Ibid.   [10] Ibid.   [11] Ibid.
[12] Benjamin Wilson, 1721–88, portrait painter, employed by Zoffany. He painted Garrick as Hamlet and later, with Mrs. Bellamy, in *Romeo and Juliet*. Both pictures were published as prints in 1754 and 1765 respectively.
[13] 7 Nov. 1757, T(ST) 383.6.

In improving Marston, and also the estate at Caledon in Ireland, Lord Cork had run considerably into debt. So confused were his affairs that Henry agreed to become a trustee for the administration of his estates in order to liquidate the many debts. Lord and Lady Cork settled in Italy and received an annual sum of £800 for themselves and their family; other revenue was used by the trustees to repay their Creditors. Relations were apparently cordial until a difference arose between Henry and Lord Cork who protested at having to support his son, Hamilton Boyle, out of the allowance. 'Who can think', wrote Henry, 'that £800 p.an. neat out of that estate is not full as much as he could reasonably expect, or the creditors grant, since their whole Dependence is on his single thread of life, save only those bonds and debts of Lord Corke which Dear Lord Dungarvan was brought in to join him in.'[14] 'I call heaven to witness that from my soul I exerted every power in me to extricate the family.' But 'these distresses Lord Corke has drawn on himself and the most shocking reflection of all is the possibility of his going into his grave without satisfying them'.[15]

This was not however the end of the matter. Unknown to the trustees Lord Cork had obtained £1422 of the money due to the creditors. This shocked Henry 'beyond utterance', as it had been appropriated to their use and benefit by a 'Solemn Deed of Trust'.[16] Lady Cork affected incredulity. 'As no uncivil letters had passed between my Lord and Mr. Hoare, we were amazed at his conduct towards us. His avoiding all intercourse kept us entirely in the dark to discover the motives of our great offence 'til by a letter that Mr. Hoare had written to his Partner in the Banker's Shop.'[17] Hardly able to contain his feelings, Henry put the banker's case. 'This deceit being detected is it to be wondered at that from that moment I altered my Conduct towards them and that I had the Spirit to show that I was not quite so tame an Animal as not to resent such treatment.' 'I then determined to adhere strictly to the terms of the Deeds of Trust and to go no further lengths for them.' 'Little did I expect...to be accused by Lord Cork of oppressions and insinuations of over-reaching him, but my Heart is Innocent as God is my judge, he will acquit me of that charge before all the World, in the great and terrible day.'[18] All the answer his Lordship returned was that 'heats and resentments was not the way to help him out of his difficulty'.[19]

The union of Susanna and Lord Dungarvan did not produce a son. Meanwhile, Henry had been planning for his younger daughter Anne (Pl. 24a) (Nanny),[20] who was then seventeen, to marry her cousin Richard[21] (Pl. 23b), whose affection, family rumour had it, was settled on her. It was clear

[14] Lady Cork, T(ST) 383.909.
[15] Ibid.   [16] Ibid.   [17] Ibid.
[18] Ibid.   [19] Ibid.
[20] Anne Hoare, 1737–59, mother of Richard Colt Hoare.
[21] Sir Richard Hoare, 1st Bart, d. 1787. Son of Henry Hoare's younger brother, Sir Richard Hoare, Knt, d. 1754.

that the inheritance of Stourhead was conditional on the acceptance other responsibilities.

> It is very obvious [Henry wrote to his brother] how absolutely necessary it is that the strictest residence and attendance We and Our Fathers have given at Fleet Street should be continued in the person of my dear Nephew who would forfeit all claim of relief from his descendants, unless by following in the steps of his Predecessors he continues that care and example which has been to the credit, support and security of us all and without which the Possession so much envy'd us must unhappily be transferred into other hands. God forbid it![22]

> Should his (Richard's) answer be favourable toward her, he may then be acquainted that her affections will sympathise with his, and that there is all reason to think there will be no love lost between them. Then the fair prospect of Worldly Interest and advantage may be laid open in a proper light so as to confirm his determination, with the indispensable necessity of their residence at Fleet Street, as urged in my letter, and of which she is so thoroughly convinced and satisfied that she makes no hesitation in cheerfully and readily consenting to whatever Her Care and Economy and example will keep up the character and established Credit of that House on which the Name and Family depends.[23]

He reiterated the theme in letters to his nephew whom he was preparing to succeed him.

> I do not doubt your particular attention to the business at all times and especially in my absence and that you will not devolve that great Care and Concern on another who may be willing enough to take it on Him that His expectations may rise higher ...but it is our interest to keep down such expectations by our own attention to what ought to be the first and last of all our thoughts and the chief happy business and employmt of our whole lives. I with gratitude must allow I have always found it so ...I will not be robbed of that pleasure by the attendance offrd by others no oftener than is necessary for me to look after my concerns here which are trifleing in comparison to that great one from whence all that we possess is derived.[24] ...Whether

22 Henry Hoare to Sir Richard Hoare, Knt, brother, 8 Sep. 1751. FS.
23 H.H. to Sir Richard Hoare, Knt, no date, FS.
24 H.H. to Richard Hoare, nephew, no date. FS. The person whose 'expectations may rise higher', was probably Richard Hoare of Boreham who was made a partner in 1758, five years later.

at pleasure or Business let us be in earnest and ever active and be outdone or exceeded by none, that is the way to thrive.[25]

But family and fortune were not all,

...As I am intent on recommending every Thing to you which may conduce to the real happyness of your Life, let me mention one thing which I and many others have drawn the Greatest Benefit from and that is the advantage which your Leisure hours at Fleet street will give you...of looking into Books and the pursuit of that knowledge which distinguishes only the Gentleman from the Vulgar and teaches Him to adorn the fortune he acquires or possesses and which, without the Lessons in History (which is Philosophy teaching by example) the most envied Height of Fortune will not be enjoyed.[26]

As for Stourhead,

What is there in creation.... Those are the fruits of industry and application to Business and shows what great things may be done by it, the envy of the indolent who have no claim to Temples, Grottos, Bridges, Rocks, Exotick Pines and Ice in Summer. When those are won by the industrious, they have the best claim to them provided their foundations is laid by the Hand of prudence and supported by perseverance in well-doing and constant cautious watchfulness over the main Chance. Without it proud Versailles thy Glory falls and Nero's terrasses dessert their walls,[27] so you could not go on your Via Charmdgiana, it is a pattern of perfection.[28]

Nanny and Richard were married on 20 March 1756. The following summer they were staying at Stourhead, and a visitor has left a description of the place as it was then. The house was convenient. The stone floor of the hall was covered with a thick Turkey carpet so that it was habitable even in winter. Outside, to the south, a lawn sloped in an easy decline to the village of Stourton, whose steeple had almost as good an effect as a ruin.

On the Brow of this Hill is a Walk of considerable Extent, of the softest mossy Turf, bordered on each Side by stately Scotch Firs of Mr. Hoare's own planting, about 24 years since; these, as well as the Wood behind them, are rather too thick set. This noble broad Walk is terminated by an Obelisk one hundred and

[25] H.H. to R.H., 28 Jan. 1755, FS.
[26] H.H. to R.H., same as 23.
[27] Cf. Pope's 'Epistle to Lord Burlington', *Moral Essays*, Ep. IV. Pope was referring to 'Sense' not 'the main Chance'!
[28] H.H. to R.H., 30 Jan. 1755, FS.

twenty Feet in Height, built on the highest Ground; it has a Mythra, or Sun, of six Feet Diameter, in gilded Copper, at the Top....Below this fine Walk, are several irregular Walks of Different Breadths leading into the Valley. These are covered by stately trees, and receive the most heightened Charms by a large piece of Water at the Bottom, on which there is a very pretty Boat....

After describing the Grotto, 'made use of as a cold bath', and other features of the garden, the writer concluded: 'Here we ought to contemplate not only what delights, but what does not shock. In this delicious Abode are no Chinese Works, no Monsters of Imagination; no Deviations from Nature, under the fond Notions of Fashion or Taste; All is grand, or simple, or a beautiful Mixture of both.'[29]

Nanny's first child died in infancy. Her second, Richard Colt Hoare, was born on 9 December 1758. But Henry was again faced with personal tragedy, for Nanny died the following May, not long before her twenty-second birthday; and Dungarvan died in September. All his hopes were now directed towards his grandson.

It is against the background of these events that the Pantheon was built, being virtually completed by 1757, with *Hercules* installed. During the years 1753–7 Henry also completed his house at Clapham, but engaged in no more major building until the early 1760s when he started the Temple of Apollo. It was the period of the Seven Years War, a state of affairs he detested and which might well have inhibited undertakings of a relatively permanent nature. Rysbrack's next commission, for *Flora*, was not until 1759;[30] the only other payment for sculpture was to Cheere 'for Busts at Barnes and Clapham'.[31] Besides commissions to Arthur Pond,[32] Henry also had pictures from Francis Harding[33] and John Wootton.[34] His interest in painting was doubtless stimulated by his friendship with William Hoare of Bath,[35] no blood relation although in 1765 his daughter married one of Henry's nephews known as 'Fat Harry'.[36] William Hoare had been a pupil

[29] *The London Chronicle*, 18 June 1757.
[30] Agreement dated 14 March 1759, T(ST) 383.4.
[31] 25 Jan. 1754, T(ST) 383.6.
[32] See I, 3, note 6.
[33] 30 July 1753, T(ST) 383.6. Francis Harding was described by Vertue as 'the landscape and coach painter'. He was said to be a successful imitator of Canaletto and Pannini. See W. T. Whitley, *Artists and their friends in England*, I, pp. 116 ff. Besides the payment referred to above, Henry Hoare also paid Harding £50 on 25 July 1745, FS(Acc.)W; and £39 12s. 6d. on 14 Aug. 1751, FS(Acc.). The painting of *The Interior of St. Peter's, Rome*, over the mantelpiece in the Music Room at Stourhead is possibly by him.
[34] 26 Sep. 1755, T(ST) 383.6.
[35] William Hoare, R.A., 1707–92. He worked mainly in Bath. In 1762 Warburton, Bishop of Gloucester, noted that he had suffered Gainsborough to run away with all his business. Despite this he seems to have prospered, for Farington noted in his diary, 16 May 1808, that he had left £37,000.
[36] See I, 4, note 100.

of Imperiali, whose *The Sacrifice of Noah* and *Rachel sitting on the House-hold Gods* were in Henry's collection. He was also a friend of Pompeo Batoni, to whom is attributed the copy of Guido Reni's *Salome*. William Hoare himself practised portraiture in pastel, and was noted for the grace of his composition and the beauty of his colouring. He was a sociable man who enjoyed the hospitality of houses such as Stourhead where he was a regular visitor. Henry paid him £1430 between 1759 and 1772.[37] According to Walpole he was employed to decorate four benches in the Pantheon with the story of Cupid and Psyche; but many examples of his work, now in the little dining-room at Stourhead, came there after Henry's death as they are portraits of Colt Hoare's half-brothers and sisters.

In a letter written to Henry in June 1760, concerning among other things a book by 'Mr. Webb',[38] William Hoare gives his views on painters and painting, approving Guido Reni, Domenichino, and Correggio, and comparing Leonardo's 'grimacing figures at his last supper' with 'the noble idea of the Apostles of Raphael'. There is a postscript: 'I know you have a favourite Sleeping Nymph in your Garden. I have made another in a dress something different, which I must beg your acceptance of, just as a memorial that I am very much in your Debt. I wait for its frame from London.'[39] The sentimentally erotic style is nearer to rococo than Henry's taste would have admitted in view of the painting he was then expecting from Anton Rafael Mengs.

The first recorded purchase from the circle of painters and dealers surrounding Cardinal Albani and Sir Horace Mann was in 1758, in which year Mann was paid a total of £571 7*s*.[40] An entry in Henry's ledger for April reads, 'To himself for a picture of Gaspar Poussin....£57. 15.' This is presumably the one referred to in a letter from Mann to Horace Walpole,[41] which Mann had bought for Henry Hoare from the Arnaldi collection at the same time as a painting by Carlo Maratta entitled *The Marchese Pallavicini conducted by Apollo to the Temple of Fame* (Pl. 28a). It was as a companion to this picture that Henry ordered the painting of *Octavius and Cleopatra*[42] from Mengs (Pl. 27).

Although only thirty-one at the time of the commission Mengs had already achieved considerable success. He had come to Rome as a prodigy from Bohemia, and in 1752 had been one of those artists recommended by Horace Mann to make copies of paintings in the Farnese Gallery for the Earl of Northumberland's house in the Strand. He had recently

37 1760 T(ST) 383.6; 1764, 1765, 1766 T(ST) and FS(Acc.); 1770, 1772 FS(Acc.).
38 Daniel Webb, *An Inquiry into the Beauties of Painting and into the Merits of the Most Cele-brated Painters Ancient and Modern* (1760).
39 William Hoare to H.H., 5 June 1760, T(ST) 383.907.
40 20 July, 2 Aug., 18 Sep., FS(Acc.).
41 See St. John Gore, 'Prince of Georgian Collectors', *Country Life*, CXXXV (1964), p. 210.
42 A second version of this painting was included in the Mengs Exhibition at the Prado in 1929, Cat. No. 3. The Stourhead Maratti and Mengs are both reproduced in M. Levey, *Rococo to Revolution* (1966).

completed a *Parnassus* for Cardinal Albani.[43] He was not a typical painter of his time, although his high seriousness accorded with Roman gravity. On his own testimony he was eclectic: 'The painter, wishing to hit upon the best taste, should learn it from the following four masters; from the antique a taste for beauty; from Raphael a taste for significance and expression; from Correggio a taste for agreeableness and harmony; from Titian a taste for truth and colour.'[44] Winckelmann, with whom his name is closely linked, claimed him for neo-classicism. David's *Oath of the Horatii*, perhaps the most famous neo-classical painting, was exhibited in Rome in 1785, the year of Henry Hoare's death. Mengs could thus be called *avant-garde*, except that some would say that David was as reactionary in paint as he was revolutionary in politics. Mengs's style, however, which aimed at unaffected masculinity, had affinities with Stourhead Palladianism, itself conservative compared with aspects of the landscape there.

Mengs was undoubtedly recommended by Thomas Jenkins who wrote to Henry, in June 1759, 'I shall take any and every step in my power to dispose Mr. Mengs to exert his utmost in order to render your picture one of his best works'.[45] Jenkins had originally come to Rome as a painter, in 1753, with an introduction from Mann to Cardinal Albani. At that time he shared a house with Richard Wilson. According to Thomas Jones, writing in the 1770s,

> his genius breaking forth in its proper direction, he luckily contracted for part of the Cargo of an English Ship at Civita Vecchia, which being disposed of to great Advantage in Rome, he thereby laid the foundation of his future fortune—from his knowledge & experience in Trade & Commerce, manufactories, etc, he became so great a favourite of the late Ganganelli that if that Pontiff had lived a little longer it is said he might have been made a Cardinal if he chose it—however by purchasing and selling at his own Prices, Old Pictures, Antique Gems & Statues, with the Profits of a lucrative banking house—he was enabled to vie with the Roman nobility in splendour & magnificence.[46]

John Plimmer, a young painter who had studied with Wilson, was also directly concerned in negotiations with Mengs. He wrote three days after Jenkins to say he had ordered Mengs to proceed immediately and be finished by Christmas. He continued, 'He hopes you will not insist on his opening the picture with arches etc.... he thinking it wide of the subject which was in a sepulchre...he has ornamented with pilasters, neaches, idols etc. in the Egyptian taste...nor do I think it will be a disagreeable

[43] Lesley Lewis, *Connoisseurs and Secret Agents* (1961), p. 201
[44] *Artists on Art*, ed. R. Goldwater and M. Treves (1947), pp. 245 f.
[45] Thomas Jenkins to Henry Hoare, 6 Jun. 1759, T(ST) 383.907.
[46] 'Memoirs of Thomas Jones', *Walpole Society*, XXXII (1951).

companion to your Carlo Maratti in the Manner in which he has treated it....'[47] Plimmer said he was obliged for Henry's advice to take classical views about Naples, as Mr. Wilson had done. 'As to what you recommend in the management of the leafing of Trees, I have endeavoured to imitate Claude and Nature with as much care as I possibly could ever since Mr. Wilson left Rome and I have been my own master.'[48] Two pictures he mentioned the previous year had been finished that spring and he would let Henry know where they could be seen in England. He added, 'I beg you will inform me if you would have me to send your copy of Claudio separate or wait till Mr. Mengs' Picture shall be finished'.[49] Jenkins assured Henry of Plimmer's excellence.

> I am glad to find my friend Mr. Plimmer is much in your good opinion. I can safely say he is without comparison the best Landskip Painter we have at this time in Italy and is allowed to be such by all the Dilletanti here. He has and does study Claude with success as I believe you will think when you see his works. The Early part of Mr. Plimmer's Education having been the study of Architecture has been of real advantage to him as it inables him to finish his Pictures with Elegance and I doubt not but you will be of this opinion when you see his works and you will find likewise that his figures have real merit in them.[50]

At the same time Jenkins was actively engaged in persuading Henry to buy other pictures, including one representing Andromeda with Perseus by Guido Reni. 'I perfectly agree with you Sir', he wrote, 'that no picture ought to be esteemed for the name of an author only, if there be not *real* merit to recommend it and I am obliged to you for the favour of your opinion on that subject.'[51]

By April 1760 Henry was still waiting for his painting and Jenkins apologized for the delay. Henry's interest in Cleopatra had obviously been stimulated by a painting by Guercino,[52] for Jenkins wrote:

> I beg you will be assured of you having an Excellent Picture, for I know Mr. Meng's real Merit, otherwise I would not venture

[47] John Plimmer to H.H., 9 Jun. 1759, T(ST) 383.907.
[48] Ibid.   [49] Ibid.
[50] Thomas Jenkins to H.H., 6 June 1759, T(ST) 383.907.
[51] Ibid. Jenkins subsequently sold the *Perseus and Andromeda* to Lord Fordwich. The episode is mentioned in Lesley Lewis, *Connoisseurs and Secret Agents*, p. 188. The engraver, Robert Strange, had said there was another version of the picture; Lord Fordwich was therefore afraid his was a copy. Fortunately it was possible to compare the two, and Strange agreed that Lord Fordwich's was original. 'Notwithstanding which', Jenkins wrote to Henry Hoare, 'there have not been wanting persons here who have given out that My Ld. Fordwich has paid £1500 for what was not worth more than £500—Knowing Sir your Good Nature and regard for truth I have taken the liberty to refer this to you, that in case you should hear it misrepresented that you may be inabled to set any person right and it is of Consequence to me that you should know the truth.' T.J. to H.H., 25 July 1761, T(ST) 383.907.
[52] Presumably the one in the Capitoline Gallery.

to say so much in his favour. The picture you mention by
Guercino formerly in the...Pallace now in the Capitol has
Merit in it, but Elegance of form or Expression was not always
that Author's good fortune to Excel in and he has been deficient
in both his Cleopatra and Augustus, his Cleopatra in Particular
has nothing lovely in her which is a Capital Error. Guercino
has great force of light and shadow and if his other talents had
been equal to that he would have been wonderful; he was
nevertheless a great Painter and so difficult it is to arrive at any
degree of Excellence in this art that great allowance ought to
be made for defects when a man arrives to a degree of excellence
in it. I speak the freer to you, Sir, on this subject being persuaded
of your *real* judgment and of course your Sensibility to the
merits of a picture. Defects will strike the Common Eye as will
a General Style of merit and expression but it is the Eye of the
intelligent only that truly distinguishes the delicacy of expression
which is the Soul of Painting.[53]

The dispatch of *Octavius and Cleopatra* from Rome, together with the
copy of a Claude, was announced by Plimmer on 12 July.[54] He died in
the course of the following twelve months, for Jenkins wrote on 25 July
1761, 'Your kindness, Sir, with respect to the heirs of poor Mr. Plimmer
is very great'.[55] The same letter acknowledged one from Henry expressing
satisfaction with Mengs's painting. 'I am very glad your Picture continues
to please, but to say the truth it is a very great good fortune when a painter
has the happiness to be imployed by a gentleman of real judgment.'[56]

That year Mengs himself accepted an offer from the King of Spain[57] of
12,000 crowns a year, an apartment in the palace and one of the king's
coaches. 'Before he left Rome', Jenkins wrote, 'I purchased everything I
possibly could from Mr. Mengs...and I am now master of his finest
work, being...the Holy Family that he painted for the King of Poland.'[58]
It was not therefore surprising that the criticism of *Cleopatra*, which Henry
had made known to him, roused his resentment.

I am exceeding glad that you have so good a Picture of him as
your Superior Judgment renders you worthy of it. As to all
objection, at least the Major part of them will by degrees fall
to the ground. If I mistake not the Person whom you mean...
he being a man who has not succeeded in his first attempts as a

53 T.J. to H.H., 23 April 1760, T(ST) 383.907.
54 John Plimmer to H.H., 12 July 1760, T(ST) 383.907.
55 Thomas Jenkins to H.H., 25 July 1761, T(ST) 383.907.
56 Ibid.
57 Charles III, who had to give up the throne of Naples to his son in 1759 on succeeding his
brother, Ferdinand IV, as King of Spain.
58 T.J. to H.H., 25 July 1761.

Painter and not being able to get up at others may endeavour
to pull them down to him. I say perhaps it is so, tho' I shall be
glad to find myself mistaken; but certainly by the method taken
by him to cover one part of a picture and then judge of the other
is *weak* and *fallacious* for the excellence of a part greatly consists
as it corresponds to the whole of a work, consequently ought
to be seen altogether by those who will be desirous of forming a
true and impartial judgement.[59]

Mengs had taken his subject from *The Life of Mark Anthony* by Plutarch.

A few days after the death of Mark Anthony, Caesar made
Cleopatra a visit of condolence. She was then in an undress,
and lying negligently on a couch, but when the Conqueror
entered the apartment, though she had nothing on but a single
robe, she arose hastily, and threw herself at his feet; her hair
dishevelled, her voice trembling, her eyes sunk; in short, her
person gave you the image of her mind; yet, in this deplorable
condition, there were some remains of that Grace, that Spirit
and Vivacity, which had so peculiarly animated her former
charms; and still some gleams of her native elegance might be
seen to wander over her melancholy countenance.[60]

The criticism concerned the figure of Cleopatra; which, some said, lacked
nobility. Mengs[61] wrote to Henry, not to excuse his shortcomings (he
was only human) but to explain his aim, which was to depart from the
conventional image of Cleopatra. His subject, he said, was a delicate,
subtle character, not someone sustained by virtue. Unlike a Doric temple,[62]
to which ornament added nothing, she was like a Corinthian temple,
which depended on ornament for its beauty, here in ruins. If she stood
by Augustus in all her splendour, then she would be like a building clad
in gold and marble, making him, the simple Doric one, seem like an
ordinary man dressed in homespun. But he had chosen to represent her
on her knees, her face upturned, her arms outstretched in supplication.
How could he represent her inner state without the prostration of her
body? He wished to make his picture unambiguous; not like Guercino's

59 T.J. to H.H., 29 Aug. 1761, T(ST) 383.907.
60 Quoted by Colt Hoare, *History of Modern Wiltshire*.
61 A. R. Mengs to H.H., 27 June 1761, in French, T(ST) 383.907.
62 Cf. Poussin, *Artists on Art*, p. 153.

The modes of the ancients were compositions of several things put together, and
there resulted from the variety of these things a difference of mode, so that it was
understandable that each one retained its own peculiar character. Thus the modes
had the power of inducing different emotions in the heart of the spectator. Because
of this the ancient sages attributed to each the quality of the effects that they saw
it produce, and for this reason they called the Dorian mode stable, serious, and
severe, and employed it for subjects that were serious, severe, and full of wisdom.

version,[63] in which it was impossible to say if Cleopatra were with Julius Caesar, Mark Anthony or Augustus.

Henry for his part,[64] although he offered praise and complimented Mengs on the strength of his arguments and the shrewdness of his remarks, had a sense of disappointment almost inevitable in view of his personal interest in the subject of which, whether from Guercino or not, he had his own pre-conceived image. Certainly Mengs had penetrated very deeply into Cleopatra's state of mind, he said; he saw the misery of a defeated woman, whose fate was to be pitied. There was only one point in which the picture fell short of 'true perfection'; the 'cursed critics' insisted she was no queen. But after all, he added, critics were not infallible, and could very easily be mistaken in so subtle an idea where, perhaps, the imagination surpasses what the brush can achieve.

Of course Mengs's arguments are a defence of the Neo-classical position; an appeal to the noble simplicity of antiquity against the decadence represented by the Rococo style. Henry, on the other hand, was looking for the Queen of Egypt in defeat, and what he had was a person of no importance caught by her master in some misdemeanour. It is hardly surprising that misunderstandings should arise; for while the correctness of external appearance and matters of historic accuracy may be established, and the symbolism implied by Doric and Corinthian may be agreed, clarity in communicating a state of mind by prostration of the body is a much more delicate problem.

The symbolic forms of art, rich in associations, crystallize ideas and feelings which otherwise escape definition. They enable individuals to participate in a collective ritual, which is open to a variety of interpretations. At the social level, gardens and picture galleries are marks of status, enhancing the prestige of the owner. At the same time other shades of meaning are conveyed by the iconography whose sources would have been familiar to Henry's contemporaries. At another level we can only guess at the significance of the pattern (later repeated in Alfred's Tower and the Convent) of raising an obelisk on the hill, while over the springs in the valley building a temple to the Mother Goddess and enclosing a nymph in a cave. This same opposition is seen in the relative positions of Augustus and Cleopatra. Augustus, according to *The Aeneid*, was descended from Aeneas. In the series of Stourhead heroes he precedes Alfred, the 'Father of his People'. And what of Cleopatra, who had previously appeared in the Grotto? She was a *femme fatale* ruled by instinct and emotion, surely that other principle of human nature with whose relation to reason Pope's generation had been so much preoccupied.[65]

[63] Presumably the painting referred to by Jenkins. See note 52.
[64] Letter in French, dated 27th July 1761. Unsigned and not in Henry Hoare's hand, T(ST) 383.907.
[65] 'Two Principles in human nature reign; Self-love to urge, and Reason to restrain.' *Essay on Man*, 2, line 53.

Of the 'eight very large pictures' which Walpole[66] saw in the great saloon at Stourhead, the room originally intended for a chapel, one was the *Family of Charles I* after Van Dyck, a second, *Midas preferring Pan to Apollo*, and a third *Wisdom accompanying Hercules*. The remaining five showed Salome, Dido, Helen, Venus, and Andromeda. Archetypal woman might be banned in the church but she was back in the house with a vengeance. Henry put *Octavius and Cleopatra* in the entrance hall, together with *Apollo conducting the Marchese Pallavicini to the Temple of Fame* and his own large equestrian portrait.

[66] 'Visits to Country Seats', p. 43.

Chapter 4

The Sublimity of Alfred's Tower

One evening, in 1760, while the Reverend Montagu Barton, Rector of Stourton, was dining with Henry, there was a disturbance in the hall. This was caused by the return of *A View of Venice* by Canaletto which Henry had given to his neighbour, the Duke of Somerset.[1] It announced the end of a match he was proposing for his widowed daughter, Susanna. The following year, however, she was married to Lord Bruce of Tottenham,[2] and for the remainder of Henry's life there were very close relations between Stourhead and Savernake, tinged on Henry's part by the deference he felt due to his son-in-law. Lord Bruce was not born to the peerage, the title, Bruce of Tottenham, having been acquired for him by his uncle Charles, 4th Earl of Elgin and 3rd Earl of Ailesbury, who also made him heir to his estates. Bruce was thirty-one years old at the time of the marriage, and a Gentleman of the Bedchamber to George III, a position he seemed to relish and for which his conscientious and meticulous disposition suited him. Henry laid out another £23,000 on this occasion, and was later able to help Bruce with ready money in his struggle to gain votes from his political rival Lord Verney, 'that Tartar Jew'.[3]

Bruce, as hereditary Warden of Savernake Forest, was particularly interested in the changes that were taking place in the English landscape. Views on estate matters were exchanged, and it was Henry who, in 1764, urged Bruce to consult Lancelot Brown on improvement and who interpreted the great man's intention with a roughly pencilled sketch.[4] 'I am glad your Lordship has got Mr. Browne', he wrote, 'He has undoubtedly the best taste of anybody for improving Nature by what I have seen of His works, He paints as He plants; I doubt not that He will remove the Damps & the too great regularity of your Garden far better to be turned into a park.'[5]

[1] R.C.H. MS. memoirs, ST.
[2] Thomas Bruce Brudenell, Lord Bruce of Tottenham, created 1st Earl of Ailesbury, 1779. Information about Lord Bruce is from the Earl of Cardigan, *The Wardens of Savernake Forest* (1949).
[3] Henry Hoare to Lord Bruce, 21 June 1766, T(TOT).
[4] A slight pencilled plan, TOT.
[5] H.H. to Lord B., undated, 1764, T(TOT).

Brown had left Stowe in 1750 and by 1762[6] was at the height of his triumphant progress through the English landscape. Stourhead, though one among many, was by then a showplace described by Walpole[7] as 'one of the most picturesque scenes in the world'. The walk round the lake 'over a wooden Palladian bridge with urns', through the Grotto 'lost in the wood', culminated in the Pantheon which few buildings exceeded in 'magnificence, taste and beauty'. But Walpole had criticized the head of Ceres, saying the features were too short and compressed.[8] Henry said that Rysbrack had left it unfinished 'till he saw it in its place with the skylight'.[9] He therefore took the old man back with him when he returned, in August 1762, from London.[10] Rysbrack was then sixty-nine, patient and industrious as ever, but bowed with dropsy so that he could only with difficulty raise his head.[11]

My dear Sukey [Henry wrote on 23 October] I wrote my last letter in a violent hurry & now I recollect I shall want Wilmot when you have quite done with him anytime before Xmas. It is to run over the alto Relievos (&) plaster Susanna with Turpentine oyl to take off the Gloss or shining & then I think they will give universal Content. I thought old Rysbrack would have wept for joy to see his Offspring placed to such advantage. He thinks it impossible for such a space to have more magnificence in it and striking awe than he found there. Had he seen Mr. Hamilton's Temple of Bacchus[12] He would not have thought so of the inside. It is an oblong, the Form of the Temple of Fortuna Virilis or the Long Temple of Balbec. The Bacchus a Noble Statue stands in the Centre & turns a profile to you as you enter. Windows are on the other end & in my poor opinion the figure (truly Antique) is lost or hurt in a Temple built on purpose for it. He was vastly struck at my Rotundo & said there was not a thought or a wish but what was not gratified in it. The outside of His Temple is in the true Greek Taste a portico to each end & columns all round the sides. The Pediments filld with Bass Relievos & as the Duchess said of mine, is all Attic Elegance. She was much pleased with the Stone Bridge (Pl. 8a) of 5 arches

6 See Dorothy Stroud, *Capability Brown* (rev. ed., 1957). Brown's first commission in Wiltshire had been at Longleat in 1757; he did extensive work for Paul Methuen at Corsham in 1760–2; and for Lord Shelburne at Bowood in 1761–8.
7 Walpole, 'Visits to Country Seats'.
8 H.H. to Lord B., 17 July 1762, T(TOT).
9 Ibid. This statue is referred to in the accounts as *Flora*. See also agreement, 14 Mar. 1759, T(ST) 383.4.
10 Ibid.
11 W. T. Whitley, *Artists and their friends in England, 1700–1799*, I (London and Boston, 1928), p. 204.
12 An antique colossal statue of Bacchus said to have cost £3000. It was eventually bought by William Beckford and taken to Fonthill. See also G. Nares, 'Painshill', *Country Life*, CXXIII (1958), p. 62; and O. Siren, *China and the Gardens of Europe in the 18th Century* (New York 1950), pl. 35.

you allways wished I would build at the passage into the orchard & the scheme of carrying the water up and loosing out of sight towards the parish. This Bridge is now about. It is simple & plain. I took it from Palladios Bridge at Vicenza, 5 arches, & when you stand at The Pantheon the Water will be seen thro the Arches & it will look as if the River came down thro the Village & that this was the Village Bridge for publick use; the View of the Bridge, Village & Church altogether will be a Charmg Gaspd picture at the end of that Water. Mr. Privets Estimate for His Stone Carrge of it is £53. The Arches I turn with my rough stone. I have one Scheme more which will Crown or Top all. As I was reading Voltaire's L'Histoire Générale lately in His Character of Alfred the Great He says Je ne sai s'il y a jamais eu sur la terre un homme si digne des respects de la postérité qu'Alfred le Grand qui rendit ces services a sa patrie. Out of gratitude to him I propose (if I can find a Quar of Stone[13] in Little Coomb which they tell me I shall) to erect a Tower on Kingsettle Hill where He set up His Standard after He came from His concealment in the Isle of Athelney near Taunton & the Earl of Devon had worsted the Danes. I propose consulting Dear Lord Bruce on the inscription over the Door or entrance. I intend to build it on the plan of Sn. Marks Tower at Venice, 100 foot to the Room which the Stair-case will lead to & 4 Arches to look out in the 4 sides to the prospect Allround. The stairs being of Stone will go up with the building & save the expense of a scaffold every 20 feet high will cost 50£ & it will be 4 years in hand about 75£ or £80 pr annm. My best Affections and Respects attend Dear Lord Bruce. It is said yesterday the Council sat on a genl. peace or War—nothing transpires. I hope in God it will be the former. Adieu, My Dear Sukey, your ever Loving Father.[14]

The naive rivalry with Hamilton over his Temple of Bacchus was to be capped by a tower nearly three times the height of the Belvedere at Painshill.[15] There were also political overtones. Peace negotiations with France, begun in 1760, had broken down, first with William Pitt's reluctance to accept some of the French clauses, but mainly because the Duc de Choiseul had signed a secret treaty with Spain, not then belligerent. On learning of this Pitt wanted to declare war on Spain immediately, to cut her off from her colonies and, incidentally, to capture the Spanish treasure fleet when it sailed from the River Plate. Failing to get support, Pitt

[13] The tower was finally built of brick, which doubtless delayed its construction.
[14] H.H. to Lady Bruce, 23 Oct. 1762, TOT.
[15] G. Nares, op. cit.

resigned in October 1761 in order, as Henry reported Beckford as saying, 'to go up & pacifye & keep minds cool & quiet forgeting that He is as he calld himself one of the Children of the Sun & warm as Indian pepper'. 'God grant us a Good peace', Henry added, 'and persons of Virtue and Ability to rule over us.'[16] The Duke of Newcastle, who remained in office, although he opposed Pitt's views, was for continuing support to Frederick of Prussia whose fortunes were at a low ebb. The strongest hope for peace was therefore with the young king who, on his accession, had declared himself against 'this bloody and expensive war'. Thus Henry's own peaceful inclinations and his new personal connections with the court strengthened his support of the monarchy. War with Spain came nevertheless. Newcastle resigned in May 1762, but successes in the West Indies encouraged those who wished to continue the war to hope for further advantages. On 20 September Henry wrote to Bruce, 'I hope in God peace will at last be restored to a people unworthy of it from the opposition given to it & insolent Clamours & abuse of the Superior powers. Such Estates have been raised out of this consuming war that contractors...and all that tribe of Traders do not chuse to end it but wish it eternal.'[17] By the end of October peace preliminaries had been agreed, but Henry saw the war transferred 'into our own Bowells'.

> The Duke of Newcastle with one foot in the Grave is setting fire to the Court to make a funeral pile to burn His Ashes in, & will draw others into the flame. The City regardless of stoping the Effusion of human blood think of nothing but the gold offered in Mexico which they flattered themselves would come into Their Coffers in two years longer continuance of War, Death and Taxes. We are all ungrateful to the Lord of Hosts who has given us Victory in the Day of Battle.[18]

The monument to celebrate victory and the peace which followed, was only completed shortly before the next disastrous war. It was to celebrate the power of the monarchy: 'As to His enemys do thou cloth Them with Shame but on himself and His posterity may the Crown flourish & God forbid they should snatch the Sceptre out of His Hand so long as He glorys in the Name of Briton & detests the German connections *as surely as Mr. P....t did*.'[19] Alfred was, of course, the successor of Augustus and 'the Father of His People',[20] as the final inscription on the tower reads. Henry communicated the first draft to his son-in-law on 18 November.

16 H.H. to Lord B., 22 Oct. 1761, T(TOT).
17 20 Sep. 1762, T(TOT).
18 6 Nov. 1762, T(TOT).
19 4 Dec. 1762, T(TOT).
20 The inscription now on Alfred's Tower. There is another longer version in MS. T(ST) 383.907.

As your Lordship is my bosom Friend & desirous of knowing the Inscription proposed on a Tablet for Alfred's Tower which I propose beginning next spring I beg leave to send you this rude undigested sketch for abler pens to alter & finish & hope Your Lordship will be so good as to consider it.

In memory of Alfred the Great, The Founder of the English Monarchy, The 1st encourager of Learning He founded the University of Oxford. The Giver of most excellent Laws, Jurys, the Bulwark of English Liberty. He instituted with a *well regulated Militia*, divided England into Shires or Countys & by a determined courage & unwearied attention to the increase of our Naval Force protected us from Foreign Invasions & extended our Trade to the remote parts of The Globe. He was the complete Model of that perfect Character, which, under the Name of a Sage, the Philosophers have been fond of delineating, rather as a fiction of Their imagination, than in hopes of ever seeing it reduced to practice.

Britons will revere the Ashes of that Monarch by whose Lessons They have (under the protection of Divine Providence) subdued Their Enemys this year with invincible Force by Land & Sea, in Europe, Asia, Africa & America, stopd the Effusion of human blood & given peace & rest to the Earth.

Erected, Anno Dom: 1762 in the 3d. Glorious Year of the Reign of our truely British King George the 3d. on that spot where Alfred settled his Standard (to this day called Kingsettle Hill) after He came out from His concealment in the Isle of Athelney (near Taunton) & gave Battle & defeat to the Danes.

I take the form of this Tower from that of St. Marks at Venice which finishes in a Pyramid. Mr. Rysbrack has a figure of Fame which he would part with on very reasonable Terms which (if) I could introduce in this Building I would; Sir William Wyndham bespoke it for His park at Orchard Wyndham. It had the Medallion of Queen Ann in its hand. On His decease Sir Charles (now Lord Egremont) would not take it so it was on His hands. After the Battle of Culloden, Rysbrack put the Duke of Cumberlands Head in the Place of Queen Ann, which provoked the Duchess of Queensbury prodigiously & she told me she hoped He never would get 1d. for it, & hates him for it. Now if I have it I shall beg leave to take out the Duke's Head & put in Alfred the Great's. Does your Lordship think this will go down with Her Grace? If not Fame shall embrace Her Head which set the World once on fire.[21] I congratulate Your Lordship on the preliminarys

[21] This refers to Kitty, Duchess of Queensberry, whose beauty was celebrated by Matthew

being ratified & am bold to say it has saved this Nation exposing its Beggary as I have good grounds to believe they could as soon have raised from the Dead all our Heroes that have fallen in Battle as have raised 12 millions more this Year. . . . Most, I may say all thinking people, even in the City, like the Peace in their Hearts well & think better of it every Day as they see the scarcity of money till the Havannah Treasures arrive.[22]

Henry did not have *Fame*[23] which was bought for Longford Castle at Rysbrack's sale in 1767; but at some time Alfred the Great was substituted for the Duke of Cumberland, as Henry proposed. Henry bought a bust of Alfred which he paid for in 1764.[24] This was Rysbrack's last work[25] for Stourhead as both he and Flitcroft died within a year of each other at the end of the decade.[26] Alfred's Tower (Pl. 8c) was thus also Flitcroft's last design for Henry and one which he did not live to see achieved. The last recorded payment to him was £100 in June 1766 'for the Temple of Apollo, Alfred's Tower etc. in full'.[27] The tower was not started for several years, and then, except for its great height, did not conform to Henry's original intention. It now has a crenellated top and Gothic detail like others of its kind, such as one built for the Duke of Argyll at Whitton,[28] or the one at Painshill to which it is related. The triangular form probably gave the least resistance to the wind, but it is of interest that Longford Castle is also triangular and Henry, who would have known it well, told a story of its being spared by Cromwell because of its unusual shape.

Peace was formally signed in 1763 and was, said Henry, 'more and more applauded daily'.[29] The Wilkes affair had roused him on the King's side, but in repeating some piece of gossip he overstepped the bounds of confidence. 'I shall never forgive myself that my zeal for His Majesty

Prior in a poem, 'The Female Phaeton' (Poems ed. 1725). Kitty, 'beautiful and young, And wild as colt untam'd', demands her freedom.

> Shall I thumb holy books, confin'd
> With Abigail's forsaken?
> Kitty's for other things design'd
> Or I am much mistaken.

She asks for a carriage in which to go out alone

> Fondness prevail'd, Mamma gave way,
> Kitty, at heart's desire,
> Obtain'd the Chariot for a day,
> And *set the world on fire!*

[22] H.H. to Lord B., 18 Nov. 1762. TOT.
[23] See M. I. Webb, *Michael Rysbrack* (1954), p. 137. At the time of Rysbrack's sale the medallion had the head of the Duke of Cumberland, although it now shows King Alfred.
[24] 12 May 1764, T(ST) 383.6.
[25] Henry Hoare bought five drawings and three bas-reliefs at Rysbrack's sale on 19 Feb. 1766, T(ST) 383.6.
[26] Flitcroft died in 1769; Rysbrack in 1770.
[27] T(ST) 383.6.
[28] See *Country Life*, 12 Dec. 1968, p. 1580.
[29] H.H. to Lord B., 6 June 1763, T(TOT).

who when He is insulted I loose all patience should make me forgetful of all other duty & caution & your Lordship must from sad experience be convinced I am never to be trusted again in secrets of State which I will ride away from & as Squirt promises to carry me as long as I live we will gallop procul discordibus armis as the Poet says & talk of Hats & Politicks no more.'[30]

The summer of 1764 was a time to relax.

> The wise tell us we shall all in the end be benefited by the Heat . . . & we must believe that whatever is, is Right. I took a Gallop over the Downs last Week with Mr. Barton cum multis aliis to Mr. Beckford & by the Vehemence of the Weather or that Gentns. oratory He has had a Fever & His Pulse has been in a Hurricane ever since till this morng. & now He is much better & the Fever gone. I hope Your Lordship will consult Mr. B. on your intended improvements. . . . He will be the only person & Witham the only Park that will send fat oxen & Bulls of Basan to Smithfield Market next Winter. I overheard Him tell Robert Dingley Esq. that the Land He then trod on was improved . . . from thirteen pence halfpenny to 20 shillings pr. Acre. . . . We never were so put to it to keep cool in this House. We dine with the Hall Doors open into the Stair Case which we never did before for the Door into the Air would let in the Heat of a Firey Furnace . . . a Souse into that delicious Bath & Grot filld with fresh Magic, is Asiatick Luxury & too much for Mortals or at least for Subjects, next I ride under the spreading Beaches just beyond the Obelisk on the Terrace where we are sure of Wind & Shade & a delightful View into the Vale & Squirt & Miss Cade alternately are the envy of all the flying Squadron that meet there; then we feed on Your Lordship's fat bounty of Venison & drink Your Health in Iced Cream.[31]

In contrast to this affluent picture, 1765 opened with the threat of a serious corn shortage. There was widespread theft of game and poultry, and of geese and ducks from the cottagers. Henry reported a hundred lost in one night. 'They held matches under them as they sat at Roost & it suffocates them.'[32] Corn was nevertheless exported, 'feeding other nations & starving our own poor',[33] said Henry. He blamed the dealers and was told, 'the Rogues in Grain enter corn for Foreign Ports receive the Bounty & carry it only into the North of England'.[34] He advocated measures to stop export, but these were not taken by the government till the following year when a bad harvest produced a crisis.

[30] Dec. 1763, T(TOT).
[31] Undated, 1764, T(TOT).
[32] 2 Feb. 1765, T(TOT).
[33] Ibid.   [34] 20 Apr. 1765.

Elsewhere the planting he had done was slow to mature. 'I am glad the Ax has been laid so properly to the Root of the Tree in your Lordship's absence; it will never happen to lay an Ax to mine, all I wish is to see them rise not fall—how sweet must Savernake Forest appear now the time of the Singing of Birds is come & the Voice of the Turtle is heard in your land.'[35] To build was quicker than to plant. In July 1765 the Temple of Apollo (Pl. 5) had 'all its Niches compleat',[36] and by December he was able to write, 'The Temple of Apollo was finished last week & the scaffold all now taking down & it charms everybody'.[37] He had bought Wood's *Ruins of Balbec* (Pl. 4a), from which the design was taken, in 1757.[38] Whether or not the conception was part of a master plan, taking the high ground beyond the Zeals road into the garden was a telling stroke, and with it the classical or Virgilian stage was over. In the same letter Henry continued, 'The Cross (Pl. 8b) is now in hand & there are so many pieces that we must I believe employ Harriet to put it together as she is such an adept in joyning the map of the Countys of England. I hope the Dean of Bristol's preferment in the News paper is true.'[39] It is interesting to note the terms in which, as late as 1733, the citizens of Bristol petitioned for the removal of this cross.

> It hath been insinuated by some this Cross, on account of its antiquity, ought to be lookt upon as something sacred. But when we consider that we are Protestants and that Popery ought to be guarded against in this nation, we make our request to you to consider if the opening of a passage to four of the principal streets in this city ought not to outweigh anything that can be said for the keeping up of a ruinous and superstitious relick, which is at present a public nuisance.[40]

It was apparently taken down and re-erected, for on 21 August 1762 several workmen were reported to be 'raising the walks in College Green and in taking down the High Cross'.[41] The pieces were deposited for two years in the cathedral when they were presented to Henry Hoare by the Dean, the Very Reverend Cutts Barton, and in October 1764, the materials were dispatched in six wagons to their final resting place in Wiltshire. The cross was the finishing touch to the 'Charmg Gaspd picture' though in truth

35 9 Mar. 1765, T(TOT).
36 6 July, 1765, T(TOT).
37 9 Dec. 1765, T(TOT).
38 T(ST) 383.6.
39 H.H. to Lord B., 9 Dec. 1765, T(TOT). 'Harriet' is Henrietta, Susanna's daughter by Dungarvan; she married the 1st Baron O'Neill of Shanes, Co. Antrim, on 18 Oct. 1777.
40 Minutes of a meeting of the Council on 21 July 1733, quoted by John Latimer, *Extracts from 'The Annals of Bristol'*, T(ST) 383.907. The same source also reports that the High Cross was transported to Stourhead in 1764; and that St. Peter's Pump was removed by an Act of Parliament, and taken to Stourhead in 1766, where it was erected near the springs in Six Wells Bottom.
41 Ibid.

the mood is nearer to Gray who, moreover, was one of the first to 'unite poetry and archaeology'[42] and to develop a true understanding and love of the Gothic. The village and the church had always, presumably, been incorporated in the view from the Pantheon, just as Kent had used the mediaeval bridge at Rousham, and Shenstone the Priory ruins and Halesowen spire.

The fashion for Gothic had been stimulated by Horace Walpole's transformation of Strawberry Hill. One stage had been completed by 1753, but in 1760 he had started to add a gallery, a round tower, a large cloister and a cabinet in the manner of a little chapel. The last of these features opened off the Gallery. 'It was', says Ketton-Cremer, 'a small room, square with a semi-circular recess in the middle of each wall; the roof, vaulted in imitation of the chapter-house of York Minster, rose to an apex formed of a large star of yellow glass. The windows were entirely filled with ecclesiastical stained glass, and the dominant light of the room was the "golden gloom" which filtered down through the great star. In one of the recesses stood an altar of black and gold, copied from a tomb in Westminster Abbey.'[43] Henry had visited it shortly after its completion.

> I was highly entertained at Mr. Walpole's last Saturday with the finest painted glass windows & Gothic Taste in the best manr. that it can be employ'd in so small a space. He has added a Gallery of 50 feet long which leads to the most Beautiful Cabinet a Room of 16 square with 4 Circles that Break from the Center, lighted from the top by a Flaming star in painted Glass which makes all the objects in the room look like a Glory & it is full of Vista, Intaglios, Cameos, Statues, Bronzes, Miniatures, Antique Urns & Lamps: in short most exquisite & will please Lady Bruce beyond all imagination; it is a Sanctum Sanctorum & tho Gothick dissolves the scene in Extasy.[44]

'tho Gothick' implies a lingering distaste, nevertheless Walpole had noted 'a greenhouse of false Gothic'[45] at Stourhead in 1762. By 1765 Henry was clearly converted and the arrival of the Bristol Cross marked his turning away from the Palladian style. The new features did not, however, intrude into the classical sequence round the lake. The wooden bridge, which some called Chinese, was Palladian.[46] The Gothic Cottage was never a feature in Henry Hoare's day. Piper does not show it on his plan; nor does it appear in Bampfylde's panoramic drawings of c. 1770 (Pl. 10). If a building was there it was probably functional and hidden by trees. The seat, porch, and possibly the window were added by John Carter after 1806,[47] when

[42] Sir Kenneth Clark, *The Gothic Revival* (1950).
[43] R. W. Ketton-Cremer, *Horace Walpole* (1964), p. 180.
[44] H.H. to Lord B., 30 June 1763, T(TOT).   [45] Walpole, 'Visits to Country Seats'.
[46] Cf. Giacomo Leoni, *The Architecture of Palladio*, III (1721), plate VI.
[47] See II, 11, footnote 16.

Nash had set the fashion for that kind of thing. Up on the hillside towards the house were later to be found a Chinese Alcove and a Turkish Tent, possibly the very one that Hamilton had at Painshill, for he had to sell his Surrey estate and move to Bath. Sometime before 1770 a Rustic Convent (Pl. 20b) was built in the woods below Alfred's Tower, following the prescription that high hills suit castles and vales near wood and water suit religious houses;[48] but there is an almost manic contrast in the height of the tower and the withdrawal of the Convent in the recesses of the valley beneath, just as these moods had elsewhere been expressed in Obelisk and Grotto, Sun Temple and Sousterrain, Augustus and Cleopatra.

In 1765, Henry Hoare was sixty. Celebrated as a gardener he enjoyed the friendship of younger men, like the energetic Bampfylde[49] of Hestercombe, near Taunton.

> Mr. Bampfield has brought me a sweet picture of His own painting a Delightfull sea and Land view.[50] He is now copying the Lucatelli[51] behind the door in the Skylight Dressing Room & is in raptures with it & in Ecstacy with His Copy of the Pamphili—says He had rather have it than all the Landscapes He ever saw in His life. I am going to assist the placing of Neptune[52] before the Dorick Temple & Captn Barton is to preside & I wish the God of the Ocean is not at last drowned in a Duckpond.[53] Mr. Hoare will on Monday enrich Bath with 3 of the finest Heads he ever did from my judgement of Hercules.[54]

All went well and ten days later Henry wrote:

> I had the satisfaction of seeing Neptune & His 4 Naggs (very fine and full of Spirit they are) landed on His Pedestal before

[48] Shenstone, 'On Gardening'.

[49] Coplestone Warre Bampfylde, 1719–91, of Hestercombe near Taunton; painter, architect, landscape gardener, collector. Bampfylde's landscape at Hestercombe included an ingenious cascade, falling from a height among rocks and descending to a series of ponds. There is a painting of it at Stourhead. On the opposite hillside was a small Doric temple containing an urn with the inscription,

Carolo K Tynte Barte et Henrico Hoare Arm
Diu spectatae memor amicitiae
Hanc urnam sacram esse voluit
C Warre Bampfylde
MDCCLXXXVI
Animae quales neque candidiores
Terra tulit, neque quis me sit devinctor alter.

This quotation from Horace, *Satires*, I, 5, equates Henry Hoare with Virgil, of whom Horace was speaking.

[50] Possibly an oval picture called *A Bay*, although this is dated 1766.

[51] The Locatellis listed in Colt Hoare's *Modern Wiltshire* are: two upright landscapes on the staircase; a landscape in the Music Room; two large landscapes (after originals of Claude Lorrain in the Pamphili Palace). The copies now at Stourhead are stylistically unlike Locatelli.

[52] There is no other record or trace of this statue.

[53] Possibly a reference to the original tank or pond shown on the map of 1722.

[54] H.H. to Lord B., 13 Dec. 1765, T(TOT).

the Arch[55] under the Dorick Temple before I decamped & it had a very fine appearance there. I also saw the first Story of the Cross put just together & repaired, now the rest will go swimmingly & be done sooner than we expected & the foundation of Stone is finished & the pavemnt forming round it, also round the Temple of Apollo & I have made the passage up from the Sousterrain[56] Serpentine & will make it easier of access facilis descensus Averno. Messrs. Bampfield & Hoare have made an ingenious model for the Cascade[57] like Mr. Bampfield's & as I have stone Quarries on the Hill just above it I hope to finish it soon in the summer. If your Lordship makes any Bricks near you I wish you could learn how much they fairly cost per Thousand. Mr. Short sent me 2 Brickmakers & they are now at work & I luckily found some excellent good Earth very handy.[58]

The bricks were probably for Alfred's Tower which was eventually begun late in 1769 or early 1770, for in April Henry wrote to Susanna,

A young lad of 18 Mr. Hoare sent from Bath has in 7 weeks finished a figure of Alfred the Great 10 feet high from a model given him to the Admiration of all the Spectators. He is a wonderful Genius & His countenance shows it. He lives with Mr. Hoare of Bath. The Tower is now about 15 feet high and begins to Figure. I hope it will be finished in as happy Times to this Isle as Alfred finished his Life of Glory in then shall I depart in peace.[59]

Next year, rather belatedly following a fashion, Henry introduced another feature in the circuit round the lake. From a letter to his grand-daughter, Harriet, we can detect the hand of Hamilton.

It is such an Age since we corresponded (I fear I owed you a Letter) that it seems to me as if the Golden Age was revived. I shall on Tuesday next send over to Tottenham Park 35 strong good Fruiting pine plants & each will have a Pot in case they should be sick in their journey & I shall gladly accept some West India plants when our Dearest Lord abounds in Them. ...I am building a Hermitage above the Rock & when you are about a Quarter part up the Walk from the Rock to the Temple

[55] Over Paradise Well, below the temple of Flora.
[56] It is not clear what this means. It could refer to the tunnel under the Zeals road. On the other hand it makes more sense applied to the Grotto and the steep serpentine steps which lead out of it. The quotation from *The Aeneid* would also confirm the analogy with Aeneas's journey.
[57] On the south side of the lake below the dam.
[58] H.H. to Lord B., 23 Dec. 1765, T(TOT).
[59] H.H. to Lady Bruce, 28 Apr. 1770, T(TOT).

of Apollo you turn short to the right & so zig zag up to it & thence go under The Trees to the Temple of Apollo as Mr. Hamilton advised. & We stop or plant up in Clumps the old Walk up the Hill to that Temple. It is to be lined inside & out with old Gouty nobbly oakes, the Bark on, which Mr. Groves & my neighbours are so kind to give me & Mr. Chapman a clergyman showed me one yesterday called Judge Wyndham's seat which I take to be of the Year of Our Lord 1000 & I am not quite sure it is not Anti Diluvian. I believe I shall put it in to be myself The Hermit.[60]

Although mainly of wood this feature, as can be seen from Piper's drawing (Pl. 13a), had the same calculated effects as the Grotto of which, in plan, it is a serpentine version. It was possibly this that led him to alter the character of the earlier structure by later adding the rocky entrance.[61]

In the same letter to Harriet, Henry wrote

I shall be impatient to see your Drawing after the fine Head of St. Cecilia. I have some pictures here of Monsr La Grennée[62] which he painted for Duke Choiseul who would not take them tho bespoken, because he was banished & They are universally & highly admired. . . . Mrs. Bampfylde has sent me some of Her work a Pheasant & Lapwing & Yellow Ham Still Life[63] most wonderfully fine, a Gold frame & plate glass is ordered for it. By Lord Arundells desire I have wrote to Monsr Vernet for 2 picture of His, a Storm and Moon Shine £200 each in value & He most politely answers He will lay aside all work to go directly on with them for my friend.[64]

Joseph Vernet was almost exactly the same age as Richard Wilson whose quality as a landscape painter he is reputed to have been the first to recognize. Vernet specialized in marine subjects, harbour scenes, storms and shipwrecks which he turned out in large numbers. From the mid 1740s onwards his work was in steady demand from British patrons[65] for whom the landscapes of Claude were in short supply. As Sir John Lambert explained when he enclosed the painters receipt,[66] two Claudes, 'a Marine and a Paysage', were to be had in Paris for 15,000 livres, whereas Vernet's prices, even though his pictures were bought by Madame Du Barry and others, were in the region of 1200. The pictures referred to in the letter

60 H.H. to Harriet, 30 Nov. 1771, T(TOT).
61 See note 56.
62 L. J. F. Lagrenée, 1725–1805.
63 A needle-work picture at present in the Italian Room at Stourhead.
64 H.H. to Harriet, 30 Nov. 1771.
65 See E. K. Waterhouse, 'English Painting and France in the Eighteenth Century', *Journal W.C.I.*, vol. XV (1952), pp. 122–35.
66 Sir John Lambert to H.H., 20 Aug. 1772, T(ST) 383.907.

to Harriot were evidently those which Lord Arundell is recorded as having bought in 1772. Although there are five references in Henry Hoare's accounts to transactions with Vernet,[67] only two pictures, a *Sunshine* and a *Moonshine*, were subsequently listed as having been bought by him. They were sold in 1883 under the titles of *Day* and *Night*.

Ingersoll-Smouse's catalogue[68] of Vernet's work lists four paintings which Vernet made for Henry, a *Marine* and a *Clair de lune* ordered in 1766 and paid for in 1767; a *Soleil couchant* ordered in 1767 and paid for in 1769; and *Naufrage à midi*, which she assumes to be the painting referred to by Vernet's father-in-law when he wrote to Henry Hoare in 1765 saying 'if you have a desire for your picture soon I shall take it as a great favour you will honour me with the Soliciting it for you and if you have not chose any particular subject leave it to me'.[69]

A *Naufrage* is the only Vernet now at Stourhead and is listed by Colt Hoare as one he bought himself. Some weeks before the letter to Harriet Henry wrote to Lord Bruce,

> I have letters from Paris that mention Monsr. Vernet's Storm which your Lordship has in miniature was thought the finest picture He ever painted & has produced Him more pictures 2 for Lord Clive & 3 for others at 300 livers (louis dors) each & He had only 500 for the 2 from Prince Palatine...I never saw that storm without I think of those fine lines in the Pleasures of Imagination,[70]
>
> > Hence when lightning fires
> > The arch of Heav'n and thunders rock the ground
> > Then furious whirlwinds rend the howling airs
> > And ocean groaning from his lowest bed
> > Heaves his tempestuous billows to the sky
>
> & think that picture greatly Superior to all His Sun & Moon-shines. Salvator Rosa never showd more Spirit than he has exerted in that uproar of Elemental War.[71]

Eight years earlier he had also indirectly referred to Akenside's poem. 'Thank God you escaped the Dreadfull Storm when lightning fired the Arch of Heaven and Thunder rock'd the ground. We had very little of it here & the Dear Harriet stood & looked at the Lightning till I desired Her to retire. We had the finest Rainbow that sprung up in the Front of the House exactly that ever mortals beheld & the round Hill & prospect appeared under it beautifull beyond description.'[72]

Vernet's romantic interpretations of shipwreck appeared regularly in

[67] 15 Feb. 1766, T(ST) 383.6; 25 Apr. 1767, 9 July 1769, 9 Aug. 1769, FS(Acc.); 1770, 'charges of a picture by Vernet', 1770, T(ST) 383.6.
[68] F. Ingersoll-Smouse, *Joseph Vernet* (Paris, 1926).
[69] M. Parker to H.H., 12 Oct. 1765, T(ST) 383.907.
[70] Mark Akenside, *The Pleasures of Imagination* (first version, 1744).
[71] H.H. to Lord B., 12 Oct. 1771, T(TOT).   [72] 29 Aug. 1763, T(TOT).

the Paris Salon between 1746 and 1789. Rosa had accustomed Henry Hoare's generation to representations of the wilder aspects of nature; but, as we can see, poetry also played a part in conditioning the mind towards acceptance of particular kinds of imagery, including the *sublime* which later had Burke's philosophic sanction as a category distinct from the *beautiful*. Akenside's poem was published in 1744 when he was twenty-three, and incidentally, at the time when Henry started work on his garden. Book III is especially concerned with the association of ideas. Knowledge, as Locke and others had reasoned, came through the senses, but immediate perception was affected by the passions, the instincts of self-propagation and self-preservation. By being associated with one or the other, objects gave rise to feelings. Thirty years before Akenside, Addison had urged the poet, in forming his imagination, to 'gain a due relish of the works of nature, and be thoroughly conversant in the various scenery of a country life'. Akenside too recommended the sights and sounds of Nature

> ...to brighten the dull glooms
> Of care, and make the destin'd road of life
> Delightful to his feet. So fables tell,
> The adventurous hero, bound on hard exploits,
> Beholds with glad surprise by secret spells
> Of some kind sage, the patron of his toils,
> A visionary paradise disclos'd
> Amid the dubious wild:[73]

'What then is taste?' he asks,

> ...but these internal powers
> Active, and strong, and feelingly alive
> To each fine impulse?

But, he continues

> ...Different minds
> Incline to different objects; one pursues
> The vast alone, the wonderful, the wild;
> Another sighs for harmony, and grace,
> And gentlest beauty. Hence when lightning fires
> The arch of Heaven, and thunders rock the ground,
> When furious whirlwinds rend the howling air,
> And ocean, groaning from his lowest bed,
> Heaves his tempestuous billows to the sky;
> Amid the mighty uproar, while below
> The nations tremble, Shakespeare looks abroad
> From some high cliff, superior, and enjoys
> The elemental war.[74]

[73] *Pleasures of Imagination*, first version. Akenside, *Works*, III (1855), lines 505 ff.
[74] Ibid., lines 547 ff.

In a later version Akenside emphasized that all could not enjoy the pleasures of imagination.

> In vulgar bosoms, and unnoticed, lie
> The pleasing stores....[75]

They were only accessible to

> ...some who, within themselves
> Retiring from the trivial scenes of chance
> And momentary passion, can at will
> Call up these fair exemplars of the mind;
> Review their features; scan the secret laws
> Which bind them to each other; and display
> By forms and sounds or colours, to the sense
> Of all the world their latent charms...[76]

The Pleasures of Imagination was widely read during the eighteenth century, so that Henry Hoare was affected by it is possibly of less interest than that, forty years later, Turner should have given it attention in his lectures as Professor of Perspective.[77]

Alfred's Tower was finished in 1772. When Mrs. Rishton, Fanny Burney's half-sister, visited Stourhead in April 1773 she was told by a gardener that Henry had never been to the top of it or visited the Convent.[78] But of course these buildings were not designed for use, nor were they ornamental in the sense that the temples of the garden were. The Convent was fairly inaccessible, not to say invisible; the bleak tower could not be called beautiful. It did, however, have the attributes of sublimity. Burke had denied that proportion, which formed the basis of the Palladian canon, could be a necessary cause of beauty which depended on smallness, smoothness, gradual variation and delicacy. Sublimity, on the other hand, produced feelings of astonishment, reverence, or awe. It arose from objects which excited ideas of pain or danger, provided these were not too immediate. It was, as he said, 'tranquillity tinged with terror'. Others, besides Burke, were concerned in philosophical refinements of the concept. Alexander Gerard's *Essay on Taste* was published in 1759, with a second edition in 1764. Editions of Lord Kames's *Elements of Criticism* appeared in 1762, 1765, 1769, 1774, and 1785. All were agreed that size was one of the factors calculated to inspire sensations of the sublime. Gerard said that objects were sublime which possessed quantity, or amplitude, and simplicity in conjunction. Kames distinguished between great magnitude, which produced feelings of grandeur, and great elevation, which produced

---

[75] *Pleasures of Imagination*, second version.
[76] Ibid.
[77] See Jerrold Ziff, 'J. M. W. Turner on Poetry and Painting', *Studies in Romanticism*, III (Boston, 1964), p. 4.
[78] *The Early Diary of Frances Burney, 1768–1778*, II, ed. Annie Raine Ellis (1913), pp. 321 ff.

feelings of sublimity. 'The emotions raised by great and by elevated objects, are clearly distinguishable, not only in the internal feeling, but even in their external expressions. A great object dilates the breast, and makes the spectator endeavour to enlarge his bulk....An elevated object produces a different expression; it makes the spectator stretch upward and stand a tiptoe.'[79] The moral significance of this had been stated earlier by David Hume.

> Any great elevation of place 'communicates a kind of pride or sublimity of imagination,' while a sublime imagination 'conveys the idea of ascent and elevation.' In running from low to high, the imagination finds an opposition, which the soul is eager to meet and overcome. The soul is ready to ascend, even if it does so with great difficulty, and thus the fancy is impelled to soar to heights above the 'natural stream of thoughts and conceptions.'
>
> 'This aspiring progress of the imagination suits the present disposition of the mind; and the difficulty, instead of extinguishing its vigor and alacrity, has the contrary effect of sustaining and encreasing it.' Hence virtue, genius, power are associated with height and consequently with sublimity. Vast objects and the difficulty of conceiving them elevate the mind, and enable it to overcome the opposition of which this difficulty is an expression.[80]

There is obviously an association between these sentiments and the lofty character of Alfred as conceived by Henry Hoare. Alfred, a 'Philosopher on the throne', as one version of the inscription puts it, has affinities with Numa, the philosopher king of Rome; and this provides the link between the tower and the garden, for Numa, it is said, derived his wisdom from the nymph Egeria who lived in a cave and after Numa's death was turned by Diana into a spring. After 1772 Alfred's Tower became part of the natural scene and therefore associated with nature's sublime phenomena. Out in the post-chaise in August 1774 Henry

> met with a most violent storm of Thunder, Lightning, Hail and Rain near the Convent, it came directly from the Tower but spared it...I have improved the placing of the Pictures in the Palm Tree Room to the approbatn of all by raiseg. the Rape of the Sabines higher so as to receive 5 pictures under in that end of the Room & I never saw the Sabines before they seem now all in motion. Have put the Storm of Jona under the Borgognone & made that section compleat. I wish we had no storms but in that Picture.[81]

[79] Quoted W. J. Hipple Jr., *The Beautiful, the Sublime, and the Picturesque in Eighteenth Century British Aesthetic Theory* (Carbondale, 1957), p. 111.
[80] S. H. Monk, *The Sublime* (Ann Arbor, 1960), p. 65.
[81] H.H. to Lord B., 29 Aug. 1774, T(TOT).

Besides sophisticated travellers, 'crowds of country people'[82] now visited the garden; but among Henry's chief pleasures was the interest of his daughter and her children. It was the latter who could probably more nearly enter into the spirit of the place and share Henry's own childlike enthusiasm. 'I am upon the entrance to the Grotto to get it finished before you come', he told Susanna in May 1776. 'It is a spot of such Romantick Pleasure as to strike everybody & nothing here ever delighted me so much. The Dear Charles has shook off his cold & trudges down to Mary Faugoin's with his Wagon twice a Day & has found the Easy path to and from it.'[83] Charles, as the 1st Marquess of Ailesbury, was to enlarge Tottenham House to grandiose proportions which his descendants have lived to regret.

Later in the month Henry was able to tell Bruce, 'Thank God they are all fine & well & now make nothing of walking round the Gardens & I mounted the Tower Thursday with the Dear Children. The Temple of the Nymph is all enchantment to Them & the Cross now new painted fills them with rapture.'[84] There were, in addition, a Chinese alcove and a Turkish tent, as at Painshill, the inside altered according to Susanna's direction.[85] Up at the house an organ was 'kept going by the charming Musicians alternately'.[86] In fact, all would have been very well if it had not been for 'the bad news from Boston'.[87]

Less than a year after the first shots had been fired at Lexington, General Howe had been obliged to retire to Nova Scotia. 'We want nothing but some refreshing showers to set Grass & Corn growing & to make the Land flow with Milk & Honey,' wrote Henry, 'Cheese will be a Dear Article else next year as the Ships carry off such Quantity. I am glad however that 6 transports arrived with provisions before Genl. Howe left Boston. I hope Quebec will not be attacked again before our reinforcemt. arrives. God only knows how that War will end, kindled and enflamed by the Vipers in our own Bosom.'[88] The ups and downs were reflected in Henry's mood. At first, with news that Howe had fresh troops and that a fleet under his brother was also there to help him, things seemed better. 'I think the face of Affairs in America now seems favourable. The Lord of Hosts is I trust with Us & they will be made to repent of their Rebellion.'[89] This, as we know, was not the case. After Burgoyne's defeat at Saratoga the war was extended by the entry of France and later Spain. Lord North who had led the government since 1770 and whose sound financial administration would have appealed to Henry, was by his very

[82] H.H. to Harriet, 18 July 1776, T(TOT).
[83] H.H. to Lady Bruce, 1 May 1776, TOT.
[84] H.H. to Lord B., 11 May 1776, TOT.
[85] H.H. to Harriet, 18 July 1776, T(TOT).
[86] H.H. to Lord B., 6 May 1776, TOT.
[87] Ibid.
[88] 13 May 1776, TOT.
[89] 1 July 1776, T(TOT).

qualities inhibited from prosecuting the war. 'I was surprised to hear of Admiral Keppel's return which seems to prove what Lord Temple told me here lately viz that the Ministry have no plan...He painted our Situation in most dismal colours.'[90] In July 1778 Keppel fought an indecisive battle off Ushant for which he was court-martialled. In August Henry wrote, 'We hear from Plymouth that Keppel's fleet is returned there after a running fight with the French who are got into Brest, poor doings indeed'.[91]

One evening in September 'the Sun set...in a Deep Crimson & in the Saloon we saw the Tower rise in it with the Majesty of awefull Darkness & it looked twice as high again as it really is. I never saw it to such advantage.'[92] If this romantic image was a symbol of his hopes they were disappointed. By the following year, 1779, the French and Spanish lay unopposed off Plymouth and all England expected an invasion. Bampfylde, who had been sketching in North Devon, wrote that the combined fleets had been seen off the Lizard. 'The accos. are so various', wrote Henry, 'we are tossed in a Sea of Troubles & uncertainty & kept in Hot Water & I pray God to deliver us.' Added to this there was turnip blight. 'I called in Mr. Farr yesterday. He says there are Thousands of Insects in the roots of those that are blighted. I wish your Lordship to order Them to be examined, tho I do not doubt the Truth of it no more than I do the enclosed Relation of the Electrifyg Eele. I am afraid to enquire after the News & wish to think of Politicks and Partys no more.'[93]

Disaster did not come, but neither did peace. In 1781 Henry was seventy-six. His hands were rheumatic, but he was nevertheless able to ride over to Savernake to 'pay Homage to the King of all Oakes & to the Queen of all Beaches'.[94] He also climbed the scaffold of the column Lord Bruce was erecting, to examine the drip on top of the cornice of the pedestal where the wet could lodge and perish the stone.[95] Twelve days later he wrote, 'We have an odd bird comes every year to us. This day I was presented with a Nicticorax or night Raven anciently so called. The Moderns call it a Night Crow, it flys in Darkness, & its Voice is like that of an Alarum going off which it continues for an hour together it is a Bird of Passage & had 2 Eggs in it. I never saw one before.'[96] It was also a bird of ill omen. Henry's mood was one of increasing pessimism, to which the seven days' rioting in June 1780[97] must have contributed. Further blows to British prestige in America and unsettled government at home were not calculated

[90] 2 July 1778, T(TOT).
[91] 3 Aug. 1778, T(TOT).
[92] Undated, 1778? T(TOT).
[93] 28 Sep. 1779, T(TOT).
[94] 16 July 1781, TOT.
[95] Ibid.
[96] H.H. to Lord B., 28 July 1781, TOT.
[97] The Gordon Riots, particularly violent in areas near the bank in Fleet Street.

to give an old man confidence in the future. He therefore decided to shed responsibility for his estates and turn his mind to his successor.

His nephew, Richard, had married again after Anne's death.[98] As next senior to Henry in the partnership, he looked forward to succession as owner of the business and the premises in Fleet Street and of the now famous Stourhead estate. But Henry had fears for the future of the business, and was determined that if a disaster befell the creditors should not lay hands on the place which he had created. He therefore decided to leave all his property to Nanny's son, Richard Colt Hoare, on condition that he left the bank and should never become a partner. When Colt proposed marriage to Hester Lyttelton[99] (niece to that Lyttelton with whom William Shenstone had so often discussed gardening in Worcestershire), Henry announced his intention of making him his heir forthwith.

This caused consternation among his nephews, for it meant that not only Stourhead but the Fleet Street premises where the business was conducted would pass to Colt Hoare. Richard's brother considered it 'most base and treacherous conduct', 'contrary to Faith, Honor and Justice'; 'it was subverting the order of Nature, Right and Justice to have the Father dependent on the will of the Son and the Uncle of the Nephew'. The shocked tones of his account,[100] and the strong feeling aroused by Henry's intention are reminiscent of his own twenty-four years earlier when faced with the perfidious behaviour of Lord and Lady Cork. It was perhaps reasonable that he should leave Stourhead to his grandson, his only direct descendant; but in depriving his nephew of the Fleet Street premises he was acting in accordance with his feeling and, as it were, introducing matrilinear descent into a patriarchal world. 'Right and Justice' were not 'the order of Nature' but perilously held concepts too easily forgotten. Henry was surprised at his nephews' reaction. He explained

> that he had by long application to business…improved and considerably increased his Estates and had formed a Beautiful Place; that his idea was that it was right for the Possessor of the Place to enjoy all the Estates about it in order to support it properly.…He had seen for some time past the Progress of this Nation's Ruin, and could not tell how soon it might happen. By leaving the House and Estates to Colt he thought it was the same as leaving them to his father…by doing this he secured to his Grandson an estate of £6,000 p.a., with a Fine House and Place, let any Public Calamity Happen, as he did not mean he should continue in the Banking Business when he came into the

98 Frances Acland.
99 Eldest daughter of Lord Westcote, Baron Lyttelton of Frankley. He was the youngest brother of Sir George Lyttelton, Henry Hoare's friend and fellow gardener at Hagley. Lord Westcote succeeded to Hagley on the death of his nephew, the 2nd Lord Lyttelton.
100 An account by Henry Hoare's nephew, Henry Hoare (1744–85), known as 'Fat Harry'. T(ST) 383.912.

possession of his Real Estates. In his state the Place was more Pain than Pleasure to him and he should resign it with the Estates with Pleasure to Colt and could finish the remainder of his Days at Clapham, living on his Income from Business, free from Care and Vexation.

Henry, however, was 'much struck' by his nephew's arguments and agreed to a compromise. A few weeks later, on 1 August 1783, he executed Deeds giving to his nephew Richard the bank premises in Fleet Street and the house where he lived in Lincoln's Inn Fields, and to Colt his West Country property, including Stourhead.

On Colt Hoare's marriage he retired, as he had said, to Clapham where having outlived Susanna, his last surviving child, he died in September 1785.

Part II

Chapter 1

Travels in Search of Antiquity

The Amiable Companion

Richard Colt Hoare, the heir to Stourhead, had been born on the ninth of December, 1758, and was six months old when his young mother died the following May. Two years later, his father, Henry's nephew Richard, married again, so Colt, as his relations called him (and as we will call him too), grew up with a family of half-brothers and sisters at Barn Elms, 'a delightful and extensive villa on the banks of the Thames' between Putney and Mortlake. His parent, as he later remembered him, was 'liberal minded...of a retired rather than of an active disposition, moral in his character, kind and attentive to his children'.[1] Colt's formal education began at Mr. Davis's large preparatory school in Wandsworth, and subsequently at a small seminary kept by the Reverend Dr. Samuel Glasse at Greenford, a pattern also followed by his younger brother Hugh to whom, throughout his life, he was devoted. Elsewhere his education proceeded informally, at nearby Clapham, with his cousins at Savernake, but above all at Stourhead where, as a schoolboy, his summer holidays were spent. Political and court gossip he may have heard at Tottenham, but what impressed him was 'the continual inspection of fine scenery without and fine paintings within doors' which inculcated into his 'tender mind a love for the beauties both of Nature and of Art'.[2] During his childhood extensive improvements were made at his father's place; Lancelot Brown was at work in Savernake by the time he was eight. He saw the building of the Sun Temple, the arrival of the Cross, and the spectacular rise of Alfred's Tower. And there was Henry Hoare himself 'tall and comely in his person, elegant in his manners and address and well versed in polite literature'.[3] Sometimes life was tedious for a boy, especially in the long winter evenings which Henry and his intimates relieved with a constant game of piquet. But in the fine season others usually assembled at Stourhead; parties to which Colt's uncle Henry, 'the very model of good humour and joviality' brought friends like David Garrick.

On leaving school Colt Hoare moved into lodgings adjoining the bank

[1] Richard Colt Hoare, MS. memoirs, ST.
[2] Ibid.
[3] Ibid.

in Fleet Street, and, while learning the business, continued his study of classical authors under a tutor. He came of age in December 1779, when an allowance of £2000 from his grandfather enabled him to set up house in Lincoln's Inn Fields, a short distance from his father's town residence.

1779 was a disturbing year. 'The state of Ireland is truly alarming', wrote Henry Hoare, 'and that of Spains moving their Naval Force to France. I pray God to deliver us from our External & Internal Enemys who will mock when our fear comes.'[4] It all seemed connected with the unpleasantness of discovering in a well at Stourhead, from which workmen had been drinking, the skeleton of a man who was to have been married two years since. The weather in August was bad, 'Jupiter Pluvius has begun his reign'. Only good for turnips, 'Which promise a vast crop for the Mere people who with the colliers & other Parishes I hear make no scruple of carrying off Sacks full every day in the face of the Sun & come in such Bodys as to resist & Justice Madox actually shot at some that took his & they threatened his Life. This strikes at all improvement from that Root & next I suppose they will reap the wheat & carry it off with Sheep & Horned Cattle.'[5] It was the insects which got the roots, as he noted some weeks later. Colt was with him at the time and together they drove back to London. 'We arrived safe in 8 hours and ½ at Clapham & in the 2d Gatefield saw a fine covey of Birds which called Colt to Arms.'[6] In fact events, alarming though they were, did not seriously interfere with the course of life, or customary country pursuits. The management of estates was anyway in other hands, so that six years later Colt Hoare could leave them in order to pursue other matters to his liking. Meanwhile his uncle Henry had arranged a marriage with the Honourable Hester Lyttelton of Hagley.

The ceremony took place at Barnes on August the 18th, 1783, and the couple went to live in Adelphi Terrace. Hester Hoare (Pl. 25b) was, according to Colt, 'an amiable and very accomplished companion'. The Lyttelton family had shown evidence of superior natural endowments, and in some of its members, her cousin for instance, a certain instability or what Sir Nathaniel Wraxall described as 'constitutional nervous irritability'.[7] Hester's brother George had a period of insanity and was for some time under the famous Dr. Monro at Blackheath. She herself was evidently highly strung and this possibly went with a delicate constitution; points which are made in a letter written shortly after her marriage to her brother-in-law Hugh who was courting Maria Acland.

> Adelphi from my Boudoir Saturday the 10th. Par ma foi vous êtes un trés joli garçon or otherwise in English you are a very

[4] Henry Hoare to Lord Bruce, 5 June 1779, TOT.
[5] 7 Aug. 1779, TOT.
[6] 28 Sep. 1779, T(TOT).
[7] Sir Nathaniel Wraxall, *Memoirs*, I (1815), p. 316.

pretty boy, I mean for making such a speedy answer to my last letter. As I pretend to be an excellent Christian I exercise as far as I am able every precept that is to be found in the Good Book, and if I mistake not, among the number there is this to be met with, *Do as you would be done by*, which *circumbendibus* (or Sir come bend I buss) of expressions is only to lead to the simple fact of my writing to you direct, that you may do the same by me again as you have already done. Now if I don't deserve a *patent* for that *rhapsody of Nonsense*, I don't know who doth. I am sorry you was stupid when you wrote, but why do you *court melancholy* with the soft *strains* of *Mary's Lamentations*, you had better upon all occasions bid *mirth and all her train appear*. I don't wonder that Dame *Patience* preaches to you so constantly, she is a *cold unfeeling* creature, and those who have most of her are generally too *Phlegmmy* for my *Taste* tho' I believe they are the happiest of people. If I was you I would not listen to *her dictates*, but like the heros we read of in days of chivalry or like Acland Junioso, seize the divine Angelica and mounting her *in groppa* on *crop* then all powerful fly to *Gretna Green*. I will now though endeavour to proceed in the dull track which *common sense points to me....* We dined last Sabath day with your Parentage at the Elms. Your Mammy we thought much improved in Health and Spirits and greatly delighted with your Epistles and Miss Maria's Purse—This morning I went in quest of a velvet. Much as I wish'd to oblige you, I have bought one exactly the reverse of what you desired, but prithee do not object, for in the first place t'is thirteen shillings per yard cheaper than you wd. have had it at prime cost. In the second t'is a lovely colour, and precisely similar in that respect to one the P. of Wales has order'd for the Birthday and thirdly by way of conclusion it is a *perishable commodity* and if you are determined to dislike it will have the goodness to leave your back long before your back can leave it—I hope you will on the contrary be pleas'd with it, & I send you a bit to shew to the beloved, whom I beseech to admire it for my sake—Farewell I am going to *adornize* my charms for the opera which bye the bye is *spik* and *span new* and wonderfully pretty—almost as *pretty* as *Lady Gormanstone* says you are. I wd not have you be vain but she whispered to me yesterday, that she thought you a mighty pleasing (I could say *pretty*, but that wd. be tautology) *young man*

The letter continued on Thursday the 15th when the change in style of handwriting graphically illustrates the change in mood.

Since I lay'd down my pen on Saturday I have been very ill and unable to resume it. I am now better God be praised, and not *bare bones* tho very near the matter. I feel almost ashamed of sending this mad performance of a letter, but it is more trouble than I am equal to to compose another, so be to its faults a little blind.—L'Epoux cheri is well and delighted and desires to greet you with a holy kiss,—farewell, Dear Hugo, write to me e crede-temi sempre your affectionate

Hester Hoare

I have got no velvet to send.[8]

Colt would have shared her appreciation of quality in material things, and a sensuous taste which took pleasure in clothes and surroundings. It was from this that he derived his enjoyment of the landscape and which made him an observant traveller. But in the considerable volume of his writings he reveals little of his personal life or what he felt about people, except in a general way. There was always a tendency to withdraw from society, in spite of its attractions. His repeated detailed lists of things seem like a ruse to tie them down; just as, in later life, the patient accumulation of facts may be seen as an attempt to grasp reality, when, in fact, his tendency was to slip into a fantasy. Not only is his subsequent taste in pictures evidence of this, but often in his travels he could only enjoy a scene by associating it with some remote or mythical event.

Colt was never quite reconciled to the enforced leisure which the terms of his grandfather's settlement had imposed on him; nor to the loss of a share in the profits of the business. However, having moved to Stourhead with his wife, he declared himself inclined to the 'repose and occupations of a country life' and found the change in his fortunes 'agreeable though less profitable'. His father, who was overlooked by the settlement, took it hard, and the Baronetage he received in 1786 came too late to compensate. Hester wrote to Hugh from Stourhead in May 1785,

as my Spouse is writing a tender Epistle to his Papa I feel it unnecessary for me to address any of my precious lines to your mother or anybody else at the Elms. . . . Both my good man and I are vex'd to think that your Father should feel he had been slighted and not invited hither, God knows it was a foolish excess of Delicacy which stopped our mouths when we parted in London, for we found it painful to our feelings to name this place more than was absolutely necessary either to him or your mother, and of all things particularly disliked asking them in a formal way to visit us at it. I think it would have been kinder had they taken it for granted that their son's doors would be at

---

[8] Hester Hoare to Hugh Hoare, 1783/4, FS.

all times open to them and I can answer for it that my dear man would feel no joy greater than that of receiving them. I wish he had gone with me to the Elms....He has determined to go to Town in the winter to see him, and in the meanwhile he will be able to convince him by his letters that *indifference* or *slight* never can find admittance in his heart when he is in question.[9]

Colt Hoare's first child had been born the previous September and Hester was pregnant again. The child died and her own condition was serious. Colt wrote to Hugh in July,

Having of late had so much real cause of Anxiety owing to Hester's dangerous situation, I have neither had time or spirits to write to you but, thank God, the prospect is now much fairer: her fever has left her and with it, I hope, all danger; she is still and of course must continue for a long while very weak before she regains her natural strength not being of a very robust constitution; she was taken up out of her bed for the first time yesterday and bore it much better than she expected— she has now rheumatic pains flying about her, which disturb her rest in the night....If all goes well and Hester recovers her strength sufficiently to remove from home, we intend to pay a visit to Killerton in the course of the Autumn or Winter and perhaps we may eat our Xmas pies there *together*—You must soon think of getting your Nags in order to mount the Devonshire Hills—I shall content myself with looking down upon you from some High Torr: I begin now to count the days to the first of September when my favourite diversion begins; the Coveys are very large and in tolerable plenty; Still has given me Deverill Longwood, a noble wood for game if I can protect it—where do you mean to *murder* this year?

...I am afraid this addition to the Game Laws, will tempt the farmers who shoot to destroy the birds.[10]

They were safe from Colt that year. Hester 'had foreboded her death before her accouchement and frequently had said she should never recover from it'.[11] And so it was. Colt blamed the superintendent and the nurse, of whose disagreement he had known months before. 'Our dear unhappy Friend', wrote Mr. Barton, Rector of Stourton, 'sent to me Wednesday Evening and I spent near an hour with him, and had sufficient command of myself not to distress him. He set me an example of fortitude wch I endeavoured to imitate....I am afraid the mourning wch is ordered is of

9 May 1785, FS.
10 R.C.H. to Hugh Hoare, Jul./Aug. 1785, FS.
11 R.C.H. MS. memoirs, ST.

such variety & in such abundance that it will delay the last Ceremony till the latter end of next week—no less than 25 suits of men and women's mourning.'[12] From Killerton Colt's sister Henrietta, now Lady Acland, so far forgot herself as to sign herself Hoare. 'I shall not write to Colt at present as I think it will only distress him. We did mean to have asked him here but as you have told me his intention of going abroad it is out of the question.'[13]

The death in September of his grandfather Henry, hastened perhaps by this last melancholy event, clinched the matter. On the nineteenth of that month, with Captain Meyrick, a friend of the Lytteltons, as a companion Colt Hoare sailed from Dover. Except for a brief period in 1787, he did not return to Stourhead for six years.

[12] Rev. W. Barton to Hugh Hoare, 27 Aug. 1785, FS.
[13] Lady Acland (Henrietta Hoare) to Hugh Hoare, 29 Aug. 1785, FS.

Chapter 2

The Road to Rome

During the next twenty-two months, driven by a restless curiosity which was his pattern for many years to come, Colt Hoare travelled 6571 miles (not including local excursions) by 580 stages, each one of which he recorded with a comment on the state of the inn. 'From having become one of the most settled men in the world, I am become one of the most fickle; I hardly know where I shall sleep the next night.'[1]

The crossing to Calais took two and three-quarter hours. 'Having never quitted England before I found myself among a people, differing as much from my own countrymen in appearance, dress and customs, as perhaps the inhabitants of America.'[2] Hogarth's *Calais Gate* was nevertheless an extravagant caricature. There was certainly a Capuchin monk who begged alms at the inn, but 'most of the soldiers whom I saw are far different from those pictures of famine which he has drawn. They are well made, good looking men; and many wear whiskers, which give them a manly and military appearance.' Dessein's Hotel, a building of two or three quadrangles, had a garden surrounded by pleasant apartments, and a theatre where 'one of Molière's pieces was performed very decently'.[3] The following morning the party left on the first stage of their journey to Naples.

Those who could afford it equipped themselves with an English coach, chaise, or barouche. Those who could not had to be content with a French cabriolet, a large assortment of which, either for hire or sale, were always kept at the Great Inn at Calais. New ones could always be bought in Paris and, for a long journey, it was prudent not to rely on second-hand. Colt and his companion presumably had their own post-chaise, bought and paid for in September,

> Neatly run with raised beads, painted dark carmelite colour with Cyphers in Mantles on the doors, the leather japand and plated beads round it, plated lock handles and brace buckles, the body lind with fine light colourd cloth trimd with lace the same colour,

---

[1] R.C.H. to Hugh Hoare, 13 Feb. 1786, FS.
[2] Richard Colt Hoare, *Recollections Abroad*, I (1815).
[3] Ibid.

> plate glasses and Venetian blinds in the front and doors, a large
> oval glass in the back and a plated frame round it, a wainscot
> trunk under the seat, double steps and carpet in the bottom,
> hung on a light strong perch carriage with iron axle trees screwd
> at the ends, wrot boxes and hoop tire wheels, a set of steel
> springs, a platform and wing irons covered with leather and a
> leather cover with plated buckles to the fore part of the carriage
> and wheels painted yellow and varnished...£97. 10.[4]

Extra were a pair of lamps with silver reflectors and convex glasses, 'an
Imperial to the roof', a large leather trunk, locks to the doors and bolts
to the blinds, trunk cover, trunk chain, drag chain, and tool budget.

The post to Paris took six days. 'The mode of travelling in France is
novel to an Englishman,' wrote Colt, 'the postillian equipped with immense
jack-boots, with his hair tied in a long queue, and a cocked hat, drives
three horses abreast in a rope harness; and as he speeds away, endeavours
to crack a tune with his long whip.'[5] The roads were paved and planted on
each side with trees. The farmers were industrious and neat in their
method of husbandry; the crops were superior to those in England. Arthur
Young, some eighteen months later, travelling in a more leisurely way from
Boulogne, until his mare caught cold and he had to complete the journey
to Paris 'as other travellers in Post-chaises do, that is to say, knowing
little or nothing',[6] commented differently. The husbandry, he thought, was

> full as bad as the country is good; corn miserable and yellow
> with weeds, yet all summer fallowed with lost attention. If the
> French have not husbandry to show us, they have roads; nothing
> can be more beautiful, or kept in more garden order, if I may use
> the expression, than that which passes through a fine wood of
> Monsieur Neuvillier's; and indeed for the whole way from Samer
> it is wonderfully formed; a vast causeway with hills cut to level
> vales; which would fill me with admiration if I had known
> nothing of the abominable *corvées* that make me commiserate
> the oppressed farmers, from whose extorted labour this magni-
> ficence has been wrung.[7]

At Chantilly Colt saw his first example of French garden art, laid out
in parterres with copious fountains and part 'disposed á l'Anglaise;
though so unlike anything I ever saw in England that I should not have
observed the peculiarity without an explanation'.[8] Four full days of
sightseeing in Paris. Girardon's *Richelieu* in the Sorbonne was 'one of the

[4] Wright Lukin & Co., Account, 2 Sep. 1785, T(ST) 383.57.
[5] *Recollections Abroad*, I.
[6] Arthur Young, *Travels in France and Italy, 1787, 1788 and 1789* (Everyman ed. 1906).
[7] Ibid.
[8] *Recollections Abroad*, I.

finest pieces of sculpture in the world'; the pictures in the Louvres not
equal in merit to those in the Royal Academy. Visits to the opera, Comédie
Française, and the Italian theatre. Then on to Lyons; five days by way of
Pontheiry and Fontainbleau, Moret, Fossard, Villeneuve-la-Guyard, Sens,
and Villeneuve-sur-Yonne; Joigny, Auxerre, Vermenton, Cussy-les Forges,
Rouvray, Saulieu, Chagny, Chalon, Tournus, Mâcon, and Villefranche-
sur-Saône.

At Lyons the party paused to hire *voituriers* for the journey over Mont
Cenis to Turin. This was by now a commonplace experience. But forty-five
years earlier Horace Walpole found the horrors accompanied by too much
danger to give time to reflect on the beauties. 'Such uncouth rocks, and
such uncomely inhabitants!' The passage over the mountain was accomplished by mules and in low chairs slung from poles; the descent reputed
rapid and dramatic. Colt found it less difficult and romantic than it had
been painted. Arthur Young, proceeding in the opposite direction, felt
the same.

> To those who from reading are full of expectation of something
> very sublime, it is almost as great a delusion as to be met with
> in the regions of romance; if travellers are to be believed the
> descent *rammassant* on the snow is made with the velocity of a
> flash of lightning; I was not fortunate enough with anything so
> wonderful. At the *grand croix* we seated ourselves in machines
> of four sticks, dignified with the name of *traineau*; a mule draws
> it, and a conductor, who walks between the machine and the
> animal, serves chiefly to kick the snow into the face of the rider.
> When arrived at the precipice, which leads down to (Lansleburg)
> the mule is dismissed and the *rammassing* begins. The weight of
> two persons, the guide seating himself in the front and directing
> it with his heels in the snow, is sufficient to give it motion....
> As it is at present, a good English horse would trot as fast as we
> *rammassed*.[9]

Turin was reached on 14 October; Florence on the 26th, where Colt's
party was received with great civility by Sir Horace Mann, then with but
one more year to live. They were now approaching those parts of Italy
which for various reasons affected the imagination most strongly. In a
sense Colt Hoare's education fitted him especially for travel of this kind.
He was prepared not only by the Latin authors he had studied but the
pictures and scenes at Stourhead, his grandfather's reminiscences and the
practical lessons in painting he had recently received from 'Warwick'
Smith.[10] Leaving Florence by way of the Lake of Trasimene they were
detained for a whole day on its banks at Toricella, 'a miserable little inn',

[9] Young, op. cit.
[10] Receipt from John Smith, T(ST) 383.4.

which nevertheless enabled Colt to contemplate the classic ground where Hannibal had so dramatically defeated the Romans under Flaminius. Colt returned there in 1789, when he noted 'Nature has rendered the Lake of Thrasymene a beautiful scene; agriculture by its cultivation, a rich one, and history by the events that transpired on its banks a classical one'.[11] 'The inequality of hills renders the country near Toricella very picturesque, that on the opposite side, adjoining the Val di Chiana, is much less so, owing to its flatness. The mountains in this district being well wooded with oak contribute much to the general beauty of this scenery around this lake. It is studded with three islands and its circumference is stated at thirty miles.'[12] As a fisherman he was interested in tackle and found that the hooks used at Toricella were of brass wire, sharpened and bent, but without barbs, so that fish might be sent alive and unhurt to Rome. The use of steel hooks was punished with the galleys.

Although on this occasion he did not linger on the road from Perugia to Rome, the attention he subsequently gave to it is evidence of the impression which it made. 'Of all the various provinces of Italy which I have yet visited, that of Umbria appears to me the most pleasing and picturesque, uniting the rich and cultivated scenes which its fertile plains produce, to those of a more dignified and majestic nature.'[13] 'I question if any one local district throughout Italy can within the interval of a hundred miles, produce so many objects worthy of attention as the country lying between Arezzo and Narni.'[14] Perugia, Assissi, Foligno, Spoleto, Terni, Narni; it was certainly a much travelled road, and, thanks to the attention of the Pope, a good one. Almost a year after Colt, to the day, Goethe having sent his carriage on to Foligno, found the walk one of the most enchanting he had ever taken. Nevertheless the different currencies, the vetturini, the prices, the wretched inns were a daily nuisance. 'Anyone who travels alone for the first time, hoping for uninterrupted pleasures, is bound to be often disappointed and have much to put up with.'[15] 'The inn here in Foligno is exactly like a Homeric household. Everyone is gathered in a large vault around an open fireplace, shouting and talking. They all eat together at one long table, as in a painting of the Wedding Feast at Cana.'[16]

The beauty of the Nera valley (Pl. 32a) had long been celebrated. Colt Hoare was deeply impressed and returned in a more leisurely way the following May. He was then able to leave the road to visit some of the more sublime spectacles. Augustus's bridge at Narni was the most immense

11 *Recollections Abroad*, II.
12 Ibid.
13 Ibid., p. 250.
14 Ibid., p. 257.
15 J. W. Goethe, *Italian Journey, 1786–1788*, trans. W. H. Auden and Elizabeth Mayer (1962), p. 111.
16 Ibid., p. 110.

and magnificent he had ever beheld; he made drawings and detailed observations, and quoted Martial,

> Sed jam parce mihi, nec abutere Narnia Quinto
> Perpetuo liceat sic tibi ponti frui
> (Preserve my Quintus, Narni, from all harm,
> So may thy noble bridge withstand the shock of all
> devouring time.)[17]

Four or five miles from Terni (to the north-east of Narni), the reputed birth place of Tacitus, the River Velino (Pl. 31a) falls into the river Nera. 'The cascade', said Colt, 'is reckond the highest in Europe, and the water is a very white hue which Virgil mentions.

> Audiit et longe Triviae lacus, audiit amnis Sulphurea Nar
> *albus* aqua, fontesque Velini!'[18]

Salvator Rosa had called it 'cosa da far spiritare ogni incontentabile cervello per la sua orrida bellezza'.[19] Richard Wilson exclaimed more succinctly, 'Well done; water, by God!'[20] Boswell had visited it. And Smollett found it 'an object of tremendous sublimity', though it lost effect from lack of a proper point of view. This was not the only disadvantage. J. E. Smith, the botanist, having hired a calash to take him to the cascade, 'A cicerone fixed himself on the back of our chaise, and we were pestered with boys bringing trumpery petrifactions to sell, all which impertinences are very disagreeable when one comes to contemplate a grand natural object'.[21] On the last occasion Colt Hoare visited Terni in October 1789, he determined to see it from 'a more advantageous point of view, at least in one more congenial to the eye of an artist'.

> Scorning the assistance of a cicerone, and considering myself no longer a stranger on this classic ground, I proceed on my ride to the banks of the Nera. Leaving my horses at the desolated village of Papignia, and descending towards the river, I crossed it, over a picturesque bridge, adjoining the delightful villa of Signor Gaziani, I pursued my walk on the left bank of the Nera, the scene varying each moment. At one time I found myself surrounded with lofty rocks and mountains, adorned with the most beautiful foliage; at another time buried in the deep recesses of a high grown forest called La Macchia piana, with an impetuous torrent roaring at my side; at last I entered into a thick and gloomy copse of evergreen oaks which bade defiance to the

[17] R.C.H., MS. Journal, Wiltshire Archaeological Society, Devizes, p. 77.
[18] Ibid., p. 80.
[19] Elizabeth Wheeler Manwaring, *Italian Landscape in Eighteenth Century England* (London, 1965), p. 169.
[20] Ibid., p. 74.
[21] J. E. Smith, *A Sketch of a Tour on the Continent* (1807), II, p. 319.

cheering rays of Phoebus, still pursuing my anxious course, till at length emerging from this dark retreat, the long expected object of attraction burst upon my sight, and left no further scope for imagination; for the fall of the Velino into the Nera is one of those wonderful works of nature, which no mind can fancy, nor pencil delineate with appropriate grandeur.[22]

Pictures of this scene and others on the road from Foligno to Rome form part of the Stourhead collection of Ducros's work.

Most travellers approaching Rome were affected not only by its historic importance but, whether Protestant or Catholic, by its religious and political overtones. For Goethe, in 1786, the dreams of his youth had come to life. 'The first engravings I remember—my father hung views of Rome in the hall—I now see in reality, and everything I have known for so long through paintings, drawings, etchings, woodcuts, plaster casts and cork models is now assembled before me. Wherever I walk I come upon familiar objects in an unfamiliar world; everything is just as I imagined it yet everything is new.'[23] Such anticipations were bound to invite an anti-climax, and when for the first time, on 4 November 1785, Colt Hoare entered the imperial city his heart 'beat with enthusiasm, curiosity and impatience increased'. 'But when I saw only the same appearances as in other Italian towns which I had recently visited the romantic ideas which my mind had long been forming suddenly vanished; the Scipios and Caesars were transformed into abbés and cardinals, and the marble palaces and triumphal cars into hotels and hackney coaches.'[24] After five days rushing from one famous building to another he was in no mood to appreciate them and being unwilling to attach ideas of disgust and disappointment to scenes which had for so long been objects of his most ardent wishes, he continued to Naples which he reached on the 11th of November. On Sunday the 18th, Captain Meyrick, who had been such a sympathetic companion at the time he most needed one, died of malaria caught in the Pontine marshes.

On Wednesday the 21st, in the evening, attended by many of the English, Colt performed the last sad office to his friend. He then sought new lodgings and prepared to settle in Naples for the remainder of the winter.

[22] *Recollections Abroad*, II, p. 252.
[23] Goethe, op. cit., p. 116.
[24] *Recollections Abroad*, I.

Chapter 3

Naples

'Naples is a paradise,' wrote Goethe, 'everyone lives in a state of intoxicated self-forgetfulness.'[1] The country seemed to satisfy all basic needs and breed a people, happy by nature, who could wait without concern for tomorrow to bring them what they had to-day. The many-coloured flowers and fruits added to the impression of universal gaiety. All who could afford it wore silk scarves, ribbons and flowers in their hats. In the poorest homes the chairs and chests were painted with bright flowers on a gilt ground; even the one-horse carriages were bright red, their carved woodwork gilded, and the horses decorated with artificial flowers, crimson tassels, and tinsel.

Sir William Hamilton, who had come as English minister in 1764, said that if he were compelled to be a king he would choose Naples for his kingdom.

> Here a crown has fewer thorns than in any other country. His very want of political power ensures his repose; and the storms which desolate Europe pass over his head. Placed at the extremity of Italy he is removed out of the way of contest and hostility. A delicious climate, shores to which the Romans retired, when masters of the world, in order to enjoy a luxury unobtainable elsewhere...all the productions of the Levant, blended with those of the Mediterranean; a splendid capital, palaces, wood, game, everything seems assembled in this enchanting bay that can conduce to human enjoyment.[2]

When, in 1734, Philip V of Spain had ceded to his son Charles all his rights to the kingdom of Naples and Sicily, Neapolitans of all classes had welcomed enthusiastically a king of their own, after years of Spanish and Austrian domination. Charles had a passion for hunting and building which infected his subjects, so that in twenty-five years Naples became one of the finest capitals in Europe. But in spite of extravagance revenue increased, taxation diminished, and intellectual freedom was permitted to an extent unknown in Italy.

[1] Goethe, op. cit., p. 198.   [2] Sir Nathaniel Wraxall, *Memoirs*, I, p. 253.

On the death of his brother Ferdinand VI, in 1759, Charles became King of Spain, and had to cede Naples and Sicily to his third son, Ferdinand, who was then a minor. On coming of age in 1767, Ferdinand had been married by proxy in Vienna to the Archduchess Maria Carolina of Austria, sister of Marie Antoinette. Maria was cultivated and ambitious, and on her arrival in Naples the court became a lively cosmopolitan social centre. She was far more suited to a throne than Ferdinand, who was without ambition and of childish simplicity. Sir Nathaniel Wraxall wrote: 'He always reminded me of a rustic, elevated by fortune or accident to a crown; but it was an amiable, honest, sensible, well-intentioned rustic, not altogether unworthy of such an elevation.'[3] Nor did Ferdinand show defect of natural understanding, though he was altogether destitute of that elegance and art, which frequently veil the want of information.

Sir William Hamilton thought no European sovereign, without exception, so ill-educated as the King of Naples. His ordinary Italian was a Neapolitan dialect, such as the lowest of his subjects spoke. He understood French but rarely read or wrote that language. Indeed he scarcely ever read anything, and considered as the greatest of misfortunes a rainy day, when the weather was too bad for him to go out to the chase.

J. E. Smith, the botanist, who visited Naples in 1787, adds another touch to this picture.

> As to the character of the king, two traits may serve to give an idea of it. He is a great billiard-player, and adjoining to the billiard-room has a small oratory, with a figure of the Virgin, to which he addresses himself when any great sum is depending. He is extremely fond of hunting the wild boar, and partakes of that amusement almost every day. The least appearance of a thunder storm alone used to interrupt him. But of late his royal courage braves this danger undaunted, for he is provided with a little image of some anti-electric saint, which, being worn in his bosom, is a sure protection. These little foibles, however, do not lessen his character as a benevolent and well meaning sovereign.[4]

This amiability did not extend to the animals he pursued with a grisly and persistent malevolence. Colt Hoare was present at a Royal Hunt given for the English benefit on 29 January 1786. They met in the morning at a forest about fifteen miles from the Royal Palace at Caserta. Tents were pitched and breakfast served after which they went to the scene of action, a square field, surrounded on three sides by canvas and on the fourth open to the forest, through which the game were driven by a multitude of beaters. In the middle of this arena were the carriages the ladies and other spectators, while the king and others joining in the sport were stationed at the corners

3 Wraxall, p. 233.
4 J. E. Smith, op. cit., p. 136.

of the wood. Dogs of various kinds were kept in readiness. As each deer, fox, or hare appeared, greyhounds were loosed to destroy it.

> At last a herd of wild boar came out, who were pursued by Bulldogs who soon seiz'd them and held them fast till the King or some one of his attendants came up and stuck his spear into its chine; a chasseur afterwards takes up the Boar by the legs and the King sticks him with his couteau de chasse in a more mortal part.[5]
>
> These Wild Boar by no means deserve such a name, for they are by no means fierce and are constantly fed in the woods and I have heard will come when you whistle.[6]
>
> There were only 28...kill'd this day a very mortifying number to his majesty.[7]
>
> For my own part, I was so thoroughly disgusted with this scene of slaughter and butchery that nothing would tempt me to be present at it a second time. The lamentable cries of the Deer and the howling of the dying Boar would I think induce me to throw away the knife...yet the King and his court seem to receive great pleasure from the acts of cruelty, and to vie with each other in the Expertness of doing them.[8]

As Colt justly and prophetically observed, in view of what was enacted fourteen years later under stress of war and revolution, 'These repeated acts of Barbarity must tend to harden the heart of those who commit them, and to deprive them of all feeling and humanity.'[9]

Across the bay, the plume of smoke from Mount Vesuvius was an ever present reminder of 'tranquillity, tinged with terror'. To men in search of the sublime and the beautiful Naples it seemed offered both in full measure. If the natives were content to learn to live with it, the volcano exercised a compulsive fascination over others. Sir William Hamilton was as passionately addicted to it as he was to Emma Hart. Few travellers could resist making the journey at least once to look down into the crater. Vesuvius was particularly active about this time, a major eruption occurred in 1794, when lava flowed 650 yards into the sea, causing it to boil. In between times the journey was uncomfortable rather than dangerous, depending on the extent to which providence was tempted. Goethe went near to it on more than one occasion.

> So long as there was space enough to remain at a safe distance, it was a grand, uplifting spectacle. After a tremendous thundering roar which came out of the depth of the cauldron, thousands of stones, large and small and enveloped in clouds of dust, were

[5] R.C.H., MS. journal, Devizes, p. 49.
[6] Ibid., p. 45.   [7] Ibid., p. 45.   [8] Ibid., p. 44.   [9] Ibid., p. 45.

7—L.A.

hurled into the air. Most of them fell back into the abyss, but the others made an extraordinary noise as they hit the outer wall of the cone. First came the heavier ones, struck with a dull thud and hopped down the slope, then the lighter rattled down after them and, last, a rain of ash descended. This all took place at regular intervals, which we could calculate by counting slowly.[10]

Observing this he thought there might be time to reach the mouth and return between two eruptions. Unfortunately they could see nothing because of the steam rising from the fissures, and having delayed in the hope that it would clear, forgot to count. 'We were standing on a sharp edge of the monstrous abyss when, all of a sudden, thunder shook the mountain and a terrific charge flew past us. We ducked instinctively as if that would save us when the shower of stones began. The smaller stones had already finished clattering down when, having forgotten that another interval had began, and happy to have survived, we reached the foot of the cone under a rain of ashes which thickly coated our hats and shoulders.'[11] Not everyone was so exhilarated. Goethe's companion, Tischbein, the painter, 'grew more depressed than ever when he saw that the monster, not content with being ugly, was now threatening to become dangerous as well'.

Colt Hoare made the ascent shortly after his arrival in Naples. The first part was by mule, and then by foot over the loose cinders to the summit, 'as high as it was possible to go without running a great danger'. Hearing that there was a flow of lava on the other side, he continued to climb, but when he came near it 'the smell of sulphur being as strong as a lighted match under my nose it was impossible to proceed any further'.[12]

> I walk'd over the old crater which is now at the foot of the new one, it is quite a level surface, in which there are many smoking chimneys and in one part of it there is a boiling cauldron of lava which makes a loud bubbling and hissing noise, from this cauldron the lava goes underground, and perhaps is the source of that which makes its appearance on the other side of the mountain. Between the crevices of the old lava I saw some of it as red as a Blacksmith's Furnace.[13]

The version in the notes and journals which he wrote at the time sometimes differs from that published many years later, where the experience is embroidered and his efforts after literary style not an improvement. Thus: 'The present eruption is quite sufficient to give me a very good idea of what a much greater one is; it roar'd very much and vomited out a great

---

[10] Goethe, op. cit., p. 184.   [11] Ibid., p. 185.
[12] R.C.H., Journal, p. 17.   [13] Ibid., p. 17.

deal of smoke mixed with stones,'[14] became: 'The mountain was in a state of ebullition, and the eruption sufficiently great, to give a competent idea of its fury when aggravated in a high degree. It roared tremendously and vomited forth thick volumes of smoke mixed with stones, some of which fell at my feet, and others beyond me.'[15]

Herculaneum had been rediscovered early in the century but was over-shadowed by the later revelations at Pompeii. These had occurred within the lifetime of most travellers, who made a point of visiting the sites. Charles III had encouraged excavation. A whole street had been uncovered but Colt lamented that Ferdinand was not zealously bent on the work, and only continued it by his father's order. 'Thirty men only are at this time employed; and I believe it is the business of one half of them to over look the other.'[16] This, and the visit to the Royal Museum at Portici where he could 'examine utensils of every kind, discovered in those houses, and made use of by the Romans', are his first recorded interest in antiquities of this kind. But another trivial incident probably throws more light on his character and motivation. Shortly after his ascent of Vesuvius he visited the Catacombs at Capo di Monte. In common with others of his time Colt liked to reflect on death. He had, indeed, recent cause and the mixture of objectivity and sentiment is characteristic.

'It is impossible for anyone, I think, to go through this immense repository of the Dead, where thousands of skulls are dispers'd about, without being forceably struck with awe and horror. . . . For my own part, I never saw the few skulls and bones thrown upon the stage in the play of Hamlet without some sensation, how much stronger then were my feelings, on walking thro' this dark arched vault (by the light of a *funereal* torch) strewed with thousands of relics of my fellow creatures.'[17] The facts follow as an afterthought. 'The form of the Catacombs cut in the Rock, is like this', followed by a sketch. 'There are two stories of these vaults, in one part there is a large funnel to convey the putrid air away.' 'In the year 1764 there was a great mortality at Naples and these vaults were used to deposit the poor who suffered by it.'[18] And so on.

Goethe objected to the mixing up of past and present and rebuked his guide in Sicily for the 'odious evocation of defunct ghosts',[19] especially when these disturbed peaceful dreams by recalling scenes of savage violence. Colt Hoare's sentiment was towards the past. Italy particularly invited 'the recollection of former times, and a comparison of those times with the present'. The object of travel was 'to restore to our minds the classical studies of our youth; to visit those places recorded in history as the residences of illustrious characters of antiquity, or rendered interesting by historical facts or anecdotes, to admire and reflect upon those remains of

[14] Ibid., p. 17.
[16] Ibid., p. 35.
[18] Ibid.

[15] *Recollections Abroad*, I, p. 31.
[17] Journal, p. 26.
[19] Goethe op. cit. p. 222.

polished architecture and sculpture'.[20] In these early topographical excursions myth and history were confounded.

> From a high spot of ground close to the *Arco felice* you may see the Roman coast, the ancient river Cocytus and *Palus Acherontia*; and a square tower near the sea which was built on the spot where the tomb of the great Scipio Africanus stood on which was the follg. inscription,

> > Ingrata Patria, ne quidem ossa mea habes

> It is now called *Torre di Patria* owing to the word *Patria* being the only one legible on the tomb at the time when Linternum (the ancient name of the place) was beseiged by the Vandals in 455.

> A little farther is a hill on which the citadel of Cuma stood, on the very summit of it are a few remains of the famous temple of Apollo mention'd by Virgil.

> > At pius Aeneas, arces quibus altus Apollo
> > Praesidet, horrendaeque procul secreta Sybillae
> > Antrum immane petit...

> I afterwards visited this famous cave

> > Excisum Euboicae latus ingens rupis in antrum,
> > Quo lati ducunt aditus centum, ostia centum,
> > Unde ruunt totidem voces, responsa Sybillae.

> The present entrance into it is near the Lake of Avernus; there was a passage thro' it from thence to Cuma; on entering into it you observe a long straight and vaulted passage; about the middle of it you turn to the right and by the help of a flambeau and a man's shoulders, you are led thro' a long dark and narrow passage, which is up to a man's knees in water, into a small apartment in which is a stone trough, by some antiquarians said to be the sibyl's bath and by others her bed: this is the only room at present discover'd, but as such revolutions have been occasion'd in this country by volcanoes and earthquakes, if the *aditus centum* and *ostia centum* ever existed, most probably they have been choked up.

> The *Lake of Avernus* is a large round piece of water surrounded with hills and from its shape very probably once the crater of a volcano; in some places it is 25 fathm deep. On the banks of this lake are the ruins of an ancient temple, built of brick; it is not certain to whom it was dedicated; some say to Neptune or

---

[20] Richard Colt Hoare, *A Classical Tour through Italy and Sicily* (1819), p. viii.

Mercury; and others to *Juno inferna* by which latter name it goes at present. From its situation I should imagine it was sacred to some of the infernal Deities, near this spot being the descent into Hell, thus painted by Virgil.

> Spelunca alta fuit, vastoque immanis hiatu,
> Scrupea, tuta lacu nigro nemorumque tenebris,
> Quam super haud ullae poterant impune volantes
> Tendere iter pennis; talis sese halitus atris
> Faucibus effundens supera ad convexa ferebat
> Unde locum Graii dixerunt nomine Avernum.[21]

The remains of antiquity about Cuma were so very trifling that, had they not been so beautifully described by Virgil and other classical authors, Colt thought they would have been very uninteresting. As it was, the two days he spent there afforded him the greatest satisfaction. On 4 February he made drawings of the Lake of Avernus (Pl. 29b), which were later used by Turner in a painting representing *Aeneas and the Cumaean Sibyl* (Pl. 29a).

It may be suspected that to begin with Colt was not socially at ease. He had lost his companion, and not until the arrival of his friend Dr. Warner[22] did he find another. He filled the gap with frequent visits to the English Club, the theatre and the opera. Naples was famous for its music; singers, instrumentalists and other virtuosi from the *Conservatori* were in demand in all the courts of Europe. The opera house, completed in 1738, had six tiers of boxes, thirty in each. They were long and narrow, so that although they held twelve people only three could sit abreast. As most people did not go to hear music, but to meet and talk to one another, this was immaterial. The boxes were leased to individuals and furnished like drawing-rooms to their taste. It was customary for a lady to make appointments to receive visitors in her box on a particular night, when they would remain with her during the whole opera, and be regaled with iced fruits and sweet-meats. Once she was seated, a lady did not leave her box; but gentlemen ran from box to box, even during the performance.

The Neapolitans, Colt found, preferred 'external splendour' to 'internal comfort'. They took little exercise, and every class of people gambled. The nobility inhabited the upper stories of their houses; visiting involved climbing many, often filthy, stairs. 'The pot doth not boil, neither doth the spit labour, as in England, in the cause of hospitality. Though great dinners are occasionally given, the friendly intercourse of the small but social board is scarcely known.'[23] He had, however, begun to enjoy himself

[21] Journal, pp. 40 ff. The conclusions on the Virgilian associations of the lake at Stourhead were written and published before reading Colt Hoare's journal. Colt Hoare made some alterations in the Temple of Flora and he may have caused the inscription, *Procul, o procul este profani* to be cut, although I do not personally think so. Author.
[22] John Warner, D.D., 1736–1800, later Rector of Stourton.
[23] *Recollections Abroad*, I, p. 51.

after his inauspicious start. 'I have spent my time here much more pleasantly of late,' he wrote to Hugh on 13 February, 'and have got into a very tolerable society which will be continued at Rome—to which place I remove myself and baggage on Friday next—in all probability I shall stay there till the end of April, as its antiquities, environs, etc. cannot be seen *properly* in a much shorter time.'[24]

[24] R.C.H. to Hugh Hoare, 13 Feb. 1786, FS.

Chapter 4

Rome

'In Rome I was glad to study; here I only want to live', said Goethe in Naples. Colt Hoare, in the reverse direction, arrived just in time for the Carnival. On 2 March, he settled down to a steady diet of antiquities; four hours a day.

> My mornings have been constantly employed & will be for three weeks longer in visiting the Antiquities etc. with a Cicerone— you may judge of the number of objects worthy of notice when six weeks are but just sufficient to see them. When this part of my education is over, I shall take my horse (whom I brought with me from Naples & is a very good little fellow) & recon- noitre the Environs of this once famous city—I shall spend most, probably the last three weeks, of my time in the country which will *then* be delicious, though now there is scarcely any appear- ance of spring at Rome, the climate being much backwarder than at Naples—The amusement I find here suits me so well & there is so much work for my pencil, that I know not when I shall be able to get away: I hope to have satisfied my curiosity by the middle of May, when I shall proceed towards Switzerland visiting a few places in my way.[1]

The guides through 'the immense labyrinth of antiquities and rarities' were 'Mr. Byres and Mr. Morrison, two Scottish gentlemen...well qualified by abilities and experience....' James Byres, the son of a Scottish Jacobite, was educated in France and was for some time in the military service of that country, until he returned to claim estates which would otherwise have been forfeited. After a year or two in Britain he went to Rome to study architecture and in 1763 adopted the profession of guide–antiquary. 'Mr Byres being already engaged with a party,' wrote Colt, 'I put myself under the tutelage of Mr. Morrison; and had every reason to be satisfied with his remarks as a scholar and an antiquary, and his attentions to me as a traveller.'[2] Morrison's tour, which lasted until 8 April, Sundays

[1] R.C.H. to Hugh Hoare, 19 Mar. 1786, FS.
[2] *Recollections*, I, p. 70.

excepted, included not only the ruins of Rome but some thirty palaces, villas and galleries, and two dozen churches.

Soon after his arrival in Rome, Colt visited the house of his grandfather's old friend and agent, Thomas Jenkins. Although petitioners no longer lined his gate and stairs, kissed his hand and called him *illustrissimus*, Jenkins was still a well-known and influential person. Jenkins and Byres between them controlled the taste and expenditure of Englishmen who visited Rome. Thomas Jones recollected that,

> Each of these Gentlemen had a party among the Artists, and it was customary for everyone to present a specimen of his Abilities to his Protector, for which he received in return an Antique Ring or a few sechins—These specimens were hung up in their respective Rooms of Audience for the inspection of the Cavaliers who came—Each party likewise, by established custom, dined with its Patron on Christmas Day—by accident I was first introduced to Mr Byers as I happened to travel from England with Norton his partner and coadjutor—But being first invited to the Christmas Dinner by Mr Jenkins I was looked upon as being enrolled under his Banner—this custom however began to wear away as the last holy days a Party dined by Subscription at my Apartments & Mr Jenkins sat down to a Sumptuous Entertainment attended by only one Person.[3]

In 1777 James Northcote had found it absolutely necessary to get an introduction for permission to copy in the Vatican. He also found that men like Byres exercised such control over the picture market that it was impossible to get commissions except through them. 'Those cursed antiquaries who are of late years established here have all the power in their own hands, and one or two miserable wretches who are sycophants to them make all the copies for the English nobility at very small prices.'[4] Byres had purchased for the Duke of Rutland a group of pictures by Nicolas Poussin; the removal of such works was forbidden by law in Rome and a sensation was caused by their exhibition in London in 1787. The Marquess Bonapaduli let Byres have his Poussins as copies were made to put in their place. Joshua Reynolds said that the Marquess made it a condition of the sale that Byres 'should bring strangers as usual to see the copies, which he says he is obliged to do, and I suppose, swear they are originals, and it is very probably these copies will be sold again and others put in their place'.[5]

Colt Hoare corresponded with Byres and Morrison during the whole period he was in Italy. Morrison acted as his agent, and received pictures,

---

[3] 'Memoirs of Thomas Jones', *Walpole Society*, XXXII (1951).
[4] W. T. Whitley, *Artists and their friends in England*, II, p. 308.
[5] Ibid., p. 76.

books and other things for dispatch to England. The only painting that Colt Hoare recorded having bought from him was certainly not genuine, although Colt never doubted that it was, for in the published edition of his travels there is a footnote concerning a ceiling by Veronese in San Nicoletto dei Frari in Venice, 'I afterwards purchased of Mr. Morrison at Rome, the original design in oils for this ceiling'.[6] Morrison also mentioned this in a letter to Colt Hoare in Florence, shortly after he had returned to Italy for the second time by way of Germany.

> No doubt your journey must have afforded you much entertainment, particularly in the line of fine arts. The Flemish school must always command our admiration but seldom engages our attention, their charms are but momentary, Non satis est pulchra esse poemata dulcia sunto. I am persuaded the many acquisitions you mention to have made have been selected with a just criterion and will afford repeated pleasure when added to your collection....I do not remember any other commission you were pleased to favour me with beside the monument, unless it be the casts from the antique Farnese Calender which I procured before its departure from Naples and is still in my possession....Let me know when and where I am to send your picture of P. Veronese which you desired me to keep until your arrival in Italy.[7]

In this aspect of patronage Colt Hoare followed the tradition already established at Stourhead except that for Italian pictures he either did not have Henry Hoare's flair or he was not so well served. Many were wrongly attributed and in any case the supply was beginning to dry up. His purchases were mainly made between 1788 and 1791. Perhaps the most important, Ludovico Cigoli's *Adoration of the Magi*,[8] was also one of the last before he finally returned to England. He saw a vast number of paintings in Italy. On the whole, his taste was conventional. Before Raphael's *Transfiguration* we can almost hear Morrison at his elbow; 'Justly considered as the masterpiece of art.' 'Few subjects more arduous...success of the artist has been more admirable than in most of his other works.' 'Many of Raphael's works,' Colt went on, 'like treatises on philosophy, appear to me to be too deep to be understood at first sight; but to a steady and persevering attention....What dignity and variety does he display in his characters; what grace in the disposition of his drapery, what harmony in his colouring! In his works man is not merely dignified, but almost deified.'[9]

[6] *Recollections*, I.
[7] Colin Morrison (unsigned) to R.C.H., 12 Feb. 1789, T(ST) 383.4.
[8] Receipt, 21 Feb. 1791, T(ST) 383.4. See also E. K. Waterhouse, *Italian Baroque Painting* (1962), p. 154.
[9] *Recollections*, I, p. 84.

At the Vatican Michelangelo got an honourable mention, but it was Raphael's *School of Athens* which Woodforde had to transpose into the library at Stourhead.

When he was moved it was often by some story which art recalled, as with the group of Niobe and her children, in Florence; or to make some comment of a personal, rather than general significance. 'The rape of a Sabine woman, by Giovanni di Bologna; a beautiful group, in which the distress of the female sufferer, the joy and passion of the vigorous ravisher, and the grief of the father who in vain attempts to rescue his daughter are admirably contrasted.'[10] Female distress, if not rape, was a recurring image; the lines, for instance, which he attributed to Thomson, on the confluence of Rhône and Saône:

> She meek and modest, with a virgin grace
> Winds round and round, as shunning his embrace,
> He rushes rapid with a bridegroom's air,
> And pours his torrent in the yielding fair.[11]

The man of taste and man of sentiment were never integrated, which explains the unevenness of his judgement. Topography was his real preference and it is here he made his most important contribution as a patron, and his claim to have assisted the progress of the English water-colour school.

On Saturday, 8th of April, Colt wrote in his journal. 'Finished with my Antiquarians went to Artists etc.'[12] These were almost certainly Louis Ducros, Philipp Hackert, and Carlo Labruzzi, whose acquaintance he had previously made. Labruzzi was subsequently his companion when he studied the course of the Appian Way in November 1789. The project was never completed, because of bad weather and Labruzzi's ill health at the time, but many of the latter's drawings are now in the British Museum. They are interesting as records made on the spot, loosely done in pencil and monochrome and tinted with colour.

Philipp Hackert was a Prussian who had come to Rome in 1768 and made his name as a specialist in Italian Landscape. In 1777 he had accompanied Charles Gore on a tour through Sicily in which Richard Payne Knight was of the party. Hackert was well known to many Englishmen. When Thomas Jones was seeking patrons in Rome, in 1779, he was asked by Sir Thomas Gascoigne whether he prepared his canvasses himself, and whether his colours were all minerals. 'I innocently told him that I bought my Cloths & Colors I made use of ready prepared at the Colorshop, & were the same that all other Painters used: "Oh no," reply'd he, "Mr. Hackert at Rome always prepares his own Cloths & bleaches them in his

10 *Recollections*, I.
11 Ibid.
12 MS. Journal, W.A.S.

Garden half a year before he begins painting them—that *all* his colors were prepared from Minerals, & procured at vast Labour & Expence from the different Mines in Germany."'[13] Hackert was later asked by Lord Bristol to visit Jones in Naples to see how some commissions were progressing. Jones was greatly surprised, as 'the great Mr. Hackaert' had never once deigned him that honour all the time he was in Rome. 'He was pleased to pay many Compliments on my progressive Improvement in paying due attention to the Detail—that is to say, minute finishing, which bye the bye, was more congenial to his own taste, who like most German Artists, study more the Minutiae than the grand principles of the Art.'[14]

Goethe, who got to know him well and enjoyed his company, wrote: 'Though Hackert is always busy drawing and painting he remains sociable and has a gift for attracting people and making them become his pupils. He has completely won me over as well, since he is patient with my weaknesses and stresses to me the supreme importance of accuracy in drawing and of a confident and clearheaded approach.'[15] Hackert's extensive landscapes, with every detail clearly defined, do not fall into a sophisticated category. 'When he paints he always has three shades of colour ready. Using them one after the other, he starts with the background and paints the foreground last, so that the picture appears, one doesn't know from where.'[16] Later, in June 1787, Goethe found Hackert an invaluable guide.

> Hackert and I visited the Colonna Gallery where paintings by Poussin, Claude Lorrain and Salvator Rosa are hung side by side. Hackert has copied several of them and studied the others thoroughly, and his comments were most illuminating. I was pleased to discover that my judgments of these pictures are still pretty much what they were when I paid my first visit. . . . What one needs to do is to look at them and then immediately look at Nature to learn what they saw in her and in one way or another imitated; then the mind is cleared of misconceptions, and in the end one arrives at a true vision of the relation between Nature and Art.[17]

Colt Hoare did not record that Hackert helped him in this way although it is improbable that so inveterate a teacher would have withheld advice from someone so obviously seeking it. Colt met Hackert again at Naples in 1790, when they made an excursion together to the festival at Isernia[18] which gained some notoriety by Payne Knight's dissertation on the worship of Priapus, distributed to the Dilettanti Society in 1786. Colt bought a

[13] Memoirs of Thomas Jones.
[14] Ibid.
[15] Goethe, op. cit., p. 197.
[16] Ibid.
[17] Ibid., p. 343.
[18] *A Classical Tour through Italy and Sicily*, pp. 224 ff. Also *Recollections*, IV.

Hackert painting and some drawings, including one made on another excursion in search of the picturesque at Piedimonte,[19] near Naples. At the end of a narrow glen called Vallone del Inferno, 'a river of the most transparent water rushes from a Cavern under a lofty mountain'. 'Of this cavern and river I have a very correct drawing in my collection, made by my fellow traveller, Filippo Hackert.'[20]

But Colt's enthusiasm was for Ducros, a discovery he believed would revolutionize English water-colour painting. After his third visit to Rome in 1787 he wrote to Hugh, 'Du Cros an artist...whom I think I mentioned to you last year has done four drawings for me which (if they arrive safe in England) will be the admiration of the whole town & put all our English artists, even the great Mr. Smith to the blush: I flatter myself he will add much to my improvement, for he has not only taught me the management of his colours but shewd me a very easy method of engraving drawings in the brown tints—'[21] In a note-book he recorded

Water colors us'd by Du Cros

Carmine	Prussian blue
Gamboge	Venice Indn Ink
Bister	Sepia

Sometimes Red Chalk

The Carmine & Gambouge mix'd make the strong vigorous tints like dead leaves—Gambouge & Sepia make a strong & vigorous green—Blue seldom used in the first plan—
The distances carmine & blue, if wanted, warmer a little gamboge—Water do in the great shades a little Carmine added to the Sepia.[22]

Ducros[23] was ten years older than Colt Hoare; that is to say, he was thirty-eight when Colt first met him in 1786. He had come to Rome about 1772, from Geneva via Flanders settling first at Tivoli. The four paintings to which Colt Hoare referred in his letter, *The Lake of Thrasymene*, *The Tomb of Munatius Plancus*, *Civita Castellana*, and *View at Tivoli* (Pl. 31b) are *tours de force* in the medium, all about 30 × 40 inches. They are elaborately worked in superimposed washes to give an appearance of density comparable to oil. Of the eight paintings Colt bought subsequently some are even larger. Besides the more celebrated Roman ruins they included his favourite scenes on the river Nera, Augustus's bridge at Narni, and the falls of Velino. Colt sometimes commissioned artists to paint pictures from his own drawings, which may have been the case here, and would account

19 Ibid., pp. 240 ff.   20 *Recollections*, IV.
21 R.C.H. to Hugh Hoare, 21 Feb. 1787, FS.
22 R.C.H., notebooks relating to tours, T(ST) 383.919.
23 Biographical details from D. Agassiz, *A. L. Du Cros, Peintre et Graveur, 1748–1810* (Lausanne, 1927).

for the unevenness. Some, like the *Subterranean falls of the Villa Maecenas* (Pl. 40), are impressive; in others the accumulation of insensitive and repetitive schema, for trees for instance, becomes monotonous. The rendering of storm in the Nera valley (Pl. 32a) pulls all the sublime stops, buildings struck by lightning, floods, peasants in distress. Ducros's Swiss friend de la Rue wrote in 1784.

> A force de vouloir être grand il devient un peu vague, a force de vouloir être harmonieux et clair il devient un peu faible d'effet, mais il rachète cela par des choses vraiment admirables. Il compose avec gout et seulement dans un style heroique. [And in 1785] Du Cros, cet amy dont je t'ay tant parlé n'est pas aimé ici, il est craint et évité par tout le monde. On lui trouve le caractère faux et la langue mauvaise....Son talent pour la peinture est bien réel mais il se fait aider prodigieusement par des peintres d'histoire pour ses figures et par des architectes pour ses monuments.[24]

This reputation did not help him when French-speaking foreigners came in for persecution in 1793. He moved to Naples from where he made journeys to Sicily and Malta, and prospered until the failure of his banker in 1808, when he returned to Switzerland. He died of apoplexy in 1810.

Colt Hoare was constant in his friendship for Ducros and thought the enmity with which he was regarded due to jealousy of his superior merit.[25] He wrote to him often when in Italy but the only surviving letter is one from Ducros in 1800, soliciting commissions for his views of Malta.

> Je voue prie d'avoir La complaisance de recomander ce Projet a vos bons amis, Et de me Procurer La connoissance des meilleurs Marchands Libraires ou Topographiques, come c'est un sujet national et que Malthe Minorque et Giberaltar sont les Boulvards de la Puissance Britanique.... En May on attend L'arrivée de My lord Elgin au quel un amy avait envoyé a Constantinople deux de mes grands dessins dont it est fort content. Il veut avoir de moy les monuments de l'Empire Romain, comme Don Tito Lussier lui fait ceux du Levant. Cela me tiendra ques tems en Romanie que j'aime toujours cependant je suis charmé de voir de nouvelles choses et de varier un peu Les Jouissances Pytoresque. Celles de Malthe me transportent de Plaisir et l'admiration et je voudrais vous y voir pendant qques Semaines. Vous les employeriez bien agréablement. Il me semble qu'on m'ait oté le vesuveu dessui les Épaules. Je respire en liberte sous un Gouvernement qui me connoist....[26]

[24] Ibid.   [25] R.C.H., *Modern Wiltshire*, I, p. 82.
[26] L. Ducros to R.C.H., 1800, T(ST) 383.907.

At the end of April 1786, feeling the need 'for the retirement and tranquillity of the country', after weeks of social life in Rome, Colt visited
Tivoli (Pl. 31b). 'I never mean to quit this place, indeed it has temptations
enough to seduce any man who has a proper taste for the beauties of
Nature. This small spot, which is not above seven miles in circumference
contains more picturesque scenes & a greater variety of objects than any
place I have ever seen.'[27] In addition who could not 'feel a degree of
enthusiasm, on breathing the same air as Brutus, Cassius, Sallust, Horace,
Propertius, and many others'. Yet, he noted, Tivoli was 'unnoticed and
unfrequented, except by artists in search of improvement, or foreigners
in search of novelty'.[28]

About eighteen miles to the north-west the site of Horace's Sabine farm
had not long since been identified by the Abbé Capmartin de Chaupy. 'I
always felt peculiar partiality to this poet, at a time when I little thought
I should tread the same soil, and drink the same spring'—[29]

> By numerous allusions to this villa and its pleasures, we are
> enabled to trace (his) character, habits and inclinations....
> Patronized by the great, and associated with the fortunate, the
> affluent, and the powerful, he never lost the native moderation
> of his taste and character: an humble farm, a garden watered
> by the limpid stream, and the friendly shelter of the grove....
> Thither he repaired from the turmoil of the capital, and sought
> health and pleasure in the rational occupations of a country life,
> unmoved by the derision of his more dissipated neighbours.[30]

This free rendering of Horace was a fair description of life as he imagined
it at Stourhead, for which the Sabine farm was the archetypal pattern.
On the way the journey was broken at Vicovaro (the *Varia* of Horace)
where he 'found ample employment for his pencil, in the many picturesque
views which the village and its environs, with the Convent of St. Cosmato
afforded'.[31] A drawing by Labruzzi of this place, at Stourhead, suggests
that he accompanied Colt Hoare.

In the same letter from Tivoli Colt wrote, 'I make but a short stay at
Rome at present, being on the point of making another excursion to
Albano Frascati etc. & shall take Woodford with me'. This is the only
mention made of this artist who subsequently worked so much at Stourhead. Samuel Woodforde was twenty-three at the time. His talent had
been recognized and encouraged by Henry Hoare, who had sent him to
study at the Royal Academy schools. On Henry's death Colt's father

27 R.C.H. to Hugh Hoare, 29 Apr. 1786. FS.
28 *Recollections*, I, p. 97.
29 Ibid., p. 101.
30 Ibid., p. 99.
31 R.C.H. to Hugh Hoare, 29 Apr. 1786, FS.

offered to send Woodforde to Italy and to allow him £100 a year for three years. When his father died in 1787 Colt continued the annuity and Wood-forde travelled back with him through Germany to England in 1791. The association continued until Woodforde's death in 1817. He told Farington that in all he received £1500 to £2000 from the Hoare family. Henry Thomson, whose work Colt Hoare also bought, said that at the time of his death Woodforde, 'by his narrow economy...had £1200 in the 3 pr cents accumulated'. 'He also had a child some years ago, for which he allowed 4 shillings pr. week. He has left the person to whom it is said he was married & who went to Italy with him, £170 pr annum.—She now says she was married to him at Rome. If so,' Farington smugly added, 'she left England as his mistress. Such is the sad way in which some proceed in life.'[32]

To anyone brought up with the images of classical landscape a pilgrim-age to Albano was necessary. 'I make no doubt but Claude Lorrain, Gaspar Poussin and Salvator Rosa, the three greatest landscape painters, fixed on this spot as the fittest for their studies.'[33] For the artist to compare the model with the image was part of his education. Scenes like the Lake of Nemi were widely familiar. It was already represented by Wilson at Stourhead; and Colt subsequently acquired another drawing by J. R. Cozens, apart from those he made himself. 'On the border of the lake was formerly a temple dedicated to Diana to whom the adjoining groves were sacred. Here also I found ample occupation for my pencil and quitted these classical scenes with regret.'[34]

Apart from classical diversions Rome held another interest for English travellers.

> I have this evening been presented to the Duchess of Albany, daughter of the *Pretender*. She is a very pleasant woman & rather handsome. I have not yet seen her Father, but being asked to dine there next Sunday, I hope to have the honor of seeing *his Majesty*—His Lamp I believe is almost burnt out. Do not think that I am turn'd Jacobite, but impute this visit of mine partly to curiosity of seeing a man who once made so much noise in our Country—& partly to the benefit I may reap from an acquaintance with the Dutchess—I will certainly send you an account of my *Reception*—at this *Gingerbread Court*.[35]

J. E. Smith, who was in Rome the following year, saw Charles Edward at the Carnival, where, at the Corso, he had a coach in the centre, a privilege accorded only to sovereign rank, although the only one he

[32] *The Farington Diary*, VIII, ed. J. Grieg (1922), p. 154.
[33] R.C.H., MS. journal, W.A.S.
[34] *Recollections*, I.
[35] R.C.H. to Hugh Hoare, 19 Mar. 1786, FS.

enjoyed. 'Here the "exiled majesty of England" might be seen every afternoon, lolling in his coach, the very image of a drunken Silenus, more
asleep than awake, and apparently tottering on the brink of that grave
to which he is since gone. The small remains of expression to be seen in
his face, wore the appearance of good nature. He was often accompanied
by his legitimated daughter, the duchess of Albany, a lively and unaffected
woman, but without any personal charms.'[36] Colt attended the duchess's
dinners on several occasions. The dangers against which his progenitor
and namesake had warned John Hoare were in fact no longer seriously
regarded. Sir John Leicester, who became acquainted with Colt at this
time and was subsequently his life-long friend, wrote to his mother that
the Pope was unfortunately receiving no-one. 'If he does before I leave
Rome I mean to kiss his Holiness's Toe.'[37] In Holy Week the English
flocked to the ceremonies, whereas at home they would not have dreamed
of attending. The performance of the *Miserere* in the Sistine Chapel was
among the high spots; Goethe found it 'unimaginably beautiful'. 'The
moment when the pope is stripped of his pontifical pomp and steps down
from his throne to adore the cross, while all the others stay where they
are in silence, until the choir begins—*Populus Meus quid feci tibi?*—is one
of the most beautiful of all these remarkable rites.'[38]

Smith admitted that he did not know which setting of the *miserere* to
prefer. 'Each seemed the perfection of harmony and left nothing to be
desired but that its impression might last for ever.'[39] When the Pope went
to pay his devotions to the illuminated cross Smith got upon the steps of
the high altar to have a good view of him, and could not forebear some
sceptical observations.

> At this altar was now an assemblage of the most distinguished
> foreigners, collected there to see his holiness, particularly their
> royal highnesses the duke and duchess of Gloucester, the duke
> and duchess of Buccleugh and the several ladies of their parties,
> to all of whom the pope seemed actually to be kneeling; and this
> had an extremely ludicrous effect. It was a matter of debate
> among some of us, what could most probably occupy the holy
> father's thoughts at that moment. Could so many lovely, though
> heretical, forms be totally unregarded?[40]

In retrospect Colt found the Benediction pre-eminent.

> Let the reader picture to himself the grandest modern building
> in Europe, flanked on each side by a magnificent colonnade, a
> spacious area, ornamented with Egyptian obelisks etc. crowded

---

[36] J. E. Smith, *Sketch of a Tour*, p. 48.
[37] Sir John Fleming Leicester to his mother, Tabley House.
[38] Goethe, op. cit., p. 482.
[39] J. E. Smith, op. cit., p. 281.   [40] Ibid., p. 282.

with thousands of spectators, waiting impatiently for the appearance of their *divinity* to shower down blessings upon them. Let him suppose he sees the Pontiff move gradually towards the balcony of his palace, seated on a golden throne, adorned with superb plumes of white feathers, habited in his costly robes, the tiara glittering on his head, and preceded by a long procession of officers and attendants bearing crosses and other symbols of religion. Behold him rise from his throne and with all the dignity of the most graceful actor, move majestically forwards. See him spreading his hands, and extending his arms, as if drawing blessings from heaven to dispense them on the multitude beneath; while the effect is heightened by the sounds of martial music, and the thunder of artillery.[41]

At the time he thought the ceremony might be improved 'by having more martial music and a louder Peal of Ordnance; yet considering it in its present performance it certainly for *a moment* impressed you with great awe—& converts you into a Catholic'.[42]

The Feast was followed by a general exodus; many went on to Venice for the Ascension which began on the 25th of May. Departures had to be arranged, Sir John Leicester told his mother, so as not to interfere with one another, there being always a scarcity of post horses.

Colt had prepared to leave Rome at the beginning of May. He gave instructions to his brother Hugh, who arranged his credit.

You may send letters to me at Rome, chez Mons[r]. Byres till the middle of April, afterwards to Louis Porta at Lausanne—Pray desire Samuel to leave the above directions at the Post Office & desire them to observe them. Pray send me a Letter of Credit for £200 on Mess[r] Rougiert Co.—at Milan—Another for £200—on Valerio Morelli at Bologna—Another for £200 on Weber, Gouhard & Co.—at Genoa—

I have mentioned the above people as I do not think you have any correspondents at those places—I find also that I have no Letter for Lausanne so you may send a Credit for me to L. Porta for £500—as Lausanne will be my direct Summer Residence.[43]

Hugh also had instructions concerning his affairs in England.

I am much obliged to you for your accounts of my affairs in the West—and am surprized at having receiv'd only one Letter from Charlton since my absence from England. . . . With respect to holding the Tenants Audit at Stourhead, I am convinced it the

41 *Recollections*, I, p. 95 ff.   42 Journal, W.A.S.
43 R.C.H. to Hugh Hoare, 19 Mar. 1786, FS.

best measure when their Landlord is at home, but when they have not his face to meet, I doubt whether the coming to the house only would produce any better effect—Besides the expense of the Liquor they drink is not inconsiderable. By Charlton's account of the Audit, I find they paid their rents much better than I expected, for last summer was certainly a very distressing one to most of them, and they generally avail themselves of every disadvantage to plead in their favour— I expected that would have been the case much more than it has. ...Pray let Ann Gleadah's bill be paid—I am quite surprized to find that Gauntlett's is not...write to him with my apologies & tell him that I not only *meant*, but concluded that I *had* plac'd the money to his account almost immediately on the receipt of the wine.[44]

The bill for oysters must be paid—but I am surprized at the Postilions demand, having paid every servant to the first day of October before I left Stourhead—there can be therefore no demand for wages otherwise the coachman & the other servants would have made a like demand.[45] (I) am made very happy by the good accounts you send me of yourself & my dear little Boy....I am glad to find that Switzerland is still in your thoughts & hope it will not get *out* of them.'[46]

Soon Hugh and Maria had decided on the trip and Colt was looking forward to meeting them. 'Lausanne will be *my chief* residence when I am not on my horse riding about the Country....I think it would be adviseable for me to take a house either out of the Town of Geneva, or Lausanne against the time of your arrival, where we might be together, & see as much of each other as possible.'[47]

I will not trouble you to bring me an uniform, but if you can find room for the following articles they will be very serviceable to me—

> a dark brown coat, plain white buttons—
> a dark blue do—plain yellow do—
> a plain light drab color'd do—white buttons made with breast lappel, no lining, & the fashionable sleeve—
> 3 strip'd yellow & white dimity waistcoats of the latest pattern—stripes crossways—
> a blue & buff stripd sattin waistct—to wear with the blue coat—stripes crossways—
> a few spare buttons to each—and a cock'd Hat—

Now if any of these are the least impediment to you I beg you will without any ceremony leave them out—I advise you to have

[44] 13 Feb. 1786, FS.   [45] 19 Mar. 1786, FS.   [46] Ibid.   [47] 29 Apr. 1786, FS.

a tin travelling case made for your hats which will fix on to the top of your Imperial—[48]

To these commissions he added a gold watch chain, a 'dozen of black lead pencils' and in a further letter,

> I beg you will bring me two boxes of Bayleys Shaving Powder & half a dozen tooth brushes of this form — [sketch] also if it will not be too great an incumbrance to you, a little box of laced ruffles which my Mother has lock'd up in some [] of her Drawers in L.I.F. I have desired Charlton to send you every

'You had better take the ruffles out of the box & put them in paper—least they should think them new—& smuggled—& if any are very dirty not to bring them.'[49]

Colt excused these requests by saying that it was difficult to get anything good abroad; but he advised Hugh to lay in a stock of winter and spring clothes at Lyons, where they could be had for half the price and 'much more elegant than in London'.

Colt left Rome on 17 May, by the road along the Nera Valley where he stopped at Civita Castellana and made the observations quoted earlier on Augustus's bridge at Narni. Crossing over to Ancona on the Adriatic he hardly paused at Rimini, Bologna, and Modena until he came to Genoa on 31 May. It was, he thought, one of the cleanest places he ever saw. Although commerce prevailed (even the nobility did not think themselves degraded by trade) he found plenty of pictures and churches to see in the four days he was there; and outside the town the gardens of the Lomellini and Doria families.

> These are the two best specimens of Italian taste in Gardening; they endeavour to imitate the English as much as possible, but the heat of their climate will ever be an effectual obstacle to them, & prevent their obtaining that constant verdure which is the greatest ornament of our country seats. . . . But they are still crowded with buildings, grottos, fountains etc. From a Chinese temple in the Lomellini there is a view towards the sea which would be an ornament. . .even in England. In the middle of this garden there is a field covered with chesnut trees in the middle

[48] Ibid.   [49] 15 May 1786, FS.

of which there is a *Dairy* with yellow ware in it à l'Angloise & close to it a *Water Closet* à l'Angloise too, which they do not fail to show to all foreigners. I met the owner of this villa who was exceedingly civil & highly pleased with my praising this *child of his own creation.*[50]

On 3 June Colt hired a felucca, embarked for Marseilles, and thence via Aix, Nîmes, Arles, and Romans came to Grenoble on 13 June. Here he stopped to make the customary visit to the *Grande Chartreuse*, and to add his ecstatic comments to those of Gray, Wilkes, Beckford, and others who had been there before him. He later stayed in many monasteries, particularly in his second tour abroad between 1788 and 1791, partly because they provided good and cheap accommodation for travellers. In Sicily, during 1790, he was dependent on them for lodging, and only once did the letters of recommendation he carried fail to get him a bed. He was generally well pleased, but in October 1786 he stayed with his brother-in-law Lyttelton at Montserrat, near Barcelona, where, although the room and the beds satisfied him, he complained that every trifling necessity had to be bought at an exorbitant price. 'We were almost starved for want of fire; and the friars to whom we brought letters of recommendation never presented themselves to us, as if apprehensive of an appeal to their civility. How different was the conduct of the worthy Carthusians, near Grenoble, whose friendly roof and hospitable table were ever open, without distinction to rich and poor, contributing to their comforts or alleviating their distresses, without any fee or reward, except that of gratitude.'[51]

Monasteries like the *Grande Chartreuse* were, of course, visited for the spectacular scenery in which they were situated; and because the retired religious life had a sentimental fascination for Colt and many of his contemporaries. After seeing many more he was able to make comparisons and reflect on the experience.

On this occasion he was content to acknowledge that a poet had been there before him and to paraphrase his words. 'Gray, who visited this spot in 1741, has painted its beauties and horrors in the most glowing colours. For myself I do not remember to have proceeded ten paces without an involuntary exclamation. Not a precipice, not a torrent, not a cliff, which does not inspire the enthusiasm of religion and poetry. Here are scenes which would awe even an atheist into belief.'[52]

A violent storm of thunder and lightning accompanied him on his return to Grenoble. On the next day, 17 June, he arrived at Lyons. He left there for Geneva on 7 July.

[50] Journal, W.A.S., pp. 106–7.   [51] *Recollections*, I, p. 264.
[52] Ibid., p. 129.

Chapter 5

Switzerland and Spain

> The sociable manner in which the Swiss seem to live, cannot fail
> to strike any traveller just come out of Italy; they seem to have
> no affectation; their manners are natural and obliging. The *gouté*
> is the time when they all meet and afterwards spend their evening
> comfortably together; the *gouté* is like a tea drinking party with
> us,—but on a more extensive plan; for it not only consists of
> tea, but of all sorts of fruit, cakes, pyes, wine and sometimes of
> meat—To the people of the Country who dine at a very early
> hour, such a repast is very acceptable—but upon us it is thrown
> away—As soon as the *gouté* is over—card tables are immediately
> introduced & in the course of five minutes everyone of the com-
> pany is engaged in a party. Whist is the prevalent game at which
> they play very low being not desirous of playing for profit but
> amusement.[1]

Colt's first two weeks at Geneva were mildly spent in social life of this
kind (sight-seeing and excursions in the neighbourhood, to Voltaire's
house at Ferney for instance). He had been joined on 11 July by Hugh and
Maria, Lyttelton, and other friends, who, on 25 July, accompanied him
in the first part of an extensive tour of the country.

Switzerland had begun to attract the English in increasing numbers as
the cult of Nature, particularly the sublimer aspects, spread. Rosa and
Thomson had assisted in the growth of a taste for wild mountain scenery;
the glaciers of Chamonix and Grindelwald were added to the repertoire
of Nature's spectacles and the avalanche (Pl. 32b) to the stock of horrific
imagery. J. R. Cozen's serene and more poetic Alpine paintings, made
during a visit with Richard Payne Knight in 1776, were among the first
of their kind.

Francis Towne, returning from Rome in 1781 with 'Warwick' Smith, had
made some fine drawings of the Source of Arveiron, thus described by Colt.

> The sources of many rivers are interesting, but none surpasses
> that of the Arveron. . . . It has the air of a supernatural creation,

[1] MS. journal, W.A.S., pp. 131 ff.

of a retreat raised by the power of the nymphs and naiads; indeed poetry itself has never assigned them a more romantic and appropriate abode. . . . It is a beautiful grotto of sea-green ice, broken into the most fantastic forms. The river rushes from its deep recesses; above is the glacier which descends from Mont-anvert; and beyond rocky mountains and groves of pine.[2]

The poet Colt had in mind was most likely Thomson, whose lines on the abode of winter he quoted when describing the scene from the *Col de Baume*, looking towards Mont Blanc. But the imagery foreshadows another poem conceived ten years after the experiences Colt described, by a poet who had never been to Switzerland.

> And from this chasm, with ceaseless turmoil seething
> As if this earth in fast thick pants were breathing
> A mighty fountain momently was forced:
> Amid whose swift half-intermitted burst
> Huge fragments vaulted like rebounding hail,
> Or chaffy grain beneath the thresher's flail:
> And 'mid these dancing rocks at once and ever
> It flung up momently the sacred river.

Thought and feeling are here fused in an image which is one of the mysteries of art, in the same way that Turner transcended Rosa and topography. Nevertheless, the experiences on which the great romantics drew were still, at one level, those which Colt Hoare could understand.

> Nothing could exceed the wildness of the scenery through which we passed; we were surrounded with lofty pines, huge rocks, tremendous precipices, and continually overlooked the Rhone, which foamed in endless cascades down the rapid descent. I thought that no addition could be made to this grand and romantic picture; when suddenly appeared a most beautiful glacier, which is the origin of the Rhone, and a parent worthy of so noble a stream. With joy I beheld the source of a river, whose wanderings I had traced from Avignon to Lyons and Geneva, and through the whole length of Valais, and whose banks had delighted me with a rich variety of grand and picturesque scenery. It is interesting to follow the windings of great rivers and trace them to the spot from which they derive their birth; but in this respect none surpasses the Rhone. Few are more fantastic in their course, or display more variety; few flow with more rapidity, or traverse countries more picturesque. Issuing from the glacier under Mount Furca, it waters the whole Valais, precipitates itself into the Lake of Geneva, and is dis-

[2] *Recollections*, I.

tinguished for a considerable distance by its dusky hue. At the farther extremity of that beautiful sheet of water, it bursts forth in two channels, near the town of Geneva, and is soon swelled by the stream of the Arve. It is curious to observe these two rivers coalescing, as it were, with reluctance, and each preserving its different channel, and peculiar colour; the Rhone appearing of a beautiful sea green; and the Arve, yellow and turbid. Descending towards Lyons, the Rhone buries itself under ground near Avranches; and then suddenly bursting from the rocks, as if from a new source, continues uninterrupted, till it unites itself with the Saône at Lyons. Thence it flows to Avignon; and below Arles, empties its tributary waters into the sea.[3]

Colt's more ornate attempts to convey sublimity show, however, the all-pervading influence of Rousseau. Rousseau's *Julie ou La Nouvelle Hélöise, Lettres de deux amants Habitants d'une petite ville au pied des Alpes* had been published in England in 1760. Apart from the anglophile tendencies expressed in the character of Milord Edouard Bomston, his attitude to nature coincided with the English mood and his description of Julie's Elysée with the ideal of a cultivated wilderness.

The affinities the English felt for Rousseau had not, in individual cases, survived when face to face with him. Even so, George III had granted him a pension, and the legend of 'L'Homme de la Nature at de la Vérité' produced a cult almost in his lifetime. This had been fostered by the Marquis de Girardin who, inspired by the description of Julie's garden, had made in his park at Ermenonville a similar earthly paradise. In 1786 it had only been eight years since the death of the philosopher there and his burial on *L'Ile des Peupliers*. 'A boat conveyed us to the isle of Poplars,' wrote J. E. Smith in 1787, 'the repository of the remains of Rousseau. His tomb, of white stone, is of an elegant form, and embosomed in a grove of those trees. . . . It was impossible to contemplate this monument without various reflections and emotions. Many people may wonder that I should bring away a little portion of moss from its top; but I knew some gentle minds in England to whom such a relic would not be unacceptable.'[4] And, as with Colt, objectivity in Smith went alongside sentiment.

That the intelligent observer of nature may have a just conception of the magnificent scale of these gardens, and that he may be well satisfied they are no paltry unnatural jumble of grottoes and rock-work, and 'plantations raised in a garden pot'; I shall give a most decisive proof of their genuine wildness, in truly saying, that even a botanist would here almost think himself on the Alps. The rocks and crags are covered with a profusion

[3] Ibid., pp. 149 ff.
[4] Smith, *Sketch of a Tour*, I, pp. 103 ff.

of the rarest mosses and *lichens*, which for the most part shun the haunts of men, and flourish only in the purest air and most alpine stations. Among others I gathered the true *Lichens Deustus* of Linnaeus, figured in Vaillant, not that of Dillenius, tab. 30, fig. 117, which is *polyrrhizos*, and possibly also *velleus*, of Linnaeus. It grew abundantly just below Rousseau's hut, nor did I ever find it in any other place.[5]

Smith also visited Thérèse, who was happy to entertain tourists and converse about her late husband. The views which Smith expressed on this occasion counted against him later when his appointment as royal tutor was in question. By that time sympathy with the Jacobins' philosopher was suspect.

In his *Recollections* Colt Hoare felt obliged to defend *La Nouvelle Hélöise*.

On this book I well know the opinion of the world is much divided; but the writer has his admirers as well as his critics. He has his virtues as well as his defects, his merits as well as his faults; and what author has ever attained a high degree of celebrity, without first passing through the rigid ordeal of criticism! Having read with delight, mingled with tears, the affecting tale of Julie and St. Preux, suggested by a heart of sensibility, drawn by the pen of nature, and decorated with the graces of language; having surveyed the scenes which Rousseau has selected for the exile of the suffering lover; having seen and felt the justness of his pictures, and sympathised with the imaginary sorrows of his hero, I have no sentiment but concern for his wayward fortunes, and admiration of his genius. Heavy objections have certainly been made to the morality of his book; but its beauties are so natural, so bewitching, and so congenial to the feeling heart, that in the contemplation of his excellencies I overlook his defects. *Heloise* accompanied us during our excursion, and we all were equally interested for our fair companion.[6]

In Switzerland *Julie* was an essential handbook.

At times huge rocks hung like ruins over my head. At times I was deafened by the sound of lofty waterfalls and drenched in their thick spray. At times beside me an endless torrent ran in depths I dare not contemplate. Sometimes I was lost in the gloom of a thick wood. Sometimes on emerging from a dark recess I was cheered by the sight of a pleasant meadow. The astonishing

[5] Ibid.
[6] *Recollections*, I, pp. 209 ff.

mixture of wild nature with cultivation revealed everywhere the hand of man where one would not have believed he would have penetrated: beside a cave, houses; withered leaves where one would only have expected thorns, vines in wasteland, excellent fruit growing in the rocks, and fields among the precipices.[7]

Rousseau not only described mountain scenery, he formulated the emotions which should accompany it.

That day I arrived on less elevated mountains whose rugged contours contrasted with the lofty peaks above. Having walked in the clouds, I reached more sheltered places, where, in season, the thunder clouds gathered above one; a true image of the sage's life, for which there was never a model, except in those places which have been taken as a symbol for it.

There I became keenly aware that the purity of the air around me was the true cause of my change of mood and of the return of that inner peace which I had lost for so long a time. In fact, it is the general experience of all men, although they do not always notice it, that on high mountains, where the air is rare and pure, breathing is more easy, the body feels lighter and the spirits calmer; pleasure there is less intense, and the feelings temperate. In such places thoughts take on a certain greatness and sublimity associated with their surroundings, a certain voluptuous tranquillity, in which there is nothing bitter or sensual. It seems as if, in being raised above the place where men dwell, all base and earthly sentiments are left behind, and, as one draws near the ethereal regions, the soul catches something of their inalienable purety. There one is serious without being melancholy, still without being indolent, content to be and to think: appetites too keen are blunted; they lose that sharpness which makes them painful; all emotion that remains is light and pleasant, and thus the passions which elsewhere torment man, in a favourable climate contribute to his happiness.[8]

These feelings, Colt found, corresponded with his own as he journeyed to the Valais (Pl. 30b; but he could not go all the way with Rousseau. 'I can easily conceive the happiness and content of these people; but I cannot speak in high terms either of their hospitality or disinterestedness; for in every part of this district we were exposed to great imposition as to our charges. The *auri sacra fames* seems to pervade every rank of people, from the haughty Genevois to the humble Valaisan.'[9]

Colt's expectations may have been aroused by his friend and mentor,

---

[7] J. J. Rousseau, *Julie ou la Nouvelle Hélöise*, Part I, letter XXIII. Quoted in French, *Recollections*, p. 155.
[8] Ibid., pp. 151 ff.   [9] Ibid., p. 153.

William Coxe, whose book, *Sketches of the Natural, Civil and Political State of Swisserland*, he had studied beforehand. 'Swisserland', wrote Coxe, 'is a most delightful country, and merits the particular observation of the traveller, as well for the diversity of the several governments, as for the wonderful beauties of nature: but the impositions of the inn-keepers, the difficulty of procuring horses, and the exorbitant price one is obliged to pay for the hire of them, are the taxes one must inevitably be subject to, for the enjoyment of its delights.'[10] Indeed the discomforts of this kind of travel were self-imposed, and some provision was made by the Swiss in the most unpromising places. For instance, just below the Grimsel Pass a hostel was maintained to receive all travellers, provided they could pay. In the winter months, when there was no landlord, stocks of 'cheese, hard bread, salted provision and fuel' were left, in case any unfortunate wanderer should happen to come that way. 'This hovel', Coxe continued, '(besides the store-houses for the cheeses, of which they make here a large quantity, and of a most excellent sort) contains only a small kitchen, and one room, in which we are now sitting. We occupy nearly one side of it; the other is taken up by our servants, the landlord and his wife, and half a dozen honest labourers: the latter are eating their homely supper, with all the relish that well-earned hunger can give; and are enjoying a short respite from their toil, with that noisy mirth which characterises the gaiety of this class of people.'[11]

Colt's route took him roughly in a figure eight, on a north-east south-west axis with Lucerne at its intersection and its northernmost point the fall of the Rhine at Schaffhausen. At Zurich, as Coxe had done, he visited the physiognomist Lavater.

> We found him civil and communicative, especially when I started the subject of his book. His countenance is animated and full of expression; and to judge from many of his sentiments, he is a man of great benevolence. In the evening he returned our visit and supped with us. He seems partial to the English, and said that he wrote his book principally for our nation, as it requires much study and thought. When pastor to the House of Correction, he had frequent opportunities of examining the characters of those confined there, and was gratified to find, even in those who were reckoned the most abandoned, some favourable trait. The result of his inquiries did not lead him to conceive a bad opinion of human nature. . . . During the time he filled the office of pastor a couple were brought before him to be married, who had the most inveterate aversion to each other, for which they could assign no satisfactory reason. For this, however, the

---

[10] William Coxe, *Sketches of the Natural, Civil, and Political State of Swisserland* (1789).
[11] Ibid.

physiogomist accounted; one having a round, the other an oblong face. It was necessary, he said, that the tempers of man and wife should be contrasted, for if cast in the same mould they would never agree so well. He instanced own wife and himself, whose dispositions were very unlike. He has great faith in the virtue of christian names, and does not believe in the slightest degree of chance. No traveller, he said, could be just and true, without being indiscreet; for which reasons he has been deterred from writing his own tours.[12]

Making a subsidiary loop through Berne, Interlaken, and the Grindelwald glaciers, and omitting no opportunity to turn aside for anything that promised to be interesting, Colt proceeded to Basle, and arrived back at Geneva on 1 September. He had travelled mainly by horse or mule, sometimes by boat. In the latter part of his journey he had been alone. On 19 September he wrote to his father.

I have been living for these last two months amongst Rocks, Cataracts, Precipices, etc. & amongst a people only communicative *to me* by signs; by which means my eyes have been informed more than my ears—It would be impossible to send you any description expressive of the variety of the beautiful scenes which have been presented before by eyes during a tour of above twelve hundred miles. I will not therefore attempt it, but will defer it till I open my budget of drawings, which tho' but very humble imitations of the beauties which nature has displayed throughout this Country, may perhaps give you a better idea than anything I could say in writing. Lyttelton, Greville & myself made an excursion to Vevay, Meillerie & its environs rendered so interesting by the stories of Julie & S. Preux so finely described by Rousseau in his Heloise—about the middle of next month my two friends meet me at Lyons, from whence we shall all proceed together to Marseilles: Lyttelton thinks of wintering at *Nice*, but we shall proceed to Florence & Rome. . . . I hope the weather has been finer in England than here, otherwise the harvest must have suffer'd considerably—it begins now to have a more settled appearance—I was glad to hear that my crop of Hay was very fine.[13]

He added a post-script: 'I am quite charm'd with the accounts I hear of my dear Boy, and am not a little anxious to see him.'

But this pleasure he was willing to postpone for another ten months. After some weeks at Geneva and Lyons, he left again, with Lyttelton, for

---

12 *Recollections*, I, pp. 161 ff.
13 R.C.H. to Sir Richard Hoare (father), 19 Sep. 1786, FS.

a quick visit to Barcelona. He found social life there dull because of the austere character of the governor and his lady, who were great bigots, and thought it more meritorious 'to indulge the pomp and mummery of superstition, than the amusements of innocent gaiety'.[14] As we have seen, he found the monks of Montserrat rapacious, but this was compensated by the natural surroundings of their monastery, which gave opportunity both for interesting observations and sublime reflections.

> This singular mountain deserves the notice of every admirer of the rude and savage features of nature. . . . The whole mass is a composition of pebbles, cemented so strongly as to form a compact body, of that species which is vulgarly called pudding stone, varied into the most singular shapes. Some of the rocks rise from the surface like insulated obelisks of gigantic proportions; while others bear on their summits large balls of stone, which appear as if restrained from falling by magic. The interstices are filled with every species of evergreen, particularly the tall and dwarf ilex, laurustinus phylerea, cistus, box, besides a great variety of the erica, and numerous aromatic plants which both perfume and adorn this romantic abode.[15]

On their return they left early. 'The morning being cold, I did not mount my mule, but continued walking till break of day.' (He often spoke as if he were alone, when he did in fact have a companion.)

> The moon shone forth in all her lustre, and, by the varied effects of strong light and deep shade on the huge masses of impending rock, added considerably to the majesty of the scenery. On the right opened an extensive prospect; and the clouds, undulating amidst the hills, by their silver hue and even appearance, recalled to my recollection the aspect of the Swiss glaciers. The murmurs of a stream, at a considerable distance beneath, and the faint sound of the bell which roused the monks to early matins, at length interrupted the awful silence which marks the repose of nature.

> > With quicken'd step
> > Brown night retires; young day pours in apace,
> > And opens all the lawny prospect wide:
> > The dripping rock, the mountain's misty top,
> > Swell on the sight, and brighten with the dawn.

> Such scenery as that which stretched around me is calculated, under every aspect, to awaken the noblest feelings, but on the retreat or return of day the impression it produces is peculiarly

14 *Recollections*, I.
15 Ibid.

sublime. At the close of an autumnal evening, when every object is heightened by the clearness of the atmosphere, and the landscape diversified by the beautiful and variegated tints of the season; when the sun gilding an extensive plain, watered by a meandering stream, and bounded by rocks and mountains, seems to withdraw reluctantly from a theatre of transcendent magnificence; when the sober tints of evening are gradually deepening into the shade of night; or before the dawn, when the moon sheds her pale lustre, and imperceptibly fades at the approach of a nobler planet; at such times, the mind appears to sympathise in the majestic serenity of nature; and wrapt in silent wonder, turns with awe and gratitude to the Being who has created the objects of its admiration and endowed it with such elevated powers of enjoyment.

In spite of the ponderous style we can discern that it was quite an experience.

In two hours and a half we reached the place where our calashes were waiting. The road by which we had descended, though rather longer, was much better than that which we had taken in the ascent, and indeed practicable for a carriage; but it is disliked by the muleteers and guides, who endeavoured to dissuade us from choosing it, by telling us that the descent would employ five hours. By thus varying the route, we made nearly the whole circuit of the mountain.

On settling accounts with our muleteers, they asked so exorbitant a price for the use of their beasts, that we could not think of complying with their demand. They immediately armed themselves with stones and began to threaten us; but the sight of our pistols soon reduced them to reason.[16]

By 3 December he was in Leghorn where he wrote to Hugh that he had come to Italy by felucca from Antibes.

I slept on board my vessel two nights and at a little port where we put in to rest the watermen, I was surprised to meet another Felucca which contained my friend *Greville*. I could hardly believe my eyes on seeing him, for he had left us before our expedition to Barcelona & intended to make the best of his way to Italy—he had been detain'd fifteen days at *Marseilles* and twenty-one at *Monaco* a miserable little sea port in the Mediteranean. I took him into my Felucca & we travell'd together to this place—we dined today at *Piza* a very handsome town where there is the famous leaning tower you may have often heard of—
After having seen what is worthy of notice in this town I shall

16 Ibid., pp. 264 ff.

proceed to *Florence* where I expect to find quite a folio volume of English Letters—not having receiv'd one since I left Switzerland—I shall not stay long there as the town will be very dull since the death of our Embassador Sir Horace Mann—from thence to my favourite Rome where all the world is to be assembled.[17]

Christmas was spent in Florence with truly English weather, 'the snow a foot deep in the streets'. 'I met with great civility from Sir Horace Mann & from another English family there & got acquainted with many Florentines, to whom I spouted Italian very boldly—I played at whist every evening & strange to tell *for once* fortune favor'd me, for I departed winner of *One hundred pounds*.'[18] The famous envoy, as Colt had previously mentioned, died on 16 November 1786; this Sir Horace was his nephew, namesake, and heir who had hurried to Florence at the news of his uncle's decline.

Colt stayed in Rome during January and most of February. 'All the Beau Monde is flown to Naples...so that you see Rome is not the gayest place in the world—there are six operas open all bad—or middling.'[19] Society was limited to his old friends James Greville and Sir Cecil and Lady Bishop, the latter a charming companion, but not much to be expected from her husband. Lord Clive's family was there but were very retired and unsociable. If the pursuit of art and antiquities had not engaged him he would not have remained there even though it was 'the most bewitching place in the Universe'. His thoughts were turning homeward, where he hoped to be by the middle of July.

> Grove wrote me word of the sport he had had at Stourhead. I hope we shall all partake of it next season. I shall make but a poor & ridiculous figure on horseback after two years disuse, but I will attend you to cover & if I can't follow you, will return home.... I hope you have begun to think about my one horse chaise—I sent you word that I would have all the ornaments of brass with plain neat harness for two horses (one before the other, in case I should drive them with a postilion). Do not let them engrave the plates of the harness till my arrival, or make the saddle—in all other respects I would have it as simple & as little expensive as possible—we agreed that the light grey with Etruscan ornaments would be preferable to the dark blue.—I am very much vex'd to hear the account you send me of the Game, particularly as the preservation of it is my Great Hobby Horse, & my chief amusement in the country—I do not know which to complain of most—the Parsons or the Poachers.[20]

[17] R.C.H. to Hugh Hoare, 3 Dec. 1786, FS.
[18] 5 Jan. 1787, FS.   [19] Ibid.   [20] 21 Feb. 1787, FS.

He heard five weeks later that the 'Whisky' was built; 'but my intention was to line it either with our livery blue or a grey suitable to the color of the carriage with orange & black fringe & lace corresponding to the mouldings & ornaments—if the drab colord cloth is already put in, you must match the fringe & lace with the border etc.—if not, I leave it to you either to line it with dark or light blue'.[21]

Colt left Florence on 31 April when, by way of Siena, Bologna, and Venice, where he stayed a fortnight, he again crossed Mont Cenis, revisited the *Grande Chartreuse* and came to Lyons. Here he took the opportunity to order some more clothes:

> A suit of mourning;
> A summer suit of green silk with an embroidered waistcoat;
> A blue silk suit with a fur lining;
> A spring velvet suit and waistcoat;
> A frock of green and bronze and a silk one also;
> Two pair of boue de Paris breeches; and yellow silk for two
>   more;
> Five gilets, two striped silk and one for winter.

Giro, his servant, also had to have a jacket and waistcoat of Nankeen with white buttons. He ordered to be sent to England:

> An embroidered suit of scarlet and white,
> A winter velvet and a muff,

And lest he should forget he noted,

> Begin to wear Velvet coats 1 November
> End at Easter
> Begin to wear fur linings at Xmas
> End as above
> Begin to wear demi-saisons at Easter—22 Septr
> Begin to wear silk at Whitsuntide, 1 June.[22]

He had also accumulated other possessions, particularly books and pictures deposited with various agents. At the end of June he started on the return journey; impatient to arrive he did not stay in Paris as long as he at first intended. He had begun, as he said, to inhale his native air, and felt the *maladie du pays*. On Friday 13 July 1787, he landed at Dover, and noted

> the manners dress etc. totally changd. Struck with the carriages,
> Cleanness of the Inns—Civility of the people etc—the master of
> the inns not above their business—find myself in a country where
> every object shews me the effect of Industry, Commerce, etc.

[21] 1 Apr. 1787, FS.
[22] Notebooks, T(ST) 383.919.

Custom house officers not rigs. Houses well built, clean streets, Tomb stones in C. Yards. Master at going in & leavg. the Inn. Postilion whips ears spared & humanity. Bedrooms separate, chairs, tables etc.,

> Lend a hand to the plow
> Beauty of Women
> Neat farmer's Wives, Market Sign posts—footpath.[23]

It was almost two years since Hester's death; his son would be three in September. He himself was twenty-eight.

[23] Ibid.

Chapter 6

Interlude in England

Colt Hoare returned to Stourhead in the first week of August. After so long an absence there were many people to see; the Aclands at Holnicote and Killerton in Devonshire; the Lytteltons at Hagley. Friends from abroad reassembled and old friends like the Bampfyldes came visiting. But on 2 October Colt was called to Bath where his father was ill. Sir Richard, who had received a baronetcy the previous year, died on 11 October. Colt, succeeding to new dignities and responsibilities, accompanied his step-mother to Barn Elms. The following September *The Gentleman's Magazine* observed 'what the rational appropriation of superfluous riches, the influence of example, and, zealous endeavours' had effectuated there. 'Much, indeed, has been owing to the late Sir Richard Hoare, bart. He might be truly styled the father of the wretched, the patron of every under-taking in the Parish, calculated to relieve distress, and promote religion and morality. . . . In addition to a well-regulated workhouse, there is a charity-school for twenty children.'[1] These, on this occasion, after 'a pious and enforcing discourse', preached for their benefit sang, 'in a very affect-ing manner', a hymn to Mercy.

> To Mercy's Throne your voices raise!
> For blessings, join in hymns of praise!
> For them your grateful offrings bear—
> The Widow's hope, the Orphan's prayer![2]

Colt, as the eldest son, clearly benefited by more than a title; there was for instance, a house in St. James's Square, which he now took as his town residence. For the time being he returned to Stourhead for the shooting. Snow fell over Christmas and lay for a week. He made another visit to Hagley, and in the middle of February returned to town.

London was supreme as a fashionable centre, the tone set by the Prince of Wales. Colt, like others of his age and station, dined and gambled, once, twice, or three times a week. Attendance at the opera was regular, Tuesday and Saturday. In spite of the crisis caused by George III's first illness in

---

[1] *The Gentleman's Magazine*, Sep. 1788.
[2] Ibid.

9—L.A.

November, politics were stable, with the younger Pitt firmly in power. Warren Hastings's trial caused a stir when it opened at Westminster Hall on 13 February. During the following week Colt went on two occasions; by the time Hastings was acquitted, seven years later, interest had flagged or was more fully engaged by events across the channel. And it was there Colt wished to be; perhaps because the memory of events at Stourhead was still too painful; perhaps he had found interests he wished to follow. Or was it that life in Italy was warm and easy, and this time he had experience, rank, and friends waiting to receive him? He planned to go by Holland, Germany, and Austria and his departure was unhurried.

Among matters concerning his father's estate, inventories of wine, linen, and china at St. James's Square, annuities to be continued (Woodforde's £100 included) he noted,

Cloaths to take abroad.
2 new winter suits.
1 blue lin'd with fur
1 Ratteen
1 Demi-saison velvet
1 cloth   do   with steel
2 Summer silks mourning
4 new leather breeches
2 winter   fustian
2 summer   do
4 washing linen   do
6 Kersemere winter
6   do   summer
1 pair of black silk
1 do of Sattin
2 do of Boue de Paris
6 pair of new boots
8 do of shoes
2 cock'd hats
1 round do black
1   do   white
2 Chapeau bras
2 dozen new shirts
2   do   thread stockings
6 pair worsted
2 dozen white handkers
1   do   color'd
Silk color'd stockings
socks, night caps etc. etc.
blue   frock edg'd
brown   do
Scarlet frock
Striped french cloth
Striped stuff
Striped silk
Blue frock & red cape

Green   do
Blue plain   do
Brown   do
Winter—bath coating
Walking great coat
4 flannel winter waistcts
6 Dimity Summer do
4 Striped stuff   do

In addition there was other equipment:

Coffee Pot, Kettle, Case of Knives and forks, Candle sticks and candles, Case for tea pot and saucers, Soy, Tea, Sugar and Garden seeds.
Bathing Caps & dress—Gloves
Gun, Powder horn & shotbelt
L. glass
Umbrella, compass, harness, scales.
Medecines, glass smelling bottles,
Green toothpick cases.
300 pens, a box of Wafers for sealing letters and a quire of Blotts.
6 quarto books, 12 duodecimo and 6 drawing
2 reams of paper gilt and plain

and twenty-two quires of other shape and size, antiquarian, atlas, imperial, tracing, botanical and bank post. There were of course, watercolours, inks and pencils and also books;

Swinburne's Spain & Sicily
Brydone's—Sicily
Reisbecks Germany
sketches of Austn Netherlds
Scipio Maffei abt Pola
Nugent & Keysler

Virgil, Ovid, Horace
Maps of Germany, Holl^d, Sicily
Louisa—Man of feeling
     Atlas—Stackhouse
     Pliny—Frontinus
     Lucretius, Lucan, Polybius
     Martial—Livy—Strada
     Caesar—Emmeline—
     Vertots Roman, Portugal &
       Swedish Revolutions

Revolutions of Denmark
Danvilles Geography—
Kirchers Latium—
Goldsmiths Roman & English History—
Gibbons Roman   do
Felsina Pittrice
Watson's Philip 2^d
Hists of United Provinces
Charles the Fifth[3]

Some of this was doubtless dispatched to Italy; with the rest, Colt Hoare embarked for the second time at Dover on 30 June 1788.

[3] Notebooks, T(ST) 383.919.

Chapter 7

The German Route

On the road from Calais to Dunkirk 'Numbers of poor children, clamouring for *la petite charité*, and the melancholy notes of frogs, seemed to bespeak the wretched situation of both man and animals.'[1] The port and harbour dismantled at the Treaty of Utrecht, were being rebuilt. Bruges contained nothing worthy of mention, but at Ghent there were paintings by Rubens and Van Dyck and 'a curious piece by John van Eyck, the first inventor of oilcolours'. 'Curious' was also his comment on the paintings of 'Quintin Matsys, the Blacksmith' which he saw in Antwerp, a city which, in spite of evidence of former affluence appeared depopulated and presented a wretched and melancholy appearance. Most of three days there were spent in churches and galleries and in visiting contemporary artists. He did his best, but with the exception of Rubens and Van Dyck, the Flemish School was alien to his taste:

> Although I avow my partiality to the Italian school, I am not so far prejudiced in its favour, as to ascribe to it the whole merit of the art. Both the ancient and modern Flemish painters are certainly deficient, with regard to grace and dignity of expression, in their historical pieces; and in their landscapes are more attentive to the nice discrimination of objects than to the general effect, yet their just representation of nature entitles them to attention and applause. The picture dealers are numerous, and I think exorbitant in their demands; though from the information I received, their traffic is one of the most active and profitable which is now carried on.[2]

On 7 July, dragged slowly over barren heath, or through deep sand, and passing over four rivers, three of which were very considerable, he entered Holland. 'Imagine a large meadow surrounded by a canal of stagnant water, with a mill or two, generally employed to carry off the floodings after the melting of the ice. Conceive it covered with the finest and handsomest cattle imaginable, peopled with a variety of wildfowl, and occasionally a solitary stork stalking about. Imagine a succession of these meadows,

[1] *Recollections*, II.   [2] Ibid., pp. 16 ff.

and add a few distant steeples, and poplar trees; and you have the general appearance which the face of Holland exhibits.'[3] Why, he reflected, did the English prefer the rude and savage features of nature to the rich and cultivated scenery which other nations favoured?

> It is not, I hope, from barbarity of mind, or a want of feeling and civilization, that nature in her gayest trim is less attractive to us, than when surrounded with her horrors; it is not, I hope from a want of the milder virtues, that our eyes dwell with eager attention on the tremendous precipice, the foaming cataract, the barren rock, or the desolate regions of eternal snow, while they carelessly glance over the smiling plain, or the rich and cultivated valley. Nor is it, I trust, from a want of civilization, or a remnant of savage nature lurking in our bosoms, that to us the rugged and romantic scenes of Helvetia minister more delight than the golden plains of Campania Felix; or that the wild, and I may say, unnatural landscapes of Salvator Rosa, find among us more admirers than the serene and tranquil views of Claude Loraine and Gaspar Poussin. As an Englishman, and feeling the full force of this remark, I will not admit that this peculiarity of our taste proceeds from any deficiency of good qualities in the heart. On the contrary, I would urge, that we prefer the great and wonderful features of nature, because they are more congenial to the energy of our national character, and inspire us with a superior elevation of mind. Majestic and awful scenes are like the traits of a noble and generous spirit, which at once awaken pleasure and admiration; which captivate and sink deep into the heart; while ordinary landscapes which are marked by no striking feature, like the ordinary cast of human character, may perhaps amuse and detain us for a moment, but leave no lasting impression behind.[4]

These attitudes remained with him; they account for the fact that although Constable visited Stourhead none of the paintings found a home there, or were even mentioned. Not that Colt was unusual in this neglect for, as Constable's friend John Fisher said, it was because his pictures did not *solicit attention* that they were not popular.

Such are the contradictions of taste that the very things which rendered nature picturesque, were those which in other circumstances, were objectionable. In the Dutch villas 'all the beauties of nature are neglected or excluded, and her rights invaded; mathematical symmetry is the standing order'.[5] However, the main square in Brussels was 'a striking instance of bad taste, and the violation of every rule of architecture. Not the

[3] Ibid., pp. 36 ff.   [4] Ibid., pp. 34 ff.   [5] Ibid.

slightest trace of regularity is to be observed in the houses.'[6] The towns
Colt found monotonous; the smallest village Amsterdam in miniature.
Only at the Hague, where he stayed with the British Minister, Sir James
Harris, did he find 'the pleasures and advantages both of good society
and retirement' with 'persons distinguished for rank and abilities', unlike
'other Dutch towns where traffic absorbs the attention of the inhabitants'.[7]
He was however curious about aspects of Dutch life and tried to penetrate
outside his social circle; in particular two episodes impressed him. In
Saardam, outside Amsterdam, he made many attempts to enter houses
and, hardly surprising, was met with surly refusals. To one in Brock he
was however admitted.

> The passage or entry was covered with India matting; but I must
> not omit to observe, that instead of a carpet or mat to wipe the
> shoes, a clean napkin was laid at the door. The first apartment
> we saw was a bed-room; but the beds being enclosed in closets,
> it bore no appearance of the use for which it was designed. It
> was ornamented with a beaufet of fine china, arranged in the
> nicest order; the walls were pannelled, and, with the ceiling,
> painted and varnished.
>
> The most striking object in the next room, was the fire-place,
> which was lined half way up the chimney with Dutch tiles; and
> the hearth so highly polished as to cast a reflection like a mirror.
> So far was the excess of cleanliness carried, that an inlaid box
> was placed by the fire-side to contain the peat and wood for
> burning.
>
> The third room was more elegant than either of the two pre-
> ceeding. It was fitted up with gilt leather, and adorned with a
> beaufet of china, still more valuable than the former, as well as
> many silver trinkets, with pieces of very substantial plate,
> intermixed.
>
> The fourth and last room, though containing fewer objects to
> attract the attention at first sight, proved the most curious,
> because it led to the knowledge of some customs peculiar to
> North Holland, and gave rise to a very interesting scene. A
> custom prevails here, almost universally, which is extremely
> singular. There is a particular door in each house, which is never
> opened, except on two occasions: at the marriage of a young
> couple, or at a funeral. After pointing it out, our hostess took
> us into an adjoining room, where there was a pink and white
> bed, finely laced and worked, which was appropriated only to
> the wedding night. She afterwards shewed us a cradle, which,
> with the bedding belonging to it, was adorned in the same

[6] Ibid., p. 39.   [7] Ibid., p. 21.

manner, and which with pleasure she told us had held many of her family. These she shewed us, with a countenance highly expressive of the happiness derived from her own marriage, and little family. Partaking of the satisfaction the good woman evidently felt, I little expected that her pleasing reflection on past happiness would soon be effaced by the recollection of a recent loss. A doll, or image, dressed up after the likeness of a beloved daughter, ten years old, who had lately died, wrought so powerfully on her feelings, that she burst into a flood of tears, and rushed out of the room.[8]

The other experience concerned the *Musicaux* in Amsterdam.

In fact, these are no other than licensed brothels. Such resorts, in a country no less celebrated for the regularity of its police, than for its systematic discouragement of idleness, have awakened the astonishment of foreigners; and induced many to visit these assemblies. I shall describe the two I saw, which are reckoned the most genteel in the place. The rooms were long, with benches down the sides, occupied by women, whose profession was obvious from their appearance. At the farther end were two or three scraping fiddlers exalted in a balcony; and opposite, were as many waiters, dressed in white jackets and aprons, whose office was to supply the company with wine, pipes, &c. The middle of the room was destined for those who chose to dance, or walk about. Unfortunately for me there was little or no dancing; for only two of the frail sisterhood once attempted to make out something like a dance; but there are times when the rooms are full of dancers. The price of admission is a guilder, for which you are supplied with a bottle of wine; and immediately on entrance a waiter offers a glass and a pipe. It might be naturally imagined that such an assembly would not be distinguished for decency; yet strange as it may seem, I did not observe the slightest tendency to the contrary, while I staid; and what is still less credible, honest, good, and modest citizens' wives frequently accompany their husbands to these houses of entertainment. The mixture of Jews, sailors, officers, grave senators, and burgomasters, in such a place, afforded a scene equally ridiculous and amusing.[9]

Neither Brussels nor Liège detained him, but he stopped a week in Spa where play, intrigue and dissipation were stronger attractions than the powerful quality of the waters. Five days through dreary heaths and desolate forests, averaging forty miles a day, brought him to Hanover.

[8] Ibid., pp. 26 ff.
[9] Ibid., pp. 29 ff.

The villages he passed gave the appearance of great poverty. Near Osna-brück was the corpse of a man broken on the wheel. After six more days through Brunswick and Magdeburg he reached Potsdam. The streets were mathematically straight, the squares capacious, the buildings elegant and on the Greek and Roman model. Colt almost thought himself in Italy. He approved. He noted the composition and pay of the Prussian Army. Frederick the Great, not long dead, lay strapped down in his tomb, buried with his boots, cane, clothing; his savings by him, fourteen million dollars, and the precept: 'Regardez ceci—faites comme moi'.

Possibly one of the reasons why Colt Hoare felt at home in Potsdam was the pervading Palladian influence into which Frederick the Great had been persuaded by the Venetian, Francesco Algarotti,[10] who, between 1742 and 1753, had played an important part not only in Prussia, but at Dresden in Saxony. The collection there was already one of the finest in Europe, due to the purchases made by Augustus III and his minister, Count Brühl.[11] They included for instance, the hundred finest pictures from the collections of the Dukes of Modena. Algarotti persuaded Augustus to purchase paintings by great contemporaries such as Tiepolo; but more important was his proposal for extending and completing the art gallery so that instead of merely reflecting the collector's personal taste it should include examples of all schools and thus represent the history of painting as a whole. It was natural, therefore, that Colt Hoare should stay in Dresden longer than in any other German city, that it should remind him of Florence and that he should find there 'inexhaustible rescources to a lover of the arts'. Seidelmann, who had 'brought the art of copying in bistre to the highest perfection', provided for his collection reminders of pictures by Rembrandt, Raphael and Barocci. He himself also spent much time in study; and to this was added congenial society, particularly Charles Gore, an older man, friend of Hackert, who settled near Weimar and died there in 1807. On 21 September Colt moved into Bohemia. On the way to Dresden his phaeton had been overturned, through the somnolence of a postillion, and being apprehensive of a similar occurrence on the rough mountain roads, he left his carriage and sketch book in hand went forward alone. 'I was at first enveloped in a dark forest of firs, the gloom of which was deepened by a thick fog, floating heavily around. Suddenly it was dissipated by gleams of sunshine, and one of the noblest views which imagination could form, opened before me; an immense cultivated plain bounded by dark blue mountains, of the most varied, singular, and picturesque forms. To the painter, indeed, scenes less extensive are prefer-able.'[12] Although the poet dwelt on such prospects with peculiar rapture, the painter found confined views 'more congenial' to his 'limited faculties'.

[10] Concerning Algarotti see Francis Haskell, *Patrons and Painters* (1963), pp. 347 ff.
[11] Ibid., p. 294.
[12] *Recollections*, II, p. 78.

Colt settled for 'an ancient castle in ruin, enclosed on three sides with woods, while on the fourth an opening enabled the eye to catch a glance of the distant country, and beneath a passage cut through the rock, with a road winding through a dark forest of firs'.[13] Arrived at Töplitz (now Teplice) he spent a day visiting the Castle and the estate of Count Waldstein, the only residence he had found out of England which combined the beauties of nature and art with the comforts and necessary enjoyments of life. There was a good library, collections of prints, fossils, minerals, antique coins, and cameos. The gardens were adapted to every taste; parterres and straight avenues for the French; fountains and green (*boschi*) for the Italian; a kitchen garden for the Englishman. There were also an aviary, a conservatory and a stable stocked with English grooms and horses. This was the current rage of the Count whose previous passions had included the study of antiquity (in Italy) and the collection of weapons and warlike instruments of different ages and nations.

> At times he has had at once an hundred and fifty English horses in his stables. Most of these he sells, and then replaces them with others. He crops, nicks, and docks them himself; hunts his own hounds, blows the horn, &c. &c. Every year he repairs to England to purchase horses; and not content with buying them at Tattersal's, or of the London dealers, he travels post into Yorkshire to traffic with the original breeders. In short, he seems to consider this species of commerce as a science, and penetrates into all its mysteries. He now talks of visiting Spain and Africa; and then I doubt not but his active mind will be inflamed with some new pursuit.[14]

Colt was received with great civility by the Count, who urged him to prolong his stay. However, the next day he left for Prague and by 30 September was in Vienna.

> In no city in Europe can a foreigner find a more ready admission into society, or spend his time more agreeably. . . . The French and Russian embassadors give weekly suppers and dinners; to the first of which there is a constant, and to the last a frequent, invitation. Every evening the houses of Prince Kaunitz, Madame de Thun, and Madame de Pergan are open, and visitors admitted without the least restraint or ceremony. There are, besides, an excellent Italian opera, and a good theatre in the suburbs. Both sexes are extremely attentive and obliging to strangers; and the women are handsome as well as agreeable.[15]

During his stay Colt made an excursion into Hungary, to see Esterhazy where Haydn was 'master of the band'. The broken pales and weeds

[13] Ibid., p. 79.   [14] Ibid., p. 83.   [15] Ibid., p. 101.

contrasted with the splendour within the palace. He regretted that such vast sums of money had been lavished on so worthless and barren a spot, on the border of an extensive marsh which contributed little to health, comfort, or beauty. Doubtless thinking with some satisfaction of his own house and park, he reflected how a much less sum, judiciously spent, could have made it a more delightful place. In Vienna for just over two weeks he had 'staid just long enough to taste the bitters, without enjoying the sweets'. The longer he remained the more difficult it was to part, and October being far advanced he had to decide whether to winter in Germany or Italy. The climate of Vienna, which he found disagreeable, and his ignorance of German decided him to proceed. So, through 'majestic woods of larch, fir and beech, heightened with the rich tints of autumn', noting with approval 'the industry of the peasantry', turning aside to see the caves of Adelsburg, he reached Trieste. From here he went by boat to Pola, on the Adriatic, in order to see and record the remains of the Roman port. On November the 5th he continued from Trieste to Mestre, where, leaving his carriage with the post-house master, he took a gondola to Venice.

Chapter 8

Etruria and the Appian Way

Colt Hoare's arrival at Venice completed what was generally understood by the Grand Tour, which, as he said, was as much as the tourist thought necessary to perform, the general object being to see as much in as short a time as possible. Lacking neither time nor 'a proper sense of curiosity', Colt was more thorough than most. His second visit to Italy was, therefore, less of a tour than a period of residence during which he undertook systematic antiquarian excursions into less frequented places. 'Having gained a sufficient knowledge of the Italian language to enable me to interrogate without the aid of an interpreter, I quitted the road for the path, the capitals for the provinces, and proceeded with increased confidence, and I need not add with increased delight.'[1] Thus, during 1789, he investigated the remains of Etruscan civilization, and traced the course of the Appian Way as far as Benevento. During 1790, when he was mainly resident at Naples and Palermo, he made two tours of Sicily and visited Malta. At the end of the year he returned to Rome by the Via Latina; and in 1791 he visited the Lake of Celano in order to examine 'the emissary', a canal constructed by the Emperor Claudius to relieve flooding.

The details of his antiquarian journeys, which occupied, at the most, seven months out of thirty, are fully described in *Recollections Abroad* and *A Classical Tour Through Italy and Sicily*; whereas the barest outline is given in the diaries of life in Siena, Naples, Palermo, and Rome, 'the abodes of ease and dissipation' where he spent three-quarters of his time.

After his arrival in Italy he was in Venice for three weeks. While there he bought a painting of Doge Lando[2] which subsequently hung at Stourhead over the library fireplace. He thought it was by Titian but probably it was not. There is an entry for 9 November 1788, 'Music at the Mendicanti. Dined with Mahon. Went to the opera in the evening'.[3] There may be some connection between the Mahon mentioned here and an attempt in 1809 to blackmail him. A Mr. May had then acquired the 'manuscript memoirs and original letters from her professed admirers' of Mrs. Gertrude

[1] R.C.H., *A Classical Tour through Italy and Sicily* (1819), p. x.
[2] *Recollections*, II, p. 154.
[3] Diaries, T(ST) 383.919.

Mahon, 'celebrated by the appellation of the Bird of Paradise'. 'You, Sir,' wrote Mr. May, 'are one of those personages alluded to...if you are not ambitious to have your name recorded with Mrs. Mahon's quondam Gallants, you can, at the expense of a little *trouble*, supress it entirely and recover your letters. If I do not hear from you at the expiration of a few days I shall conclude you have no objection to shine in the Histoire, and consider myself justifiable in giving all the effect I can to your Epistles when I submit them to public Animadversion.'[4]

From Venice Colt proceeded to Florence; and on 19 February 1789, to Siena, which was his centre for most of the year. Indeed, the largest part of his time during his second tour was spent there. 'In many respects Siena has claims superior to any other town in Italy, particularly as an eligible Summer residence. Its situation amongst the Apennines is airy and healthy; the heat of its climate, even in the midst of summer, is not oppressive; its society is agreeable and unaffected; and the purity of its language and accent is generally allowed to surpass that of any other province.'[5] Even so, we may guess there were other attractions. For some months he lived a settled, almost domestic life; a drive or walk in the morning and 'as usual in the evening'. On 17 July a series of entries[6] record, 'T/ere ill', 'At home all day. Ta ill', 'All day at Bucci's. Ta ill', 'Out in Phaeton alone. Ta ill', and so on. Finally on 19 August, 'Fever returned to Ter'a B'i'. From the amount of time he spent with the Bucci family, we may conclude that the lady was Teresina Bucci. After he had gone to Sicily he wrote her thirty-two letters; more than to anyone else, even his beloved Hugh.

He had a great number of correspondents;[7] 116 are recorded between December 1788 and April 1791, totalling 465 letters. Some of these were concerned with business and doubtless many were acknowledgements of the hospitality he everywhere received. Apart from Teresina and Hugh, he wrote most frequently to his brother-in-law Lyttelton; and, of course, regularly to his agent, Charlton, at Stourhead.

It was while staying at Siena that he first combined tourism with a specific archaeological aim: to identify the sites of the twelve Etruscan cities mentioned by classical authors. Interest in the Etruscans had been stimulated by the publication in 1723 to 1726 of *De Etruria Regli* by Sir Thomas Dempster (1579–1625). Illustrations of Sir William Hamilton's collection of Etruscan, Greek, and Roman antiquities were published by D'Hancarville in 1766/7; although the pottery which captured the imagination of Josiah Wedgwood was mistakenly attributed. G. B. Piranesi took an active part in the rehabilitation of Etruscan sculpture. His fantastic series of 'prison' engravings might well bear some relation to what Colt

---

[4] Copy. Whereabouts of original unknown.
[5] *Classical Tour*, I, p. 1.
[6] Diaries.   [7] Ibid.

Hoare called 'the striking and gigantic character of the Etruscan architecture' (Pl. 33a). Colt visited not only existing towns of Etruscan origin, such as Volterra, Populonia, and Saturnia, but, with Cluverius as a guide, explored the sites of Vetulonia, Ansedonia, and Roselle (Rusellae). The first of these he failed to find; the last he discovered after a second attempt.

> Early in the morning [of May 15th, 1789] I left Grosseto, accompanied by Signor Bondoni, an inhabitant of the place, in search of the ruins of Rusellae, which I had before failed to find for want of a proper guide. I have already observed that the remains I had seen at Moscona did not in any way correspond with the description of Cluverius, and therefore I was convinced that I must look for this ancient city elsewhere...at present the place is totally uninhabited, and continues only a shelter for cattle and wild animals. It is so overgrown with wood, as to be not easily approached, or even discovered. Besides the walls, nothing of a very antique date remains except a circular building, supposed by antiquaries to have been an amphitheatre.[8]

Colt's opinion was that it was not of Roman construction and probably later.

> But it is of little consequence to enter into the age or intent of this structure, when we find such striking evidence of the remote antiquity and former splendour of Rusellae within the compass of its walls, which for so many centuries have bid defiance, and for many more may yet bid defiance, to the ravages of the great devourer, Time. The quantity of trees, thorns and coppice wood, which render the approach difficult, may at the same time have contributed to their preservation. Of these remains the most noble and perfect part is exposed towards the north, and faces the great road, leading to Siena. Here we may see the works of a nation, who by several centuries preceeded the Romans, and on whose ruins the Romans laid the first foundation of that mighty power, which afterwards overshadowed the whole civilised world:

> > —sic fortis Etruria cessit
> > Scilicet et rerum facta est pulcherrima Roma.

> with wonder and amazement we may here contemplate the traces of a people, who flourished before the dawn of authentic history....In exploring these awful remains of so remote an age, we shall find ample cause for astonishment, at the profound knowledge of mechanics, which must have been employed in raising and placing stones of such extraordinary magnitude.[9]

[8] *Classical Tour*, I, p. 63.   [9] Ibid., pp. 65 ff.

Compared with those at Saturnia, Ansedonia, Populonia, etc. these walls showed little attention to symmetry, and the stones, whether square, oblong, or triangular, appeared to be laid in the order they were drawn from the quarry. Some which Colt measured, one at the summit of the wall, were as much as nine feet by six; and these were not the most massive.

> The height of the walls appeared to be about twenty feet, or at least above fifteen; but of this it was difficult to judge from their mass and position.
>
> On considering the situation on the Etruscan cities, I find that they were generally built on eminences, of which the summits were purposely levelled. They seemed to have begun by rendering the ground even, and raising the walls, before they erected dwellings; and probably the stones thus dug up were employed in the construction of the walls. Hence the mechanical labour of moving such masses was diminished; for the stones were lowered not raised.[10]

Although Colt Hoare's travel books have not the style or human interest of others of his famous contemporaries they contain much topographical information. The visit to Elba, not yet notorious, for which he interrupted his Etruscan journey, is still relevant to the modern traveller. The village where he stayed, in the mountains above Rio, is (in 1966) 'very much as Hoare found it and completely unvisited by tourists'.[11]

He left Siena early in October, stopping at Florence and then proceeded to Rome along the road through Arezzo and Narni, revisiting Trasimene and Terni as we have already seen.[12] On 31 October he set out along the Appian Way with Labruzzi[13] as a companion, making many drawings and indulging what R. E. Sandell calls 'his mania for copying classical inscriptions'.[14] This was, in fact, necessary because of 'the barbarous practice of stripping every antique monument of its recording tablet, which, when removed, becomes an useless piece of lumber, and if left, would throw most important light on many now obscure historical events'.[15] As usual topography was invested with the romance of history; the pursuit of Caius Marius through the marshes of Minturnae;[16] or the defeat of the Romans at Caudium,[17] described by Livy. Colt, contemplating the defiles blocked by the Samnites to entrap the legions, doubted the feasibility of such an

---

[10] Ibid., p. 68.

[11] MS. commentary by A. J. Chatterley on Hoare's *Tour of Elba*.

[12] See above, pp. 79–82.

[13] See Denys Sutton, 'An 18th Century Artist Rediscovered', *Country Life*, 23 June 1960. Also Catalogue, *Carlo Labruzzi (1748–1817)*; Exhibition of Water Colour Drawings of the Appian Way (London, 1960).

[14] R. E. Sandell, 'Sir Richard Colt Hoare', *Wiltshire Archaeological and Natural History Magazine*, CCIX, vol. 58, p. 2.

[15] *Classical Tour*, I, p. 118.

[16] Livy, book LXXVII (Summary).

[17] Livy, book IX.

operation in the distended valleys as he found them. In the church of S. Erasmo at Gaeta he found a font formed from an antique vase with a relief showing the story of the infant Bacchus conveyed by Mercury to be educated by Leucothea. This so pleased him that he had it reproduced on the chimney piece in the picture gallery he built at Stourhead.[18]

He had intended following closely the track of the Appian Way, but heavy autumnal rains forced him to follow the usual road to Naples. For the same reason, and due to the ill health of Labruzzi, he had to abandon the idea of continuing to Brindisi, and remained at Naples a month before sailing for Sicily.

Besides going over some of the ground he had covered in 1786, Colt visited Capri, where he lodged at the Carthusian convent. The island was used by the King of Naples for shooting quail which were plentiful in the spring; and it also abounded in classical remains, although the twelve villas supposed to have been erected by Tiberius were destroyed by the Romans on his decease so that no stone should stand as a memento of the abominable vices and cruelties which had transpired.

Relatively new as a place of pilgrimage were the temples at Paestum. Through these, and others in Sicily, Greek architecture was becoming familiar and fashionable. Piranesi's drawings were made in 1778; John Soane visited it the following year. Stuart and Revett's study of the Acropolis, the second volume of *The Antiquities of Athens*, was published in 1788. Paestum was not easily accessible even from Naples. Henry Swinburne, in 1780, went by sea. Colt considered the journey from Salerno could not be made under twelve hours, excluding time spent there. Unlike Willey Reveley, with whom he corresponded while in Italy and who subsequently did work for Stourhead, he did not stay overnight. Reveley was an enthusiast for Greek architecture, but otherwise he was not impressed.

> The people all looked miserable & unhealthy. The place abounds with snakes, vipers, knats & other venomous animals & the wolves in the neighbouring mountains, during my last visit to Paestum came into the town if so wretched a place can be so called & devoured a living mule left out to graze near the cottages. . . . As strangers rarely go to Paesto the people whenever they do come impose upon them as much as possible, & will bully & might murder any person if they chose it, for it is out of the way of all justice or enquiry, therefore all travellers going should be well armed for their own safety & to secure the civility of people whose unhappy situation reduces them to a level with the beasts of the field.[19]

[18] *Classical Tour*, p. 126.
[19] Willey Reveley, MS. Notes on Architecture, R.I.B.A.

Chapter 9

Sicily and Malta

The most impressive Greek ruins of Sicily were the temples at Segesta, Selinunte, and Girgenti (Agrigento). The spectacular site of Segesta, in the bleak western corner of the island, was vividly described by Goethe in 1787.

> Standing on an isolated hill at the head of a long, wide valley and surrounded by cliffs, it towers over a vast landscape, but, extensive as the view is, only a small corner of the sea is visible. The countryside broods in a melancholy fertility; it is all cultivated but with scarcely a sign of human habitation. The tops of the flowering thistles were alive with butterflies; wild fennel, its last year's growth now withered, stood eight or nine feet high and in such profusion and apparent order that one might have taken it for a nursery garden. The wind howled around the columns as though they were a forest, and birds of prey wheeled, screaming, above the empty shell.[1]

Colt, three years later, noted that Segesta was very unfavourably situated, on rocky and uneven ground, surrounded by sterile mountains, and exposed to the violence of the winds. The wind and rain were so violent that he feared his litter would be blown away. He was torn between his picturesque expectations and the facts which, as always, he faithfully recorded. Although the temple seemed majestic in its barren setting he lamented the want of trees to render the landscape more agreeable; and admitted he got more pleasure from the scattered ruins at Selinunte than these which were well-preserved.

> For this, [he wrote] it is easy to account. Works of architecture, as well as statuary, when executed with just proportions, lose their apparent magnitude in their symmetry and harmony.... But amidst the ruins of Selinunte the eye wanders with astonishment over the huge masses, scattered on the ground in the wildest confusion; and the painter may find an almost inexhaustable

---

[1] Goethe, *Italian Journey*, p. 255.

variety of subjects to employ his pencil in these remains, which are the most gigantic and picturesque I have ever seen. In proof of their magnitude one instance may suffice. On the ground, at some distance from the temples, is a stone twenty-six feet in length, which, from its form, was probably intended as part of the architecture of the largest temple.[2]

Vaster and more numerous were the temples of Agrigento. Payne Knight, in 1777, counted the remains of fourteen.[3] Goethe could not span a triglyph of the Temple of Jupiter with outstretched arms; the flutings of a column barely touched his shoulders as he stood in it; and he estimated that twenty-two men, shoulder to shoulder, would be needed to encircle it. Colt Hoare found eleven temples in different stages of dilapidation. And if Selinunte was more majestic, Segesta grander in its proportions, Agrigento united the beauties of landscape with the elegancies of art, so that the ruins awakened more admiration and delight the more they were contemplated. Colt, however, was never a Greek enthusiast in architecture. The nearest the Grecian style came to Stourhead was a design for Terrace Lodge by William Wilkins[4] which was not executed. Colt himself increasingly inclined to a mediaeval taste, perhaps to match the monastic one.

Five of Colt Hoare's eight months in Sicily were spent in and near Palermo, which 'from its beautiful situation, delightful rides and walks, pure and enlivening air, from the hospitality and politeness of its inhabitants, and the ease and freedom of their mode of life, is among the most pleasant of the Italian cities for the residence of a stranger'.[5] Here he became acquainted with the principal nobility, who were so numerous that a private *cavaliere* was a being almost unknown. Not everyone was so acceptable. Henry Swinburne, whose book Colt had taken with him, found his letters of introduction ignored and said he was shewn no civility, nor was he invited to break bread under a single Sicilian roof.[6] This was not entirely true as he acknowledged two exceptions; the learned antiquary Prince Lancellotti of Torremuza and Monsignor Severino of Naples, Archbishop of Palermo and Monreale. Perhaps it was the ladies who offended him, for he remarked they were 'little favoured by nature'.[7] Payne Knight, who was there about the same time, found that 'the generality of women are lively and agreeable. . . . Their manners are not inordinately fine, but easy and natural and not corrupted by that stupid imitation of the French, through which Italians of rank render themselves so ludicrous

[2] *Classical Tour*, II, p. 82.
[3] Richard Payne Knight, Sicilian Diary; reproduced by N. Pevsner, *Art Bulletin*, XXXI, Dec. 1949.
[4] Letter and account from William Wilkins (1778–1839), T(ST) 383.4. Drawing, R.I.B.A. These remarks do not apply to furniture, where Grecian influence is evident in the work of the younger Chippendale.
[5] *Classical Tour*, II, p. 352.
[6] Henry Swinburne, *Travels in the Two Sicilies*, II (1785), p. 192.   [7] Ibid., p. 206.

and from which, indeed, our own countrymen are not altogether free.'[8]
Female society was not so circumscribed as in other parts of Italy; the
young were not doomed to languish in a cloister to await a husband, but
were introduced into company by their mothers. Nor were they coupled
as elsewhere with a *cavaliere servente* or male chaperon. Should the men
have been so whimsical as to expect the strictest fidelity from their wives,
they must often have deluded themselves, for the blood of the fair Sicilians
was too hot for them to resist an opportunity which was never lacking.[9]

Brydone found the Sicilians much fonder of study than their neighbours
on the continent; and the nobility, instead of the frivolities which usually
constituted conversation, liked to talk of literature, history, and particularly poetry. He was surprised to find many of the young men intimately
acquainted with the work of English philosophers and poets.[10]

Payne Knight, however, complained that in some parts of Sicily, notably
Agrigento, although a tradition for hospitality persisted from ancient
times, attention and courtesy became tedious without the wit to entertain
or the knowledge to instruct. He found it intolerable to have to squander
his time either replying to trivial enquiries or in attending to insignificant
observations.[11] Without Payne Knight's intellectual arrogance Colt also
indulged a sense of moral superiority. Though he enjoyed the company of
Sicilians he censured their habits and manners; too much show and too
little domestic comfort; a rage for gambling which had ruined the theatre;
and a belief that a life of ease and indolence constituted happiness. To
prove that this was not so he set out on 1 March 1790, round the perimeter
for two months.

His suite consisted of: a litter, with two mules ('by no means uncomfortable and the only vehicle practicable in the Sicilian roads which are
beyond any descriptions or ideas of imagination');[12] another mule, carrying a driver and half a load; a third with his bed, kitchen furniture, and
many other articles; two other mules for servants and two campieri as
guards. His residence in Palermo had procured him so many excellent
letters that he was never in want of a good night's lodging, often in a
monastery.

Besides those antiquities already mentioned Sicilian topography was
rich in classical allusions and Colt was able, not only to fill his portfolio
with drawings, but to indulge his fancy in contemplating near Mount
Eryx the place where Aeneas landed, where Anchises died, the scenes of
the games held in honour of his memory and the burning of the Trojan
ships.[13] Or, at Syracuse, on a hill overlooking the site of Ortygia, he

[8] Payne Knight, op. cit., p. 313.
[9] Ibid.
[10] P. Brydone, *A Tour through Sicily and Malta*, II (1773), p. 251.
[11] Payne Knight, op. cit., p. 315.
[12] R.C.H. to Lord Ailesbury, 24 May 1790, TOT.
[13] *The Aeneid*, book V.

recalled the defeat of the Athenians and the scenes of slaughter attending it.[14] 'The cries of the wounded; the hymns and exhortations of the spectators on the walls, or their moans and lamentations according to the events of the battle; the shock of vessels rushing against each other, or driven on shore; the mangled heaps of dead and dying; and the shattered wrecks floating on the water; all combined to form a scene, the most awful and horrible which imagination could conceive.'[15]

More recent devastation was evident at Messina, still largely in ruins after the earthquakes of 1783. Not far away were the traditional sites of Scylla and Charybdis. 'While I was examining the situation of this strait, enjoying the beautiful and classic scene before my eyes, and musing on the terrors with which it had been invested by the magic of poetry, a large vessel, under full sail, glided through the centre of the passage. All my reveries vanished; and I contemplated with exultation so common, yet so striking, a proof of the improvement of science, and progress of naval knowledge.'[16]

May was spent at Bagheria with the Prince of Trabbia, who kept open house for a large company. A curiosity of the place was the villa of the Prince of Pallagonia. The grotesque statuary outside and the still more bizarre interior provoked most travellers who saw it. The avenue of monsters leading to the house was three hundred yards long, and terminated in a circular court 'crowded with stone and marble beings, not to be found in any book of zoology'.[17] They lined the battlements in menacing attitudes, and the walls were cased with 'basso-relievos, masks, medallions, scriptural subjects, heathen gods, emperors and posture masters'.[18] Indoors it was the same. 'The ceilings of the rooms are of looking glass; the walls lined with china and delf baubles, monkies hold up the curtains, horses mount guard, and devils wait at the foot of the stairs. The ball room remains imperfect, though intended for the chef d'oevre; round it runs a marble bench, which upon examination I found to contain a great number of night tables....'[19] Goethe adds a final touch to this picture of proto-Dada.

> The legs of the chairs have been unequally sawn off, so that no-one can sit on them, and we were warned by the castellan himself not to use the normal chairs, for they have spikes hidden under their velvet-cushioned seats. In corners stood candelabra of Chinese porcelain, which turned out, on closer inspection, to be made up of single bowls, cups and saucers, all glued together. Some whimsical object stares out at you from every corner.

[14] Thucydides, *History of the Peloponnesian War*, VII, lxix–lxxii.
[15] *Classical Tour*, II, p. 170.
[16] Ibid., p. 210.
[17] Swinburne, op. cit., II, p. 215.
[18] Ibid.
[19] Ibid.

Even the unrivalled view of the sea beyond the foothills is spoiled because the panes of coloured glass in the windows either make warm tones look cold or cold tones blazing. I must not forget a cabinet. Its panels are made from antique gilt frames which have been sawn in pieces and then put together again. The hundred different styles of carving, ancient and modern, crammed into these panels, from which the gilt was peeling when it wasn't smothered in dust, made it look like a mangled piece of junk.

A description of the chapel alone would fill a book. Here lies the clue of the whole madness. Only in the brain of a religious fanatic could it have grown to such rampant proportions. I must leave you to imagine how many caricatures of a perverted piety have been assembled here, and only mention the most conspicuous one.

A carved crucifix of considerable size, painted in realistic colours and varnished and gilded in places, is fixed to the ceiling. Into the navel of the Crucified a hook has been screwed from which hangs a chain. The end of this chain is made fast to the head of a man, kneeling in prayer and painted and varnished like everything else. He hangs suspended in the air as a symbol of the ceaseless devotions of the present owner.[20]

The author of this creation had spent forty thousand pounds before his relations took over the administration of his estates. Brydone found him a poor, miserable, lean figure who seemed to be afraid of everyone to whom he spoke, but who, surprisingly, talked speciously enough on occasions. From time to time he could be seen in the city collecting ransom money for the slaves captured by Barbary pirates. He appeared walking down the middle of the street, through all the dung and dirt, with an air of unperturbable dignity, an elderly gentleman in a freshly curled and powdered wig, his hat under his arm, and wearing a silk coat, a sword, and neat shoes with jewelled buckles. He was accompanied on either side by runners with silver salvers. The collection never amounted to much, but it served to remind people of the plight of the unfortunate captives. The Pallagonia arms were a satyr holding up a mirror to a woman with a horse's head. Colt spent some evenings at the villa. He thought it all in poor taste.

A month after his return to Palermo Colt started on a journey across the interior. This was a more uncomfortable undertaking than the last. Brydone, who had toured the coast mainly by boat was horrified by the poverty. 'The sight of these poor people has filled me with indignation. Surrounded by the finest country in the world, yet there was neither bread

---

[20] Goethe, op. cit., p. 233 ff.

nor wine to be found in it, and the poor inhabitants appear more than half-starved.'[21] The poverty, as Goethe discovered, was reflected in accommodation for travellers. The inn at Caltanissetta provided only an unclean room, no furniture, food, or even facilities for cooking.

Colt, as we have seen was well equipped, and experienced no such difficulties. He passed by Caltanissetta, lodging at the Franciscan convent of Castrogiovanni (Enna), not far from which is a lake, traditionally the place where Proserpine was gathering flowers when Pluto snatched her into the underworld. Now, there were no signs of perpetual Spring. 'Except a few scattered trees, which feather the southwest side, its banks and declivities are totally naked. Its borders are stinking and loathsome, and in the Summer months exhale an air, which is pestilential and fatal to those who approach them…at times it abounds in fish, particularly tench and eels; but at others they all perish, and without any apparent cause.'[22]

Crossing to the south coast beyond Vittoria, he boarded a merchant vessel and sailed for Malta, returning on 17 June, after nine days, to Cape Passaro. Only one major project remained to be accomplished; the ascent of Etna. This proved much more easy than he had been led to expect; and far less tiring than Vesuvius, which was a mole hill in comparison. It was believed by the inhabitants in the surrounding country to be the mouth of hell. Brydone was told in 1770 that an English queen had burned in the mountain for many years past. Her name, they said, was Anna. He could not conceive what Queen Anne had done to deserve this; but it transpired that it was Anne Boleyn, who had made a christian king into a heretic. He asked if her husband was there too, for he deserved it better than she. Certainly, he was told, and all his subjects; and if he was one of their number he need not be in such a hurry for he was sure to get there in the end.[23]

From a camp in the Grotto delle Capro Colt began the last climb at one in the morning, by bright moonlight, and in three hours reached the summit just before sunrise. As day dawned over the mountains of Calabria, his journey lay below him as on a map. Mounting half a mile higher, he at last looked down into the crater (Pl. 34), 'one vast unfathomable abyss …so close beneath me that I stood within a few paces of its dreadful verge. Beyond was another, infinitely greater, throwing out so dense a vapour, that its circumference, and precipitous border were seen only as through a thick fog. From hence issued a continued roar, like that of a tempestuous sea. These two gulfs are separated by a narrow ridge of rock; and above the last, towers a lofty pinnacle, the highest point of the mountain, incessantly vomiting forth a thick volume of smoke, mixed with

[21] Brydone, op. cit., II, p. 20.
[22] *Classical Tour*, II, p. 252.
[23] Brydone, I, p. 170.

flames.'[24] He found the air so tempered by volcanic heat that he sat down to draw, and, had time permitted, he could have remained for hours. Fully satisfied and with his imagination deeply impressed he descended the mountain on his return journey. His thoughts were turning towards England.

For the remainder of the summer he idled near Palermo, bathing daily in the sea and in the evening attending the theatre, *conversazioni* or the Marino (Pl. 33b), the summer rendezvous of the Sicilian nobility. This was an open space between the city wall and the sea from which, even in the hot season, there was always a cool breeze. In the evenings, before the assembly, the company would drive up and down the quay, where music and refreshments were provided. The orchestra was housed in 'an elegant kind of temple', and the concert began at midnight when the walk was crowded with carriages and people on foot. The better to favour pleasure and intrigue, all lights were extinguished. 'The whole company generally continue an hour or two together in utter darkness, except when the intruding moon, with her horns and her chastity, comes to disturb them. The concert finishes about two in the morning, when, for the most part, every husband goes home to his wife. This is an admirable institution, and never produces any scandal; no husband is such a brute as to deny his wife the Marino and the ladies are so cautious and circumspect on their side, that the more to avoid giving offence, they very often put on masques.'[25]

The concerts were preceded by general *conversazioni* where people played cards, ate ices or just talked. They were, said Brydone, held in apartments lighted with wax candles, kept cool and agreeable, and were altogether the most comfortable institutions. There were, besides, special *conversazioni*. 'These are always held in the apartments of the lying-in ladies; for in this happy climate, child-bearing is divested of all its terrors, and is only considered as a party of pleasure. . . . This conversation is repeated every night during her convalesence, which generally lasts for about eleven or twelve days. The custom is perfectly universal, and as the ladies here are very prolific, there is for the most part three or four of these assemblies going on in the city at the same time; possibly the Marino does not a little contribute towards them.'[26]

However contemptuous the Protestant might be of Catholic superstition, he always enjoyed the spectacles associated with it. Brydone considered those held to celebrate the Feast of S. Rosalia at Palermo superior to Holy Week in Rome or the Feast of the Ascension at Venice. Indeed, the illumination of St. Peters was no more to be compared with them than the planet Venus to the sun. 'The whole church, walls, roof, pillars, and

[24] *Classical Tour*, II, p. 324.
[25] Brydone, op. cit., II, p. 36.
[26] Ibid., p. 38.

pilasters were entirely covered over with mirror, interspersed with gold and silver paper, artificial flowers, etc. done up with great taste and elegance, so that not one inch either of stone or plaister was to be seen. Now, form an idea, if you can, of one of our great cathedrals dressed out in this manner, and illuminated with twenty thousand wax tapers....'[27] 'The whole church appeared one flame of light; which, reflected from ten thousand bright and shining surfaces, of different colours and at different angles, produced an effect, that, I think, much exceeded all the descriptions of enchantment I have ever read.'[28] The feast began on 12 July, a week of other illuminations, fireworks, ceremonies and horse races. On 29 August, at ten o'clock at night, Colt Hoare sailed in the Lyon packet; and at eleven o'clock in the forenoon of 3 September he arrived once more in Naples.

[27] Ibid., p. 123.
[28] Ibid.

Chapter 10

A Passing Look at the Contemplative Life

It was on this last occasion, besides visiting Ischia, that Colt made the short excursions, already mentioned, with Hackert. One of these was to Isernia (Pl. 30a), where the fair and festival had attracted notoriety. The ceremony in honour of Priapus as the principle of fecundity had first been described by Sir William Hamilton in 1781. As the festival became better known a degree of scandal was attached to part of it, and certain phallic offerings were prohibited by royal decree. Colt, however, procured a specimen which, though indelicate in itself, he said, was curious to an antiquary as proof of the deep hold which this originally heathen ceremony had taken on the public mind. He also defended Payne Knight's dissertation on the worship of Priapus, which had been privately circulated to members of the Dilettanti Society in 1786, when it was strongly criticized and soon afterwards withdrawn. Horace Walpole, then Lord Orford, was particularly scornful of Payne Knight's attempt to 'prove the lascivious designs of antiquity to be merely emblematic of the creative power'.[1]

Colt finally left Naples on 28 October, this time recording the monuments and inscriptions along the route of the ancient Via Latina. He claimed, on the way, to have introduced the potato to the monks of Monte Cassino. By way of Teano, Conca, Aquino, Frosinone, Ferentino, Agnani, and Valmonte he made his way to Rome where he arrived on 27 November.

He spent January, February, and March of 1791 in Siena, returning to Rome on 26 April. From there he made a final antiquarian expedition into the Abruzzi, unfrequented by the generality of travellers and unknown even to the inhabitants of the neighbouring districts.[2] His particular intention was to visit the Lake of Celano (the Fucine Lake) and the emissary of the Emperor Claudius mentioned by Tacitus[3] and Suetonius.[4] This was an attempt to regulate flooding by constructing a canal, three miles in length, partly by cutting through and partly by levelling a mountain. Thirty thousand men were employed in the work during eleven years.

[1] *The Farington Diary*, I, ed. J. Grieg (1922), 29 Apr. 1794.
[2] *Classical Tour*, I.
[3] Tacitus, *Annales*, XII, lvi, lvii.
[4] Suetonius, *Vitae Duodecim Caesarum*, V, xxi, 'Divius Claudius'.

To celebrate the opening, Claudius arranged a naval combat with fleets manned by malefactors. According to Suetonius, a difficulty arose, for when those on board the ships cried, 'Health attend you, noble Emperor; Dying men salute you,' Claudius replied, 'Health attend you too;'[5] at which, taking him to mean that they were excused, they all refused to fight. It was only by leaping from his seat, running along the side of the lake with his ridiculous staggering gait, that Claudius, by fair words and reproaches, persuaded them to engage.

At first the channel was not sufficiently level for the water to flow, and further work had to be done to clear it. But when it was last opened, the rush of water was so great that it threatened to overwhelm the sumptuous banquet which had been prepared at the mouth by the lake. Part of the works were carried away. The roar of the torrent, and the crash of materials falling in, spread general alarm. As confusion and noise filled the place, the Empress accused Narcissus, director of the work, of incompetence, and Claudius stood astonished.

At the time of Colt Hoare's visit the work of clearing and restoring the emissary was in progress.[6] Writing about it some years later he was overcome by one of his periodic fits of heart-searching.

> I may appear tedious and diffuse in recapitulating these particulars; but what is the object of history and antiquarian research? And in what does their interest consist, if it be not in collecting and combining scattered and insulated facts, and elucidating them by local investigation? Without the aids which may be drawn from history and antiquities, what sensations would the Lake of Celano inspire beyond those excited by the sight of a transparent sheet of water, surrounded by mountains? Sensations which might please for the moment, but would be soon obliterated by new impressions?

Whatever the future might say to this fundamental question, Colt was only able to answer that, in Italy at any rate, 'every scene bears a classic character, and every district acquires double interest, from the recollections it calls forth'.[7]

In the spring of 1791, after spending a few weeks at Siena, he started homewards from the Bucci's country house at Armajulo, in the Appenines. His last thoughts on Italy were for the monasteries. During his travels he had frequently received from them 'generous and disinterested hospitality'. On his last journey along the Via Latina the Padre Guardiano of St. Antonio, near Teano, had given up his own apartment in the *ospizio* with its magnificent view over the autumn woods towards the bay of Naples.

[5] This is how Colt Hoare tells the story. According to Suetonius, Claudius said, 'Aut non'.
[6] Henry Swinburne recorded a visit in 1780, when he found the opening of the emissary choked. Op. cit., II, p. 517.
[7] *Recollections*, IV.

Colt also turned deliberately aside to visit Casamare and Trisulto. The former, of the Trappist order, he found oppressive. 'The situation of this establishment is devoid of every charm; for it is exposed to a scorching sun, surrounded by a country moderately hilly, and destitute of wood.'[8] Such was the austerity of the rule that life there, Colt thought, could merely be existence.

> Dreary, indeed, is this abode; occupied by men condemned to perpetual silence, devoted to fasting and prayer, cut off from the society of parents and friends, dead to all the joys and comforts of life, and consigned to cheerless labour and increasing mortification. Such a retreat seems fit only for those wretched beings who, in the language of Shakespeare,
>
> > have within them undivulged crimes,
> > Unwhipp'd of justice,
>
> not for those who, animated by a true but fervid devotion, wish to retire from the cares and temptations of life, and the noise and bustle of the world, that they may the better prepare themselves for an hereafter; for surely the ALMIGHTY never intended that religion should be the parent of such unnatural privations, or assume so stern and repulsive an aspect.[9]

Colt was received in silence, and conducted round with great civility by the abbot who pressed him to stay the night, adding, as an additional temptation, that at two in the morning he would awake and summon him to the choir. Colt felt so little of the spirit of the order that he begged leave to decline. He did not feel this way about the Carthusian establishment at Trisulto; nor about Lavernia, Camoldi, and Vallombrosa, in Tuscany, which he visited after finally leaving Siena. He was, in fact, attracted by them, although what his motives were he could not say. 'Certainly not for the sake of historical, or even secular, information, of which little can be gleaned from the secluded inhabitants; nor from any predilection for these now useless establishments. I can only ascribe it to a love of those scenes, where nature exhibits her original and undisguised character; scenes which furnish gratification to the eye and employment to the pencil. Such are the sites generally chosen by those who devote themselves to a life of solitude and contemplation.'[10] 'Thick and gloomy forests present a retreat suited to those who have renounced the gaieties, pomp and luxuries of the world; while the convent standing alone, far from the dwellings and turbulent occupations of man, affords no object to interrupt the silence of meditation, or to divert the attention of the

[8] Ibid.
[9] *Recollections*, IV, p. 71.
[10] Ibid.

voluntary recluse from the duties and occupations of his solemn profession.'[11] This may sound like conventional sentiment of the kind which
prompted the little folly built by his grandfather in the woods below
Alfred's Tower. On the other hand there was no doubt of the hold which
the monastic past had over the romantic imagination, nor of the part it
still had to play.

It is probable that part of Italy's attraction was the ubiquity of the
Mother Goddess and the complementary institution of monasticism.
Brydone, man of science though he was, observed the Sicilians' warmth
of enthusiastic devotion before their favourite saints, particularly the
female ones, resembling 'the pure and delicate sensations of the most
respectful love'.[12] He admitted that he sometimes envied them their feelings, and 'cursed the pride of reason and philosophy, with all its cool and
tasteless triumphs, that lulls into a kind of stoical apathy these most
exquisite sensations of the soul'.[13] These overtones were sought in visiting
the nunneries. 'There is no artificial ornament, or studied embellishment
whatever, that can produce half so strong an effect, as the modest and
simple attire of a pretty young nun, placed behind a double iron grate. . . .
The pleasure of relieving an object in distress is the only refuge we have
against the pain which the seeing of that object occasions; but here, that
is utterly denied us, and we feel with sorrow, that pity is all we can bestow.
From these, and similar considerations, a man generally feels himself in
bad spirits, after conversing with amiable nuns.'[14]

Colt did not visit nunneries; at least, he did not say that he did. He
justified the monasteries primarily because the literary world was indebted
to them for 'valuable records and collections, rescued from oblivion by
their indefatigable industry'. Some he admitted were useful because they
cultivated 'extensive wastes or desert mountains' and maintained a
numerous population. The rigid orders were not essentially beneficial to
society, but at least their endowments made them independent. Those who
had none, mendicant friars and such, in whom he considered religion was
'a plausible pretext for idleness', would be more usefully employed in
trade, husbandry, or manufacture.[15]

The monk in his cell could also be taken as man alone with ultimate
reality. Colt shrank from this interpretation, and monasticism for him was
only attractive when, as at Vallombrosa, it was tempered by cheerful
prospects without and ease and opulence within. The seemingly ideal
existence which he was able to lead brought its own problems, in that when
there is no need to care for everyday necessity, nor even to think twice
about having what you want, the question of the meaning of existence is

[11] Ibid.
[12] Brydone, op. cit., p. 148.
[13] Ibid.
[14] Ibid., p. 57.
[15] *Recollections*, IV, p. 183.

likely to insistently intrude. Some temperaments might seek to distract from this impingement by constant titillation of the senses; others by feverish activity. The artist might search for the inward pattern in the outward form of things. But Colt Hoare, in spite of all his drawing, was not an artist; and his search for meaning turned to curiosity about an increasingly remote past.

Colt left Italy with some reluctance, yielding to a sense of duty rather than to inclination. His choice of route, through the Tyrol and Palatinate to Cologne and Brussels, was not entirely governed by the desire to see more places. In fact, having decided to go he was only too anxious to arrive. France, however, was now an uncomfortable place in which to travel. Numbers of French aristocrats, Colt noted, had flocked to Coblenz, including the two royal brothers, the Comte and Comtesse d'Artois, Monsieur and Madame and many others. Except for a brief period in 1802 more than twenty years would pass before the whole continent was easily accessible again to English travellers.

Twenty-four days after leaving Florence, with Woodforde as a companion, he embarked at Ostend about eleven at night, and landed the following day, 30 July 1791, in England. Unable immediately to clear his baggage at the customs he was detained at Dover until 1 August; and on Tuesday the 2nd was back in his house at St. James's Square.

On the 9th he wrote to his uncle at Savernake that he hoped to be at Stourhead by the 20th to prepare to receive friends for the shooting season. Woodforde, he said, paid his respects. He was glad to think their protection had not been thrown away on an idle subject, for during five years' residence in Italy he had not only made very rapid progress in his studies but had maintained an irreproachable conduct. He thanked his uncle for the kind and generous offer (of what he did not specify). 'I must beg leave to refuse', he wrote, 'as I wish to preserve my Liberty & Independence without any incumbrance whatever. My time is so pleasantly occupied with my favorite pursuits of reading & drawing that the introduction of any new one & particularly one of so important a nature, would interrupt if not totally annihilate those which are far more congenial to me.'[16]

16 R.C.H. to Lord Ailesbury, 9 Aug. 1791, TOT.

Chapter 11

Transformations

During his brief residence, before his flight abroad, Colt had had little time for innovation; Stourhead therefore remained virtually as his grandfather had left it. But now that the lines of his personality were set, he turned with enthusiasm and energy to making a place conformable with his own tastes and way of life. In 1791 he owned over 11,000[1] acres, most of them adjoining Stourton and Gasper, but with outlying estates in Wiltshire, Somerset, and Dorset. His gross annual rental was between £9000 and £10,000,[2] which put him high in the group of 300 wealthy men immediately below the great landed nobility.

One of his first acts on returning to England was to order a wide range of ornamental trees for the pleasure gardens. In the woodland he deplored Henry Hoare's method of mixing beech and fir; 'The former a spreading tree...to be seen in perfection ought to be suffered to grow uncontrolled; the other of a spiral nature, and dying *downwards* as it grows upwards. A more unnatural combination could not be imagined; yet for many years this mode of planting continued in all this neighbourhood.'[3] Henry Hoare had used the simplest means to achieve a visual effect.[4] There is no evidence that he was influenced by Hamilton's more novel departures at Painshill.[5] Colt belonged to a more sophisticated generation of plantsmen, and numbered among his friends such pioneer botanists as A. B. Lambert.[6]

[1] Schedule of Lands, 1827, T(ST) 383.
[2] Rent books, T(ST) 383. 29–46, 50.
[3] R.C.H., *History of Modern Wiltshire*.
[4] See II, 4, p. 31.
[5] J. C. Loudon, *Arboretum et Fruticetum Britannicum* (1838), of Painshill:

> Among the trees remaining are some remarkable fine silver cedars, pinasters and other pines, American oaks, cork trees and ilexes, a tupelo tree, tulip trees, deciduous cypresses, Lombardy and other poplars etc. Here some of the first rhododendron and azaleas were introduced into England by Mr. Thorburn, who was gardener to Mr. Hamilton, and who afterwards became an eminent nurseryman at Old Brompton.

I am indebted to Mr. Miles Hadfield, who quotes this in *Gardening in Britain* (1960), for this and other information regarding plants.

[6] A. B. Lambert, 1761–1842, of Boyton, Wilts., where he collected an herbarium with 30,000 specimens. He was a founder-member of the Linnean Society in 1788, and was responsible for introducing many species of pine. His chief work, *The Genus Pinus* appeared in 1803. A second volume (1824) is dedicated to Colt Hoare.

His choice of trees was not, however, particularly original, although it included some of the more unusual specimens which nurserymen now had on their lists. The bills from Miller and Sweet of Bristol in 1791 show that he bought a wide variety.[7] The existing pattern at Stourhead was reinforced by 1000 beech, 425 horse chestnut, and 250 Spanish. Other familiar trees were added in variety; five kinds of ash, three of birch, four of elm, five of holly; specimens of red Virginian cedar and varieties of cypress, maple, oak, sycamore and thorn gave an ornamental character to the woodland. But plane and tulip-trees, catalpa, chionanthus, snow-drop tree and nettle-trees, were of a different character and changed the emphasis in Henry Hoare's garden from landscape to arboretum. Colt also introduced *Rhododendron ponticum*, possibly the ancestor of those vast plants which still spread on the border of the lake.

In subsequent years, up to 1799, a massive planting programme was fulfilled, mainly of ash, beech, hazel, fir, and larch; so that by 1803 something like 90,000[8] trees had been established. There were 1036 acres of woodland at Stourton and Gasper and 1173[9] acres elsewhere. In 1798 and 1799, 9700[10] laurels and hollies were planted in the garden, on Apollo's hill and round the churchyard. The rates for digging holes varied, presumably according to the tree; in 1798 they were 4s. 2d. a hundred for beech, fir, and larch, 2s. 6d. for hazel. The rate for laurel was 1s. 8d.[11] Acres of woodland were underplanted with this shrub which, Loudon noted some years later, gave a monotonous effect.[12]

While in general applauding his grandfather's design, Colt disapproved of 'nature overcrowded by buildings', particularly if these were not in harmony with one another. Thus the Gothic greenhouse (Pl. 10c), Chinese temple, and Turkish tent were removed from the hillside nearest the house, together with the Palladian temple (Pl. 13b), at the end of the terrace, whose urn and marble busts were transferred to Flora. His object, Colt wrote, was to render the design of the gardens as chaste and correct as possible, and to give them the character of an Italian villa.[13] In 1794 he was making gravel paths so that he could go round the gardens with a dry foot.[14] The wooden Palladian bridge, across the north arm of the lake, was finally taken down in May 1798.[15] In April 1806, John Carter, the architectural draughtsman, wrote to Colt:

> I doubt I do not sufficiently understand your instructions about the cottage and porch. . . . To have a propper explanation of what

[7] Bills for trees and shrubs are in Estate receipts, T(ST) 383.57.
[8] Estate receipts.
[9] Woods and plantations, Jan. 1803, T(ST) 383.108.
[10] Estate receipts.   [11] Ibid.
[12] J. C. Loudon. *Arboretum et Fruticetum Britannicum* (1838).
[13] *Modern Wiltshire*.
[14] R.C.H. to Lord Ailesbury, 4 Feb. 1794, TOT.
[15] Journal, 1798, T(ST) 383.924.

is to be done, there should be a ground plan...with the dimen-
tions....I do not anyways comprehend the side window and
seat. If a design is executed there must be a regular plan and
elevation (when fixed upon) and the parts at large drawn by me,
and well explained for the workmen. It is possible to do the
porch in town under my eye, and then sent down by the waggon,
the seat also and what other parts you may wish done in this
way.[16]

Although the cottage is not specified, the details correspond with the
one between the Grotto and the Pantheon, which was not shown on Piper's
plan or in the earlier panoramic drawings by Bampfylde. We may therefore
assume that if there was a building there in Henry Hoare's day it was not
intended as a feature, and that it was Colt Hoare, following the fashion
set by John Nash, who made it into one.

Meanwhile extensions were made to the house (Pl. 15a). Work on Colt's
private apartments, the principal staircase and a steward's room continued
through 1792, followed in 1793 by the major task of extending the front
by two wings, one to accommodate the picture collection, the other a
library.[17] On 13 January 1793, Colt wrote to his uncle, Lord Ailesbury,

I sincerely hope that you & all your family are well; & particularly that the accounts from the Travellers[18] are favorable. I shall
be very glad to hear some account of their late transactions, &
whether they mean to revisit Palermo again this winter—the
Italians are very much alarmed about the French Fleet on their
coast—the King of Naples & his Holiness are arming & forti-
fying—but all to no purpose if the French intend seriously to
attack them: but I rather think that they mean only to make
them sign a Neutrality—the Pope is the weakest: the Government of Rome is certainly detestable, & might be mended—I
have not been able to stir from home since I last wrote to you,
owing to company in my house; & the many occupations without
doors I must necessarily attend to—One wing is covered in, &
I am making the ground about it: I am happy it meets with the
general approbation of those who see it—and I hope to shew
it to you next summer. I mean to devote tomorrow & Tuesday
to *your service*—and hope by Wednesday Taunton coach to
send you a good supply of woodcocks—against the birthday—
unless the weather should prevent our trying our skill—We have
had no appearance of winter—the weather has been uncommonly

---

[16] T(ST) 383.907. For Carter, see below, III, 13.
[17] Summary of building accounts, ST.
[18] Charles (see above, p. 67), then Lord Bruce, who was on the Continent with his tutor. See
Lord Cardigan, *The Wardens of Savernake Forest*.

mild & rainy—a good circumstance for the poor—but the ground wants a hard frost to kill the numerous insects & worms—

On Wednesday I shall attend the Quarter Sessions at Wells—where therewith is a large meeting of the Acting Magistrates—who mean to make a public declaration (as I heard) to the Government of the state of their several districts—All is quiet in my neighbourhood—we are all loyal subjects—& are wise enough to work for no change or alteration in Government. . . . My little schoolboy has been with me for a month & returns soon to Sunbury.[19]

The mild winter was favourable to Colt's plantations. But the inevitable clash with France had come and war was declared on 1 February. 'I lament with every well wisher to Old England,' wrote Colt, on the 27th, 'that in the midst of our Prosperity we should by the perfidious behaviour of our Neighbours be obliged to take up arms—but the time has come, when we must either join the league against them & endevor to bring them to some sense of reason & justice (if possible) or risk our own property and liberties at home.'[20]

These events had no immediate effect on life at Stourhead. The work of building continued, under the supervision of Moulton and Atkinson of Salisbury.[21] An abstract of their accounts gives the cost of work completed by the end of 1794.

	£		
Sir Richds. Apartments	£237	2	6½
Principal Staircase	26	10	
Steward's Room	73	18	10½
New Wings	3466	1	½
Offices	669	3	7
Peach House	390	10	11
Vinery	265	8	4½
Privy	13	16	10
Materials left unused	40	1	1½
Drawings	10	10	
Journies etc.	198	9	
Do.	75	12	
	5467	4	3½[22]

When Colt Hoare copied this he put the last two items together as 'Moulton and Atkinson for journies etc.'[23] He also added a note saying

[19] R.C.H. to the Earl of Ailesbury, 13 Jan. 1793, TOT.
[20] 27 Jan. 1793, TOT.
[21] There is no evidence in the form of drawings or plans that they were architects. On the other hand a letter from Thomas Atkinson in 1806 suggests that he had overall responsibility for the work. T(ST) 383.57.
[22] Building Accounts, T(ST) 383.66.
[23] Summary of building accounts, ST.

that no carriage of materials was included nor a large quantity of his own timber used in different buildings. An entry in 1795, 'For 6 days Ingram travelling setting out size of pictures to picture room walls; putting up port-folio cases; hanging window blinds etc,'[24] suggests that the gallery was then ready, although when the chimney-piece was put up in 1801, additional work to the walls on either side was necessary.[25] The library chimney-piece[26] was installed in the same year, at the same time as the barrel framed ceiling. Woodforde's bill for copying 'three groups from *The School of Athens*' was presented in April 1804,[27] and Francis Eginton's, £525 for the painted glass version, in November.[28] The bookcases for the new library were made in 1801, and the old one gutted in 1802.[29] Colt's book bills thereupon increased, from £160 in the five years up to 1800, to £1317 and £1638 in the periods 1801–5 and 1806–10 respectively.[30] The majority were connected with English History, Antiquities, Topography, and Travel.

Much work was done elsewhere in the house, including a tepid bath room, and a new water closet costing £118 2*s*. 6*d*.[31] The passages from the new wings joined the cabinet and music rooms on either side. One of the last entries in the building accounts, in December 1804, reads: 'Erecting scaffold, putting up blinds to external part of upper windows in Library, assisting Mr. Chippingdale's (sic) man putting up gilt mouldings, putting organ into its recess, putting down carpet, hanging pictures etc.'[32]

The firm of Chippendale,[33] under Thomas Chippendale the younger, was regularly employed in work for Stourhead from 1795, not only making furniture, but moving it and in other work of decorating.[34] In 1804, for instance, a large iron stove for the Pantheon was packed and transported; and in 1803 Chippendale supplied a pair of battledores and shuttlecocks. But he also received perhaps the most important commissions of his life, the complete furnishing and decoration of all Colt Hoare's new rooms, and wonderfully did he rise to the occasion. The first suite of rooms was completed in 1802. The cabinet room, so-called from the cabinet of Pope Sixtus V[35] which Henry Hoare had bought, had windows draped in deep

[24] T(ST) 383.66.   [25] Ibid.

[26] Ibid. This was not the one at present in the library, formerly at Wavendon. See Francis Nicholson's painting of the library.

[27] Receipt, T(ST) 383.4.   [28] Ibid.   [29] T(ST) 383. 66.

[30] Receipts, T(ST) 383.4.   [31] T(ST) 383.66.   [32] T(ST) 383.66.

[33] After Thomas Chippendale the elder's death in 1779 the business of Chippendale and Haig continued under his son. Haig retired in 1796.

[34] Unless otherwise stated all the subsequent information about Chippendale's work at Stourhead is from the volume of accounts in the library there.

[35] According to a writer in *The London Chronicle*, 18 June 1757, 'This Cabinet formerly belonged to Pope Sixtus V. The Effigies of this Pope and the Peretti Family, from whom one of his Nephews descended, are taken from the life, and set in the Cabinet in round Recesses, with Glasses before them, in order to preserve them. The last of this Family was a Nun, who left the Cabinet to a Convent in Rome, where Mr. Hoare made a Purchase of it.' The 'effigies' to which the writer refers are probably the miniatures discovered in the drawers of the cabinet and now displayed in a showcase.

11—L.A.

blue velvet, hung with curtains of black-spotted blue satin. The alcove in which the cabinet stood was furnished with a 'large Circular Lath with Cornice thickly carved and finished in burnished gold with the Pope's tiara and other insignias'. The rectilinear emphasis in the satinwood elbow chairs, with black ebony bands and broad pannelled back, added a new touch of severity, or Greek purity, to the classical Chippendale tradition of the 1770s when the firm had worked to produce the furniture for Harewood House. Similar chairs made for the picture gallery have backs with diagonal stays in addition to the horizontal rails (Pl. 36a). The chairs and the sofa tables of satinwood and rosewood, with the 'twisted harp' motif (Pl. 36a), give a golden light to the room, even on a winter's day. Yellow and black star satin draped the windows, and 324 yards of Brussels carpet united the picture gallery, cabinet room, and passage room between. The chimney-piece had a frieze copied on Colt's instructions from an antique vase, used as a font in S. Erasmo at Gaeta di Mola.[36] It represents the infant Bacchus conveyed by Mercury to Ino, by whom the child was to be reared, disguised as a girl and thus protected from the wrath of Hera. Above the chimney-piece hung what was perhaps Colt's most important Italian purchase, Cigoli's *Adoration of the Kings*[37] (Pl. 28b), for the frame of which Chippendale made an ornament carved with a goat's head, shell and oak leaves. On either side were his grandfather's Carlo Maratta, *Marchese Pallavicini* (Pl. 28a) and *Octavius and Cleopatra* (Pl. 27) by Mengs.

It is interesting that the latter painting includes a circular table, with winged lion monopodia supports, almost identical with that in Thomas Hope's *Household Furniture and Interior Decoration* published in 1807; and that the Egyptian funerary urn foreshadows the style which was now to appear in Chippendale's library furniture. Egyptian motifs were by no means new.[38] Egyptian antiquities were illustrated in the supplement to Montfaucon's *L'Antiquité Expliquée*, the English version of which (1725) is in the library at Stourhead. At the time Mengs was completing his Cleopatra, Piranesi had been decorating the English Coffee House in Rome with Egyptian figures, animals, hieroglyphs, etc. There was an Egyptian Society in England in 1741; but the main impetus for the Egyptian taste came from France. De Caylus's *Recueils d'antiquités égyptiennes, étrusques, grècques et romanes* began to appear in 1752; the craze, however, arose after Napoleon's Egyptian campaign of 1798. The short peace of 1802 opened Paris again to English travellers, and with a new wave of French fashion Vivant Denon's *Voyages dans la Basse et la Haute Egypte* was published in London in the same year. These influences were evident in Sheraton's *The Cabinet Directory* in 1803; it is not therefore surprising that a marked change in style should appear in the furniture delivered to Stourhead in 1805.

[36] R.C.H., *Classical Tour*, I, p. 126.   [37] Receipt, 19 Feb. 1791, T(ST) 383.4.
[38] See N. Pevsner and S. Lang, 'The Egyptian Revival', *A.R.*, May 1956.

The library furniture is not, however, derived from any particular source, but is highly original and successful. The large mahogany pedestal table with columns and supports carved with Egyptian and philosophers' heads (Pl. 37), 'the whole made to take to pieces'; the very large mahogany table to hold portfolios, with fluted pilasters, panelled ends and doors with brass grilles; the eight mahogany chairs with round backs, broad sweep-panelled tops with circle elbows and carved Egyptian heads (Pl. 37), have a weight and proportion which contrast with the flat book-lined walls and plain barrel ceiling, and exactly suit the character of the room (Pl. 35). They have a solidity which matches the scholarly environment, and a degree of fantasy which is an appropriate accompaniment. The overall design is Roman; the philosophers look back to Greece, the Egyptians to more exotic antiquities. Even the vertical stays in the chair backs are turned in a manner reminiscent of an English past, except that there is no uncontrolled Carolean exuberance, and in plan, elevation and perspective they proclaim the classical tradition of the firm which made them. The two matching upright chairs are less successful. Each chair had a thick quilted cushion covered with fine Athenian red cloth, tied down with yellow and black tufts and covered with yellow leather. The three tall windows overlooking the south lawn, through which the afternoon sunlight comes, were draped in blue silk damask hung from carved and gilded cornices with an eagle as a central ornament. Over the fireplace hung the portrait of Petrus Landi, *Doge of Venice*, supposed to be by Titian; on either side, one above the other, ten views by Canaletto of the principal buildings with which the functions of the Doge were associated.[39] A finishing touch to the room was given by the green carpet with a design based on a Roman tessellated pavement.

For those who like imposing fronts the addition of the wings (Pl. 15a) may be an improvement, but architecturally Campbell's north and south (Pl. 14b) elevations were ruined. Inside it is a different matter. The library is probably Colt Hoare's supreme achievement as a patron, as complete in conception as his grandfather's garden; and it represents the introverted way of life he found in the Italian monasteries without any of the attendant disadvantages.

For all the work which Chippendale did up to 1805 the cost was £2719 15s. 11¾d. The highest price paid for a single piece of furniture was £115 for the library table; the very large one for portfolios was £72, and the set of eight chairs £76. The curtain material was much dearer, £125 for the picture gallery and £186 for the library. Chippendale was made bankrupt in 1804,[40] and it is evident, from a letter he wrote to Colt, that things did not go too well after his failure.

---

[39] See painting by Francis Nicholson in the library at Stourhead. The portrait and the Canalettos were sold in 1883.
[40] Whitley, *Artists and their friends in England*, II, p. 262.

Sir Richd

According to your request have sent your account up to the time of my stopping, the Curtains will be a fresh account, and I have sent them this morning to Brown & Brices Taunton Waggon, I should have sent them sooner but was disappointed by the Fringe Maker.

I am very sorry the pole of the screen has cast and I wonder at it as it was made of old dry wood. I will send down another if you have any one that can fix it. I think a joiner could do it if not the Block must come up again. You will please to direct me in St. Martin's Lane as I shall now be enabled to go on again, and shall hope for a continuance of your favor & recommendation which I will always endeavour to merit by my strict attention could I but be fortunate to get such an order as you was pleased to hint to it would be the making of me. I beg your excuse for mentioning this but one word from a Gentleman of your known taste might do a great deal for me. I am Sir

Your most hbe Servt.
Thos. Chippendale

5th May 1808
No. 60 St. Martin's Lane.[41]

A bill for £24 10s. 10d. was annexed, which included two lounging chairs; otherwise he had little work to do for Stourhead until 1811–12. It was then he delivered the suite of furniture now in the Italian room, formerly Colt's bedroom. This was perhaps the order he referred to in his letter. It comprised ten chairs of Spanish mahogany with hollow panelled backs, part carved with scrolls and bands, armchairs en suite (Pl. 36b), and a pair of music stands with scroll heads and drawers (Pl. 36b). As Clifford Musgrave writes, they display 'classicism in a rich and florid mood, but still retaining dignity and good proportion. . . . The armchairs have a large and striking *guilloche* ornament around the sides and backs, while tapering reeded legs look back to Chippendale's earlier inspiration from the French, but have taken on a new sturdiness.'[42] There is nothing quite like them in Regency furniture.

Chippendale made many other single pieces for Colt; besides the masterpieces which have been mentioned there is the sideboard carved with laurel leaves, leopards' heads, and lions' feet and inlaid with ebony (1802); the big library steps (1804); 'a large Mahog Dressing Table to fit into the recess of a window with a large Dressing Glass to rise, two drawers fitted up for razors, a Cupboard with folding doors and 4 drawers under fitted with divisions' (1812); and in 1816 four caned hunting chairs, now in the

[41] Thos. Chippendale the younger to R.C.H., 5 May 1808, T(ST) 383.4.
[42] Clifford Musgrave, *Regency Furniture* (1961), p. 75.

entrance hall. He made plantstands in the form of sarcophagi, candelabra, firescreens, innumerable boxes, and many footstools, for throughout his later years Colt suffered with the gout. In 1815, besides £252 for cabinet work, Chippendale's bill included £169 for paperhanging, £383 for carpets, and £406 for upholstery. One of his last recorded commissions, in 1818, four years before his death, was to cut and polish a piece of petrified oak. This, he wrote to explain, 'was so hard that we could not make the least impression on it, therefore I took to a Mason and a Man after 8 days could do not more than what you will perceive and gave it up, saying they never met with any stone or marble so very hard'.[43]

Work about the house went on for ten years, and it seems likely that it was not completely transformed to Colt's liking until the library was finally furnished in 1805. By then the pictures he had bought in Italy were hung, including the eleven large Ducros assembled in the Column Room. He had discovered Turner, who was doing work for him; Woodforde had painted the large portrait[44] (Pl. 24b), with his son, in which, at thirty-seven, Colt already looks elderly. Building proceeded elsewhere on his estates; £493 for a farmhouse at Bonham in 1797; £487 for stables and ox-stalls in 1798; new cottages at Stourton in 1802; and a new bridge at Woodbridge Mill which in 1803 cost £1066 16s. 3d.[45] He recorded having built ten lodges,[46] but only one, Tower lodge, is mentioned in the accounts.[47] Willey Reveley certainly designed some of these, as a letter dated 1 December 1797 begins, 'Herewith I trouble you with the designs of the lodges.' These activities did not of course fill all Colt's time, and meanwhile he was occupied in other ways.

[43] Chippendale's accounts, ST.
[44] 'Mr. Woodford is now here making a sketch for a whole length of Mrs. Hugh Hoare—a fine Newfoundland Dog, & her eldest son are introduced—when you see it, I think you will like the disposal of the figures—he is to paint a whole length of me & my son at Stourhead.' R.C.H. to the Earl of Ailesbury, 27 July (1794?), TOT. The portrait is inscribed 'R. C. HOARE BART, AETAT XXXVII H. R. HOARE AETAT XI'.
[45] Summary of building accounts, ST.
[46] Lodges at Stourhead built by R.C.H., T(ST) 383.250.
[47] Summary of building accounts.

Chapter 12

Spas and Other Men's Estates

To a large extent the pattern of life which Colt had formed abroad persisted. Part of the year, not usually more than half, he resided at Stourhead.[1] Family life made no demands on him. His son, Henry, who was at boarding school, first at Sunbury and then at Eton, came home for the holidays. Except when he was High Sheriff for Wiltshire in 1805 his only public office was that of magistrate, which meant spending nights away at Salisbury, Wells, or Taunton. For one month or two, between January and April, he stayed in London where he visited his family and dined out every night, although most frequently with Lyttelton, his brother-in-law, or Sir John Leicester, whose friendship he had made in Italy and with whom he continued to be intimate. He was admitted to the Dilettanti in 1792[2] and as a Fellow of the Society of Antiquaries in March of the same year.[3] His brothers Hugh and Charles, and his older friends, Archdeacon Coxe and Sir Abraham Hume, were already Fellows. In February 1794 Colt presented the Society with the first number of *Via Appia Illustrata* which Labruzzi was publishing in Rome with engravings from the original drawings then at Stourhead.[4]

Each spring Colt set off on his travels, within the British Isles perforce.

> The mind and eye which for five successive years had been indulged, could not remain fixed on one spot however captivating. The serious disturbances which prevailed over the continent constrained my rambling thoughts, and confined them within the limits of my native land. The love of drawing, and of picturesque scenery, which most frequently influenced my motions induced me to turn my thoughts towards Wales in the summer of the year 1793.[5]

[1] R.C.H. recorded his movements between 1794 and 1837 in diaries which contain little else but notes of where he was at any time, the people he visited or who visited him. There are some gaps. T(ST) 383.924, 926, 936, 937.

[2] Joan Evans, *A History of the Society of Antiquaries* (Oxford 1956), p. 93 note.

[3] Minutes of the Society of Antiquaries, 16 Feb. 1792, 22 Mar. 1792, Burlington House, London.

[4] Ibid., 20 Feb. 1794.

[5] MS. memoirs, ST.

Many other thwarted travellers also turned in that direction. The number of books on the subject increased enormously between 1790 and 1810.[6] Quantities of unpublished manuscripts besides lie in various archives, among them the journals which Colt Hoare wrote in 1793, 1796, 1797, 1798, 1799, 1801, 1802, 1803, and 1810.[7] There are also his account of the North in 1800 and a book on his Irish tour of 1806 which, Colt said, the travelling accounts of that country being so scarce, and many incorrect, he thought it his duty to contribute. As Farington remarked, it did not do much for him as an author.[8]

With Wales, even before 1790, it was otherwise. Colt's friend H. P. Wyndham published his *Tours in Wales* in 1781, with illustrations by Samuel Hieronymous Grimm. But Colt himself relied more heavily on the work of Thomas Pennant whose Welsh Tours, published in 1778 and 1781, included much historical background of the places he visited. And there were Gilpin's *Observations...relative chiefly to Picturesque Beauty*, especially, in the present context, those on the Wye and South Wales published in 1782.

Conditions in the late eighteenth century favoured intimate exploration; the horse, as an alternative to the chaise, could penetrate where the motor car cannot. Roads, of course, varied; that from Nantwich to Whitchurch 'so bad, so heavy & so sandy';[9] that from Trecastle to Llandovery, 'made in lieu of the old one which traversed a steep and tedious mountain',[10] was excellent. In Yorkshire the roads were very full of loose stones and bad for horses. 'In making them they do not give themselves the trouble of breaking them.'[11] In Pembrokeshire too they were rough and stony.[12] On turnpike roads travel was not too difficult except after heavy rain. Under these conditions it took Colt four and a half hours, in 1801, to get from Llandrindod Wells to Builth.[13] Hilly country always slowed things down, four horses being sometimes necessary, as in the long drag from Dolgellau to Machynlleth, four hours to make eighteen miles.[14]

The character of much of the country, especially the wilder parts of Wales, remains unchanged today; other parts would now be unrecognizable. The approach to Bridgnorth, for instance, was 'over a heath—desolate—a rabbit warren on one side—a gibbet on the other—long winding ascent up to the town—picturesque hovels built in the rocks—fine rich view on the left'.[15] The scene was changing yearly. In 1801, from the top of the Malverns, Colt found the face of the country altered, since his visit five years previously, 'by means of a very extensive enclosure'.[16]

In England there were no monasteries to accommodate him. He could

[6] See bibliography, Esther Moir, *The Discovery of Britain* (1964).
[7] Cardiff Municipal Library, MS. 3.127.
[8] *The Farington Diary*, V, p. 228.
[9] R.C.H., Tours, 1801, Cardiff.
[10] Tours, 1793.
[11] 1801.   [12] 1802.   [13] Ibid.   [14] 1796.   [15] 1801.   [16] Ibid.

perhaps have stayed in private houses, but the independence of an inn, however homely, had charms for him which the stately mansion often failed in affording.[17] His homely standards were quite high; good beds, a private parlour, wine, and post-horses essential. In the absence of all these there were sometimes compensations.

> We found at Buttermere a small inn—What was wanting... was amply made up to us in the cleanliness & civility of the landlords—This little inn is kept by two old people who have now one only daughter left—their sons having followed the Sea Service & there lost their lives—Tourists have proclaimed aloud the beauty & form of the Fair Maid of Buttermere & with justice—for such a form & such a face & such a head of hair, are rarely found, even in more cultivated & civilized spots—her face is truly Graecian—her hair of a fine dark brown—of an extraordinary length—done up with great taste. She reminded me of a fine Italian Beauty, both as to the form of her features & the method of dressing her hair. This little inn furnished one double bedded & one single room & one small parlour—they have no wine. We could procure no straw to litter our horses with. Notwithstanding these inconveniences we spent the night here.[18]

This was a good deal better than Henry Wigstead at Llanymynech, 'accommodated with the state room, which was a cockloft, at the very brink of a step-ladder staircase';[19] or at Ffestiniog, where he mistook the inn for a barn or outhouse. 'Our bedrooms were most miserable, the rain poured in at every tile in the ceiling. The state room was decorated with two tressels, on which was nailed a common garden mat, on which lay a sort of feathered bed. The sheets were literally wringing wet, with much difficulty we had them aired, but we thought it prudent to sacrifice to *Somnus* in our own garments between blankets.'[20] Wigstead distinguished between Snowdonia, where the people were 'almost in a state of simple nature', and South Wales, where the 'landscape evinces the more civilised state of the inhabitants'. Though even near Swansea he complained of a cook with unwiped hands and a child in the dripping pan. 'I devoted my attention to a brown loaf, but on cutting into it, was surprised to find a ball of carroty coloured wool; and to what animal it had belonged, I was at a loss to determine.'[21] Perhaps travelling with Rowlandson had predisposed him to such scenes. Colt made no observations of this kind; but he was probably more careful of his comfort. He had, too, his own laconic classifications. *Magnificent* (the Talbot at Pyle); *very good* or *good*; *tolerable*; *indifferent* (Brecon); *miserable* (St. David's probably); and *wretched*.

[17] 1802.   [18] 1800.
[19] Henry Wigstead, *Tour to North and South Wales* (1800).
[20] Ibid.   [21] Ibid.

The problem of getting to Wales from Wiltshire remained the same until the recent building of the Severn Bridge; whether to face the inconvenience of the ferry at Aust, or circumvent it by Gloucester, Cheltenham or Hereford. In Colt's day there were two ferries, known as the Old and New Passages. James Baker, writing in 1794, said the New Passage

> is so called to distinguish it from the passage of Aust, or Old Passage; the New Passage house on the Gloucestershire side of the Severn, is about ten miles from Bristol, at which place a boat regularly attends to convey to the opposite side, the Welch Mail, and such travellers as go thither for that purpose, by the coach that leaves the Rummer Tavern, near the Exchange, Bristol, about half an hour past one o'clock each day. Such as do not come in the coach, are only admitted into this boat on courtesy. There is besides a common passage boat of larger construction, that attends each day at low water for all descriptions of passengers, to either shore, with their equipages, horses, etc. etc., and is as commodious as most vehicles of its kind.[22]

The Old Passage was shorter, Colt said, but the New much better for embarking carriages; and the small passage boat was recommended as the large was loaded with cattle and horses. The time varied from a 'rough & tedious passage of two hours and a half'[23] to a quarter of an hour. To Gilpin, fortified by the rules of picturesque beauty, circumstances like a delay at the ferry-house could be profitably turned.

> Our windows overlooked the channel, and the Welsh-coast which seen from a higher stand, became now a woody, and beautiful distance. The wind was brisk, and the sun clear; except that, at intervals, it was intercepted by a few floating clouds. The playing lights, which arose from this circumstance, on the opposite coast, were very picturesque. Pursuing each other, they sometimes just caught the tufted tops of the trees; and sometimes gleaming behind shadowy woods, they spread along the vales, till they faded insensibly away.[24]

If he went the other way, Colt usually spent some time in Cheltenham, touring the countryside from there. Lodgings in the High Street cost him 6 guineas a week in 1799, but in 1801 he paid $2\frac{1}{2}$ guineas, and 18 shillings for a cook and housemaid, in a 'quiet retired house in the center of the town'. They were in general very neat and clean; provisions were plentiful and not extravagantly priced. The Spa opened at seven in the morning. There was a Coffee Room, with newspapers, for ladies only at the Bowling

[22] J. Baker, *A Picturesque Guide through Wales and the Marches* (1794).
[23] R.C.H., Tours, 1793.
[24] William Gilpin, *Observations on the River Wye and Several Parts of South Wales* (1782).

Green, which was also open for tea on Sunday and a public breakfast on Thursday. The gentlemen's Coffee Room, with newspapers, was at the Plough; subscription, five shillings for the *Sun*, *Star*, and *Morning Post*. Rooms for cards were open every night. Plays were performed on Tuesday, Thursday, and Saturday; balls took place on Monday and Friday. For the water, ostensible reason for Cheltenham's existence, the usual price was a fee of five shillings a week to the lady who drew it. Baths ended at eleven o'clock at night.[25]

But Colt did not go to Cheltenham for his health as he later went to Bath when crippled with the gout. Nor did he go to Abergavenny because invalids found goat's milk and pure air beneficial, but for salmon fishing and sketching. In fact, the Angel at Abergavenny gave bad attendance, and he stayed at 'a tolerable little inn', the Bear, Crickhowell. Health at Malvern was restored by climbing rather than by springs, and by a view superior to Cleeve. Harrogate, on the contrary, had not one beauty to recommend it.

> It is bleak, exposed & cold—but, I believe, healthy—to those who can bear so sharp an atmosphere—at a very short distance, you feel quite a different climate—it abounds with springs of different qualities—Calybeate, sulphur—and the two united. Fashion, certainly not convenience, has made upper Harrogate the general rendez-vous of the best company—the lower town is objectionable in hot weather from the strong smell of the waters. And perhaps the walk of a mile to the well may be beneficial, tho' as a daily task it is certainly not very pleasant. ...Notwithstanding its long establishment, & the great resort of company, there is neither pump room to shelter the company from the rain or any building over the well to shelter the women who serve the water, of whom one attends from each house to attend their different guests. In bad weather you must either go down in a chaise, or take the water at home—where it loses much of its spirit & good quality, & is infinitely more nauseous —such a composition surely can scarcely be found—except sea water, which I think is still more disgustg.[26]

The supposed advantage must certainly have been offset by overeating. Colt lodged at the Granby, superior in point of company to the Dragon or Queen's Head.

> Our party was small & pleasant. The method of living at these houses is well arranged & comfortable. About eight o'clock the company begin to make their appearance at the well—breakfast about ten—dine at four—tea at seven—supper at ten—retire at eleven. People generally breakfast at separate tables—dine

[25] Tours, 1796.   [26] 1800.

together, the last comer sits at bottom and rises gradually to the top. Each person has his own bottle of wine with his name fixed on a label to it. If you invite a friend you pay for him. The house consists of two large rooms, in one you dine, the other you sit morning and evening. Those who do not take a private parlor have no other place, except their bedroom.[27]

In 1796 he discovered Bala, to which he afterwards returned each year, and took a house (now the Golf Club) overlooking the lake. Bala is on the western point of a triangle whose other points are Chester and Birmingham. To the east of Chester is Knutsford (Mrs. Gaskell's *Cranford*) and near to it Tabley (Pl. 39b), the seat of Colt's friend Leicester, later to play an important part as a patron of Turner and other British artists. Colt stayed there each year on his way from Bala, often during Knutsford races. To the south is Hagley, another call on his return home. Apart from such usual intercourse, visits to other country seats were common, as between equals, to compare and criticize one another's houses, gardens, and collections. Not far off Colt's route to Bala were the estates of Uvedale Price and R. Payne Knight with whose views on landscape Colt was naturally familiar. In 1796, when in Aberystwyth, he noted that 'Mr. Price of Foxley, Herefordshire—author of the Essay on the Picturesque has built a house in the form of a castle, projecting immediately over the rocks near the castle.' The chief beauties of Foxley were, Colt thought, the extensive views, the irregularity of its hills and woods, the different trees and the variety of grouping. Price argued for an aesthetic category, distinct from the sublime and beautiful,[28] which would account for the satisfaction which derived from scenes and objects having none of Burke's attributes. If beauty was characterized by smoothness and gradual variation, what of those painters who used intricate and broken form and colour? How was the appeal of a Gothic building justified? Or Henry Hoare's 'gouty nobbly oakes?'[29] These, rather, were distinguished by their irregularity, roughness, and sudden variation. In landscape the followers of Brown, who had intended to restore nature, had created a new formality of clumps and curves. In practice, therefore, a certain shagginess should be encouraged, either by judicious planting or allowing nature to run wild, to blur distinctions and to make a visual connection between one part and another. Repton, Price, and Knight, the protagonists in the picturesque controversy, were in no deep disagreement over the management of landscape in practice; in fact they had all moved in a similar direction before the argument began, and did not hesitate to approve of one another's work. They all believed that nature should be assisted rather than controlled by

[27] Ibid.
[28] For a full discussion of the theories see W. J. Hipple Jr., *The Beautiful, the Sublime and the Picturesque in Eighteenth-century British Aesthetic Theory* (Carbondale 1957).
[29] See above, p. 62.

art, but that common sense should prevail in the interests of convenience and comfort; what Repton called the principle of *utility*. Thus formality was justified in the immediate vicinity of the house; and garden should be considered as essentially different from landscape. These ideas were expressed in Knight's poem, published in 1794, the same year as Price's *Essay*. The greatest art, Knight wrote,

> ...is aptly to conceal;
> To lead, with secret guile, the prying sight
> To where component parts may best unite,
> And form one beauteous, nicely blended whole,
> To charm the eye and captivate the soul.[30]

On the other hand,

> Oft when I've seen some lonely mansion stand,
> Fresh from th'improvers desolating hand,
> 'Midst shaven lawns, that far around it creep
> In one eternal undulating sweep;
> And scatter'd clumps, that nod at one another,
> Each stiffly waving to its formal brother;
> Tir'd with th' extensive scene, so dull and bare,
> To Heav'n devoutly I've address'd my pray'r—
> Again the moss-grown terraces to raise,
> And spread the labyrinth's perplexing maze;
> Replace in even lines the ductile yew,
> And plant again the ancient avenue.
> Some feature, then, at least we should obtain,
> To make this, flat, insipid, waving plain;
> Some vary'd tints and forms would intervene,
> To break this uniform, eternal green.[31]

These sentiments Colt echoed two days after visiting Payne Knight at Downton when he went to Powis Castle and wrote,

> The gardens were laid out in the foreign style with terrace above terrace, vases, statues, parterres, fishponds etc. the traces only of these remain at present—I regret that the modern taste of gardening has entirely put the old mode of laying out grounds out of countenance—for certainly it has a great dignity of character in it—it will not suit *all* situations but it is the only one fit for Powys Castle, from whence you could descend by no other means into the gardens but by a long flight of steps. This still remains as an approach from beneath the walls overhung with fine ivy...but the gardens & terraces are in a very neglected state.[32]

[30] Richard Payne Knight, *The Landscape* (1794).   [31] Ibid.   [32] Tours, 1799.

And the following year, at Burleigh,

> The Park is very finely wooded with a variety of aged trees of
> all sorts—a particular treat to me after the dreary flat & fenny
> country which I had lately traversed for many miles—there is
> also a fine piece of water, & a handsome bridge over it—from
> this spot looking up the water, the form of it is too serpentine
> in its shape,—& the banks on that side near to the house would
> be improved by planting some trees near them, in order to break
> the uniformity of the lines.—In modern gardening—many
> people wishing to avoid the formal appearance of a straight
> line, have fallen into a worse error—by making their walks &
> water into too serpentine a direction—Nature points out the
> *nearest* way—but then her lines are always sufficiently varied
> and irregular—art too often...falls into the very errors she
> wishes to avoid...the very curves she makes in order to avoid
> formality appear much more studied than a straight line—
> which is certainly the line of nature—in going from one object
> to another.[33]

Payne Knight and Colt Hoare, though perhaps not friends, were
certainly acquainted as fellow Antiquaries and Dilettanti. Knight was eight
years Colt's senior, a tough personality with a considerable intellect, who
did not suffer fools gladly. His *Discourse on the Worship of Priapus*, published in 1786, a treatise on comparative religion before its time, brought
many charges of obscenity and was probably the reason he was blackballed
at the Literary Club in 1795. Colt Hoare, nevertheless, admired this work,
and, as we have seen, followed Knight in his journey to Isernia.[34] Lord
Orford (Horace Walpole) could not stand him. He told Farington in 1796,

> I cannot go to Mr. Payne Knight's to see his antique bronze,
> which I exceedingly admire, because I have abused his literary
> works. I think him as an Author, arrogant and assuming; his
> matter is picked up from others having little originality....His
> dictatorial manner is very offensive, and His placing Goldsmith
> in the rank which He has done is a proof of want of judgment.
> Goldsmith in his *Deserted Village* has some good lines, but his
> argument, that commerce destroys villages, is ridiculous.[35]

The number of references to Knight in Farington's diary is evidence of the
impact which he made, particularly after the publication in 1805 of *An
Analytical Inquiry into the Principles of Taste*. Colt's friend Sir Abraham
Hume thought Knight well-informed but in manner dictatorial. 'When
observations are made upon the subject on which He has spoken, He hears

[33] 1800.   [34] See above, p. 140.
[35] Farington Diary, 24 July 1796.

witht. condescending to answer any objection, but repeats his own opinion.'[36] Lady Oxford found Knight 'very learned, but Mr. Price more elegant and agreeable'.[37] In other respects Knight was considered temperate. Banks spoke of him in 1812 'as being the person who of all others regulated Himself the best so as to have as much indulgence of every appetite as his constitution would bear witht. suffering injury from it. He would eat, He wd. drink as far as consideration for His health wd. admit but would never exceed so as to suffer from it.'[38] All the same, at sixty-seven, he was seen to take five or six eggs at breakfast. Price, on the contrary, 'has not that self command & feels the disadvantage arising from the want of it'.[39]

Downton Castle, designed by Knight after buildings in Claude's pictures,[40] of which he had a valuable collection, was 'Gothic without and Grecian within'. The most conspicuous room, Colt found, was 'an elegant rotundo used as a dining room—fitted with niches supported by columns representing Porphyry—in each nich is a bronze figure holding a light—the cieling (sic) is ornamented with compartments—the whole room is very similar to the Pantheon in my gardens at Stourhead & I have heard that the idea was taken from thence.' However gratifying this might be, Colt did not think the building was 'quite adapted to the Genius of the place... neither an ancient Castle nor a Modern House'.[41] The landscape he approved, and his account can be compared with Thomas Hearne's drawings.

> From the House I descended to a stone bridge over the River Teme—& entering a narrow walk followed its left bank for a mile & a half—till I came to a rude and picturesque wooden bridge thrown across the river:—on this spot the scenery is grand, pleasing & romantic. The rocks on the opposite bank are of a considerable height & perpendicular—the scene is animated by some picturesque cottages & a mill & a waterfall occasioned by a weir—where the water is penned up in the mill—Above the bridge it flows in a clear & tranquil stream—Crossing over the bridge, the Path leads back on more elevated ground above the river—the trees are fine—& the scenery totally different from that on the opposite side. This walk of three miles affords a constant succession of natural beauties—here nature reigns alone—the works of art are scarcely discernible—except in the forming of the walks, which are done with great judgment & the most picturesque Eye.[42]

[36] Ibid., 25 June 1809.   [37] Ibid., 21 June 1806.
[38] Ibid., 22 Oct. 1812.   [39] Ibid.
[40] See N. Pevsner, 'Genesis of the Picturesque', *A.R.*, XCVI, Nov. 1944; and 'Richard Payne Knight', *Art Bulletin*, XXXI, Dec. 1949.
[41] Tours, 1799.   [42] Ibid.

As might be expected, Colt gave particular attention to the management of trees in the landscape. Perhaps he hesitated before so renowned an authority as Knight, but often he was more critical. Hafod, the seat of Knight's kinsman Thomas Johnes, was not to his taste. He thought the beauty of its situation greatly exaggerated when he visited it in 1796, two years before Turner.

> After crossing some of the most dreary & barren mountains imaginable, you enter a valley apparently well wooded at a distance, but on nearer inspection all the trees have been distorted and blasted by the effect of sea breeze—at the bottom of this vale runs the river Ystwyth, a mountain torrent—furious in winter—but in summer presenting a spacious bed of stones, & but a moderate stream. . . . The house is of a singular and not an elegant species of Gothic architecture—one room fitted up with very fine Gobelin Tapestry—the library circular in its form with a Gallery supported by marble columns of the ancient Doric order without vases—the proportions *much too heavy*. . . .[43] The house is certainly not very advantageously placed—facing a barren mountain—nor do I think (owing to the small extent of this woody valley) could it have been placed so as to have had the barrenness of the adjoining country totally concealed— The largest trees are sycamore—which I have always thought the hardiest of all trees.[44]

Later on he did modify this rather sour impression by saying that 'the rich groves of Havod' were some compensation for the many tedious miles he had crept over rough and dirty roads.[45] Apart from those estates already mentioned, Hafod (1796), Downton and Powys (1799), Burleigh (1800), and Foxley (1802), Colt visited others, mainly in the north and west of England. His more interesting comments are on Chirk Castle in 1798; Belvoir, Plumpton, Rydal, and Studley in 1800; Corsham and Hawkstone (Shropshire) in 1801. He was of course familiar with his brother-in-law's estate at Killerton; and Luscombe, where Nash and Repton worked for his brother Charles about this time.

In 1806 Farington described, from another point of view, Colt's visit to his neighbour, Beckford, who was then being ostracized by all the local gentry for supposed moral aberration. The account was given by Jeffrey Wyatt, nephew of the architect of Fonthill Abbey.

> Jeffrey sd. that about 4 months ago He (Jeffrey) was at Fonthill & saw the Abbey which is so strictly forbidden to be shewn that His Uncle, who was then there, could not undertake to shew it to Him. He therefore threw Himself in the way of Mr. Beckford

[43] 1796.   [44] Ibid.   [45] 1802.

who asked him to go to the Abbey where He dined & staid the night. . . . Not long since Sir Richard Hoare of Stourhead applied to Mr. Beckford to see *the Abbey* (Pl. 54b) which Mr. B. granted and attended Sir Richard when He came for that purpose. These civilities which passed between them were reported to the neighbouring gentlemen who took such umbrage at it, as concerning that Sir Richard was giving countenance to Mr. Beckford that a gentleman wrote to Sir Richard in His own name & in that of others to demand of Him an explanation of that proceeding as they meant to regulate *themselves towards Him accordingly.* Sir Richard applied to His friend the Marquiss of Bath upon it, & represented that He had no further desire but to see the Abbey & the meeting with Mr. Beckford was accidental.[46]

Colt said he thought Beckford was not at home and was surprised to find him at breakfast. 'Jeffrey said that he concluded Mr. Beckford had heard something of what had passed, as at breakfast He said before Jeffrey "He wondered how He could be such a d. . . .d fool as to allow Sir Richard to see the Abbey." . . . Mr. Beckford sd. that Sir Richard Hoare while looking over the Abbey made some good observations but He afterward sd. "Sir Richard had no taste".'[47]

[46] Farington Diary, 16 Oct. 1806.
[47] Ibid.

litcroft, Temple of Flora, *c.* 1745

2a. Earlom after Claude Lorrain, *Landscape with Egeria*

2b. Claude Lorrain, *Aeneas at Delos*

ake with Flitcroft's Pantheon, *c.* 1754

4a. Temple from Wood's *Ruins of Balbec* (1757)

4b. Vasi after Richard Wilson, *Temple of Clitumnus*

R. Wilson disegnò *Veduta del Tempio, e Fiume del Clitunno nello stato presente* *Giuseppe Vasi intagliò*

5. Flitcroft, Temple of Apollo, 1765, with view of Temple of Flora

6a. View of Stourton Church and Stone Bridge from Grotto

6b. The Pantheon, *c.* 1754 and Gothic Cottage, *c.* 1806

J. Cheere, attributed to, *Sleeping Nymph*

J. Cheere, *River God*, 1751

7c. Rysbrack, *Hercules*, 1756

8a. Stone Bridge after Palladio, 1762

8b. Bristol Cross 1373; Stourhead 1765

8c. Flitcroft, Alfred's Tower, 1772

9a. Map of Stourton 1722

9b. Map of Stourton 1785

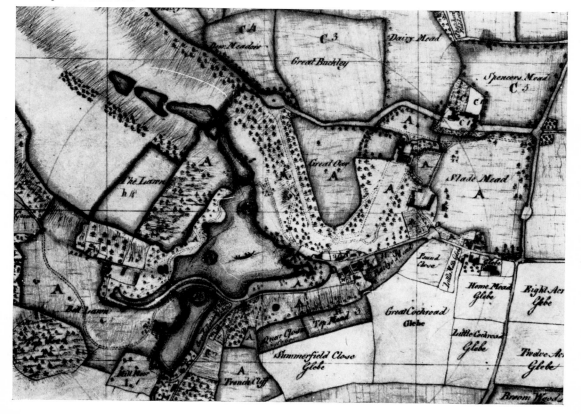

10a. Bampfylde, *Panoramic sketch with Pantheon, Grotto, Wooden Bridge and Obelisk*, c. 1770

10b. Bampfylde, *Sketch with Temple of Flora, Cross, Stone Bridge, Church and Temple of Apollo*, c. 1770

10c. Bampfylde, *Sketch with Grotto, Wooden Bridge, Obelisk, Temple of Flora, Gothic Greenhouse and Stone Bridge*, c. 1770

11a. Piper, *View from Chinese Umbrella*, 1779

11b. Piper, *View from Hermitage*, 1779

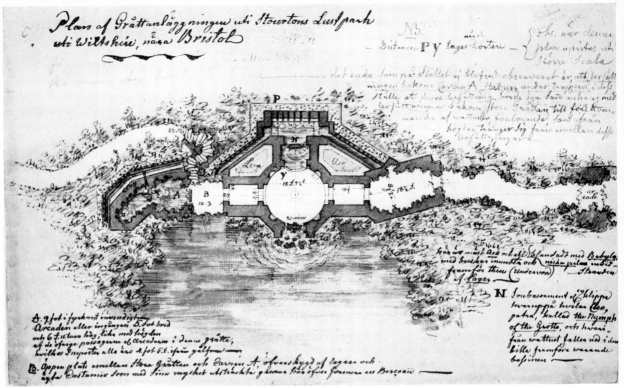

12a. Piper, *Plan of Grotto*, 1779

12b. Piper, *Section of Grotto*, 1779

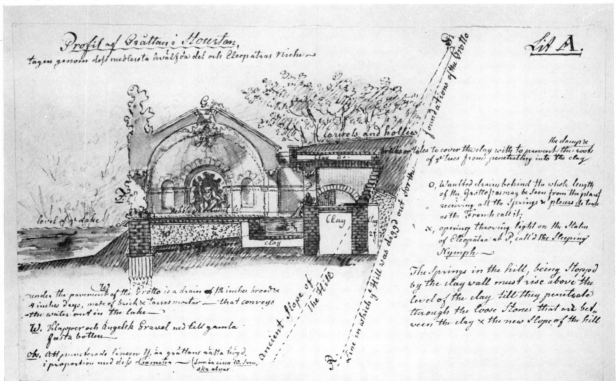

13a. Piper, *Hermitage, plan and section*, 1779

13b. Piper, *Temple on Terrace*, 1779

14a. Campbell, *Stourhead House*, east elevation

14b. Campbell, *Stourhead House*, south elevation

15a. Nicholson, *Stourhead House, c.* 1813

15b. Stourhead House from the north-east

16a. Turner, *At Stourhead*, *c.* 1800

16b. Constable, *Stourhead*, 1811

17a. Nicholson, *Lake from the Cross*

17b. Nicholson, *Lake from the Dam*

18a. Nicholson, *Temple of Flora*

18b. Nicholson, *Interior of the Grotto*

19a. Nicholson, *The Pantheon and Gothic Cottage*

19b. Nicholson, *Temple of Apollo*

20a. Nicholson, *View of Alfred's Tower*

20b. Nicholson, *The Convent*

21b. Dahl, *Henry Hoare I*, d. 1725

21a. Richardson, *Sir Richard Hoare*, d. 1718

22b. William Hoare, attributed to, *Henry Hoare II*

22a. Dahl and Wootton, *Henry Hoare II*, d. 1785

23b. Cotes, *Sir Richard Hoare, father of Colt Hoare*

23a. Wootton, *Henry Hoare II and Benjamin Hoare with hounds*

24a. Cotes, *Anne Hoare*, daughter of Henry Hoare II, mother of Colt Hoare

25b. Woodforde, *Hester Hoare, wife of Richard Colt Hoare*

25a. Prince Hoare, attributed to, *Richard Colt Hoare as a young man*

26. Carpenter, *Henry Hoare*, d. 1836, son of Richard Colt Hoare

27. Mengs, *Octavius and Cleopatra*

28b. Cigoli, *Adoration of the Kings*

28a. Maratta, *Apollo and the Marchese Pallavicini*

29a. Turner, *Lake Avernus with Aeneas and the Cumaean Sibyl*

29b. Colt Hoare, *Lake Avernus*

30a. Colt Hoare, *Isernia*

30b. J. R. Cozens, *Pays de Valais*

a. Ducros, *Falls of the Velino*

b. Ducros, *Tivoli*

32a. Ducros, *Storm in the Nera Valley*

32b. Nicholson after de Loutherbourg, *Avalanche*

33a. Colt Hoare, *Etruscan Structure near Cortona*

33b. Colt Hoare, *The Marino at Palermo*

34. Nicholson after Colt Hoare, *The Crater of Etna*

35. The library

36a. Chippendale, chair and sofa-table, *c.* 1802

36b. Chippendale, armchair and bookstand for music, *c.* 1812

hippendale, library chair and desk, *c.* 1805, with model of *Hercules* by Rysbrack

38a. Nicholson, *Storm by land*

38b. Grimm, *Llanthony Abbey*

39a. Turner, *Kilgarran Castle, hazy sunrise*

39b. Turner, *Tabley, windy day*

40. Ducros, *Falls of the Villa Maecenas, Tivoli*

41. Turner, *Ewenny Priory*

42a. Turner, *Salisbury Cathedral, West Front*

42b. Turner, *Salisbury Cathedral, South View*

Turner, *Salisbury Cathedral from the Cloister*

44. Turner, *Transept of Salisbury Cathedral*

45b. Turner, *Entrance to the Chapter House, Salisbury Cathedral*

45a. Turner, *Lady Chapel of Salisbury Cathedral, from the Choir*

46. Thomson, *Distress by land*

7. Jones, *The Bard*

Woodforde, *William Cunnington*

48b. Edridge, *Sir Richard Colt Hoare*

48c. Crocker, *Cunnington and Colt Hoare barrow-digging*

Group of Barrows, South of Stone Henge.

49a. The Wansdyke, looking east from Morgan's Hill

49b. White Sheet Down, Neolithic causewayed enclosure and other antiquities

a. Marlborough Downs near Barbury Castle

b. Barbury Castle

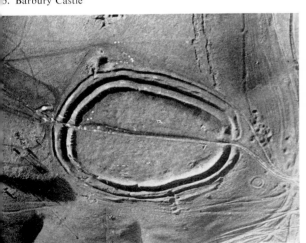

50c. Barbury Castle, engraving from *Ancient Wiltshire*

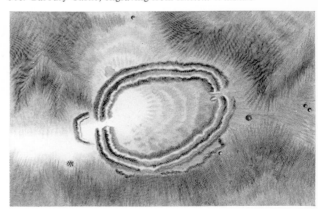

51a. The Stonehenge Urn

51b. Ground Plan of a British Village on Steeple Langford Down, surveyed A.D. 1822. From Hoare's *Modern Wiltshire*, "Hundred of Branch and Dole"

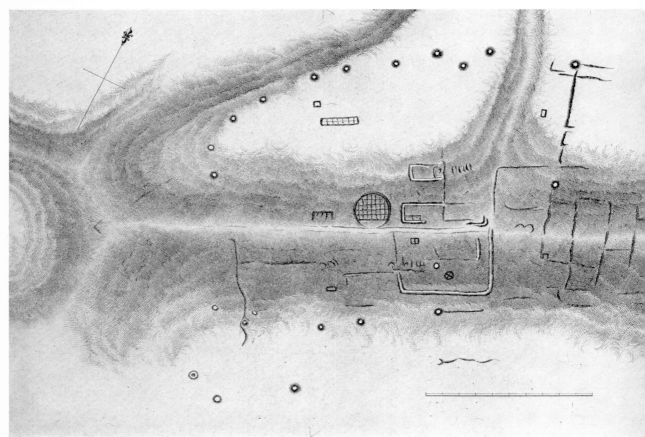

O. G. S. Crawford, Aerial photograph, SU 037395

The discovery of these earthworks, too late for inclusion in *Ancient Wiltshire*, was attributed by Colt Hoare to the Rev. Mr. Seagram of Steeple Langford. The plan shows "pillow mounds" and other mounds of unusual shape overlying "Celtic" fields. Colt Hoare, considering the possibility that they were barrows, could not account for them, as not one "contained a single interment" and they were "ranged in a more regular line than usual". O. G. S. Crawford suggests they may have been connected with Yarnbury Fair, though elsewhere he suggested that "pillow mounds"

as a class were associated with rabbit farming. In 1810 John Parker reported a British Village between Yarnbury Camp and Stapleford (Letters, R.C.H. 88). If this is the site in question he did not get the credit. There is, however, another site to which Colt Hoare refers. "At a short distance from this village, to the east, is another decided British settlement, in which our spade brought to light the usual indicia of ancient residence in excavations, pottery, coins etc." (*Modern Wiltshire*, "Hundred of Branch and Dole", page 171.)

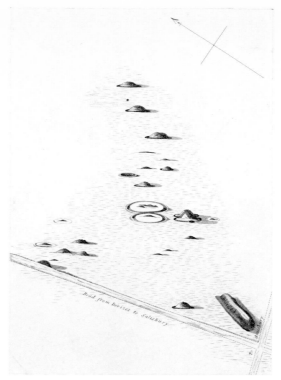

53a. Group of Barrows on Winterbourne Stoke Down. From Hoare's *Ancient Wiltshire*

Basire's engraving after Crocker of this well-known group near Stonehenge shows examples of Hoare's long, bowl, bell, Druid and pond barrows.

53b. Group of barrows at Winterbourne Stoke Crossroads

54a. Buckler, *Fonthill Splendens*

54b. Buckler, *Fonthill Abbey*

55. Buckler, *Fonthill Ruins*

Salvaging the Middle Ages

The Vale of Llangollen is still recognizable as the place Colt knew when driving to and from Bala each year; and it is perhaps a consequence of the love of scenery which men of taste professed that much of what they admired has been preserved. The state of our industrial cities is also, possibly, a consequence of their neglect. 'Birmingham', said Henry Wigstead in 1797, 'by no means prepossesses the traveller in its favour... a confused mass of brick and tile rubbish piled together, enveloped in an almost impenetrable smoky atmosphere, is by no means an agreeable object to a picturesque eye....It is computed to contain 80,000 inhabitants, and 13,000 houses, and is, perhaps, the greatest manufactory for hardware in the universe.'[1] And Colt: 'For one whose taste & pursuits do not lead him to examine into the Mechanism & state of Manufactures, Leeds is an uninteresting town.'[2] Nevertheless the signs of prosperity were impressive and his curiosity overcame distaste. There were estimated to be 3240 broadcloth manufacturers, 'generally men of small capital...dispersed in villages & houses over the whole face of the country—not a single Manufacturer is to be found more than one mile East or two miles North of Leeds'.[3] The road from Bradford to Halifax was very bad and hilly, necessitating four post horses; but on either side were finely cultivated dales and great population. 'In this short stage I saw *more pretty faces*, than in *all* my preceeding tour—fair complexions & a general appearance of good health.'[4] And approaching Halifax along a ridge, with a bird's eye view of the town beneath, 'a most rich & gratifying scene of Commerce, Riches & Cultivations'. He found much to admire there, especially the Piece Hall, 'such a building as does not find its equal in England'.[5] The situation of the town reminded him of Bath, 'the same color'd stone—hills around it—fine valley—not the seat of luxury & dissipation—but of Industry & Commerce—& in this respect widely different'.[6] Rochdale was 'a nasty town, built of brick & rendered more unpleasant to me from being

[1] Wigstead, op. cit.
[2] R.C.H., Tours, 1800.
[3] Ibid.   [4] Ibid.
[5] 1800.   [6] Ibid.

a Market day. In many places in the North, the traveller finds much inconvenience on these days—he finds the inns full—people busy—& his wants unsupplied.'[7] The road to Manchester was 'too much peopled to be picturesque'. Manchester was very populous, had many good streets and a handsome square, but it could afford little amusement to those who had not a turn for 'Mechanics & the Minutiae of Manufactories'.

> I wished however to see some of the processes, two of which appeared to me remarkably curious—the passing the velvets—callicoes & even muslins & the finest silk handkerchiefs over a red hot cylinder to give them a gloss, & take off the rough outside nap—the other, cutting the ribbs in velvet, plush, corderoy etc—which is performed by a long narrow instrument resembling a sword & performed with the greatest rapidity & dexterity. The cylinders made use of are of cast iron, semicircular & hollow within—in which part they are heated, & kept constantly hot—one of these will last about a week—this is one of the most curious operations I ever beheld—& many who did not see it, would disbelieve it.[8]

The Bridgewater Arms boasted 120 good beds, but Colt complained of bad attendance, uncleanliness and such a noise and bustle of people continually running up and downstairs during the night that sleep was effectually prevented.

> I have in general found large Manufacturing towns the most unpleasant halting places—you find less attention—less urbanity of manners.—Self interest & business occupy the minds of the inhabitants & prevent that polish which the inhabitants of other towns, where dissipation takes the lead of trade, more frequently have in their manners—but, however more unpleasant these towns may be (to) the tourist who travels for his amusement—the country profits—and, as a well wisher to the interest of my Country, I by no means wish to see the honest blunt Tradesman transformed into the modern Fine Gentleman.[9]

Fortunately for Colt industrial scenes, especially in Wales, were infrequent. Cardiff was 'large & neat & rendered more interesting to the inquisitive Traveller by the remains of British Antiquity which it contains.'[10] Neath, although 'a populous & commercial town with iron, copper, tin & coal works', was 'seated in an extensive vale & surrounded by well wooded hills & mountains'.[11] There were also scenes which industry enhanced, such as Amlwch in Anglesey where 'what most strikes the eye is the very singular color of the rocks adjoining the port, which assume the most

[7] Ibid. [8] Ibid. [9] Ibid.
[10] 1802. [11] Ibid.

beautiful tints, from the brightest orange color to the most delicate pale yellow—this singularity arises from the adjoining copper mines'.[12] These, Colt thought, were one of the most beautiful sights he ever saw, although he noted that the men employed in such unhealthy occupation, exposed to pernicious fumes, suffocating heat and draughts of cold air, received only 16 pence for a 12 hour day.

The salt mines of Northwich,[13] belonging to his friend Leicester, were also a sight hardly to be surpassed. The caves of rock salt, resembling brown and white sugar candy, mixed occasionally with specimens of a fine red colour, were broken at intervals by massive columns, left to support the roof, and illuminated with some hundred lights. Even if a man of taste had directed the work he could not have produced more picturesque forms.

By contrast all manufacturing towns, especially those in the iron trade like Brecon and Coalbrookedale, had a 'dirty and dreary appearance', however beautiful their natural situation might be. At Coalbrookedale there still remained much to admire in the hanging woods and shady well kept walks of Mr. Reynolds, where retirement and solitude were interrupted only by repeated strokes of the hammers in the furnace beneath, and even the roaring explosions of the Cannon Factory produced a fine effect. But the beauty of the vales was certainly much injured by the great population, extensive iron works, and other manufactories. The Iron Bridge was not, in Colt's opinion, a picturesque object as it was wanting in solidity.

> The whole scenery is also (in point of beauty) much diminished by the brick buildings which are general—I have always had the greatest aversion to them, & particularly when viewed in a picturesque light—they admit of no variety of tints, no effects of light or shade—& have therefore a dull & heavy appearance —N.B. Painting the window & doorcases green—with the addition of blinds of the same color—tends to give them a better effect—by releiving (sic) the eye from the heavy mass of dull red. Cover them with a wash of a soft cream color—retaining the green windows etc. & they become at once cheerful & pleasing objects.[14]

For Colt at any rate, scenery had to be enjoyed in solitude, free from signs of industrial activity. Relative solitude; a comfortable inn did not detract from its appeal. The Hafod Arms at Devil's Bridge, in point of situation, stood unrivalled perhaps with any in Europe. The scenery round there was 'very grand & truly Alpine',[15] Colt's highest praise, for he had exhausted all his Rousseauesque superlatives in Switzerland. Barren moors and woodless bogs he endured getting from one place to another, but he

[12] 1801.   [13] 1800.   [14] 1801.   [15] 1802.

did not seek them out, except to find a lake in which to fish. Llyn Conwy, for instance, which was 'full of trout which are red, firm and good'. 'The distance to this pool from Yspythy is (as near as I can guess) about five miles—& the nearest place from which it is accessible—but the accommodations here are so indifferent—that no one but a great Lover of Flyfishing, would put up with them for the chance of sport so very variable & uncertain.'[16] Colt took his rod everywhere and fished any convenient lake and some inconvenient. With luck he got scenery and fish, but sometimes a strenuous ride went unrewarded, as at Llyn Cwmorthin where 'the mountains slope regularly down—without any of those abrupt & perpendicular rocks which render several of these mountain lakes so striking,...it is full of trout which rise freely at a fly—& are also caught with a worm— they are white, soft & bad'.[17]

It was on his way back from Llyn Conwy to Bala that he met with hundreds of Methodists[18] returning from an annual meeting. He came across them again at Beaumaris eight days later, when he found the town crowded with them and their followers. 'The first sight was a preacher elevated on a stage on the green near the sea—preaching sub dio to two or three thousand people, & ranting away his prose extempore as readily as an Italian Improvisatore would his verse: fortunately I got a bed & good sitting room at the Bull Inn—I would recommend to every Traveller who consults comfort & quiet during his tour in the principality, to avoid *Fairs* & *Methodist* Meetings, particularly the *latter*—when every private & public bed is engaged.'[19]

Colt's notion of religion, as we know, was allied to solitude and scenery. The site of a monastery not only satisfied his sense of picturesque beauty, but stirred vague thoughts of an existence which escaped him. He never failed to turn aside and visit one and to note, as at Valle Crucis, 'A little rapid brook runs near it—it is backed by a lofty mountain coverd with fine wood—& the situation is such as the monks generally selected for their habitations—who in this respect at least knew how to mix the *utile* with the *dulce*—a good soil, fine water—& a shelterd & secluded spot.'[20] To Llanthony he returned more than once reporting with regret its gradual dilapidation. The first time was the 26 June 1793, when he wrote:

This day I spent amongst the ruins of Llanthony Abbey (Pl. 38b) —the road I went (on horseback) is calculated at eight miles [from Crickhowell], but the badness of it heightened the distance considerably—indeed this noble ruin is accessible only with difficulty....This abbey is still magnificent even in its ruins, though daily decaying from the neglect of its owner—it presents a mixture of Norman and Gothic Architecture—the lower arches of the latter—the upper of the former order. The West

[16] 1801.   [17] Ibid.   [18] Ibid.   [19] Ibid.   [20] 1797.

Front is tolerably perfect, as well as the inside of the Nave—Aisles etc. The Eastern & Western fronts varied in their architecture—the former was decorated with one large Gothic window: the latter with three smaller—with great regret I heard (that) the beautiful arch of the Eastern Front had fallen last year: of which a very exact view by Grimm, together with an inside view of the nave etc. has been given by Mr. Wyndham in his Tour through Wales.—Few ruins present themselves in a more striking manner to the Eye, chiefly owing to their isolated situation, where all the surrounding objects appear characteristic of the building to its original destination. There is nothing but a miserable little Ale House—where the Traveller who is not over nice may eat his cold meat within view of the ruins—or if he wishes to be better accommodated, he may use his endevors to prevail on the farmer to receive him into his house, which is annexed to the Abbey.[21]

Five years later:

After breakfast, went to Llanthony Abbey—turned off to the left by the side of an old decayed oak—road narrow & bad—I had visited the ruins three times before—& viewed them again with fresh pleasure—they owe their beauty to a variety of causes & effects. In the first place, no natural situation can be more appropriate to the holy institution formerly established there, surrounded by fine mountains—a rich cultivated (vale) water'd by a limpid stream—the Religio Loci—The architecture is grand & simple; the breadth & massive appearance of the tower has a good effect—rising in the midst of the vale, & relieved by the mountains in the background—The fine mellow yellow tints with which the grey stone is tinged, add much to the general effect of the building—many parts of it disjointed by trees & other plants growing in the fissures between the stones threaten a speedy dissolution. I must own they received in my eyes an additional good effect by not being coverd with ivy as the ruins in Wales generally are—I approve of ivy when it hides deformities —not when it conceals beauties—

We dined at the door of a little public house in full view of the ruins—on a cold collation we had brought with us—a necessary precaution for every traveller—as nothing can be procured in this remote & solitary spot.[22]

Colt's last record is dated 17 May 1803:

Visited once more & probably for the last time the ruins of Llanthony Abbey, which are now alas approaching rapidly to

[21] 1793.   [22] 1798.

dissolution. I was informed that last year a part of one of the fine Gothic windows in the western front had given way—and now I had the sad mortification to find that all these three windows—(by far the most elegant part of the whole window) had in the course of the preceding winter fallen to the ground— the Saxon Tower, I fear, from the present unconnected state of the stones which compose its masonry, will soon follow the same fate—It is a melancholy sight to the traveller who frequently revisits the same ground and objects of Antiquity, to witness the progressive ruin of these fine specimens of ancient architecture.[23]

Colt had visited Margam the year before, warned of the change it had undergone.

That chef d'oevre of elegant Gothic Architecture is now alas! no more! and every passing traveller will weep over the sad relicts. . . . In the year 1793 its dissolution had commenced but even then, with a little care and trifling expense it might have been sav'd from the ruin which daily impended over it—two of the arches had only then fallen—the central column which supported the roof still stood firm: & the remaining groins & arches would have been a sure and easy guide to any workman who might have undertaken its reparation—but *that* happy moment passed by—the central column gave way & with it the whole roof fell in—so that nothing but the shell or skeleton of this *unique morceau* now remains.[24]

In the itinerary on the fly-leaf of his South Wales sketchbook the young Turner noted, opposite *Margam*, 'Part of the Chapter House fallen since 1795'.[25] 'How often has the possession of this beautiful ruin been envied?' wrote Colt, ' & how little care would have preserved it for many more centuries in its original state of perfection—Hundreds & perhaps thousands have been spent on the same ground in conservatories & greenhouses.'[26]

It was the Antiquaries, confined within their island, who turned their attention to the discovery and preservation of the English past. Part of this interest was directed to the primitive, as in Douglas's *Nenia Britannica or Sepulchral History of Great Britain*, etc. Druids, who had been a preoccupation for so long, still lingered in Colt's imagination at St. David's Head in 1793 where

on the western point, where the land contracts itself into a very narrow point, and is on three sides surrounded by a deep precipice of perpendicular Rocks, is a druidical Monument differing

[23] 1803.   [24] 1802.
[25] *Complete Inventory of the Drawings of the Turner Bequest*, 2 vols. (Stationery Office, 1909), XXVI.
[26] Tours, 1802.

from any I have yet seen. It consists of six distinct circles of no very large dimensions, with stones set around them, most of which are now displaced—I have seen a similar Druidical relict described in Rowlands's account of Anglesey—a triple wall surrounded them on the only side by which they were accessible —on the outside of this wall is an altar or cromlech similar to those before described near Newport & Nevern, but smaller than either of them; the broad Stone at the top has fallen from its original position, and rests only on one small one beneath & this, like all the others I have seen, points in its narrowest part towards the North. No place could ever be more suited to retirement, contemplation or Druidical mysteries: surrounded by inaccessible rocks—open to a wide expanse of Ocean, nothing seems wanting but the thick impenetrable groves of oak, which have generally been thought concomitant to places of Druidical worship, and which, from the exposed nature of this situation, could never, I think, have existed here even in former days.[27]

Objectivity could not overcome the disposition to see in the rocks 'the most perfect profile of a venerable old head—such as I could have fancied a Druid's character'.[28] In 1800 he reluctantly dismissed the claims of Hayman Rooke and others that Brimham Rocks in Yorkshire were idols, dolmens and oracular stones fashioned by the Druids. 'Prejudiced as I was in favour of their system, and anxious by wishing to find evident existing proofs of it—I could not, on the partial survey I took of these rocks, attribute their formation to any hand but that of Nature.'[29]

The main interest of the Antiquaries lay, however, in mediaeval church architecture, still crudely classified as Saxon, Norman, or Gothic, with the first two styles generally confused. J. Rickman's *Attempt to discriminate the Styles of English Architecture* did not appear until 1819. The English past had been the subject of extensive studies during the seventeenth century, and the records published. William Dugdale's *Monastici Anglicani* was translated in 1718, with supplements in 1722 and 1723; enlarged editions of Thomas Tanner's *Notitia Monastica or An Account of all the Abbies, Priories and Houses of Friars heretofore in England and Wales* were issued in 1744 and 1787. Nevertheless after 1730, mediaeval studies had been neglected for a variety of reasons; and, as we have seen from the story of the Bristol Cross, Gothic monuments were popularly regarded with disfavour. In 1736 Sir John Clerk[30] thought them 'only the degeneracy of Greek and Roman Arts and Sciences'; by 1768 Richard Gough[31] regretted 'the little regard hitherto paid to Gothic Architecture of which so many beautiful models are daily crumbling to pieces before our eyes'.[32] Gough

[27] 1793.   [28] Ibid.   [29] 1800.
[30] Sir John Clerk of Penicuik, 1684–1755, Scottish Antiquary.
[31] Richard Gough, 1735–1809.   [32] Quoted by Joan Evans, op. cit.

was Director of the Society of Antiquaries from 1771 to 1798. His *Sepulchral Monuments of Great Britain*, published between 1786 and 1796, reflected the genealogical orientation of the interest in parish churches. Colt examined those of almost all the places he visited, noting in detail the monuments they contained and little else besides, although he did say of Peterborough, 'However destitute of monuments & inscriptions the inside of this building may be—its beautiful architecture will ever command the attention of the curious traveller.'[33]

It is clear that not only the abandoned abbeys were in disrepair. Skenfrith church, in Monmouthshire, Colt found 'in a most shameful state of neglect & almost ruin'.[34] Llandevi Brevi, in Cardiganshire, was more like a ruin than a building still appropriated to the Service of God. 'Four lofty Gothic arches supporting a massive square steeple bespeak its ancient grandeur: the South Aisle only remains, divided from the nave by three arches supported on octagon pillars. . . . The appearance of this once celebrated Sanctuary is really melancholy—no pavement—but the plain earth—no ceiling—but the rafters & beams as in a barn—which it certainly ressembles more than a church.'[35]

But some attempts at restoration were also unnacceptable.

> The love of innovation, and the bad taste, or perhaps I might better say ignorance of the most intelligent of our Architects, have robbed many of our Churches and Cathedrals of their original beauties—during my various excursions, it has been my misfortune to witness the many absurdities which have been committed in the *modern* repairs of our Cathedrals—& which is now called *beautifying*. It is singular, that Architects, having the finest examples of pure Saxon & Gothic architecture dispersed throughout the Kingdom, from which they might improve or rather form their taste, should put rules at defiance, and produce such a motley unmeaning farrago of Architecture as I have seen frequently collected in the modern production of their Art.[36]

John Wood's additions at Llandaff he thought 'beneath criticism'. 'An Italian building rears itself within the walls of a Gothic shell—nothing can be more discordant or ridiculous.'[37] Likewise at St. David's: 'The *old* West front was much admired for its Saxon workmanship—but the *modern* one, like the adjoining Chapter house, is beneath criticism. Such an heterogeneous mixture of Saxon Gothic and castelled architecture I never before beheld.'[38] He added a note: 'The architect was Mr. Nash—then a young man—now much improved in his art as an architect.'

These remarks are echoes of a dispute about Wyatt's restorations which

[33] Tours, 1800. [34] 1798. [35] 1802.
[36] Ibid. [37] Ibid. [38] Ibid.

had raged among the Antiquaries for ten years previously.[39] The spearhead of the preservationist attack was John Carter, the architectural draughtsman, to whom Colt probably paid more altogether than to any other artist.

Carter, the son of a stone-carver, was born in 1748. His father dying when he was fifteen, he got employment with a surveyor and mason, and about the same time made drawings of the ruined Herald's Tower at Windsor. During the 1770s he was said to be supervising some building work for Wyatt; but although he made designs for the Sessions House on Clerkenwell Green, Alms-houses erected at Wrotham in Kent, and for the Great West Window at Exeter Cathedral, executed by Coade under Soane, his career developed mainly as a draughtsman and illustrator, particularly of mediaeval church architecture. The writer of an obituary in *The Gentleman's Magazine* said: 'His education was very inferior even to what, in the time he was educated, might have been given to qualify him for those pursuits in which he subsequently engaged. He knew no language but his own, and never could read or explain any inscription or epitaph that was not written in English. This threw him into a very unpleasant state of dependence in his subsequent pursuits, and was the cause of much uneasiness to him in the course of his life.'[40] This was why, on the title page of his work *Specimens of the Antient Sculpture and Painting now remaining in this Kingdom*, he stated that some of the descriptions were by 'Gentlemen of Leterary (sic) abilities, and well versed in the Antiquities of this Kingdom'. The dedication was to Horace Walpole. Richard Gough thought highly of Carter's abilities, and some of his drawings were included in the *Sepulchral Monuments*. In 1780 Carter was employed by the Society of Antiquaries, of which he became a Fellow in 1795. He was the only one, except John Buckler, to appear on the list as 'Mr' not 'Esquire', a courtesy which was only extended to professional artists who were also Royal Academicians. Carter was described as 'frugal even to parsimony, and very temperate...tall and thin...capable of enduring privations and hardships which many men would have sunk beneath'.[41] His principles were sound; his integrity incorruptible; his manners reserved; his temper irascible; his resolution sometimes bordering on obstinacy.[42] From 1798 to 1817 he contributed articles to *The Gentleman's Magazine* under the title 'Pursuits of Architectural Innovation'. In his chosen cause, the inviolacy of ancient fabrics, he gave no quarter and expected none. He was not intimidated by threats or diverted by ridicule. Nor, if he were mistaken, could he usually be persuaded to change his opinions. It was in 1795 that he joined in the attacks on Wyatt for his ruthless restorations at Salisbury and Durham. Carter had been employed at the latter place, making drawings for the Antiquaries, and when he exhibited his sketches to the Society

[39] Details of this dispute are given by Joan Evans, op. cit.
[40] *The Gentleman's Magazine*, Mar. 1818.
[41] Ibid., Oct. 1817.   [42] Ibid.

on 20 November he remarked on the drastic alterations Wyatt was making and suggested that an appeal should be made in high places 'to stay in time this innovating Rage and prevent interested persons from effacing the still remaining unaltered Traits of our Ancient Magnificence which are but faintly to be imitated and perhaps never to be equalled'.[43]

Wyatt presented himself as a candidate for election to the Antiquaries in 1797. He was blackballed. But factions had arisen pro and con, Gough, the Director, supporting Carter against Wyatt. Among other strictures, Carter accused Wyatt of intending to destroy the twelfth century Galilee, a Lady Chapel placed unusually at the West entrance, in order to make a walk round the cathedral. Wyatt said he only proposed a partial demolition and rebuilding; to which Carter replied that the East End of the Chapter House had been pulled down and that even supposing it had undergone but little alteration it was not now the original Chapter House of Durham Cathedral and that 'the long Train of historic Ideas which lately filled the minds of the Beholders, are now no more'.[44] He added, for good measure, that such buildings were memorials to those whose heroic courage in defence of their King and Country could not fail to excite emulation in their posterity at a time when invasion was threatening. Later in the year, when Wyatt again presented himself he was elected. Gough, taking it as a personal defeat for his defence of Carter, resigned as Director.

Where Colt Hoare stood in all this is evident from his subsequent patronage of Carter, who, between 1799 and 1807, received £781[45] for drawings made mainly in South Wales. Carter continued to work for Colt after this date, and in 1808, prickly as ever, wrote, 'I waited on Ld. Milford this day, but he did not want to see me; sent word down for me to leave the drawings which I could not do, as most people when examining drawings handle them with the same indifference as they do a news-paper. Perhaps Sr. Rd. My lord will call on me, or send for me in a day or two.'[46]

Colt also gave specific views on the restoration of Durham when he went there in 1800.

> I have as yet seen no building of such grand & perfect Saxon architecture—much however of its effect is lost, by the modern alterations & improvements (as the Bishop & his Architect Mr. Wyatt would wish them to be called)—I wish I could think them so—repairs, if necessary, should certainly be *done*—but not in the manner they are *here* done—In entering these grand Gothic Structures—the mind should be impressed with a religious awe suited to the place—here no such effect—no fine mellow tints— on the columns no effect of light & shade—no relief to the Eye—

---

43 Quoted Evans, op. cit.
44 Ibid.
45 Statement of account, T(ST) 383.4.
46 John Carter to R.C.H., T(ST) 383.4.

one general glare—one general *yellow wash* has been unmerci-
fully placed over the walls cieling & every part of this reverend
building—Even the marble monuments have not been spared—
for the two Tombs of the Nevilles have been equally daubed
over—This puts me in mind—when at Milan—going to see the
celebrated fresco Painting of Leonardo da Vinci in the Refectory
of a Convent—which, in cleaning up the Convent, had been
covered with whitewash—but luckily for the lovers of the fine
arts has been since uncovered. The same bad taste in both cases
—In many things the *lucidus ordo* may be pleasing—but I shall
never think it applicable to an old Cathedral like that at Durham
—Neither do I approve of the scraping system without—if stones
are wanting, they might be replaced, and if they did not soon
gain the color of the old—they could never look half so bad—
as the new in toto. . . . The Cathedral of Durham should both in
its outside & inside appearance bear the Character of the aera in
which it was built—it would be just as ridiculous in a collector
of medals to clean & brighten those of Syracuse or Rome—and
in my opinion, it is just as great presumption in Mr. Wyatt to
attempt the restoration & improvement of a fine old Saxon &
Gothic Cathedral as it would be in any modern painter to
retouch (with an idea of amendment) a picture of Raphael or of
Claude Lorrain.[47]

[47] Tours, 1800.

Chapter 14

Young Turner

The fashion for picturesque pursuits and Gothic enthusiasms had involved someone whose significance even yet has not been fully understood. Turner,[1] at seventeen, made his first journey into Wales in 1792, going from Bristol to Chepstow, presumably by the Aust passage, and thence to Rhayader and the falls of the Mynach at Devil's Bridge. On his way he visited Tintern, Llanthony, and Crickhowell, where he made a small water-colour drawing of a cottage with a mountain behind, now in the Ashmolean Museum. The pictures arising from this tour were exhibited in the Royal Academy in 1794, among them the *Inside of Tintern Abbey* and *Second fall of the river Monach, Devil's Bridge, Cardiganshire*. The latter, together with *Christ Church Gate* and *Porch of Gt. Malvern Abbey* were described by the critic of the *Morning Post* as 'amongst the best in the present exhibition; they are the productions of a very young artist, and give strong indications of first-rate ability; the character of Gothic architecture is most happily preserved, and its profusion of minute parts massed with judgment and tinctured with truth and fidelity'.[2] Such a notice would not have escaped Colt, even if he had not visited the exhibition and formed an opinion for himself, as it was his custom at this time to be in London during part of April or May. Turner had been exhibiting since 1790.

Colt, as we have seen, was first in South Wales in 1793, when he visited Llanthony from Crickhowell. He did not mention Tintern till 1797. Turner's drawings of Llanthony,[3] seen across a meadow with a mountain behind, remained unfinished; but his interiors of Tintern were among the most successful of his early finished water-colours, cashing in, as it were, on the fashionable view expressed by Gilpin in his *Observations on the River Wye* that 'when we *enter it*, we see it in most perfection'.

By 1793, Farington reported, Turner had a ready market among collectors for his drawings, though at very moderate prices. It is not therefore

---

[1] A. J. Finberg, *The Life of J. M. W. Turner, R.A.* (Oxford 1961).
[2] Finberg, op. cit.
[3] Complete Inventory of Drawings, XII F, XII G. Dr. John Gage tells me there is a finished version, TB XXVII R, dated 1794.

surprising that among the orders for drawings noted in his South Wales sketchbook should be two views of Hampton Court, Viscount Malden's house in Herefordshire, for Sir Richard Hoare.[4] Other orders followed. In 1798, when Turner again set off to Wales, to visit Richard Wilson's country on a pony his friend Narraway had given him, he went by way of Malmesbury, and on the back of drawings of the Abbey wrote 'Sir Richard Colt Hoare, Bart.'.[5] That year Colt left Stourhead on 24 June, with Sir John Leicester, to fish at Bala and in Snowdonia.[6] He was at Tabley on 25 July and home ten days later, only to leave again on 20 August to make drawings in Monmouthshire for his friend Coxe's forthcoming book.[7] Turner, according to Finberg, started his tour after the close of the Academy exhibition, that is to say in August. His route was Chepstow, Tintern, Brecon, Cardigan, Aberystwyth, Dolgellau, Harlech; then across Traeth Bach to Criccieth, Beddgelert, Carnarvon, Bettws-y-Coed, Conway, Denbigh, Llangollen, and Ludlow. So his path crossed with Colt's but never met.

Along the valley of the Towy Turner attended to all the landmarks[8] familiar to each; the spectacular ruin of Carreg Cennen on its isolated crag; or Dinevor, by Llandeilo, celebrated by Dyer in Grongar Hill.[9] 'The ruins of this ancient castle', wrote Colt, 'still crown the summit of a high hill, majestically clothed with wood, and form the principal feature in the beautiful grounds at Newton. To view this fine object in the most favourable point of view, it is advisable to go into the meadows on the other side of the Tywy, where the hill, castle and river, form a most enchanting landscape'.[10] Cilgerran[11] on the Teifi impressed Turner as much as it did Colt five years before, 'No description can give an adequate idea of the beautiful scenery on the banks of this river, nor could the most ingenious artist, or man of the greatest taste, have placed a ruin on a more happy spot—the river though influenced by the tide, still preserved its beautiful sea-green color, it winds in various turnings through a narrow channel, surrounded by hills, feathered with wood to the water's edge.'[12] It was however Colt's friend Leicester who bought *Kilgarran castle on the Twyvey, hazy sunrise, previous to a sultry day* (Pl. 39a), which Turner exhibited at the Academy in 1799. In fact Colt bought none of Turner's interpretations of the scenes he so much admired and, with one exception,

[4] Ibid., XXVI.
[5] 'Hereford' sketchbook, 74, 86. Complete Inventory, XXXVIII.
[6] Tours, 1798.
[7] Historical Tour in Monmouthshire.
[8] 'Hereford' sketchbook.
[9] Deep are his feet in Tywy's flood,
   His sides are cloth'd with waving wood,
   And ancient towers crown his brow,
   That cast an awful look below.
[10] R.C.H., Commentary to *Giraldus Cambrensis*.
[11] 'Hereford' sketchbook; several water-colour versions.
[12] Tours, 1793.

his commissions were purely topographical. The most important were the series of large water-colour drawings of Salisbury Cathedral[13] (Pl. 42–45). The first of these, *North Entrance with a funeral procession* and *The Lady Chapel* (Pl. 45a) (Choir), were exhibited in 1797. The last two were completed sometime after 1802, when the forceful and technically brilliant *Trancept* (Pl. 44) shows Turner's mastery of an awkward subject.

In volume one of the *History of Modern Wiltshire*, published in 1822, Colt maintained that 'the advancement from *drawing* to *painting* in water-colours did not take place till after the introduction into England of the drawings of Louis du Cros...his works proved the force as well as the consequence, that could be given to the unsubstantial body of water-colours, and to him I attribute the first knowledge and power of water-colours. Hence have sprung a numerous succession of Artists in this line; a Turner, a Glover, a Nicholson, Reinagle, De Wint, Nash, cum multis aliis.'[14] His contention was, presumably, that these artists became familiar with Ducros's work through the examples he himself introduced into England and of which, in 1787, he had written to Hugh that they would be 'the admiration of the whole town & put all our English artists, even the great Mr. Smith to blush'.[15] Apart from Turner, Colt employed Nash and Nicholson. Francis Nicholson, who was an older man than Colt, did a lot of work at Stourhead about 1813; there is no evidence he was there before then. Nash made a water-colour painting of the Porch at Malmesbury Abbey which Colt bought in 1815. If the influence of Ducros's work at Stourhead was felt it must have been through Turner. A water-colour drawing of the Bristol Cross[16] and a sketch and unfinished painting[17] of the sun rising over the lake are evidence that Turner was at Stourhead sometime about 1800.[18] Finberg thought that this visit was probably made in the summer of 1800 when Turner was at Fonthill. But on 27 May of the preceding year Farington wrote that Turner was to go to Fonthill and was also to make views of Salisbury Cathedral for Sir Richard Hoare. Turner called on Farington before he went and on his return. We do not know what caused the conversation to take that particular turn, but on both occasions Turner seemed preoccupied with technique. 'He told me', wrote Farington on 21 July, 'he has no systematic process for making drawings. He avoids any particular mode that he may not fall into manner. By wash-ing and occasionally rubbing out, he at last expresses in some degree the

---

13 See note A at end of chapter.   14 R.C.H., *Modern Wiltshire*.
15 See above, p. 96.
16 Complete Inventory, XLIV e.
17 Ibid., XLIV f and g.
18 There is also a water-colour, *Rise of the River Stour at Stourhead*, exhibited 1825:

> From his two springs in Stourton's woody glade;
> Pure welling out—into a lake,
> He pours his infant stream. [Finberg, op. cit.]

Dr. Gage has pointed out that Turner made versions of paintings by Teniers and Rembrandt at Stourhead in 1796 and 1797.

idea in his mind.' And on 16 November: 'Turner called. He reprobated the mechanically systematic process of drawing practised by Smith and from him so generally diffused. He thinks it can produce nothing but manner and sameness.' This certainly describes Colt's own work, and Smith, it will be remembered, was his master; until, that is, he was superseded by Ducros, in whose pictures Colt would have rubbed any young artist's nose. But this one, however anxious to succeed, had arrived; already, in 1798, he 'had more commissions...than he could execute and got more money than he expended'. Ducros's paintings at Stourhead were systematic and mannered and would have been unlikely to appeal to Turner in his then state of mind. Of the two drawings Turner made, the rather insipid Bristol Cross shows some system. But the *Stourhead, Sunrise over the Lake* (Pl. 16a), even though a failure, shows Turner driving the colours about till he has expressed the idea in his mind, as Farington put it. Of course Turner might have seen the Ducros on an earlier occasion, for his acquaintance with Colt dated from at least 1795. In which case we should consider the nature of the influence Ducros's example may have exerted, and which of Turner's paintings could show it. When Colt spoke of the change from drawing to painting in water-colours he makes it clear by using words like 'force' and 'consequence' compared with 'unsubstantial' that what he admired was the approximation to the solidity of oil. It was also a question of size; Ducros's paintings must have been among the largest of their kind at the time. Some of Turner's paintings of Salisbury, which in 1822 Colt thought would never be surpassed, are also large and consequential and in their heavy gilded frames may well have been an attempt to emulate Colt's paragon. However, in 1797, when *The Lady Chapel* or *Choir* (Pl. 45a) was first exhibited, Turner also showed *The Trancept of Ewenny Priory*[19] (Pl. 41), which Finberg considers 'significant of the direction in which Turner's powers were turning'. The subject matter, composition and disposition of light and shade are similar in both paintings. But there are important differences, for whereas at Salisbury the architectural detail is of the first importance, the Ewenny painting, as far as can be judged, was made from the barest information in the smaller South Wales sketchbook of 1795,[20] and some details in the so-called 'Swans' sketchbook.[21] Architectural accuracy is, however, immaterial, for the subject of the picture is the light which floods improbably through the presbytery and from the door in the south transept opening into the Turbeville's garden.

The critic of *St. James Chronicle* thought it one of the grandest drawings he had ever seen, and equal to the best pictures of Rembrandt. He added, 'There is mind and taste in everything the man does'. Although Rembrandt is the more apt comparison, yet Turner could have had in mind Ducros's

[19] National Museum of Wales.   [20] Complete Inventory, XXV.
[21] Ibid., XLII, 48, 49, 54.

Subterranean Falls of the Villa Maecenas (Pl. 40) at Stourhead, which also treats of light penetrating a dark interior. In both paintings the intense shadow is made up of transparent washes of blue and brown; but in the Turner, in contrast to his earlier blue paintings, warm browns and yellows predominate. Comparing the vaulted interiors in both paintings, and the way the light is broken as it strikes through the rounded apertures, one cannot but think that Turner may have taken a hint.[22] Incidentally, in another connection, he could have seen Vernet's *Naufrage* at the same time.

There were other painters who could have known Ducros in Italy; J. R. Cozens comes to mind. Turner had copied many of his drawings when at Dr. Monro's with Girtin between 1794 and 1797; he must therefore have learnt much about painting in water-colours from him. Turner had a drawing by Cozens with a note in Colt's writing on the back; Colt also had two drawings by him. About this time Turner started exhibiting paintings in oil. One cannot help thinking, looking at *Ewenny Priory*, that if the example of Ducros influenced him in any way it must have been to persuade him that oil was a more appropriate medium for what he was trying to do; it might even have suggested to him that he could use oil like water-colour rather than the reverse.

What was the common ground between patron and painter? Chiefly perhaps that in one particular field Turner did superlatively what Colt aspired to do. But in serving them Turner also adopted some of his patrons' attitudes and habits, the picturesque tour for instance. When he was staying at Tabley in 1808 Turner was said by Henry Thomson to have been occupied in fishing rather than painting. There were common interests which took both Colt and Turner to Ewenny. Colt said the river on which it was situated abounded in trout. On entering the priory for the first time he found it 'one of the most ancient complete and interesting specimens of "Saxon" architecture' he had ever seen. 'The only Gothic work I could see was the wooden skreen separating the choir from the transept: to me this building had double charms, as I could fancy it had existed nearly in its present state at the time when Giraldus travelled through Wales.'[23] Some such feelings must also have stirred Turner, who then made only the briefest sketches to remind him of the image. Colt recorded all the details and concluded, 'My second visit to the Priory was attended with success—for I then deciphered the two old inscriptions which I believe till now have never been clearly understood'.[24] The starting points were the same, the ends so different.

It was in 1798, the year after the exhibition of Ewenny Priory, that Turner first attached lines of poetry to his paintings. Most of these were from Thomson, the poet of a previous generation and one most often

[22] Compare also Turner's study of a cottage interior exhibited the previous year. Complete Inventory, XXIX, 10. Turner's *The Fall of the Clyde* (1802), now in the Walker Art Gallery, Liverpool, shows compositional similarities to Ducros's picture.

[23] Tours, 1802.   [24] Ibid.

quoted by Colt although he was not much drawn to poetry. Turner was at one time much preoccupied with the relation of poetry and painting[25] for, as Reynolds had said, 'Poetry addresses itself to the same faculties and the same dispositions as painting, though by different means. The object of both is to accommodate itself to all the natural propensities of the mind.' He was further encouraged by the literary culture of his patrons, to which he naturally aspired; and it is significant that he studied Akenside whose exposition of associationism had once attracted Henry Hoare. When Colt had stood by the Lake of Celano and wondered what, apart from its historical associations, could give a transparent sheet of water meaning he had found no other answer. We have only to look at the titles of Turner's pictures to see that for him too associations were important; but they were also more rich and complex. 'The painter (as opposed to the poet) must adhere to the truth of nature', he said; and added to his titles 'Sunrise after a squally night', 'Thunder storm approaching', or 'Calm morning'. But what was nature? A compound of Cuyp, Claude, Richard Wilson, and what Hazlitt calls his own 'powers of eye, hand and memory'. Looking at the titles *Trancept of Ewenny Priory* and *Choir of Salisbury Cathedral*, who would suspect the difference?

Turner's inclination was towards imagery associated with the sublime rather than the picturesque, if such categories can be thought to apply to him. In this respect too he was in accord with his patron's professed taste.[26] When, with many others, he hurried across the channel in 1802 he found that Switzerland surpassed Scotland, as Scotland had done Wales. There, like any tourist, he followed where Colt and others had been before; Grande Chartreuse, Devil's Bridge, the Source of the Arveiron, the Mer de Glace, and the Fall of the Rhine at Schaffhausen. He interpreted these sublimities in unfamiliar ways. Mr. Dashwood junior, of Cley in Norfolk, told Farington that the *Waterfall of Schaffhausen* was 'a wild, incoherent production, the froth of the water being like a brush of snow'. James Boaden of *The Oracle* looked at it and said, 'That is madness'. Sir John Leicester procured it, giving in exchange *The Shipwreck* he had bought the previous year and fifty guineas more. This was in 1806. By that time Colt was possibly out of sympathy; and Turner too, soldiering on with architectural commissions. His letters of 1805–6 are a suitable concluding record of dealings with his patron.

64 Harley St April 6th 1805[27]

The time being past which Sir Richard Hoare mention'd that
I was to send my account of the Drawings finished I now take

[25] See Jerrold Ziff, 'J. M. W. Turner on Poetry and Painting', *Studies in Romanticism*, III, 4, (1964).
[26] See II, 7, p. 179. For a discussion of picturesque theory in relation to Turner, see John Gage, 'Turner and the Picturesque', *Burlington Magazine*, Jan. and Feb. 1965.
[27] T(ST) 383.4.

13—L.A.

the liberty of so doing. The two outsides 25 Guineas each, the trancept 30 Guineas and the close gate 10, making the whole 90 guineas. The remaining two to complete the set of Salisbury can with confidence be promised to be sent to Stourhead by the latter end of the Summer. I wish I could say sooner; perhaps I may be able before I go to Devonshire—but even then I fear the Summer will be far advanced—hoping to have the pleasure of hearing from you soon allow me the honor

to remain
your most truly obliged svt
J. M. W. Turner

Sion Ferry House, Isleworth
Novr. 23 1805[28]

Sir Richard

I have as you desired sent the following account of the Salisbury set

Trancept View Cloister do General View and the Close Gate	Charged as per letter of April last	95 guineas
Wilton front New Market House	Drawings orderd Novr 21	20 guineas

£120. 15

I could wish you to refer to my letter of April for the first drawings and if it (will) not trouble you when you favour me with the draft to say—if Lord Coningsby Monument is (I think I can find the sketch) requisite to your History of Marden if so it shall be done by January tho it is neither a pleasant or can it make a pleasing drawing from its formality.

I have the honor to be
your most truly obligd
J. M. W. Turner

March 4 1806[29]

J. M. W. Turner with his respects to Sir Richard Hoare has sent the Drawings of Hampton Court and Sir Richard Hoare having desired that the Bill should be (advised) it is therefore

[28] Ibid.
[29] Ibid. Marden, Herefordshire, near Hampton Court, the former seat of the Coningsbys.

subjoin'd. Yet JMWT begs leave to say that the charge for the Malmesbury expenses (e.g. five guineas) is *only* added if Sir Richard declines having the sketches finished that were made at Malmesbury.

The two Drawings of Hampton Court S.E. and W views 7 guineas each	14. 14.
Expenses at Malmsbury	5. 5.

64 Harley St   To Sir Richard Hoare Bart.
Note in Colt Hoare's handwriting: 'paid p draft 14. 14. deducting 5. 5. overcharged on last account.'

64 Harley St.
Saturday April 19 1806[30]

Sir Richard Hoare
    Mr. Woodforde call'd yesterday with your favour dated the 6 of March for 14. 14. together with copies of my letters of April and the last one respecting the overdraft of 5 pounds and allow me to say I feel perfectly satisfy'd in the deduction you have made to agree with my letter of April last

your most truly obligd
J. M. W. Turner

Except in the 'Hereford' sketchbook of 1798 there is no trace of the Malmesbury drawings so perhaps Turner never got his expenses eight years overdue. It was not till 1815 that he had another order, 'One hundred and fifty guineas for a landscape representing the Lake of Avernus'[31] (Pl. 29a). There is no mystery as to why this picture should have been bought for Stourhead as it represents Aeneas and the Sibyl, and in the *Modern Wiltshire* catalogue of paintings Colt wrote: 'Classical subject painted from a correct sketch taken by Sir Richard Colt Hoare (Pl. 29b) when in Italy, and represents the Lake of Avernus in the foreground, with the temple on its banks; above is the *Monte nuovo*, which was thrown up by a volcanic force in one night. In the next distances are the Lucrine Lake, beyond it the castle of Baiae, and the lofty promontory of Misenum, with the island of Capri at the extremity of the horizon.'[32] The painting was sold at Christie's in 1883 and is now in the Collection of Mr. and Mrs. Paul Mellon. The curious thing is that Turner's sketch from Colt's drawing was made about 1800, and a version painted about the same time is now in the Tate Gallery. Turner, we have seen, was at Stourhead about 1799. The

[30] Ibid.
[31] Receipt, 25 Feb. 1815, T(ST) 383.4.
[32] R.C.H., *Modern Wiltshire*.

reference to the Sibyl on the Temple of Flora would not have escaped him; perhaps Colt talked to him of it and of the original Avernus in Italy. The painting seems never to have been at Stourhead, and the most probable explanation is that Turner did it for his own purposes in the manner of Richard Wilson whose work he was studying at that time. In 1800 Colt was not interested in that kind of picture; but in 1815 the end of the Napoleonic War, and a wave of nostalgia for the past, was prompting him to publish the journals of his tours in Italy. For some reason this coincided with Turner's interest in subjects from *The Aeneid*.[33]

The war passed hardly noted in Colt's journals. Even the invasion scare (and a landing had actually been made at Fishguard) was passed off as a joke.

> A late event has rendered this place more conspicuous in history, than it was when I last passed through it. I allude to the landing of the French in its neighbourhood on the 22 Feby 1797...to the number of between twelve & fourteen hundred—their place of landing was a point of land called Cerrig Gwastad to the West of Aberfelin Bay—This was on the 22nd inst and they surrendered their arms on Goodrick Sands near Fishguard on the 24th to the English troops far inferior in number. The object of the French expedition hitherto remains a mystery—My friend Mr. Fenton[34] told me a circumstance in which Providence seems to have almost miraculously interfered to save the neighbouring country from their depredations—for a short time only before their landing, a ship laden with wine was wrecked near that coast —every cottager profited of the spoils attending the wreck—so that the French on plundering in their turn the cottages drank so freely of the wine that they were in a complete state of intoxication, & were heard exclaiming Vive le Roi d'Angleterre etc etc—& suchlike loyal expressions.[35]

As the war progressed the depressing news on land was to some extent offset by other news from sea; as when at Chippenham, on 16 April 1801, Colt read 'with that heartfelt satisfaction which ever animates an Englishman on hearing the Naval Exploits of his countrymen recorded, the account of the memorable and gallant action performed by Lord Nelson before Copenhagen'.[36]

When peace came, while Turner went abroad, Colt spent the summer following the route of Archbishop Baldwin through Wales when he preached the third crusade. Colt's translation of Gerald de Barri's account

---

[33] *Dido and Aeneas*, exh. 1814; *Dido building Carthage*, exh. 1815.
[34] Richard Fenton, 1747–1821; author of *Tour in Search of Genealogy, Historical Tour through Pembrokeshire*, etc. Colt Hoare first met him in 1793, after which they became close friends.
[35] *Tours*, 1802.   [36] *Ibid.*

of this itinerary appeared in 1806,[37] with a commentary based on his own topographical observations. He felt some justifiable pride in this achievement; but by then he had become involved in another project with which his name is still primarily associated.

Note A

In *Modern Wiltshire* Colt Hoare refers to 'eight exterior and interior views of Salisbury Cathedral' which hung with the Ducros in the Column Room. Christie, Manson, and Woods's catalogue of the sale of the Stourhead heirlooms, 1 June 1883, lists:

18 The West Front of Salisbury Cathedral, Exhibited 1799.
     (Finberg No. 56; coll: Harris Art Gallery, Preston).

19 South View of Salisbury Cathedral.
     (Coll: Birmingham City Art Gallery).

20 The North Entrance of Salisbury Cathedral, with a funeral procession.
     (Finberg No. 38, North Porch of Salisbury Cathedral, exhibited 1797; private collection).

21 South View of Salisbury Cathedral, from the Cloister.
     (Coll: Victoria and Albert Museum).

22 The Transept: entrance to the Choir.
     (Coll: Lady Agnew).

23 The Lady Chapel.
     (Finberg No. 36, Choir of Salisbury Cathedral, exhibited 1797; coll: Lady Agnew).

24 The Entrance to the Chapter House, exhibited 1801.
     (Finberg No. 73, Chapter House, Salisbury Cathedral; coll: V. & A. Museum).

25 Interior of the Chapter House, exhibited 1799.
     (Finberg No. 55; coll: Whitworth Institute, Manchester).

Turner's letters to Colt Hoare, refer to 'Trancept View, Cloister do., General View and Close Gate;' also 'Wilton Front' and 'Market Place'. Apart from 'Hampton Court' and 'Malmesbury' it is clear that Turner had other commissions from Colt Hoare. Cf. two lists in Turner's hand at the British Museum (Turner bequest) headed 'Size of the drawings at Salisbury for Sir Richard Hoare'.

I am indebted to Dr. Gage for the information that nine drawings of Salisbury, the *City Series*, were bound in one volume and sold among the books from the Stourhead library in 1883. They were (1) *The Bishop's Palace*, (2) *Ancient Arch in Mr. Wyndham's Garden*, (3) *St. Martin's Church*, (4) *Ancient Market Place*, (5) *St. Edmund's Church by Market Place*, (6) *Wilton House*, (7) *New Council Room*, (8) *Poultry Cross*, (9) *Close Gate*. They were sold again, as separate lots, in the Rev. J. A. Ellis's sale at Christie's, 28 July 1927. Nos. 2 and 3 are now in the British Museum; no. 9 in the Fitzwilliam Museum, Cambridge. The rest are untraced.

[37] *Giraldus Cambrensis.*

Part III

Chapter 1

The Rape of the Barrows[1]

The Mighty Dead

The front of Stourhead House faces the western extremity of the bare Wessex chalk hills, a landscape very different from the sequestered valley to the south. White Sheet Down (Pl. 49b), the nearest point and some mile and a half away, is surmounted by an earthwork older than Colt could ever guess.[2] While his attention had for so long been directed to the sights and antiquities of foreign lands, he had been apt to defer taking a single look at what he could have seen as often as he pleased. 'But the tide has ebbed', he wrote, 'and the stream is diverted into its native channel.'

The river Wylye, which gives its name to Wiltshire, rises just to the north-east of White Sheet, cutting a valley through the Deverills towards Warminster and isolating a bleak block of down known as Cold Kitchen Hill, appropriately enough when the wind is in that quarter. This, as Colt said, was to prove a most interesting object, abounding in '*tumuli*, ditches and excavations, denoting ancient habitation'.

These features of the landscape had not of course gone unnoticed; who could ignore the great iron age forts of Battlesbury and Scratchbury dominating Warminster? Or Yarnbury to the east and Bratton to the north? And further still, across the Pewsey valley at the northern edge of the Marlborough Downs was Barbury where, in 1723, William Stukeley had passed and written, 'This mighty camp stands on one of the western eminences of this ridge, running east and west; very steep to the north and west, separating the high ground or downs from the fertile country below, which...lies under the eye like a map, as far as the Welsh hills beyond the Severn....A little beyond, upon the same ridge, is Badbury Camp (Liddington); and the whole is well planted with stout camps and frequent, the eye-sore and terror of the plain.'[3]

Although a Lincolnshire man Stukeley has a special place in Colt Hoare's county, not only for his records of Stonehenge and Avebury, but for his enthusiastic descriptions of the downs and the well-being they engender.

[1] For a note on the Source Material for Part III, see the Bibliography (p. 283).
[2] A neolithic causewayed enclosure of c. 3000 B.C.
[3] William Stukeley, *Itinerarium Curiosum* (1776), p. 140.

When we contemplate the elegance of this county of *Wiltshire*, and the great works of antiquity therein, we may be persuaded, that the two atlantic islands, and the islands of the blessed, which *Plato* and other ancient writers mention, were those in reality of *Britain* and *Ireland*. They who first took possession of this country, thought it worthy of their care, and built those noble works therein, which have been the admiration of all ages.[4]

Nought can be sweeter than the air that moves o're this hard and dry, chalky soil. Every step you take upon the smooth carpet (literally) your nose is saluted with the most fragrant smell of *serpillum*, and *apium*, which with the short grass continually cropt by the flocks of sheep, composes the softest and most verdant turf, extremely easy to walk on, and which rises as with a spring under one's feet.[5]

These were sentiments which Colt Hoare was frequently to echo as, three-quarters of a century later, he rode upon the same ground, possessed with some of the romantic infection of the older antiquary.

It was in this spirit that, on 10 May 1724, Stukeley chose a hill over-looking Stonehenge from which to view a total eclipse of the sun, and to describe in detail, as darkness came on and the shepherds hurried their flocks into the fold, the disappearing features of the landscape.

Salisbury steeple, six mile off southward became very black; the copped hill quite lost, and a most gloomy night with full career came upon us. . . . The whole compass of the heavens and earth looked of a lurid complexion . . . there was likewise in the heavens among the clouds much green interspersed, so that the whole appearance was really very dreadful, and as symptoms of sickening nature.

Now I perceive us involved in total darkness and palpable, as I may aptly call it; the horses we held in our hands were very sensible of it, and crowded close to us, startling with great surprise. As much as I could see of the men's faces that stood by me, had a horrible aspect . . . the whole appearance of the north and sky was intirely black. Of all things I ever saw in my life, or can by imagination fancy, it was a sight the most tremendous.[6]

Stonehenge even now is a mystery; and mysteries, particularly ancient ones, touch a deep vein of fantasy in the human mind. To this Stukeley[7] was prone, especially in later life. Thus, in spite of his valuable observations, he was inclined to see things which were not there; at Avebury, for

[4] Stukeley, *Abury* (1743), p. 14.   [5] Stukeley, *Stonehenge* (1740), p. 9.
[6] *Itin. Cur.*, pp. 179 ff.
[7] For Stukeley's life and ideas, see Stuart Piggott, *William Stukeley* (Oxford 1950).

instance, a snake proceeding from a circle, with its tail at Beckhampton and its head on Overton Hill. Or perhaps it would be truer to say that once his fancy was taken by the Druids he interpreted what he saw in terms of supposed Druidical lore. Geoffrey of Monmouth, in a spurious account of early British history (1136), mentioned Stonehenge and recorded the magical transport of the stones from Ireland by Merlin. William Camden repeated his story. During the seventeenth century the monument attracted increasing attention. Some writers (Edmund Bolton, 1624; John Gibbons, 1666; Robert Plot, 1686) considered it the work of the Britons; Bolton suggested the 'Tomb of Boudica'. For Aylett Sammes it was the work of the Phoenicians; for Inigo Jones of the Romans, a temple of the Tuscan order. Dr. Walter Charlton, from descriptions of Danish Monuments by Olaus Wormius, thought it a similar work. Sir William Dugdale and John Dryden also thought it was built by the Danes. There were still those in the early eighteenth century who held Jones's views that it was Roman; and to the other supposed originators, Georg Keysler, in 1720, added the Saxons.

Avebury, however, was unnoticed until John Aubrey came upon it while hunting and identified what had hitherto been regarded as a natural phenomenon as the work of man. Later, speculating on the nature of the early inhabitants of Britain in a sketch for a history of ancient Wiltshire, he wrote: 'Their priests were Druids. Some of their temples I pretend to have restored as Avebury, Stonehenge etc.' Thus stone circles became associated with these shadowy figures, whose tenuous roots were in the writings of Caesar, the elder Pliny, and Tacitus, the texts of which were available to educated men from the end of the sixteenth century.

Stukeley seized on Aubrey's suggestion, and Druids became firmly established in his mind, and through him in the minds of his contemporaries. Justification is not here in question. The fact is that people believed in them, and thus a great deal of energy was generated which went not only into antiquarian researches but literature as well. This was not always profitable; from failing to see the work of man it became a habit to see a Druid's hand where it was not, resulting, as we have seen, in Colt's wild-goose chase to Brimham Rocks. But at least he was stimulated to look.

The Druids,[8] like other archetypal figures, had two aspects; they were both black and white magicians. On the one hand they were the source of wisdom, and Colt saw in the rocks of St. David's 'the most perfect profile of a venerable old head—such as I could have fancied a Druid's character'.[9] For Stukeley they had represented all that he found best in life; the Church of England or the scene from Haradon Hill, above Amesbury.

> Whoever is upon this spot cannot fail of a great pleasure in it;
> especially if the sun be low, either after rising or before setting.

[8] See Stuart Piggott, *The Druids* (1968); T. P. Kendrick, *The Druids* (1927); and A. L. Owen, *The Famous Druids* (Oxford 1962).
[9] See above, II, 13.

For by that means the barrows, the only ornaments of these plains, become very visible, the ground beyond them being illuminated by the sun's slaunting rays. You see as far as *Clay Hill* beyond *Warminster* 20 miles off. You see the spot of ground on the hill, whereon stands *Vespasian's* camp, where I conjecture the avenue to *Stonehenge* began, and where there was a *sacellum*, as we conceive. From hence to that spot a valley leads very commodiously to Radfin, where the original ford was.... 'Tis a pretty place, seated in a flexure of the river, which from hence seems to bend its arms both ways, to embrace the beginning of the avenue. The place is very warm, shelter'd from all winds, and especially from the north. I am persuaded it was originally a seat of an Archdruid or Druid.[10]

On the other hand, from references by Caesar to human sacrifice, and by Pomponius Mela to secret meetings in remote places, a quite different picture arose of a cruel and sinister brotherhood. Edward King, whose *Munimenta Antiqua* were published between 1796 and 1805, wrote:

I chanced, the first time I visited this structure, to approach it by moonlight; being later on my journey in the evening, than I intended. This, however, was a circumstance advantageous to the appearance: insomuch, that although my mind was previously filled with determined aversion, and a degree of horror, on reflecting upon the abominations of which this spot must have been the scene; and to which it even gave occasion in the later periods of Druidism; yet it was impossible not to be struck, in the still of the evening, whilst the moon's pale light illumined all, with reverential awe, at the solemn appearance produced by the different shades of this immense group of astonishing masses of rock:[11]

Even Wordsworth, not often associated with the horrific, could write,

> Fly ere at once the fiends their prey devour
> Or grinning, on thy endless tortures scowl
> Till very madness seems a mercy to thy soul
>
> For oft, at dead of night, when dreadful fire
> Unfolds that powerful circle's reddening stones
> Mid priests and spectres grim and idols dire,
> Far heard the great flame utters human moans,[12]

[10] *Stonehenge*, p. 37. Stukeley is here describing the site of Amesbury Abbey. It was here that Bridgeman, in improving the Duke of Queensberry's Park in 1738, included in his scheme the iron-age fort known as Vespasian's Camp, and the barrow which it encloses. See above, I, 1.
[11] King, *Munimenta Antiqua*, p. 160.
[12] 'Guilt and Sorrow', *Works*, XIV, ed. Selincourt, i, pp. 100–1.

which shows how deep the druid myth had taken hold; and also the ambivalence of it, for on another occasion he referred to himself as 'A youthful Druid taught in shady groves',[13] thus identifying the cult with his own brand of nature mysticism.

Thomas Jones, visiting Stonehenge in 1769, could not help thinking that its situation added much to its magnificence, 'the vast surrounding void not affording anything to disturb the eye, or direct the imagination'. If it were situated 'amidst high rocks, lofty mountains and hanging woods',[14] it would lose much of its grandeur. He painted a picture[15] (Pl. 47) to show this, 'the subject taken from Gray's ode, and I think one of the best I ever painted'.[16] The ode, published in 1757, refers to the tradition that Edward I, when he completed the conquest of Wales, ordered all the bards who fell into his hands to be put to death. The painting illustrates the lines,

> On a rock, whose haughty brow
> Frowns o'er old Conway's frowning flood,
> Robed in the sable garb of woe,
> With haggard eyes the Poet stood;
> (Loose his beard, and hoary hair
> Streamed, like a meteor, to the troubled air)
> And with a Master's hand, and Prophet's fire,
> Struck the deep sorrows of his lyre.[17]

The henge-like monument in the middle background illustrates how druid-ism had been appropriated by students of Welsh mediaeval poetry, who claimed that the bards were a direct continuation of the druid hierarchy. *Specimens of the Poetry of the Ancient Welsh Bards*, by the Reverend Evan Evans, was published in 1764. Certain obscure poems by Taliesin were called by him 'Druid's Caballa'. Later, Edward Williams, called Iolo Morganwg, claimed that the Glamorganshire bards had preserved the wisdom of the prehistoric Druids. Poems of Taliesin, he declared, exhibited a complete system of Druidism; to prove his case he forged aphorisms defining Druidical doctrine and philosophy. Williams, who was born in 1747, worked as a stone-mason in London where he was an active member of a group of Welshmen interested in their national culture. In 1792 these met as an Assembly of Welsh Bards on Primrose Hill, setting up a circle of stones round an altar (Maen Gorsedd). During the traditional Eisteddfod at Carmarthen in 1819 Williams, or Morganwg, produced stones from his pocket and set up the Gorsedd Circle in the garden of the Ivy Bush Hotel, thus establishing a connection between 'Druidical rites' and that festival.

---

[13] Quoted A. L. Owen, op. cit., p. 164.
[14] 'Memoirs of Thomas Jones', *Walpole Society*, XXXII. Entry for 1769.
[15] Thomas Jones, *The Bard*, National Museum of Wales. I am indebted to Mr. John Ingamells for pointing out the connection between the picture and the entry in the journal.
[16] Jones, Memoirs, entry for 1774.
[17] *Poems of Thomas Gray*, ed. A. L. Poole (1966 ed.), p. 56.

In 1761, shortly after Gray's poem, *Fingal* appeared, claimed by James Macpherson as the translation of a lost Celtic epic by one Ossian, an almost unrelieved tale of battles and slaughter in the mists of Northern Ireland. Others followed. The deeds of these heroes were set in an indefinite past and received great acclaim as indigenous achievements, particularly from the Reverend Hugh Blair who set them beside the works of Homer and Virgil.

> There was nothing about druidism in *Ossian*, [writes T. B. Kendrick] there was nothing directly about druidism in *The Bard*, but they advanced the cause of the druids and promoted a popular affection for them more thoroughly than any archaeological treatise could have done. It is, in fact, to this early *romantic* poetry that we should properly attribute the astonishing success of the laborious theories of Stukeley and other archaeologists. Such poetry was an evidence of the turning of men's minds away from the old familiar classical mythology and the rigours of the classical formulae in letters and art; and the signal for a movement towards freedom of Keltic wildness, of the chill grand landscapes of the north peopled with hoary bards and with rude chieftains, and the mysterious haunting creatures of Keltic mythology.[18]

And for all the information that existed, it might as well have been people such as these[19] whose remains lay in the burial mounds on Cold Kitchen Hill, on either side of the Wylye valley and, in increasing numbers, within sight of Stonehenge. Over two thousand are listed in the *Victoria County History of Wiltshire*. In fact they range from neolithic longbarrows some 5000 years old to round barrows of various shapes and sizes made in the so-called Early and Middle Bronze Ages of about 1900 to 1400 B.C. No such classification was made until after Colt Hoare's death in 1838. Wisely, perhaps, he assigned no date to the grave goods he recovered and knew the original inhabitants of this island merely as the Britons.

The contents of these barrows Colt was now meticulously to record. But in opening up the past he could not altogether escape stirrings of conscience as he ravaged in the mounds whose roundness and beauty he

[18] Kendrick, op. cit., p. 26.
[19] In a note-book he used to record sources of information on ancient burial customs and the early inhabitants of Britain, Colt Hoare wrote down several extracts from Ossian. Among these are:

> Raise high my grave Vinvela. Grey stones and heaped up earth shall mark me to future times, When the hunter shall sit by the mound and produce his food at noon 'Some warrior rests here' he will say, and my fame shall live in his praise.

> Behold that field, O Carthon! Many a green hill rises there with mossy stones & rustling grass; these are the tombs of Fingal's foes.

> They are now forgot in their land: their tombs are not found in the heath; the green mounds are mouldered away.

almost inevitably destroyed. 'Our *impious* hands', he would say; and the
opening of a fine bell-shaped barrow near Woodyates in a thunderstorm
was 'attended by many awful circumstances'.[20] The poet Bowles,[21] who
was present, sent Colt some verse the following morning.

> 'Let me, let me sleep again:'
> Thus, methought, in feeble strain,
> Plain'd from its disturbed bed
> The spirit of the mighty dead.
> 'O'er my moulder'd ashes cold
> Many a century slow hath roll'd,
> Many a race hath disappear'd,
> Since my giant form I rear'd;
>
> .   .   .   .
>
> 'Shall the sons of distant days
> Unpunish'd, on my relicks gaze?
>
> .   .   .   .
>
> Hence! yet though my grave ye spoil,
> Dark oblivion mocks your toil.'[22]

[20] *A. W.*, I, p. 239.
[21] William Lisle Bowles (1762–1850), Rector of Chicklade, 1792–7; Vicar of Bremhill, 1804.
[22] *A.W.*, I, p. 239.

Chapter 2

The Ingenious Tradesman

The unfolding of the story of Ancient Wiltshire began in the valley of the Wylye, which flows north through the Deverills, turns southeast at Warminster until it joins the Nadder twenty miles further on. On one side is the mass of Salisbury Plain; on the other a triangular wedge, its apex at Wilton, its western extremity the escarpment overlooking Stourhead. The line of a Roman road follows the ridge through Groveley Wood, Stockton and Snail-creep Hanging; it passes Cold Kitchen Hill and Stourhead, crosses the Fosse just north of Shepton Mallet and ends in the lead mines of the Mendips. There are many barrows and earthworks along its course, and other signs of early settlement. On the floor of the valley too, are, or were, a number of great barrows, which led Colt to call the Wylye 'the *dilectus amnis* of the Britons'. At Wilton, the seat of Stukeley's friend and patron the Earl of Pembroke, a barrow had been used to terminate a vista. 'This, questionless, is a Celtic tumulus:' Stukeley had written, 'and the very name (King Barrow), inherent through long revolutions of time, indicates it to be the grave of a king of this country of the Belgae; and that Wilton was his royal residence, which for goodness of air, of water and soil, joined with the most delightful downs all around it, must highly magnify his judgement in choice of a place second to none for all the conveniencies and delicacies of life.'[1]

At the opposite end of this territory were the estates of Longleat and Stourhead; to the south of it Fonthill where the ostracized Beckford was building his fantastic abbey. And in the pleasant villages tucked in beneath the chalk were smaller seats of lesser gentry. Men like these governed Wiltshire; and because the majority of Englishmen still lived in villages and country towns, they controlled Parliament too. The Britons, it must have seemed, belonged to them. It is therefore all the more delightful to record that the genius of this story was not a man of leisure but a tradesman.

William Cunnington (Pl. 48a) had migrated in 1775 from Northamptonshire to Heytesbury, just outside Warminster where, in 1800, he lived with

[1] *Itin. Cur.*, p. 136.

his wife and three daughters. He had prospered as a wool merchant and owned, in addition, a mercer and draper's shop. After twenty-two years assiduous attention to business his health deteriorated and he was advised to 'ride out or die'. He preferred the former, and in doing so acquired an interest in antiquities and fossils. With the latter we are not here concerned; but in 1798 he wrote to the young John Britton,[2] about to start *The Beauties of Wiltshire*, describing discoveries made on the Knook and Upton downs overlooking Heytesbury. These included many fragments of pottery, nails, small pieces of bronze and iron, a curious bead, and Roman coins of brass and silver. He had also found several human bones and large quantities of coarse pottery, by which he judged that the last inhabitants must have been surprised and perhaps the greater part destroyed on the spot. A few years previously, adjoining but not in a barrow, there had been found two urns full of human bones.

> I have also visited Stonehenge since I saw you, where in digging with a large stick under those two very large stones which fell down about three years ago, I was much surprised to find several pieces of black pottery similar to those on the above downs... which I used to think was Roman. I also found several bones of deer or sheep. From these specimens of pottery, the magnitude of this stupendous structure, and other circumstances, I am of opinion our ancestors (if I may so call them) were not so barbarous nor so ignorant of the Arts, as some suppose them when the Romans first invaded this isle....[3]

Britton was a Wiltshire man, from Kington St. Michael near Chippenham, where his father was a small farmer, maltster, baker and shopkeeper. After a desultory education he was apprenticed to a tavern in Clerkenwell as a cellarman; but having early acquired a taste for reading he was able to obtain the post of clerk in an attorney's office. Meanwhile, having had some success in writing he was asked by the publishers of a dramatic miscellany to which he contributed, to undertake *The Beauties of Wiltshire*.

When he first met Cunnington in 1796 Britton had been collecting material for this, and had stayed, 'by pressing solicitation' with Beckford at Fonthill.[4] On his return to London he wrote that, with the blessings of health and assiduous application, he hoped he could complete the work in no disreputable manner. Indeed, hope brightened the distant horizon and promised a reward for his industry. He was evidently in need of this as shortage of money and other difficulties pressed on him at this time. Cunnington used to send him honey, which Britton took instead of butter. But more especially he acted as a good-natured and mature friend to the touchy and volatile author, who was always prone to think he had been

2 John Britton, 1771–1857, antiquary, topographer, writer.
3 Letters, W.C. to J.B., 25 Nov. 1798, W.A.S.   4 Letters, J.B. to W.C., 15 Nov. 1796.

slighted and whose demands for reassurance that this was not so invited the very consequences he wished to avoid.

It was Britton's intention to write a *History of Wiltshire* which eventually brought him into conflict with Colt, in whom ambition for authorship was as strong as the passion for knowledge. The struggle, if such it can be called, was for the information which Cunnington possessed. 'Pray will you favour me with a few observations on Wool—the Agriculture of the Plain in your district, and any such other remarks which you deem valuable or worthy of being made public', wrote Britton in 1800. 'I wish to embrace all the information which I can give upon *every* subject connected with this county.'[5] So far Britton had no competitor, although even at this stage Cunnington did not quite see eye to eye with him. 'Your beauties and my antiquities will not do well together', he wrote, '—you must deal sparingly with the latter.'[6]

In 1800 Colt was preoccupied with his Welsh travels and the idea of translating *Giraldus Cambrensis*. But his friends Henry Penruddock Wyndham,[7] Member for Wiltshire, and William Coxe,[8] who was presented with the living of Stourton that year, were already promoting Cunnington's researches. Apart from a thin volume on his tours in Wales, Wyndham had published *Extracts relating to Wiltshire from Domesday Book* (1788) in the preface to which he had outlined a proposal for a county history. Coxe was a scholar with an established reputation, based chiefly on his *Life of Sir Robert Walpole* (1798), although, as we have seen, he had published accounts of travels in Switzerland and elsewhere. At this time he was busy on his *Historical Tour in Monmouthshire* for which Colt had done the illustrations.

Coxe and Wyndham were both interested in excavation, but they had other occupations. One of the things which attracted them to Cunnington, apart from his evident intellect and sympathetic personality, was his willingness to do the work necessary in making discoveries. They assumed that he had the time to supervise the digging of barrows while they attended the sessions, or even went about their social life. Coxe, for instance, would excuse himself from a major barrow operation at Stonehenge, which he himself had sponsored, on the grounds that he had company. Or he would ask Cunnington to arrange for a tent and cold meat because he expected a party of gentlemen.

Ultimately the whole business of excavation depended on those who would do the hard physical work. This also required some skill, as Coxe wrote, 'It will be proper to have some careful labourer who has been accustomed to such business, to superintend and assist. Could you recom-

5 Letters, J.B. to W.C., 6 Oct. 1800.
6 Letters, W.C. to J.B., 25 Nov. 1798.
7 H. P. Wyndham, 1739–1819. Topographer, M.P. for Wiltshire, 1795–1812.
8 William Coxe, 1747–1828, author and antiquarian. Rector of Bemerton, 1788; Rector of Stourton, 1800–1811; Archdeacon of Salisbury, 1804.

mend one who could be spared for 10 days or a fortnight, in case I should want him.'[9]

Sometimes much labour was required. Opening the great flint barrow in Kingston Deverill field involved moving fifty to a hundred cartloads of flints and putting them back again. Eight men were employed in opening Hatfield Barrow at Marden, the largest artificial mound in the country next to Silbury. It was twenty-two and a half feet high and made of sand which kept slipping back into the cavity. In spite of this, twenty-four square feet of the floor were exposed. With smaller barrows fewer men were employed; usually just Stephen Parker and his son John, who became experienced and indispensable. It was one of Cunnington's gifts that he could gain men's interest and affection, whereas Colt, for instance, could only petulantly say, 'Tell John he must be in a *sweet temper* & await my pleasure for I will have no sulks'.[10]

Equally, people like Wyndham were necessary to Cunnington, especially in obtaining permission from other landowners. Usually there was no difficulty; but in 1802 Coxe wrote that 'the Duke of Queensbury has refused permission to replace the trilithon (at Stonehenge) and he is such an extraordinary man that I begin to be apprehensive lest he should retract the permission granted to me to open the barrows; for which reason I should be glad if you spare thursday and friday next week for that purpose, provided the weather is fine.'[11] Sometimes farmers were difficult. Searching for a barrow in 1809 on the Great Ridge, overlooking Fonthill, Cunnington reported that the field was planted with turnips. 'And had not this difficulty occured, others of a more serious nature stood in our way, for young Candy who rents the land & whose brother is Lord of Chicklade, threatened us with a prosecution; he told me it was not the first time he had seen that fellow (John Parker). I talked to him very civilly, but he took us all for poachers.'[12]

Wyndham also provided Cunnington with books from his library; Coxe tended to press his own. 'You need not be in a hurry to return the travels in Switzerland, but when you have done with them I will lend you my Travels into Poland, Russia, Sweden and Denmark, and the Memoirs of Sir Robert Walpole if you chuse to read them.'[13] Coxe was so busy that it was difficult to remember what he was about. 'The work in which I am now engaged', he wrote in 1801, 'is not the Account of the Roman Roads in Wiltshire of which I am not yet nearly master; but the memoirs of Lord Walpole, brother of Sir Robert.'[14] In fact he was temperamentally more inclined to movement than to the rather slow business of barrow digging, and preferred riding along the tracks of Roman roads. In 1800 he was proposing to study all those in Wiltshire, to which end, in 1801, he

9 Letters, Coxe 11, 20 Apr. 1801.   10 Letters, R.C.H. 19.
11 Letters, Coxe 22, 1 June 1802.   12 Papers, XI, 1.
13 Letters, Coxe 4, 20 Sep. 1800.   14 Letters, Coxe 15, 16 Sep. 1801.
    14—L.A.

employed A. Crocker[15] & Sons of Frome to make a survey from Old Sarum to Winchester.

While Coxe inclined to Roman studies, Wyndham was particularly interested in long barrows, which we now know to be the communal graves of a neolithic people living around 3000 B.C. The unchambered kind, which were the only ones Cunnington excavated, varied in length from 60 to 400 feet. They were constructed mainly of chalk rubble, with a black stratum of some thickness above the original turf-line. In spite of their great size the interments did not exceed fifty, and the average for Wessex is about six in each. In contrast to the later bronze age round barrows, grave goods are scarce.[16]

Wyndham considered nothing new could be discovered in opening 'the common rounded barrows'.

> I should prefer the dissection of some long & irregular barrow, of which Stukeley is of the opinion that they appertained to the Arch Druids, and which is certainly contrary to mine, that they are the receptacles of Bodies slain in Battle.[17] I should like to have this brought to a decision. The long barrow at a short distance from Sr. William's[18] place, might determine the point, as neither that, nor any other long barrow has been excavated low enough for satisfaction—for the earth must have been thrown over the slain, while their corpses lay upon the original surface. I shall be happy to call upon you as early as you please to pursue this speculation.[19]

During the summer of 1800 a long barrow in Heytesbury field was opened. It yielded black earth which Wyndham assumed was animal but intended to have analysed. Otherwise the results were inconclusive. 'Our

---

15 Abraham Crocker was a man of varied interests and engaging enthusiasm. He started life as a schoolmaster at Ilminster, Somerset, later moving to Frome. With his sons he started a surveying business and was the author of *The Elements of Land Surveying* (1814). Among his other publications were *A Practical Introduction to English Grammar and Rhetoric* (1772) and *Instructions for Young People in the Public Worship of God*. He also wrote a book on making cider and a guide for measuring and valuing trees. He took a keen interest in the work of Hoare and Cunnington, with whom he corresponded. For his son Philip, who made all the surveys and drawings for *The Ancient History of Wiltshire*, see below. Further details, E. Green, *Bibliotheca Somersetensis*, ii (1902), 338–9.

16 For present state of knowledge on long barrows, see S. Piggott, *Neolithic Cultures of the British Isles* (1954). On round barrows, see P. Ashbee, *The Bronze Age Round Barrow in Britain* (1960). I am also indebted to L. V. Grinsell, *The Ancient Burial Mounds of England* (1953) and *The Archaeology of Wessex* (1958).

17 There was the authority of classical authors for this theory. Cf. also William Dugdale, *Antiquities of Warwickshire* (1656), p. 3: 'That these LOWES, or artificially raised heaps of Earth, were antiently made to cover the Bodies of such as were slain in the field, in the time of the Romans, we have the testimony of *Tacitus*, where he makes mention of *Varus'* his overthrow in GERMANY.'

18 Sir William A'Court, M.P. for Aylesbury; married H. P. Wyndham's daughter, Letitia. In 1802, at Cunnington's intercession, he commuted a sentence of death on Stephen Parker's son Stephen, for sheep stealing. For the Parkers, see below.

19 Letters, H.P.W. 3, 21 Sep. 1800.

ladies have brought home a few human bones with the black earth firmly fixed upon them. As far as I can be assured, they picked them out from some rubbish earth on a heap, about midway in the chasm digged thro'. Tho' this seems enough to confirm our conjecture, yet, I think, the pursuit should be a little farther pursued.'[20]

He then suggested that a 'huge Barrow in Bishopstrow, perhaps the largest Battle Barrow in the island,'[21] might lead to more conclusive discoveries. Known as King Barrow, this was opened by Cunnington in October and, as became his habit, he wrote a precise and circumstantial report.[22] It was 189 feet long, 54 wide and $15\frac{1}{2}$ high; originally it had been much larger. A section 28 feet long was made from the north-east towards the centre, and then enlarged to left and right. He frequently met with pieces of stag's horns, animal bones, boar's tusks and rude pottery. The floor of the barrow was nearly 3 feet below the adjoining ground, 'and of the colour of rusty iron or rather as blood appears on the roads a few days after it has been shed'; it was covered with animal bones of every description and, as he conceived, some human bones. To one side he found the complete skeleton of a horse. This proved, said Wyndham, that these were battle barrows.[23] He had no doubt that marks of carnage would everywhere be revealed. Several hundred of the slain were probably interred; and if Cunnington should, now and then, meet with parts of an urn, it might contain the ashes of an officer, who would have some distinction paid to him beyond that of a private soldier. It seemed singular that no remains of armour had been discovered in such a heap, but perhaps it was considered too valuable to be wasted. When, in another section, three skeletons were found eighteen inches below the surface, one with a sword by his side, and near them the fragment of a rude but prettily decorated urn, Wyndham's imagination ran riot.

> It is a greater confirmation to my ideas than I could reasonably have expected. . . . We cannot be surprized at the immense quantity, when we know that a carnage of a battle was much greater formerly than now—it proceeded frequently to, if possible, a general extirpation of an enemy. It is very common to find, in these Battle Barrows, skeletons and urns a little below the upper surface—These were officers of distinction who, as I have said before, were distinguished from the confusion of the common heap. The sword may indicate the skeleton near it to be that of a man of very superior rank. I am of the opinion that this huge barrow was raised by the victors of the combat which might possibly have taken place between the Saxons, encamped

[20] Letters, H.P.W. 4, 27 Sep. 1800.
[21] Letters, H.P.W. 6, 20 Oct. 1800.
[22] Papers, III, 26.
[23] Letters, H.P.W. 8.

upon the hills, and the Britons, fortified in the Roman camp below; that the Saxons gained the victory and buried the slain of both parties promiscuously in this common tumulus, and that the sword may denote a Saxon chief....I suppose the conflict to have been about the year 500, at which time the Saxons were pagans, and may account for the burning the bodies, and for the superstitious fragments of the animals found among them. Is the blade, of the sword found, perfect? I should have expected it to have been longer than 18 inches, and two-edged. ...This has been a foul morning for your operations. I hope it may mend.[24]

If Wyndham were not already convinced, other circumstances contributed to his belief. A cursory opening of Knook long barrow, in the first half of 1801, disclosed four headless skeletons not far below the surface.[25] They appeared to have been thrown there with little ceremony as two of them had their legs across each other. Wyndham found this 'curious and perhaps singular'. It was, however, known that the Danes, and perhaps other nations in ancient days...preserved the skulls of their enemies for drinking cups. 'I am glad that you have visited *Bratton Castle*', he wrote, 'and there can be no doubt that innumerable bodies have been covered by the great barrow within it, and history says that the Danes were in that castle cut to pieces by K. Alfred.'[26]

Cunnington gave cautious acquiescence. In August he wrote: 'A few days ago a farmer of Imber made an offer to assist me with two or three men to open Boles barrow....It proves an interesting barrow, and also another proof in support of your hypothesis that these very large oblong barrows are Battle Barrows.'[27] Boles barrow was 150 feet long, 94 wide and 10½ high, though it appeared higher; in shape it was like an egg cut lengthways. Making a wide section at the large east end, Cunnington first found the skeleton of a stout man, bones very sound and teeth perfect; with him were a brass buckle and two thin bits of brass, but no urn or arms. Two more shallow interments were found towards the centre. At 4½ feet they came to a ridge of flints and large stones similar to the sarsens[28] of Stonehenge. These increased in width to the floor of the tumulus, which was evenly covered with flints on which were the remains of a great number of human bodies apparently thrown together without order. Four men working for three days cleared an area of six feet by ten, a very small proportion of the whole, in which space they found thirteen skulls, and a piece of one which seemed to have been cut off by a sword. Some of the

[24] Letters, H.P.W. 10, 6 Nov. 1800.
[25] Letters, H.P.W. 14, 28 June 1801.
[26] Ibid.
[27] Letters, H.P.W. 18 (from W.C.), Aug. 1801.
[28] This is how Cunnington described them, but they were in fact 'blue stones' from Pembrokeshire.

evidence did not, in Cunnington's view, square with the theory. Why were there no arms, urn or any memorial that could throw light on its antiquity? 'It appears rather strange that the dead bodies (if of the victorious party) should have been interred with so little ceremony in this barrow; and if they were the dead bodies of an enemy they should take the pains to pave the bottom of the barrow and with such large flints and stones as composed the center, for this must have been a work of considerable labour.'[29]

Cunnington removed some of the large stones and arranged them in a circle round a weeping ash in his garden. Wyndham was delighted and on 27 October wrote, 'I hope to be in town on Monday noon next, and shall immediately proceed to bring your name forward for the Antiquarian Society.'[30] The application was supported by Coxe and the Director, Samuel Lysons, an authority on Roman villas who had visited the work at Pitmead. Cunnington was elected a Fellow in December.

[29] Letters, H.P.W. 18 (from W.C.).
[30] Letters, H.P.W. 17, 21 Nov. 1801.

Chapter 3

Pride and Affluence

Meanwhile Colt was hardly involved in these affairs. His first recorded visit to Heytesbury was in April 1801, when he was invited by Coxe to inspect a tessellated Roman pavement at Pitmead, first uncovered by Cunnington in 1798. Snow was falling and lying deep on the ground. He stayed Sunday night with Sir William A'Court, and on Monday visited Pitmead in the company of 'Mr. Cunnington, an ingenious inhabitant and tradesman'.[1] The following day, en route for Cheltenham and North Wales, he dined with Thomas Leman[2] in Bath, and met Dr. Bennet,[3] Bishop of Cloyne, who was said to have walked over almost the whole of the Roman roads of England and Wales.

Leman, who had accompanied his friend the Bishop on many of his excursions, was himself an expert on tracks and earthworks, and had written a section on the Roman roads of Leicestershire for John Nichols's history of the county (first volume 1795). He was to fill an important role in the writing of *The Ancient History of Wiltshire*, the book in which Colt was to record all that was discovered about the inhabitants from pre-historic to Roman times. Colt, Cunnington, and Leman all became acquainted about this time. Coxe wrote to Cunnington in January 1801, saying that Leman was interested in meeting him and corresponding with him; and it seems probable that it was a suggestion that Leman might help with the journeys of Giraldus which prompted Colt to make the visit mentioned above. Leman was then in his fiftieth year; Cunnington was forty-seven and Colt forty-three. It was the difference in their ages, as well as Leman's greater experience, which made Colt defer to him, and which made Leman adopt the tone of schoolmasterly irony which he often did. 'I certainly have great reason to glory in you as a Pupil! & could I turn you into any other part of England for a summer than the barren Counties of *Wales* (*or of Scotland*) I should hope from your knowledge & your assiduity, that the most creditable additions would be made to our favourite Pursuit.'[4]

[1] R.C.H. Journal, 1801, Cardiff Municipal Library.
[2] Thomas Leman, 1751–1826, antiquary.
[3] William Bennet, 1746–1820.   [4] T.L. to R.C.H., 4 Aug. 1808, T(ST) 383.907.

Cunnington was nearer Leman's age; and although he was initially prepared to accept advice, he came to resent it as his experience increased. This was partly the antagonism of the field-worker for the theorist; and Leman, whether from age, temperament, or because he had an ailing wife, was no longer inclined to explore. But there was also an element of jealousy which Colt, when he became intimate with both, was inclined to exploit, playing one off against the other. Colt and Leman both had the advantage of a classical education. Cunnington, who did not, was always conscious of his lack and suspected that his expertise was belittled. We may sometimes think that he identified with the Britons, about whom he was to know more than anyone, against the Romans. 'I must first observe', he wrote to Leman in 1809, 'that I have ever had the highest respect for people who have had a liberal education like yourself; but the information to be gathered from Caesar and Tacitus relates to the Britons in their times— therefore all theories drawn from such sources in regard to our Celtic Britons are ever at war with facts.' He added as an afterthought, 'The Book which best illustrates British Antiquities is the Bible!'[5] Thereby claiming moral superiority for them as well.

Leman was not unappreciative of Cunnington's work. When Cunnington sent him an account of opening a barrow at Codford in 1802, Leman replied: 'It is so very interesting from your having recorded the *most minute circumstances about it* that I have read it over many times with encreased satisfaction. *A few such papers* would throw more light in this very obscure part of our antiquities...than the many theoretical volumes which have been given to the world.'[6]

Cunnington, for all his enthusiasm, was apt to go after what interested him, which included fossils as much as prehistoric grave-goods. While Coxe, Wyndham, and subsequently Colt, demanded written records for their histories, Leman saw to it that finds were systematically labelled, and that both Colt and Cunnington acquired a proper attitude towards their work. Early in the researches he wrote to Cunnington:

> You will excuse me I am sure when I take the liberty of pointing out to you the necessity of *immediately pasting a small piece of paper on every piece of pottery or coin* that you may hereafter find, describing with accuracy the very spot in which you found them. The people who succeed us may possibly know more about these things than we do (or else I am confident they will know very little) but we ought...to afford *them* all the information we can, with clearness. We are too apt to suppose that even we ourselves shall know *tomorrow*, what we have learn'd *today*, & yet every day's experience has told me that I do not, & as it may

5 Papers, IX, 1.
6 Letters, T.L., 21 Sep. 1802.

possibly be so with others, I would wish you to be on your guard against this fatal error.

To collect either coins or any other pieces of antiquity without it is done with the honest zeal of being of use to others...is little better than collecting Rubbish which may impede, but cannot add to our improvement.[7]

The stimulus of Leman's mind, his incisive and often witty comment, were important to both collaborators in *Ancient Wiltshire*. That he was up against someone whose initial advantages he had not possessed was an additional incentive to keep Cunnington on his toes.

It was the year following his first meeting with Leman that Cunnington was put on the defensive through no fault of his own. Britton had published the first two volumes of *The Beauties of Wiltshire* in 1801. The second opened with a description of Stourhead, and a dedication to Colt, not only because of his reputation as a traveller and his partiality for topography, but because he had helped Britton and provided illustrations for the book. 'Affluence is too frequently accompanied by a *haughty* reserve, the result of pride and ignorance', wrote Britton. 'This...repels the advances of the humble, and intimidates the meek author at the very commencement of his labors.'[8] He had intended to go further in his castigation of the gentry, and told Cunnington what he had written would prove 'a goading lash to the illiberal, the churlish, and the ignorantly proud'.

Believe me, [replied Cunnington] there rarely comes any good to the Author of lashes....If you have introduced politicks it will create you many enemies but get not one friend. A few years peace, and Jacobinism will become as stale as Wilkes and liberty. I have considered you as a young man of parts, which if cultivated by study and conversation with people both learned and genteel, you might become an Author of consequence. I have thought you without friends and felt for you....If you have introduced much satire and politicks in your first work you are to blame.[9]

In the event, although Britton attacked housing conditions among the poor in many villages, his book was quite well received. Colt congratulated him on having laid the *first* foundation stone of a memorial to the county, criticizing only the engravings and too many italics. Wyndham said the book showed much merit, coming from so young an author.

But despite Cunnington's suggestion that he should deal sparingly with antiquities, Britton gave considerable space to theories on the origin of Stonehenge. 'It is a field where mazes of wild opinion are more complex

---

[7] Letters, T.L., 24 Sep. 1802.
[8] *The Beauties of Wiltshire* (1801), II, iii.
[9] Letters, W.C. to J.B., 12 Apr. 1801.

and intricate than the ruin', he wrote. 'I was almost deterred from making any attempt to explain what has so long remained enveloped in uncertainty; nor should I have had the courage to oppose a very prevalent opinion, but from the acquisition of some very important documents which my predecessors had not the good fortune to possess.'[10] The source had been revealed in a letter to Cunnington. 'The Druidical History of the County will make a *prominent feature*. I have examined svel. Temples, Cromlechs, etc. and have the remarks, informn. etc. of a *profound* Welsh Antiquary— W. Owen,[11] author of the Welsh Dictionary—and man of profound learning and profound good nature.'[12] Owen was the acknowledged authority on Welsh language and culture. Coxe, who thought there were affinities between Welsh and Sanscrit and that Druidism was Brahminism modified, consulted him on matters of etymology and history; and Colt Hoare regularly sought his advice when he was writing his commentary on *Giraldus Cambrensis*. But of many of Owen's fancies they were sceptical, particularly concerning the age of the Wiltshire antiquities. Owen was involved in what Professor Piggott calls Rowland Jones's 'cosy world of lunatic linguistics'. Jones, author of *The Origin of Language and Nations* (1764), *Hieroglyfic* (1768), and *The Circles of Gomer* (1771), found caballistic teaching of the Druids in words and even syllables. Their influence was discovered at Stonehenge, Avebury, and Silbury Hill, and despite arguments to the contrary, Owen was not to be moved. 'It is remarkable', he wrote to Cunnington when the latter was working at Stonehenge, 'that the names of both places, in our ancient Triads identify one as the appendage of the other. Thus Silbury Hill is called *Cludair Cyvrangon* or *Head of the Conventions*; and the circle of Abury is called *Gorsedd Bryn Gwyddon* or *Supreme seat of the Hill of the intelligent ones* (wise men).'[13]

All this Britton swallowed and produced as evidence, against 'those writers who have disdained searching for historical memorials',[14] that Stonehenge was the work of Romanized Britons about end of the fifth century. Moreover, as proof of his contention, he quoted what Cunnington had told him in 1798[15] about finding Roman pottery in the holes of the fallen trilithon.

Leman was not slow to spot this, and asked to know '*very accurately the particulars of it*, as it is by no means a trifling circumstance whether it lay at the foundation or was scattered about the outside edge and so thrown up merely by the stones falling'.[16] Cunnington hastened to urge Britton to correct his account. 'My opinion on finding the Roman pottery

[10] *Beauties of Wiltshire*, II, 118.
[11] William Owen (Pughe), 1759–1835; Welsh antiquary and lexicographer.
[12] Letters, J.B. to W.C., 6 Oct. 1800.
[13] Letters, W. Owen to W.C., 21 Dec. 1804.
[14] *Beauties of Wiltshire*, II, 130.
[15] Letters, W.C. to J.B., 25 Nov. 1798.
[16] Letters, T.L. to W.C., 21 Sep. 1802.

is as follows; I conceived they might have been fragments left on the ground as are glass bottles etc. in the present day, and worked in the earth by rabbits, and soon after the fall of the trilithon the adjacent earth containing the pottery might fall into the excavation...in this manner I wish you to represent it.'[17]

In April 1802 a party, which included Colt, Coxe, and Leman, met at Beckhampton. Cunnington was to have been there, but apparently was not. 'We found but indifferent accommodations at the Inn', wrote Colt in his journal.

> Before dinner we ascended Silbury Hill which may be called the *King of Barrows*, as it is far superior in size to any existing in our Island. Its original destination is rather uncertain. Some antiquarians have supposed it to have been a tumulus erected to the memory of some great Prince and Stukeley mentions human bones having been found within it. Others think that it may have been an altar, consecrated Mount or place of religious worship connected with the Druidical Temple at Abury. Whatever its purport may have been it is certainly a very singular object, as well as a wonderful effort of human art. In the evening we walked to Abury, distant about a mile from our Inn. This Temple may boast a much earlier existence, as well as a much larger extent than Stonehenge. . . . The Stones are erected in their natural state, rude & unshapen as they came from their native quarry. Had not the original plan of this immense building been fortunately preserved by Stukeley, modern antiquarians, I fear, would have found it impossible to have traced it, particularly the most singular part of it, viz. the majestic avenues, the snake's head etc., reduced at present to a few scattered stones. Neither is the interior part of the Temple in a much better condition, and a few years probably will annihilate all traces of this wonderful structure, except the high circular Mound of Earth which surrounded it.[18]

The next day they traced part of the Roman road from Bath to Silchester, from where it crossed the turnpike to Devizes as far as Morgan's Hill. They returned along the Wansdyke (Pl. 49a). After dinner they followed the Roman road in the other direction, towards Marlborough. Philip Crocker, a young man of twenty-one, who subsequently made all the surveys and the drawings for the plates of *Ancient Wiltshire*, was also present. He wrote enthusiastically to Cunnington. He had never experienced an excursion more pleasing or satisfactory. 'Mr. Leman is (as you mentioned) a man of extraordinary talents; possess'd of a natural bold genius, quick penetra-

[17] Letters, W.C. to J.B., Nov. 1802.
[18] R.C.H. Journal, 1802, Cardiff.

tion, and almost unlimited knowledge. These properties, assisted with affluence, seldom lie rusty.'[19]

While Colt went on to Cheltenham and South Wales, Coxe and Cunnington spent the early summer investigating barrows near Stonehenge, particularly those which Stukeley had called Druid Barrows; small mounds in the centre of a wide circular platform surrounded by a ditch and bank, now known as *disc* barrows. In July these operations were suspended so that attention could be given to long barrows at Tilshead.[20] The largest was 377 feet long, 99 wide and 11 high. 'What slaughter to occupy such an amazing space!'[21] commented Wyndham. Two others were also opened; one 255 feet long and 156 wide at the broad end; the other 173 feet long and 49 to 60 feet wide. The work went on throughout August, but apart from the usual black earth and a few skeletons nothing new was discovered. Samples of the earth were sent to Mr. Hatchett, a leading chemist, for examination. His analysis showed that it contained no animal substance. It was a blow to Wyndham's hypothesis; but he was not altogether satisfied and wrote to Cunnington: 'If you should, at any time, meet in your excavations any more of the black sooty earth, I think it would be worthwhile to dig thro' it, where perhaps you may meet with the bones or residuum of the slain, which might have been originally covered with earth or turf prior to the formation of the Barrow with the Marl of the Country.'[22]

It was, however, the end of 'battle barrows', and nothing more was deduced about them in Colt's lifetime. 'They are', he later wrote, 'so uniform in their construction, and uninteresting in their contents, that we have given up all researches in them, having for many years in vain looked for that information which might tend to throw some satisfactory light on the history of these singular mounds of earth.'[23]

By the beginning of 1802 Coxe had said *he* was going to write an account of the antiquities of Wiltshire, and he asked Cunnington not to disclose, even to the Society of Antiquaries, the mounting evidence from the barrows. At least some of this was sensational; for instance, the finding of the first example of a Deverel–Rimbury[24] barrel urn (Pl. 51a) at Stonehenge.

Colt had also begun to blow cool on Britton's project for a third volume, refusing to let him have information on the grounds that he had promised it to Coxe. 'Indeed, the papers are more calculated for a minute History than for a *Tourist*', he wrote. 'I hear Mr. Lysons intends to publish a magnificent work on a plan similar to that you propose.'[25] Britton was very

---

[19] Letters, Philip Crocker 1, 6 May 1802.
[20] Letters, Coxe 25–7; Papers, III, 39.
[21] Letters, H.P.W. 26.
[22] Letters, H.P.W. 34, 5 Nov. 1803.
[23] A.W.I. 92–3.
[24] The name subsequently given to a Middle Bronze Age Culture, c. 1200 B.C.
[25] Letters, R.C.H. to J.B., 5 Apr. 1801.

put about. 'This idea of *jealous* opposition distresses me very much', he told Cunnington. 'To think that just as I have acquired some informatn on the subject. . . . I should be watched with a jealous eye and opposed and counteracted by those persons who *ought* to patronize and encourage me.'[26]

By November 1802 plans for Coxe's book were on the way, and a meeting was held at Stourhead to discuss them. Colt, Cunnington, Coxe, Crocker, and others were present. 'Your list of camps is formidable', wrote Crocker to Cunnington, 'and when combined with a few more would greatly swell the intended work:—but where will be the spirit for its accomplishment?'[27] In December Coxe married. 'A *bold* and *unexpected* stroke', said Crocker. 'I am only fearful that it will affect the *whole county of Wilts*.'[28] Coxe assured Cunnington, however, that his wife, though ignorant of Greek, was very fond of county histories.

During 1803, while Colt was occupied in Wales and Coxe with newly married life, Cunnington, when time and health permitted, continued his researches. Opening a barrow on the north bank of the Wylye at Upton Lovel[29] he found articles of gold; eleven cylindrical beads, two decorated cones, and an ornamented rectangular plate. Among other grave goods were an amber space-plate necklace and a curious little cup perforated and studded all over with projecting knobs, now known to belong to the Wessex culture c. 1500–1250 B.C. Wyndham had seen no such things before. Cunnington ventured the conclusion that they belonged to a British chief 'near the time of Caesar's invasion'.[30]

His journeys tended to spill over into Dorset, especially down the line of the Roman road from Old Sarum to Badbury Rings, according to Grinsell 'perhaps the finest archaeological setting in Wessex'. The area round this iron age hill fort, the Vindocladia of the Romans, had many signs of early settlement; although Cunnington, influenced no doubt by Stukeley, placed Vindocladia some miles to the north at Gussage Cow Down. During the second half of 1803 he was also busy on the Deverill Downs where, among others, he opened the great flint barrow opposite Cold Kitchen Hill, 76 feet in diameter and 13 feet high.

> This tumulus has given me three times the trouble & been attended with three times the expense of any barrow I ever opened if I except the vast long barrow at Tilshead [he told Colt in December]. Had you not frequently urged me to persevere I should have desisted long ago. . . . About ten days ago I sent the two labourers to make another section. . . determining that this should close the business—after two days labour and finding

[26] Letters, J.B. to W.C., 10 Dec. 1802.
[27] Letters, P.C. 3, 4 Nov. 1802.
[28] Letters, P.C. 3, 3 Jan. 1803.
[29] Upton Lovel, 'Golden Barrow'; Letters, H.P.W. 30; Papers, I, 42; *A.W.*, I, 98.
[30] Papers, I, 42.

nothing, we gave up the pursuit,—you may therefore judge of my surprise when on Tuesday last a man from Deverell came to inform me that in consequence of the late thaw, one side of the last section had fallen in & discovered three urns standing together near the top of the barrow. I sent the two barrow men the same afternoon—on their return I was extremely mortified in learning that the urns had been ransacked and broken,—also that a brass spear or arrow head had been broken or lost, and that there was nothing to bring home but fragments of the largest urn.[31]

It was not only marauding shepherds who spoiled the record; Colt's friend, Richard Fenton, the poet and lawyer from Fishguard, took away all the articles found in the other barrows, including amber, glass and jet beads which are now lost. 'I was very willing he should take them,' said Cunnington, 'but at the same time expressing a wish that some person would make drawings.'[32]

Coxe wrote in November that Colt was 'barrow mad'.[33] Although the country had been at war with France since April, he had no fear that this would interfere with their antiquarian researches, but he nevertheless wished Bonaparte at the bottom of the flint barrow. He had meanwhile been canvassing for a vacant canonry at Salisbury so that for the time he was not interested in tumuli, Cunnington, Stukeley and Stonehenge. On 1 April 1804, Colt wrote to Cunnington, 'Now we have got the business of *exploring out* of my friend Coxe's hands, we shall go on better & more rapidly. Crocker & I shall do more in *one day* than *he* would have done in a week.'[34] He did not take over full responsibility until 1806.

Britton, convinced that Wiltshire must now be written off, regretted the time he had spent on its beauties and the thankless dedication he had made to Colt. 'As it is possible, & very probable, that I may never see you again (for depend on it I will never again ask a *favour* from you, having been several times *refused*) I shall be glad if you will remit me (per return of post) 3£ 6. for the 1st proofs.'[35] 'Paid p. draft 12 April', Colt wrote at the top. He did not care for Britton's 'intemperance' but he was still willing to promote and encourage his undertakings. This gave Britton some consolation; and although he felt he had experienced 'more incivility and contemptuous treatment from gentn. in Wiltshire than from those of *any other* county', he decided after all to bring out a third volume, to prove he had 'not been idle or inattentive to the subject'.[36]

[31] W.C. to R.C.H., 14 Dec. 1803.
[32] Ibid.
[33] Letters, Coxe 40, 1 Nov. 1803.
[34] Letters, R.C.H. 2, 1 Apr. 1804.
[35] Letters, J.B. to R.C.H., 8 Apr. 1804, T(ST) 383.907.
[36] J.B. to R.C.H., 4 Apr. 1804, T(ST) 383.907.

Chapter 4

Field-work

From now on Coxe and Wyndham virtually disappear from this story. It was tacitly assumed that Colt would write the *Ancient History of Wiltshire* from the information which Cunnington was assembling. Leman was the advisor on theoretical matters, especially concerning tracks, camps, and earthworks. Philip Crocker was the surveyor and draughtsman. Stephen and John Parker (father and son) actually did the excavations, and if more labour was required took charge of it. All these men, a cross-section of society, were caught up in the excitement of their common enterprise. The Parkers were not merely passive labourers with pick and shovel, but took an active interest in exploring the countryside for traces of the Britons (Pl. 52). 'The first thing I wish to have done...is for John to explore the Vale of Deverill as far as Kingston', wrote Colt on one occasion. 'I must come over for a day to you to examine the newly discovered villages and place them properly on our Map. John will make enough money to *build one* if he goes on as prosperously as he has hitherto. When he has done all the more important work, he must examine Ridge & Grovely Woods most thoroughly both *in* them & *round* them.'[1] And Cunnington, on another occasion: 'I was on tiptoe expecting Stephen and John on their arrival with your account of the October meeting. They were highly delighted in narrating their discoveries. Had John found a purse of Guineas he could not have been better pleased.'[2] For Crocker it was an experience which transformed his life, and he was deeply attached to both Cunnington and Colt, whose Steward at Stourhead he eventually became. But above all it was Cunnington's personality which held the group together, coping with all Colt's demands on the one hand and the Parkers on the other. It is probably the reason why, after his death, excavation almost entirely ceased.

By 1803 Cunnington had already a way of classifying barrows and a method of opening them.[3] The terms finally used were: *long*, whether

[1] Letters, R.C.H. 79, 1809.
[2] W.C. to R.C.H., 25 Oct. 1807.
[3] W.C. to Revd. Mr. Richardson, of Woolverton, Somerset, February 1803. Copies by R.C.H. in 'Collections for Wiltshire'. W.A.S. See Papers, III, 36, and Appendix I.

oblong or egg-shaped; *bowl*, the most common rounded sort; *bell*, considered an elegant refinement of the bowl, with a berm and ditch; *Druid*, after Stukeley, a small mound or mounds on a wide platform surrounded by a ditch and bank; *pond*, an inverted bowl, not considered as sepulchral. There were also variations of these basic types, including *cone* and *broad*, making twelve in all (Pl. 53). Three main classifications of round barrows in Wessex are accepted today. (A) Bowl: Hoare's common rounded sort; (B) Bell (bermed barrows); (C) Disc (Hoare's Druid barrows), with sub-types saucer-barrow (diameter much less than disc barrow), and pond-barrow (which may be a misnomer).

With the contents of the barrows it was different. 'After all the experience we have had', noted Cunnington, 'I am almost of the opinion the Britons had no regular system in regard to the tumulus nor many other things practised at the interment of their dead, but appear to have been more influenced by caprice than by established rules.'[4] He had some idea of the antiquity of his finds, although he underestimated in placing them between 500 and 1000 B.C. He conceived, by the elegance of workmanship, that the use of bronze must have preceded iron for a considerable time; also that some of the objects were imported. But he was unable to predict from the external appearance of a tumulus whether to expect inhumation or cremation, nor what grave goods might be found. Sometimes an insignificant barrow,[5] which had escaped previous notice, would yield articles of bone, pottery, copper and gold, whereas a bell-shaped barrow[6] of superior size and beauty, involving immense labour in throwing out the earth to a depth of fifteen feet, yielded only an interment of burned bones without any urn, arms or trinkets. In 'the monarch of the plain'[7] nothing was found after two attempts. No wonder John Parker had sulky fits.

Cunnington's methods are today considered to have been quite inadequate. Piggott, writing of the excavation of unchambered long barrows, observes that the 'excavations and their record fail lamentably to satisfy even the most moderate demands of the modern archaeologist'. Nevertheless the records of the contents of other barrows have been of some assistance to those who have followed. The articles were collected in a Moss House in Cunnington's garden; the urns arranged on shelves of elm, the bark still on their edges; and on the floor a model of Avebury formed of pebbles. Colt's friend, Richard Fenton, who dedicated three sonnets to Cunnington, gave a description of the Moss House in *A Tour in quest of Genealogy* (1811).

> Nothing could be more curious and systematic than the arrangement of the museum: the contents of every tumulus were separate, and the articles so disposed as in the case of ornaments, such as beads, in such elegant knots and festoons, as to please the eye

[4] Papers, V, 43, note.
[5] Mere 81133453. *A.W.*, I, 44.
[6] T.30, Stonehenge. *A.W.*, I, 162.
[7] T.40, Stonehenge. *A.W.*, I, 164.

which looks to nothing farther. The story of several was so perfectly told by the relics they contained, that an epitaph could not have let us more into the light of the rank and character of the dead. In one drawer were displayed all the utensils employed to fabricate arrow-heads, (and) other weapons and implements that required sharp points. there being various whetstones, of a coarse and a finer grit, with grooves in each, worn down by the use made of them; together with bone in its wrought and un-wrought state, evidently proving it to have been the sepulchre of an artist, whose employ this was. In another we were shown some flint arrow-heads, very similar to those I saw at Milford, which had been dug out of a turbary in the island of Nantucket.[8]

Philip Crocker was already making drawings of these objects in 1804, so that they could be engraved as plates for the history. The business of surveying had continued steadily from 1800.[9] By 1802 he seems to have taken it over completely from his father and brothers. It was not always a straightforward job as his terms of reference were often not specific. In 1804 he was tracing Bokerley Ditch through Cranborne Chase, with a local man as a guide, but could find no sign of 'supposed camps at Broad Chalk and Damerham'.[10] 'There are also three that he (Colt) speaks of at Wardour', he wrote to Cunnington on another occasion, 'which I con-ceive must be one at Dinton (of which we must enquire at Mr. Wyndham's), one at Wardour Castle and the other at Swallow-cliff or Castle Ditches, which we have surveyed—All the others on the list are, I believe, in the ancient circuit of Old Sarum, except it is Damerham; and as there are two places of this name in Wiltshire, we know not what he means—"Durnford" —as he writes it—is Ogbury Camp, but pray, where is *Sudbury*? I can find no such place in the large map.'[11]

Crocker was, moreover, employed by Colonel Mudge on the newly formed Ordnance Survey,[12] moving during 1805 and 1806 from West Sussex, through Hampshire to Wiltshire. Leave to assist Colt Hoare was sometimes grudgingly given, although this ultimately paid off in the numbers of archaeological sites marked on the Ordnance Survey sections covering Salisbury Plain, the Vale of Pewsey, and the southern part of the Marlborough Downs. Time was often short and, as Crocker said, he could not in one day go over a whole area, map in hand, inspecting every hill and dale, which is what Colt seemed to expect. Fortunately he was

8 'A Barrister' (Richard Fenton), *A Tour in quest of Genealogy* (1811), p. 251. Cunnington's museum also contained a collection of fossils.
9 Crocker received £3 3s. for a camp, £1 1s. for a plate of drawings, and 15s. for a barrow. Accounts for A.W., W.A.S., Devizes.
10 Letters, P.C. 5, 28 Sep. 1804.
11 Letters, P.C. 32.
12 Formed in 1791 for military requirements. First map in the 1 inch scale, showing south-east corner of England, appeared on 1 January 1801.

young and enthusiastic. Marriage in 1806 increased his energy and he wrote to Cunnington. 'You were somewhat wrong in your conjectures about the *month's holiday*....I am happy to say that the week I devoted to get a licence—go to church—and bring home a wife—allowed me at the same time to prepare three drawings for the engraver—since when I have made another plate for Sir Richard's collection—and finished 7 more in Indian ink.'[13]

By the beginning of 1806 *Giraldus* was finished and Colt wrote to Cunnington,

> What with Booksellers, Engravers & Printer's Devils, I am almost hurried out of my senses—otherwise I should have replied sooner to yr last letter—I wish I could indulge myself with thinking on the Britons: but I must first be delivered of my Archdeacon. It is unreasonable for *me* to expect that *you* should be at more expence than suits yr own fancy or amusement—and of this we will talk further when we meet—My plans are these, after the assizes on the 8th of March, I must go home for two or three days—I purpose sleeping at Deptford on Sunday the *16th of March*, where I shall be glad to meet you either on that evening or *early* on the next morng,—I have desired Crocker to come to you on Monday the third of March, first to finish the plates already arranged & then to proceed *with you* to Amesbury to take your directions about the district to be planned round Stonehenge, which shd extend Westwd to the circle at Winterbourne Stoke—North—to the Cursus—South to the Prophets barrows & East to the town of Amesbury—*he* must have John with him to fix his rods on each tumulus—& *you* might take the other two men to develop the tumuli in the Circle—which I beg may be done completely, as it is a singular object. It would also be gaining time if you would examine Yarnborough & Vespasians' Camp with him, the plans in your hand—I beg you will not open any more barrows till I have seen you—but Crocker must leave the plan of the environs of Stonehenge with *you*— that you & I may look it over on the spot together.[14]

Plans were followed by action. In March Colt and Crocker met at Marlborough and in a week, in spite of dreadful weather, Stonehenge, Casterley, Chisenbury, Lidbury, Broadbury, Marden, Everleigh Barrows— Chisbury and Folly Farm (Cunetio)[15] had been attentively surveyed, the latter most particularly. Colt was elated. 'Every day produces *novelty & knowledge*—we have seen what will also *stagger you*—one of the completest British Villages & what is more a specimen of *British Masonry*, it is

[13] Letters, P.C. 38.   [14] Letters, R.C.H. 15, Feb. 1806.
[15] Letters, P.C. 9, 23 Mar. 1806.

    15—L.A.

situated in the plain—immediately under *Barbury Castle* (Pl. 50)....Our Cunetio proves highly interesting, abounding both in *British* as well as Roman remains, which makes it clear (in my eyes) that it was originally a British work.'[16]

Leman joined them when the weather cleared. He did not enjoy wandering through the woods when they were dripping, or sliding down Martinsell Hill at the risk of his neck. He liked comfort. 'For my bed at Marlbro I trust that if you have any friendship for me, you will first choose me one to the South, in which there is a fireplace (as I must dress in it) & then instantly call up all the maids in the house & choosing two of the cleanest & fairest, put them both into the bed & keep them till I arrive to dinner... remember a well aird bed is my sine-qua-non.'[17] Crocker enjoyed it all enormously.

> Tuesday we pursued the Wansdyke from Morgan's Hill to Martinsell and met Mr. Leman in the evening at Marlbro':— and Wednesday the station (Cunetio) at *Folly Farm* was *decidedly established*. Mr. L. was delighted with what had been done, and entered into the spirit of the pursuit with all that fire you know he possesses....Thus, my dear Sir, the days were spent with much advantage, in knowing more of the subject that Sir Richard is now *deeply* involved in:—and in the evenings the conversation was such as to gratify the mind, and stimulate the desires to further pursuits.—Mr. L. with that ease and force of argument he at all times, and in every subject, can make use of, urged the pleasure, *and the necessity* of such an undertaking:— nay not only Wiltshire was to engage the mind of Sir Richard, but also Somerset and Dorset....But why does he not come forward himself with all the talents he possesses?—there seems to be a willingness to answer every doubt and difficulty but a reluctancy to put his hand to the plough.[18]

Cunnington, who had been suffering from 'nervous debility', was glad Colt had entered into the history of British antiquities with so much spirit. He had often longed to be with him. The discoveries at Barbury were interesting; he fancied Colt had not told him all about Cunetio. The tone continued frosty, and the reason becomes apparent. Colt had sent by Mr. Iremonger, a clergyman engaged in antiquarian pursuits in Hampshire, a plan of campaign. 'I wish *all* this summer to be devoted to the accurate investigation of the numerous British and Saxon earthen works with which our county abounds....John must be your constant attendant with his pick axe, without which *nothing positive* can be ascertained.'[19] There

[16] Letters, R.C.H. 18, 22 Mar. 1806.
[17] T.L. to R.C.H. Undated, T(ST) 383.907.
[18] Letters, P.C. 12, 11 Apr. 1806.
[19] R.C.H. to W.C., quoted *W.A.M.*, vol. LV, June 1954.

followed a list of places to be visited. Apart from those in his own neigh-
bourhood, Cunnington was to examine carefully the ground between
Heytesbury and Tilshead, and thence to Everleigh. From Upavon or
Pewsey, which had good accommodation, he was to visit all these places
Colt and Crocker had surveyed from Marlborough. From Roundway Hill,
above Devizes, he was to follow the Wansdyke along the down to St.
Ann's Hill. Continuing to Marlborough he would of course examine the
Roman site at Folly Farm. Northwards was Barbury Castle; there were
some banks in a bottom near it in which he must dig. Following the ridgeway along the northern edge he would come to Liddington Castle; and
further east to Chisbury and Membury. In addition, Avebury must be
attentively examined and the country about it.

But it was not the substance of the demands which nettled Cunnington
so much as the tail. 'In this curious investigation we must form no *previous
system* either about Britons, Romans or Saxons.

'*Our object is Truth*. Mr. Leman told me he had sent you a paper on
the subject describing the peculiarities of the British trackways, towns,
and works—If he did not, I will get him to do it.'[20] Cunnington had heard
all this before; to be precise, in December 1801. He replied: 'You recommend that when I take the field I leave all my *systems at home* & at the
same time recommend me to a system of Mr. Leman's—which system I
had from him some years ago.'[21] Colt hastened to explain. 'When I talked
to you about *systems* I can assure you I had formed *none*, either on Mr.
Leman's opinion or my own: I only wished you to be perfectly unbiassed,
and to judge only from certain proof.'[22] But Leman's system continued
to be a thorn in Cunnington's side. Colt later sent all Cunnington's accounts
to Leman for his comments; and then, rather tactlessly, back to Cunnington for his replies. The section on *Camps and other earthen works* came
in for particular attention. 'This chapter is full of very material errors',
noted Leman. 'No wonder', replied Cunnington, 'when it treats of subjects
which admit of so much dispute.'[23] Both made conjectures about the way
of life of the people whose remains they were investigating; for instance,
it was Cunnington's view that the Britons, or aborigines as he called them,
occupied the high lands because the valleys were full of wood, swamps and
probably wild beasts. 'Why not fertile and productive valleys?'[24] asked
Leman. And to this Cunnington could only assert that the Britons
descended to the valleys only after the Romans had established roads and
stations. But conjecture was a different matter from reconciling the discoveries made in excavation. Leman's system[25] was based on the not

[20] Ibid.
[21] R.C.H. 20 (from W.C.), 31 Mar. 1806.
[22] Letters, R.C.H. 21, 9 Apr. 1806.
[23] Papers, VI, 1 ff.
[24] Ibid.
[25] See letter T.L. to W.C., 24 Dec. 1801.

unreasonable assumption that the art of castramenation progressed from small irregular works to those of a regular nature. From his observations, which did not appear to include digging, he deduced that irregular works were pre-Roman; those of the Romans square or oblong, and circular works later. Extreme height in bank or depth in ditch he attributed to the Danes or Saxons; and the mark of a religious enclosure was a ditch on the inside of the vallum. Cunnington was more inclined to look for evidence in the ground; thus when Leman pronounced the outer bank at Scratch-bury Saxon, he pointed out that finding a flint celt at the entrance was an argument against this claim.[26] And of Stockton Wood, 'It is very easy to say how these things should be in the closet, but unfortunately for Mr. Leman we have twenty proofs that this place was occupied down to the latest period of the Roman government in this country.'[27]

Cunnington was not, however, the only one to have to justify his theories. Colt had one, on which he was rather set, that many of the banks and ditches found on the Wiltshire downs were sheltered ways between one settlement and another. Leman could not resist ridiculing this idea.

Many years ago, having informed a Mr. Dickenson that an old road, by which I came to his house, was a British road, I was not a little surprised afterwards at hearing him holding forth in a large assembly on *the British Trackways*, & this unfortunate road having been never repaired for the course of two thousand years, & having served as a channel or drain for all the water which had passed through it, became of course like a Ditch of many yards in depth. His fancy (for he was a Poet) immediately seized the circumstance, & he explained to the company the whole process by which the primeval Britons made their Roads: how they dug them deep in the soil to cover their marches from one place to another, & entered into the most *minute details*, as if he had been present at the whole operation. The thing being totally new, surprised the company at first, until they had time to recollect themselves when one general scream of laughter drove poor Dickenson & his hypothesis from the field. Since that time I have never heard of the ingenuity of our forefathers in their *scooping out* roads till it has been revived by you & your friend Mr. Crocker—for God's sake what would they dig into the ground for, when common sense must tell them that a road in a bottom can never be so good, or so lasting, as one on the surface of the soil—No! No! Tom Noddles as you both are the ditches you have seen are *clearly & decisively Boundaries* to mark the addition of property.[28]

[26] Papers, VII, 13.
[27] Letter from W.C., 28 Aug. 1802. Collections for Wilts., W.A.S.
[28] T.L. to R.C.H. Undated, T(ST) 383.907.

In May 1806 a party, which included Coxe and the Fentons, father and son, met to open barrows at Everleigh. Cunnington could not be there, but Crocker wrote to him that it was '*a feast of reason*, and *flow of soul*'. There had been a priest, a poet, and artist, a bard '*and a Patron of all that is good and great*...amidst the des(s)ert of fruit & the sparkling glass stood the rude relicks of 2000 years:—the "Britons" given as a toast, and drank with all the enthusiasm of true Antiquaries.'[29] From Everleigh Colt set out for Bala, via Andover, Hungerford, and Swindon. On 22 June he sailed from Holyhead for Dublin.

[29] Letters, P.C. 35.

Chapter 5

Stonehenge

While Colt was away, Cunnington rode out over most of the ground he had been asked to cover, taking John and Stephen with him to dig where it seemed expedient. During July they opened several barrows on the downs towards Enford and Netheravon; and three, one rainy morning at Golden Ball Hill, north-west of Pewsey. 'I kept John in a good temper with the history of Joanna Southcote and her prophecies; this and the meteor which luckily we saw brought us in good humour to the inn.'[1]

Crocker, who by July had left Sussex, looked forward to Colt's return.

> I am glad to hear of your continued pursuits for the Wiltshire Antiquities [he wrote to Cunnington] and your riding away from the Doctor to the invigorating breezes on your downs gives me no small pleasure—my anxiety to hear your opinion on Tilshead, Marden, Chissenbury etc. will lead me over to your house the first opportunity I have before I go into Hampshire. Sir Richard, I understand, is not yet returned from Ireland,— but as Giraldus is now given to the world, and the work off from his mind, I hope he will come back to Wiltshire with all his powers and resolutions to forward the work now collecting— *he shall not wait, nor want, for any assistance from us.*[2]

Unfortunately, when Colt got back in September he was far from well, not only from a cold 'caught in the Hibernian bogs', but from rheumatism and gout in shoulders, knee, and foot. Furthermore, instead of giving his attention to Wiltshire, he sat down to write a book on his Irish tour, in which he had especially noted the poor state of the cemeteries at Buttevant and elsewhere, whose disgusting and desolated appearance, he said, could only be equalled by a field of battle. 'I have before had occasion to remark this irreligious indecency, and in no place have I seen so little reverence paid to the dead; for here you may see coffins with skeletons exposed to public sight through the apertures of the stone; and coffins taken up

1 Papers, VIII, 30.
2 Letters, P.C. 34, 22 July 1806.

unperished, to make room for fresh interments.'[3] With this gesture to the souls of the departed, he turned anew to the prehistoric graves of Salisbury Plain.

He already had a plan for the book, in which a survey of the area round Stonehenge and a systematic investigation of all the barrows there were to play an important part. Apart from this, barrow excavation was to cease, 'otherwise *new* matter, as you well see, will daily occur & we shall never know *where* to stop'.[4] Cunnington was to receive £100 on the delivery to Colt of all his papers concerning barrows, camps, and other earthworks.

Colt's idea that autumn was to open a group of tumuli on Lake Down, to the south of Stonehenge, known as the Prophets' Barrows, from a sect of French enthusiasts who had preached from one of them in 1710. Some of them belonged to the Reverend Edward Duke, who, with Cunnington to assist him, wished to open them himself. Colt, whose strength and spirits were low, had doubts of being there, but he hoped Cunnington would make '*very large* sections, and ransack the Prophets effectually'.[5] Eventually he had to say,

> It is very great mortification to me to think that I must abandon my intended expedition to Stonehenge *for this season*—My health is such that it would be *madness* to expose myself to the cold air of the downs—I am better & getting rid of my disorder, but am still weak—tho' I am able to hobble about & take horse excercise—Still I hope something will be done—*though not on my account*—Mr. Duke is impatient to begin—and waits only for his instructions—I will write to him to say that as soon as the coursing meeting is over—*you* will give him the meeting with *your* men to put *his* apprentices in the right way—and I should recommend the *Prophets* first to your attention, but it must be understood rightly, that as *he* will have the articles discovered— *he* must bear *all* expences—*your* expences will of course fall to *my* lot—but I will not have any barrows opened on *my own* account except I can be present. . . . If Mr. Duke will enter zealously into the business & do it well, *we* shall be saved much trouble & expence—I only wish for correctness in the detail of discoveries. I had set my heart on this expedition and am truly concerned that ill health prevents my attendance—Mr. Fenton is not yet come but is expected daily.[6]

The weather proved the finest Cunnington could remember for October, and owing to the dryness of the summer the barrows opened well. 'Wednesday morning I rode to Lake Downs through a fog with no other guide

[3] Richard Colt Hoare, *Journal of a Tour in Ireland* (1807), p. 125.
[4] Letters, R.C.H. 26.
[5] Letters, R.C.H. 30, 15 Oct. 1806.
[6] Letters, R.C.H. 31.

but the different barrows I passed by, when within half a furlong of our group the sun burst out all at once and disclosed such a scene that few excepting poets could enjoy. Stonehenge never looked more grand.'[7] Fenton, who was also there, wrote three sonnets,

Auspicious morn, by prophets long foretold,
To Sarum's plain once more that calls my friend,
The dark sepulchral mysteries to unfold,
And DUKE's initiation to attend.[8]

The barrows again proved unpredictable in their contents. One of the largest contained only the skeleton of a child with a 'coarse drinking cup'; but in 'a flat mean barrow of small elevation' they found hundreds of amber beads, five plates of amber and pieces of gold.[9] In one of Duke's barrows were four small articles of bone, one black and the rest marked with a different pattern on each facet. Cunnington immediately wrote to William Owen, who replied:

I think you have guessed very happily respecting the use of the articles of bone, of which you have sent drawings—that they were used in casting of lots. For, under the druidical system many important decisions were made in this way. . . . And, as I have heretofore informed you that druidism is still preserved, so I shall now give you to understand that numberless allusions to the *coelbren*, or Lots, are to be found in the works of the Welsh Bards, and the manner of casting these lots I have seen myself, in attending the Bardic Meetings.[10]

Owen had a number of bees, including the theology of Joanna Southcott, which he found agreed with the 'druidical Triads of Divinity'.[11] About this time he inherited an estate and took the name of Pughe. As Colt drily put it, 'William Owen has succeed to £800 p.a. but the *poor* man is bit by the Prophetess Southcote'.[12]

Colt now seemed in as bad a way as Cunnington, with pains in his head as well as rheumatism and gout. He had been sadly harassed all winter, unfit, he said, for amusement or business. At the beginning of March 1807, he went to Cheltenham to recover. Uncured, he tried Bath; and that, or the advance of the season, was enough for him to set out on journeys to Dorset, Somerset, and Hagley. He found time, however, to spend a week at Amesbury at the beginning of June, presumably to disembowel with Cunnington the group of barrows on Wilsford Down. But perhaps the most interesting discovery that summer was made to the west of Stonehenge.

[7] Papers, XIII, 3 (Copy of letter to R.C.H., 30 Oct.).
[8] Fenton, *Tour in search of Genealogy*, p. 286.   [9] Papers, IV, 8.
[10] Letters, W. Owen, 27 Dec. 1806.
[11] Letters, W. Owen, 21 Dec. 1804. Owen was one of the elders appointed by Joanna Southcott.
[12] Letters, R.C.H. 35, Jan. 1807.

Little systematic study had been made of the stone circle itself since Stukeley's survey in the 1720s. In his account of it Cunnington wrote:

> I have been surprized that the following question never occured to those writers who have written so voluminously on this work. That is, how came the Britons in erecting Stonehenge to make use of two kinds of stone which are totally dissimilar to each other? Any person versed in mineralogy will perceive that the stones without the work, those composing the outer circle & its imposts, & the five Trilithons, are all raised from Sarsen stones found in that neighbourhood; whereas the inner circle of small upright stones & the interior oval of upright stones are composed of a variety of granite, hornstone etc., most likely brought from some part of Devonshire or Cornwall as I do not know where such stones could be procured nearer than the latter places.[13]

This information he probably got from William Smith,[14] the geologist, or James Sowerby,[15] the artist and naturalist whom he consulted. It is now known that the smaller stones composing the inner circle were brought from the Prescelly Hills in Pembrokeshire. Smith's views on the origin of Sarsens is an interesting confusion of biblical and scientific thinking. He supposed that a stratum of sand containing these stones had once covered the chalk land, and that this had been washed off at the deluge, leaving the heavier stones behind.[16] Cunnington thought that the flood had carried them from a stratum of sand south-east of the chalk. 'This is the direction the waters took at the deluge—according to the opinion of Sir Joseph Banks, Smith and others.'[17] Stukeley's guess had been even more curious. 'This whole country, hereabouts, is a solid body of chalk, cover'd with a most delicate turf. As this chalky matter harden'd at creation it spew'd out the most solid body of the stones, of greater specific gravity than itself; and assisted by the centrifuge power, owing to the rotation of the globe upon its axis, threw them up upon its surface, where they now lie.'[18]

However, the fact of there being two kinds of stone led Cunnington to suppose that the outer and inner circles were erected at different times. He appears to have decided that the large Sarsen circle was the more primitive of the two, and Colt Hoare illustrated it thus in *Ancient Wiltshire*. The differences in the stones had been noted by Leman in April 1806, when he wrote to Colt: 'I begin now to suspect that the *circle of stones* at Stonehenge are of *different aeras* & as I think I recollect that the stones themselves are of two kinds, I wish you to enquire of Meade or some intelligent

---

[13] Papers, IV, 53.
[14] William Smith, 1769–1839, Geologist and Civil Engineer. Lived near Bath from 1795.
[15] James Sowerby, 1757–1822, Naturalist and Artist. See Letters, 30 June 1807.
[16] Papers, IV, 54.
[17] Papers, IV, 35.   [18] Stukeley, *Abury*, p. 16.

person, whether they really are so or not, because this would be a striking feature for my new Hypothesis.' He had, of course, to fit this into his system. 'I suspect more than ever', he wrote a month later, 'that it was *first* a *Temple of the Celts* before it was altered by their successors the *Belgae*, & that the *latter* merely added the *Trilithons* which if I remember right are of a different *kind of stone* from the smaller rude stones which surround them.'[19]

Since the time when he had found Roman pottery under the fallen trilithon, Cunnington had dug in a number of places, under the so-called altar and in the ditch. Perhaps his last field expedition with Colt, in 1810, was to dig under the prostrate stone[20] at the entrance to the earthwork, popularly thought to be for the slaughter of victims. By examining the under side they showed that it had originally been upright.

In September 1807 Cunnington found Sarsen chippings in a barrow to the west of Stonehenge; and in the cist of the primary interment, which Stukeley as usual had missed, 'a large piece of one of the blue stones'.[21] Reflecting that this was not the first time he had found pieces of Sarsen in the tumuli, and that they were clearly chippings, not pieces occurring naturally in the soil, he concluded they had been scattered about before the tumulus was made. 'If this conclusion is just, it gives a higher antiquity to our British Temple than many Antiquaries are disposed to allow.'[22] Colt saw the significance. 'To what remote antiquity will this circumstance carry the temple of Abury?'[23] he exclaimed. Leman missed the point. 'Why should it be thought remarkable to find chippings of the stones of which Stonehenge is formed near the place?' 'This is a childish note', wrote Cunnington, 'if they prove that the Barrows are subsequent, we get an important piece of information.'[24]

Colt, having returned to Stourhead for the winter, planned to investigate all the tumuli in his neighbourhood about which he was not certain. Fenton, now his regular companion, came to stay, and wrote a fanciful account[25] of his visit, including the opening of the barrow known as Jack's Castle, near Alfred's Tower. The event which Colt had long anticipated, however, was the attack on the 'Monster of Marden', which he regarded as only less important than Avebury, Silbury, and Stonehenge. Although he had been given the height as 40 feet, Crocker's survey showed it as 22½. 'It is absolutely necessary *for you & me* to inspect it carefully before *Stephen & John* are set to work—for you must be aware that they are not of themselves sufficiently competent to set about it without very minute

[19] T.L. to R.C.H., 30 Apr. 1806, T(ST) 383.907.
[20] W.C. to J.D., Apr. 1810, quoted *W.A.M.*, XXIV, p. 129. See also Letters, W.C. to J.D., Mar. 1810; J.D. to W.C., 24 Apr. 1810.
[21] Papers, XII, 11.
[22] Papers, XII, 12.
[23] Letters, R.C.H. 44.
[24] Papers, XII, 13.
[25] Fenton, op. cit.

instructions—and as the undertaking will be both arduous & expensive, I do not wish to have anything done *before you & I have viewed it*.'[26] In October, 23 square feet of the floor of the barrow were exposed. Signs of cremation and bones, animal and human, were found, but the task was abandoned without conclusion, partly on account of expense, but also because of its unstable nature, being made of sand. By 1818 it had been completely levelled. The failure persuaded Colt that no major piece of information was now lacking and that he might as well start work.

[26] Letters, R.C.H. 44.

Chapter 6

The Valetudinarians

During the last months of 1807 Colt began his draft and he wrote to Cunnington: 'The tedium of the late bad weather has been somewhat alleviated by the excercise of my *pen*. Being a man of *method*, as you well know, I have begun my work in regular order—Title, Preface, Introduction —I have read a great deal this winter—of ancient times & lore but am sorry to say, the more I read, the more I am bewildered.'[1]

On 7 January 1808, he left Stourhead for London, calling at Heytesbury to collect the stone hatchets found at Knook and Upton Lovel so that he could get an expert opinion on them. 'I wish also to show the most perfect of the little *grape* urns to Wedgwood—to know if he could copy it. It will be very safe in his hands—and if you would have a little deal box made, and pack it round with wool, I could convey it in perfect safety.'[2]

Colt returned at the end of February, for the wedding of his son; in the spring he was out on the downs for those explorations which were now a seasonal occasion. 'I have had another delightful ride this morning—first to Battlesbury where I examined Crocker's *corrected plan* attentively, & found it *so incorrect* that I must have him there *in person* again. It is quite provoking to find so many *corrections* necessary....I hope to see you tomorrow on the down. I shall start at *ten*—over Arn hill near the lime kilns—& purpose my track towards Bratton—and shall look out for you on the trackway.'[3]

Crocker had a new house in Frome with 'an airy situation and a good light for drawing'. He was working on the plates for the first part of the book, which Colt said he *must* have before Cunnington went to London, a thing he did annually for a trade fair.

> Now talking of your going to London [Colt went on] I have a *request* to make you—to which *you must not say nay*—for I should be wanting in duty both to the county & myself were I not to *secure* a *portrait* of the primary and chief investigator of our British Antiquities—You must therefore *prolong* your stay

---

[1] Letters, R.C.H. 51.   [2] Ibid.
[3] Letters, R.C.H. 53.

a *couple* of days for that purpose, for *till* your *business* is completed, I conclude you cannot spare time to go to the *west* end of the town—for my artist Mr. Woodforde lives at Gt. Marlbro' Street—the arrangement we will talk of at Heytesbury—it is already in embryo.[4]

Cunnington duly attended for his picture, 'although he moaned most bitterly at the confined posture'.[5] Colt went off on 30 May, to explore the Somerset coast from 'below Wells' to Clifton. He then crossed to Wales where he met Fenton. 'Before we are many months older, we hope to ascertain the *true meaning* of the cromlech—for we mean to overturn several, & dig completely within them.'[6] The Reverend Henry Rowlands in *Mona Antiqua Restaurata* (1723) had suggested that *cromlechs* or *dolmens* were Druidical altars. Even Stukeley thought this was stretching the imagination a bit far, and that the Druid would have lost in dignity by climbing a ladder to perform his rites. We now know that they are denuded chambered tombs, as Colt might have concluded if his long barrows had been of that kind.

Colt stayed away till October. It must have seemed to Cunnington that he was left an undue proportion of the work, although there is no reason to suppose that he minded displaying his knowledge of the barrows to people for whom the opening was a social event. Of course there were moments of anxiety, especially when ladies were present. 'I had before experienced a great deal of mortification on their account at our want of success',[7] he had said on one occasion. His immediate task was the excavation, in September, of the fine tumuli which appear on the sky-line south of Stonehenge, known as the Normanton group. For once these lived up to their appearance as the graves of a Wessex aristocracy. Bush Barrow, a large tumulus 124 feet in diameter and 11 feet high, so-called by Stukeley because in his day it was fenced and planted with trees, contained an unusually rich interment. There were an axe and daggers of copper and bronze; 'curiously ornamented bones'; and articles of gold, including a wooden dagger haft decorated with small gold rivets. 'When we first discovered these shining points of gold we had no conception of their nature, otherwise we might have preserved thousands of them—but unfortunately John with his trowell had scattered them in every direction before I had examined them with a glass.'[8] There was also a polished mace-head of a rare type of limestone. Its unworn appearance and the fossil *Serpularia* it contained led Cunnington to think it might have been an

---

[4] Letters, R.C.H. 55.
[5] R.C.H. to A. B. Lambert, B.M. MSS. 28545, 17 May 1808.
[6] Letters, R.C.H. 56.
[7] Papers, IV, 45 ff.
[8] Papers, X, 9. The importance of the discoveries at Bush Barrow in establishing the existence of a distinct immigrant Wessex culture was first discussed by Piggott in 'The Early Bronze Age in Wessex', *Proceedings of the Prehistoric Society*, 1938, Jan.–July.

object of peculiar importance; even the serpent's egg esteemed so highly by the Druids, as Pliny had said.

Left to himself Cunnington wondered to what all their work amounted. His state of mind was not helped by Britton, now married, who although he found few occasions to write still nagged at what he thought avoidance on Cunnington's part.

> One might be led to suppose that your knowledge of human nature was much limited [wrote Cunnington]. What! because I cannot spend a day with you in London, & again because when at Heytesbury I did not invite Mrs. Britton & Yourself to stay at my house, I am to be blamed as slighting you. In times like the present a man in trade, to live, must make great exertions. ...Circumstances in regard to business & being obliged from poor health to get frequently on the downs I have very little time to spare with my friends. ... When in London I never have good health, therefore my great object is to get out of town as soon as I can. ... You have shewed yourself disatisfied with me ever since my connexion with Sir. Richd. Hoare & even the last time when at my house you threw out some expressions intimating that what Sir R— & myself were about would not be worth much. Now I am oftentimes of this opinion myself, yet it does not often happen that we are in a disposition to receive such hints, even from a friend.[9]

At that very time, however, the author was at last feeling equal to the task, and proposed turning his horses' heads towards the Stour, 'My health has been much improved by a life of ease, and I may almost say *idleness*—and my head can again bear the report of a gun. If my health continues as good as at present, I hope the winter will be profitably spent.'[10] By January, 'in spite of headaches', he had completed the manuscript for the first part of the book, which he took with him to London until March. During the spring and summer he spent more time than he had ever done, or was to do, out on the downs. Almost the whole of July and August he was on Salisbury Plain. Earthworks which John had reported needed verifying before they could be included in the next part. 'I wish you would send John to meet me on the trackway Wednesday morning with his axe & spade and to investigate these works. I shall be at Yarnbury Castle between 10 and 11—& shall proceed towards Overstreet from thence—so he must keep a look out for me about that time—and as he will start early, he may try his implements before I come—I shall also take the same opportunity of trying some very suspicious ground on this side of the Druid's Hut—Perhaps you may be tempted to meet me.'[11]

[9] Letters, W.C. to J.B., Sep. 1808.
[10] Letters, R.C.H. 59.   [11] Letters, R.C.H. 73.

At other times he was out with Crocker to make or check a survey; or to argue with Leman over boundaries versus scooped-out roads, but Leman could not be shifted, which inclined Colt to Cunnington's view of him.

> I agree with you that our friend the *Divine*—is often *hasty* in *thought* as well as *expression*—and *I am sure he is no Briton*—whenever I mention the subject, he avoids it, and returns to *Roman* ground where he is more at home—he is however candid & does not mind *objections* made to *his* systems—the more opinions *we* hear the better—we shall gain so little information from him on the subject of *our* researches that I could advise you not to send him any more papers—Suppose at your leisure you *write* a paper in answer to *his* notes—but do not *send* it to him—the weather is fit only for *our own* fireside.[12]

Cunnington did this. His letter, a fair summary of the theoretical basis of his researches is possibly of more interest to those concerned with the history of archaeological thought, and is therefore quoted as an appendix. His correspondence with James Douglas on Stonehenge has a similar interest. Douglas, whose *Nenia Britannica* may be said to be the prototype of *Ancient Wiltshire*, paid his first visit to Stourhead in August 1809, when he found the beauty of the place exceeded what he had been told. Douglas had been studying the Welsh Triads and had a theory that the heel-stone at Stonehenge represented Ceres and the altar-stone Proserpine, or their British equivalents. The stone circle was a temple of the sun, 'of the mithraic order',[13] dedicated to them. As 'the abbé' had explained all the mysteries, Colt said, they need think no more about Stonehenge. Leman was rather contemptuous of Douglas; a 'Ninny' he called him, for he had looked for the Roman station of Ad Decimum,[14] on the Arun, in the wrong place but had thereby accidentally discovered another. It may be, too, that Britton was not the only one to be jealous. 'Why, mon camerade', Leman wrote, 'what can give me so strong proof of your heads being affected as your desiring me to write to the *Abbé Douglas*, a pretty direction indeed! Altho' it is infinitely better than that of Coxe's who tells me only that he lives somewhere near Bognor, for *you* do specify his place of residence—: I have however found out on looking into the Noenia, that his name is James, & have accordingly this morning written to him as you desire.'[15]

Riding on the downs did not cure Colt's ailments, and in fact he thought in September it had made them worse. 'My poor head is a match for yours

[12] Letters, R.C.H. 70.
[13] Letters, J.D., 24 Apr. 1810.
[14] T.L. to R.C.H. T(ST) 383.907. No date.
[15] Ibid.

—I can neither shoot nor go on with my work, having a constant wearing pain which baffles all medicine.'[16] Eventually, persuaded by Leman, he went off to Bath to be dosed with arsenic, 'which in a few days brought forward the enemy who had hid himself in a *deep cist of bile*'.[17]

Cunnington, meanwhile, had been on a visit to his birthplace in Northamptonshire, and for a time at least had found relief.

> I left home on Tuesday the 5th inst with a pain in my head which continued all the way to Devizes where I was obliged to go to bed. The next morning on passing Shepherd's Shore into the downs about Abury I felt much enlivened as if entering the Garden of Eden, Abury, Silbury, etc. etc. all before me, here the pain in my head & all its gloomy attendants left me, & only returned for an hour or two that evening, & in the further progress of my journey I felt increase of strength & spirits.[18]

The respite was only temporary. The information he was under pressure to produce was sometimes inadequate, resulting in further questions to answer. '*John Parker* seems to *encrease in stupidity* as he grows *in years*', complained Colt, 'for he said nothing to me about his discoveries at Bonham.'[19] The reason, Cunnington replied, was that Colt had said that he knew of everything in the neighbourhood of Stourhead. Cunnington was indeed tried by the impatient author. Writing and attendance at barrows had taken up so much of his own and his daughter's time that his business had fallen behind. His head was so bad that he was obliged to retire at six or seven o'clock each evening. The pain was violent and, with few intervals, continuous.

As usual, Colt went to London in January, where his health improved under the celebrated Dr. Baillie. He worked a little every day and by February was 'in the midst of the Stonehenge tumuli'. Douglas was also in town talking about a new work on the origin of nations. 'I fear he will get beyond his depth',[20] said Colt.

The first part of *The Ancient History of Wiltshire* was ready for the press by the middle of March, and Colt pronounced himself cured. The frontispiece of the book was to be an engraving of Cunnington's portrait, but Colt was keeping this as a surprise. '*You* have nearly let *my cat* out of the bag', he told A. B. Lambert,[21] 'for the Arch Druid taxed me about *these plates* in which *you* told him *he would be particularly interested,* but I think I did away with his suspicions.'[22] But in the demands he continued to make

16 Letters, R.C.H. 75, Sep. 1809.
17 Letters, R.C.H. 78.
18 Letters, Misc., 5 Sep.
19 Letters, R.C.H. 81. Bonham is a farm and manor adjoining Stourton.
20 Letters, R.C.H. 87, Feb. 1810.
21 Aylmer Bourke Lambert, 1761–1842, botanist, lived at Boyton House, near Heytesbury, after his father's death in 1802.
22 R.C.H. to A. B. Lambert, B.M. MSS.

he showed himself unaware of the true state of Cunnington's health and mind. Had he but known it, the days in April and May were likely to be the last they would spend together on Salisbury Plain. Colt left for Cheltenham on 11 May, and from there to North Wales, to view with a fresh eye the antiquities of Snowdonia and Anglesey.[23] He was gone until September.

The first part of *Ancient Wiltshire* had appeared sometime before 31 August, for Britton wrote to Cunnington, 'I have seen *your* curious & interesting book on the Antiqua of Wilts; but have been hitherto prevented reading many pages—It is a treat I have reserved for winter—I very much object to its unwieldy, unpleasant & expensive size. My Architectural Antiquities has sold very well.'[24]

Colt returned with fresh plans, but Cunnington was no longer able to respond. 'I must again repeat the query in my last two letters which still remains unanswered...', wrote Colt, 'I shall hope to hear your health is better. We had a pleasant tho' very cold excursion and I rode away all my gouty symptoms. *Nothing like Down air* for invalids.'[25] And on 27 November:

> So long a period has elapsed since I have heard any tidings of your health, that I am induced to send a second messenger of enquiry, and at the same time some game killed on Saturday. With it you will receive an interesting letter from the Abbé—less fugitive and obscure than usual...Thank God! my head continues sound—and my time is pleasantly divided between the pursuit of the closet and the field—We are again in *the press*—and our second livraison, including Stonehenge, will be ready I hope in January.[26]

On the last day of December Cunnington died.

[23] Journal, 1810. Cardiff.
[24] Letters, J.B. to W.C., 13 Aug. 1810.
[25] Letters, R.C.H. 93.
[26] Letters, R.C.H. 92, 27 Nov. 1810.

Chapter 7

Aftermath

Cunnington had at least lived to see part of the work in print. The first volume, which appeared in three parts, covered *The Ancient History of South Wiltshire* and was not completed until 1812. For the purpose of the history, the county had been divided into stations; Stourton, Warminster, Heytesbury, Wiley (Wylye), Amesbury North, Everley (Everleigh), Amesbury South, Salisbury, Fovant, and Hindon. Excavation and field-work had not, however, been systematic, and in writing about each station Colt had often been dependent on Cunnington's memory. The second part of the work, published in 1810, although it contained an account of Stonehenge, did not apparently complete all there was to say about the area, for in the final version Colt had to say of barrows at Rollestone, 'Of these I cannot give so detailed or satisfactory account as I could wish. Some were opened by Mr. Cunnington, during the early period of his researches, when no very regular account was kept of his discoveries, and not the most distant thought entertained of laying the result of them before the public.' 'His ingenious researches are now, alas! at an end.'[1]

The true effect of this is apparent in the sketchy treatment of the area south of Salisbury and on either side of the Nadder, where there is little barrow information, except at Woodyates, which is in Dorset. Put in another way, of the 2000 odd Wiltshire barrows listed in the *Victoria County History*, a quarter are recorded in the *Ancient History of Wiltshire*. Hardly any of these are in North Wiltshire, that is, north of Salisbury Plain; and by far the larger proportion, 343 out of 683,[2] are in the area south of the Kennet and Avon canal, north of the Wylye and west of the Avon. Only 67 out of a possible 529 are east of the Avon and south of the canal. Colt Hoare and Cunnington are credited with uncovering some 320 inhumations and cremations out of a total of 660 recorded for the whole of Wiltshire. 251 out of 287 were in Salisbury Plain, west of the Avon and in the triangle of land between the Wylye and the Nadder. This was, in fact, Cunnington's home ground; and where the *County History* says 'Hoare' we must in most cases substitute his name. By contrast, the highest

---

[1] *A.W.*, I, 173.

[2] The figures represent a rough count and are not guaranteed accurate.

proportion of ditches recorded in *Ancient Wiltshire* is east of the Avon, which is the area in which Colt Hoare spent a large amount of time.

The Quarterly Review gave an extensive notice of the first two parts of Colt's work in 1811. The typography was praised as 'perhaps unrivalled'; the introductory theory was criticized as 'inconsistent with observed facts'. Where he had confined himself to recording these there was little but admiration, as well as for the perseverance and expense by which they had been obtained.

> It is a striking proof either of his own influence, or of the neglected state of the country, that he has everywhere been allowed to prosecute his researches with as little interruption as if he had been digging on his own estate. No antiquary had ever the same means or opportunities before Sir Richard Hoare; and no one ever availed himself more entirely of the advantages which he possesses. In his knowledge of barrows he certainly stands unrivalled. He has reduced the subject to a system and has nearly invented a technical language in which to describe it.[3]

On the vexed question of Stonehenge, 'we have the satisfaction of finding that he has conducted himself with all the sobriety, modesty and discretion which become a modern antiquary in treating a subject of such difficulty, in which so many of his forerunners have failed.'[4] On the whole Colt's reputation as an authority was established, although financially he was a loser. He had borne all the cost of drawing, surveying, and engraving, which amounted to £1271 14s. Crocker had received £139 11s. of this; Basire,[5] the engraver, £862 18s.; and Carey[6] £189 2s. for the maps. Miller, who had also published *Giraldus Cambrensis*, spent £1490 10s.[7] 'The sale hitherto has not come up to our expectations', he wrote on 30 November, 'but the work is *local*—its an expensive one, not suitable to every ones purchase—& its *early days* at present—& the times have been adverse.'[8] The sales, less commission, did not cover Miller's outlay. 'Although there was a particular agreement between us respecting this publication—yet I believe it was never in your contemplation that I should be any looser',[9] he said. The difference was £70 10s., and Colt was out of pocket some £1340 pounds. Miller did not, as he had done over *Giraldus*, exhort Colt not to place the *reputation* and *pleasure* he would receive against 'so trifling a sum'.[10]

3 *The Quarterly Review*, 1811, V, No. 9.
4 Ibid., V, No. 12.
5 James Basire, 1769–1822, engraver, son of James Basire (1730–1802) to whom William Blake went as pupil in 1771. Both were engravers to the Society of Antiquaries.
6 William Carey, 1759–1839.
7 Accounts for *Ancient Wiltshire*. W.A.S., Devizes.
8 William Miller to R.C.H., 30 Nov. 1812, T(ST) 383.907.
9 Ibid.
10 Miller to R.C.H., 13 May 1806, T(ST) 383.907.

Demands also came from other quarters. Cunnington's daughters assumed that the collection in the root house was their property. In 1813, being married and with the prospect of families, they began to think of selling it, believing that 'a considerable sum of money would be paid by the government & which to us who are just beginning life would be *particularly advantageous*'.[11] The British Museum declined to buy at the price which was being asked. Colt, who considered himself the chief proprietor, would not countenance a private sale; if the articles left Heytesbury they were to go to Stourhead.

> I will candidly observe to you that we wish the affair terminated [wrote Mary Cunnington at last], & should be very glad to deposit them at Stourhead, but that my sisters & myself have always expected to obtain for them at least six hundred pounds —for this I am confident you would not blame us if you were aware of the loss which as a family we have sustained from the close application of our father to the study of Antiquities, & from his having frequently expressed an opinion that the collection might after his death be a means of remuneration to us.[12]

Colt eventually bought it in 1818 for £200, which was reasonable seeing that he had paid for so much of the work to be done.

The Ancient History of North Wiltshire did not appear until 1819. Apart from a change of publisher there is no obvious reason for the delay as Colt was already in possession of most of the facts contained in it. In spite of his saying, 'My researches into the Northern district of Wiltshire, were commenced from Everley on the seventh day of June 1814',[13] these were confined to twenty-nine days[14] which he spent in the area that summer, when he opened, with little result, some barrows near Shepherd's Shore,[15] at the junction of Wansdyke and the Devizes to Marlborough road. Thereafter he made virtually no more field researches in Wiltshire. The Marlborough station contains the account of the Hatfield barrow at Marden, and the stretch of down between Devizes and Savernake along which Cunnington had ridden, as instructed, in 1806; 'one of the most spectacular experiences in British field archaeology',[16] as Grinsell calls it. It is here

---

[11] Mary Cunnington to R.C.H., 19 Feb. 1814, T(ST) 383.907.
[12] M.C. to R.C.H., 22 June 1815. T(ST) 383.907. The collection was bought from Stourhead by the Wiltshire Archaeological Society for £250 in 1883. It is now excellently displayed at their Museum in Devizes where it forms one of the most important collections of its kind in Europe. The fine golden articles from Upton Lovel and Bush Barrow are on loan to the British Museum where, at the time of writing, they are prominently displayed in the entrance to the Prehistoric Section. For details of the collection and an excellent historical background, see F. K. Annable and D. D. A. Simpson, *Guide Catalogue of the Neolithic and Bronze Age Collections in the Devizes Museum* (Devizes, 1964).
[13] *A.W.*, II, 4.
[14] R.C.H., Summary of journals, T(ST) 383.916 and 936.
[15] *A.W.*, II, 92.
[16] *The Archaeology of Wessex* (1958).

that the Wansdyke appears as a prominent feature. In 1809 Cunnington
had made a section at its junction with the Roman road on Morgan's Hill
(Pl. 49a) in order to find out which was the older. 'Although John has
completely failed in proving the Roman road anterior to the Wansdike
by digging', he wrote, 'yet from what I saw I cannot hesitate a moment
in pronouncing the Wansdike a posterior work.'[17] It is somewhat surprising that Colt makes no mention of this piece of field-work in the book,
which nevertheless shows Crocker's survey of the Wansdyke throughout
Somerset and Wiltshire.

The stations of Swindon and Calne contain a description of the camps
on the Ridgeway which runs along the Marlborough downs into Berkshire.
It was of Barbury, on this track, that Colt had written so enthusiastically
to Cunnington at the commencement of his work.[18] Also included in this
part are Avebury and Silbury, with Crocker's survey of the area made in
1812. Apart from this Colt added little new to the existing knowledge of
these places. He leans heavily on Stukeley and quotes the views of Owen
Pughe (William Owen), who wrote to him in 1814 repeating what he had
previously told Cunnington. Pughe was at that time in London, where his
'literary plans had been *superseded* by *vexations of law*'. 'In answer to a
mysterious allusion in your kind letter', he added, 'I beg leave to state that
Joanna Southcott's Mission is very near a crisis—For in her books it is
said that she is to be delivered of a son, in the 65th year of her age, before
the end of this harvest, who is to be the Prince of Peace, the Branch, the
Shiloh, and the Man-child of the Scripture—and six medical men have
given their decided opinion on seeing her, that there is no doubt of the
event being realised.'[19] The doctors had admitted that she showed symptoms similar to those of pregnancy. However, on 19 November she
announced that she was dying and directed that her body should be opened
four days after death, which occurred on 27 December. The autopsy
revealed no Messiah, or abnormality of any kind.

The last part of *Ancient Wiltshire*, 'The Roman Aera', came out in 1821.
This is largely taken up with an account of the Roman roads and the
stations on them which Colt claimed to have established; some correctly,
as at Cunetio, some not, as at Vindocladia. For much of the information
there was the authority of Thomas Gale's commentary on the *Antonine
Itinerary*, published in 1709; also the spurious account of Roman Britain
by Richard of Cirencester,[20] in whom Colt, with many others, believed.
But of some of the roads there was no record; tracing that from Old Sarum
to the Mendip lead mines was a true pioneering effort. Many had been

17 Papers, XI, 9.
18 See above, p. 213 f.
19 W. C. Pughe to R.C.H., 29 Aug. 1814, T(ST) 383.907.
20 By Charles Julius Bertram, Professor of English at Copenhagen, purporting to be an account
of Roman Britain by a fourteenth-century monk. The forgery was enthusiastically embraced
by Stukeley in 1748. See Piggott, *William Stukeley*, pp. 154 ff.

surveyed by Crocker between 1803 and 1806; the last, from Bath to Mildenhall, he followed field by field in 1819 with the Reverend Mr. Skinner[21] who had, with Colt, investigated[22] the fine chambered long barrow at Stoney Littleton, near Wellow.

The dedication of *The Roman Aera* is to Coxe:

> Twenty years have elapsed since in concert with our mutual friend Mr. Leman, we projected the History of Ancient Wiltshire, which has at length been accomplished. . . . That you may long enjoy both health and energy to add fresh laurels to those you have already so justly acquired, is the sincere wish of
> Your Faithful Friend,
> Richard Colt Hoare.

The final word is for Cunnington, 'who, from ill health, being recommended to breathe the salutary air of our Wiltshire downs, there found, in an apparently barren region, food for his intelligent mind; and to him alone, the discovery of the numerous settlements of the Britons, dispersed over our hills, must be justly attributed'.[23]

[21] John Skinner, 1772–1839, Rector of Camerton. The voluminous journals of his travels, mainly in Somerset, were bequeathed to the British Museum. Extracts have been published. (See below, IV, 2.)
[22] May 1816. See R.C.H. MS. Journal, W.A.S., Devizes.
[23] *A.W.*, II (Rom.), 126.

Part IV

Chapter 1

Sir Richard All Over

The Patronage of British Art

After 1810 Colt spent more time at Stourhead and his visits to Bala became infrequent. He was increasingly subject to attacks of gout and rheumatism, and was confined for long periods during 1812 and 1813. Other painful circumstances occurred to mar the pleasure he may have felt in the publication of his book. In February 1808 his son, Henry (Pl. 26), had married Charlotte, daughter of Sir Edward Dering. The couple went to live at the Manor of West Knoyle, where Colt added another farm to the one bought by his grandfather in 1732. He also settled £1500 a year on his son, from the rents of other estates, and £1000 p.a. on his daughter-in-law. This was not enough to meet their extravagant needs, which included visits to London to relieve the tedium of country life. As this was a pattern Colt himself had previously adopted, he might perhaps have expected his son would do likewise. Henry, however, was not interested in his estate, nor did he follow other pursuits as his father did; although it should be remembered that at the time of his marriage he was only twenty-three.

In 1811 Henry had a mental breakdown of a depressive kind, or as it was then termed *melancholia*. His symptoms were apathy, and a sense of guilt out of all proportion to the behaviour to which it was supposed to relate. Dr. Edward Fox, in whose care he was placed, noted the predisposition to instability which might have come from Hester's family (her brother George had also suffered from a period of insanity). He thought, however, that these tendencies were likely to remain dormant unless provoked by other circumstances. In Henry's case these were aggravated by 'mental and bodily inertia with an indulgent diet'.[1] It was also clear that something had gone wrong in the marriage bed; for which, it must be admitted, Henry had not been very favourably prepared. It was suggested that Charlotte might have been 'too negative in her favours';[2] but she had impressed Dr. Fox with the dominance of her personality, and the influence she was likely to have over Henry's recovery. He advised Colt to be tactful and not to enquire too closely into his son's affairs.

Colt, in his heart, blamed Charlotte, for whom his feeling had never been very warm. Moreover, his friend Champneys of Orchardleigh, who

[1] Dr. Edward Fox to R.C.H., 2 Sep. 1811, FS. [2] Ibid.

had exerted himself on Henry's behalf, strongly suggested that the marriage was a failure and the main cause of the trouble. Charlotte, for her part, disbelieved in Henry's illness and thought, possibly with some justification, that his strange behaviour was directed against her. When Colt wrote to her saying that Henry was of a warm and affectionate disposition, incapable of such a wicked motive, she replied that she had never doubted the amiableness of his disposition but had also observed 'a pertinacity of opinion very far from ductile'.[3]

When Henry did recover, his wife's ascendancy was demonstrated, and he turned on those whom he thought were trying to separate him from her. His bitterness was particularly directed against Champneys, but extended to Colt for supporting what he believed to be his friend's good intentions. We are not concerned with the complexities of feeling, recrimination and counter-charge which ensued even if it were possible to unravel them. Eventually, on 21 February 1813, Colt wrote: 'As any further discussion will only tend to mutual irritation, I shall say no more on the unpleasant topic which has for so long a period employed our pens. I am willing to forget and to forgive, and shall readily shake you both by the hand whenever you may find it convenient to ride over.'[4]

To these resentments had been added those concerning money. The visits to London which Henry regarded as essential for his comfort were quite impossible on his present income; for 'with living 5 months at Stourhead, I can barely meet the expenses of my Establishment, any reduction in which (it being as limited as can be for my situation in Life as *only* son to a Man of such large Property and consequence) would be obviously discreditable, & indeed *out* of the *Question*'.[5] Grumbling about his own building expenses, Henry's high flown style and the servants, carriage, horses, and other luxuries he permitted himself in town, Colt acceded for the time being to his son's demands.

Meanwhile there were other events which tended to keep him near home. While the Britons were being pursued on Salisbury Plain, the news from beyond the Channel was dismal indeed; best ignored, with the knowledge that at least Britain ruled the waves. Napoleon's relatives were on the thrones of Holland, Spain, and Italy; and since Russia's defeat at Friedland, Britain was virtually isolated from the Continent. However, from the time that Wellesley arrived in Lisbon with a British army in 1809 to support the Portuguese and Spanish insurrectionaries, news from that quarter was anxiously received. Thus amidst talk of Roman roads and long barrows Leman wrote: 'I am frightened a little with the retreat to Buzaco of Wellington's army. A battle must be the consequence.'[6]

[3] Charlotte Hoare to R.C.H., FS.   [4] R.C.H. to Henry Hoare, FS.
[5] Henry Hoare to R.C.H., 20 Mar. 1812, FS.
[6] Thomas Leman to R.C.H., undated, T(ST) 383.907. This presumably refers to the action at Sierra Busaco preceding the retreat to the Lines of Torres Vedras; therefore the letter was written at the end of 1810.

The more immediate results of Napoleon's blockade were rising corn prices and loss of trade. A serious economic situation had become a crisis by 1810, with frequent strikes and violence, particularly in the textile industry. This was mainly confined to the north; at Warminster things remained quiet, even though in 1809 some factories were entirely closed because of inability to sell the cloth. In Stourhead's immediate area, only protests at the enclosure of Mere Common disturbed the peace. In March 1810, fourteen were arrested for riotous assembly, but after some months awaiting trial, ten were discharged at Salisbury Assizes, and four received a sentence of one week. On 5 February 1811 the Regency Act was passed; and on 18 June the Prince, 'an aesthete decayed into grossness by habitual self-indulgence',[7] celebrated in style his accession to power with a grand party at Carlton House. 'All the royalty of Europe—such easily available guests—crowded round the long tables down whose centre a miniature canal, banked with flowers and moss and fitted with gold and silver fish, reflected all the feathers, the jewels, the gestures and the lights. . . . The old king was in his straight jacket; the Prince in his corsets seemed to rule a new kind of England.'[8]

In 1812 Douglas, who had been canvassing for the post of Curator at the British Museum, accepted instead the chaplaincy of troops at Brighton, with a parsonage and only one duty a mile away at Preston. In 1813 he had a comfortable house in Upper Rock Gardens to escape from the damps of his vicarage, 'beautiful in the fine season but absolutely not tenable in winter'. In November, among antiquarian gossip, he sent Colt news of the gay life in Brighton, and of Henry who was staying there.

> I am happy to inform you that Mr. Hoare is in excellent health [he wrote], and appears perfectly to have recovered from his most awful and perilous shipwreck, on his intended excursion to the Isle of Wight. The society here as in other places is divided in *la première, la seconde et la troisième noblesse*; every night balls and supper; my son, who is in the Prince's regiment, was not home till 5 this morning from a party where he met Mr. Hoare to whom I had taken the liberty of introducing him. Tonight there is a regular ball at Mrs. Fitzherbert's where my son is invited with Mr. Hoare; and so on every day in the week —or night rather; the young man is but a recruit and not out of the schools of the regiment which after these bivouacking parties he is obliged to attend most strictly; and on expressing the parental solicitude, I am informed it is the proper seasoning for his ensuing spring campaign in the South of France.[9]

[7] Steven Watson, *The Reign of George III* (Oxford 1960), p. 491.
[8] Ibid., p. 501.
[9] James Douglas to R.C.H., 5 Nov. 1813, T(ST) 383.907.

To his other interests Colt had added the cultivation of geraniums, starting in 1809 with the purchase of 53 species,[10] and adding many more during the following three years. By 1821 he had some 600[11] varieties. Robert Sweet[12] named plants after him; and in his *Geraniaceae* (1820–1822) there are many references to him. Thus:

> *HOAREA*[13] *corydaliflora*—Fumitory—flowered *Hoarea*. We have named it in honour of Sir R. C. Hoare, whose collection of *Geraniaceae* exceeds every other in this country, and to whom we are obliged for many useful observations, which will be acknowledged in the course of our publication.

Colt was elected a Fellow of the Linnean Society on 21 January 1812; among his sponsors were his friends Lambert and Coxe. In the minutes he is described as 'a Gentleman much attached to the Study of Natural History and the cultivation of Exotic Plants'.

Apart from some camellias and azaleas, he had not greatly extended his ornamental trees and shrubs since 1791. His initial planting was now maturing, and in 1813 he employed the painter, Francis Nicholson,[14] to record many aspects of the house and landscape at Stourhead (Pls. 17–20). This commission resulted from his topographical interest rather than his concern for painting, and it is relevant to note in this connection an event which occurred in 1811. In October that year Lambert wrote from Stourhead to his fellow Linnean, J. E. Smith;[15] 'I have been staying at this most delightful spot for some time with my friend Sir Richard Hoare.... We have now here a large party staying among whom are the Bishop of Salisbury and Mrs. Fisher & a young Artist whom the B. patronises... *Constable* by name. He is making views of this beautiful place.'[16] Constable also mentioned the visit in a letter to Maria Bicknell. 'We were not very fortunate in the weather, but the inside of the house made ample recompense. Sir Richard is no inconsiderable artist himself.'[17] Coxe was also of the party, and Constable told Farington some weeks later that he was 'a

---

[10] Bills from Sweet and Miller (44) and Colvill and Son (9), T(ST) 383.57.

[11] *A List of Geraniums in the Conservatories . . . at Stourhead* (Bath, 1821).

[12] Robert Sweet, horticulturalist, 1783–1835.

[13] These are now regarded as species of Pelargonium.

[14] Francis Nicholson, 1753–1844; founder-member of the Water Colour Society 1804; author of *The Practice of Drawing and Painting Landscapes from Nature* (1821).

With the exception of the *Interior of the Library*, which is at Stourhead, the drawings are now in the Print Room of the British Museum. They constitute a very full record of what the Gardens were like at their maturity in 1813–14. At the same time Nicholson painted *A Land Storm*, *A Sea Storm* and *Stonehenge*, all at Stourhead. '2 Views in Italy' might include *The Crater of Etna*, after a sketch by Colt Hoare, which is in 'Views of Sicily' in the library at Stourhead. The record of these commissions is in the receipts, T(ST) 383.4.

[15] Sir J. E. Smith, 1759–1828. See above, pp. 84, 99 f.

[16] Smith correspondence, Linnean Society, London.

[17] John Constable to Maria Bicknell, 23 October 1811. *John Constable's Correspondence*, R. B. Beckett ed., II, 'Early Friends and Maria Bicknell (Mrs. Constable)', Suffolk Records Society (1964), p. 50.

singular man in many respects: very little attention to others in His manners, and remarkable for His love of good eating. On His leaving Stourhead, Sir Richd Hoare said, "He is gone away well filled, as I have given Him Venison every day".[18] Coxe, however, must be credited with some perception with regard to the artist, as the following year John Fisher,[19] who had received the present of a small landscape, wrote to Constable:

> Your painting has been much criticised; disliked by *bad* judges, gaped at by *no* judges, and admired by good ones. Among these, Coxe the historian, who has seen much, was particularly pleased with it. It put him in mind, he said, 'of the good old Dutch forest painting school'. He looks at it whenever he comes into my room, which is most days. What it wants, he says, is that 'what is *depth* near, should not be *gloom* at a distance'. It is most pleasing when you are directed to look at it; but you must be taken to it. It does not *solicit attention*: and this is I think true of all your pictures, and the real cause of your want of popularity.[20]

John Fisher's enthusiasm for his friend's art was not, as Leslie points out, shared by his uncle. The Bishop's attention to Constable, 'whose art he did not appreciate, was the result of kindness alone'.[21] Sir George Beaumont, an important figure in the art world, did not understand Constable's painting either, although he was partly responsible for fostering his career. Colt's neglect is therefore not surprising; he could never, of course, have known the compliment which had been paid him. Yet there was something he shared with his great contemporaries. Constable's, 'The great vice of the present day is *bravura*, an attempt to do something beyond the truth;'[22] Wordsworth's, 'I hope it will be found that there is in these Poems little falsehood of description;'[23] and the sober tone of *Ancient Wiltshire*, 'We speak from facts not theory', talk of common values. Insularity, assisted by events, turned the English genius inward in all three.

Colt, nevertheless, had little taste for poetry; and it must be admitted that his patronage of painting was governed by loyalty rather than discrimination, when it did not come from his interest in topography. Woodforde, who had been promoted Academician in 1807, told Farington in 1811, 'Sir Richard is a shy man to strangers, but liberal and very steady in his attachments'.[24] It is thus that commissions to Woodforde predominated among Colt's purchases from British painters; he was in fact the only one whose work was bought for Stourhead between the return from Italy

---

[18] Farington Diary, 17 Dec. 1811, VII, p. 70.
[19] John Fisher, nephew of Bishop Fisher.
[20] C. R. Leslie, *Memoirs of the Life of John Constable* (1951 ed.), p. 37.
[21] Ibid., p. 79.   [22] Ibid., p. 15.
[23] Preface to *Lyrical Ballads* (1800).   [24] Farington Diary, 24 May 1811, V, p. 276.

and 1808, if we exclude the work of topographical artists like Carter and Buckler, and Turner's Salisbury series which falls into the same class. By 1811 Colt's collection of drawings must already have been considerable, especially if we add Crocker's work. He had, of course, spent large sums on building and furnishing; these, added to the expense of excavation and publishing,[25] probably left him little to spare for other forms of patronage; but between 1808 and 1816, inspired no doubt by his friend Sir John Leicester, he bought various paintings by British artists. His reason for doing so requires some explanation, which will necessitate an account of painting in England immediately before that period.

In 1800 there was no place where a painter could exhibit his work publicly except at the Royal Academy. Most leading painters were Academicians; the main exceptions were Morland, who was too drunk; Romney who was not interested; and painters in water-colour who were not eligible. The eccentric Irishman Barry had been expelled in 1799 because in his lectures as Professor of Painting he had abused not only his contemporaries but the great Reynolds whose aura still pervaded the institution. Benjamin West, at sixty-two, was President, one of the few surviving founder-members; the others were Paul Sandby and Johann Zoffany. James Northcote, Reynolds's pupil and biographer, was fifty-four; Hoppner at forty-two carried on the Reynolds tradition of portraiture in rivalry with Beechey and young Lawrence, who had been elected an R.A. in 1797 at the age of twenty-eight. John Opie, starting as a portrait painter, had also made his name with subject pictures by the 1790s. The veteran history painter, J. S. Copley, was sixty-two and had fifteen more years to live. George Stubbs had succeeded to Wootton's reputation as an animal painter, but was only an associate at seventy-six. De Loutherbourg, still the most considerable name in landscape painting, was soon to be eclipsed by Turner, already an associate at twenty-five.

The war far from stimulating a demand for English painting had a contrary effect. According to Whitley: 'As the French occupation of Italy became more complete, the owners of historic collections showed increasing readiness to dispose of their pictures. Among the English they found their principal buyers. Numbers of Old Masters were therefore imported in 1800 and their sale in London was naturally detrimental to the home artists.'[26]

The exception was portrait painting on which many artists, including Constable, depended, even though their real aspirations were to paint historical subjects, large allegorical compositions, or subject pictures of other kinds. The new generation included Opie's pupil, Henry Thomson, who became an R.A. in 1803; as Joseph Farington's confidant he appears regularly in the diary. William Owen, elected in 1806, painted portraits

25 See bibliography of works.
26 W. T. Whitley, *Art in England 1800–1820* (Cambridge 1928), p. 11.

although inclining to subject pictures of rustic life. Woodforde (R.A. 1807) and Thomas Phillips (R.A. 1808) were mainly portrait painters, although Woodforde was also employed in copying at Stourhead. The Swiss-born Henry Fuseli, friend of William Blake, became Professor of Painting in 1801 and Keeper in 1804, and was in a category of his own. No landscape painter approached Turner in reputation after his election as Academician in 1802. His methods, however, were increasingly controversial, attracting young disciples such as Augustus Callcott, and drawing censure from arbiters of taste like Sir George Beaumont, himself a painter and unshaken in his loyalty to the canons of a previous generation.

It was in these circumstances that Sir John Leicester decided to devote his patronage to British art. Colt and Leicester had remained close friends ever since in Rome they had visited painters, sculptors and musicians together, drawn the same ruins and picturesque landscapes, and examined all that was worthy of admiration.[27] In 1805 Leicester bought 11 Hill Street, Berkeley Square, intending to furnish a gallery with the work of British artists only. The completion, in 1806, was announced in *The Morning Post*: 'The pictures are hung in a perfectly novel style of elegance, suspended from chains by lions heads, splendidly gilt, and have a most striking effect. Mr. Opie's fine picture, just finished, of the *Infant Samuel*, and Mr. Turner's *Storm* have been recently added to this choice collection.'[28] The *Storm*, later called *The Shipwreck*, was bought in 1805 from Turner's first exhibition in his own gallery at 64 Harley Street. It was the first of a series of enlightened acquisitions which Leicester made from him; he later exchanged it for *The Fall of the Rhine at Schaffhausen*. Also at Hill Street,[29] presumably, was de Loutherbourg's *Avalanche* (Pl. 32b), greatly admired by Colt, and copied in water-colour for him by Francis Nicholson. Leicester had bought this too in 1805, along with *The Water Mill*, by young Callcott, which had attracted more attention than any other landscape in the Academy exhibition that year. By 1806 Leicester had a number of paintings by Northcote, including *Miss St. Clare as Miranda*, *Miss St. Clare crossing the Alps on a mule*, *Miss St. Clare with a Hawk*, and *Head of Miss St. Clare*. Emily St. Clair was apparently mistress of Leicester's house until his marriage in 1810. She was popular with artists and said to have been the model for another of Northcote's paintings, later acquired by Colt. In a letter to Leicester in 1823 Northcote wrote: 'I am informed that the picture which Sir Richard Hoare has by me named *The Dumb Alphabet*,[30] which was painted by your order and formerly in your possession, is now displayed in his house as one of his prime shows to all visitors.'

[27] William Carey, *Some Memoirs of the Patronage and Progress of the Fine Arts etc.* (1826).
[28] Quoted Whitley, op. cit.
[29] Information about Sir John Leicester's purchases of paintings and his correspondence with painters is mainly from Douglas Hall, 'The Tabley House Papers', *Walpole Society*, XXXVIII (1960–2).
[30] Sold in 1883.

Hoppner was also engaged on a portrait of Miss St. Clair in 1806; and she is said to have been his *Sleeping Venus*, yet another of the family of reclining nymphs, her arms crossed behind her head. Whether on account of the model or no, Leicester wished to buy it, subject to alteration. 'It is an insuperable objection in subjects of this kind to be *overpowered* with Beauties, being satisfied that after all, Imagination must have something left to make the thing compleate.' Hoppner saw no objection, 'provided much is not intended to be covered, he would make alterations, even before the opening of the Exhibition, as he should be unwilling to offend the Bishops, by a display of beauty finally to be veiled'.

In other letters Hoppner refers to Henry Thomson whose *Crossing the Brook* Leicester had bought at the Academy dinner in 1803, the year Thomson was elected a full Academician. The letters are undated but it may be assumed that they are of 1806.

> I see little of that wind-egg Thomson. I have been once to Vauxhall with him, and have lost all character for Virtue, by being seen in his company. 'Rak-punch and petticoats are more than his frail flesh can bear—and, with frailty in my neighbourhood, I take fire like a green cock of hay—'tis a mercy we were not both burnt to a cinder!.

Later:

> Thomson is working hard to get fishing and *other* sports that, by your account may be innocently performed by a wind-egg. I shall make it a matter of conscience however to send a kind of pastoral letter to all the maidens within ten miles of Tabley, to keep their hands on their...for I know the hunger of this blown deflowerer, and that he will fill their bellies with...notwithstanding appearances.[31]

Thomson addressed his patron as 'My dearest and best friend', and among other matters wrote: 'Mr. Parker has engaged the School Boy of me & I flatter myself I shall make it a successful Picture. Everybody that has seen it is struck with it & I might yesterday have disposed of it to Mr. C. Hoare—(the Dead of Night Gentleman). I have received a note from Sir Richard (who is in Town on Business but leaves it on Sunday) saying he will call on me tomorrow to see his snake & the Sailor.'

This may have been in February 1806; or November, when Colt was in London for a few days after his return from Ireland. One of the pictures mentioned by Thomson is probably his *Distress by Sea*, which was in the Academy of 1804 and is now at Stourhead. Colt, we have seen, was a frequent visitor at Tabley. He was there for a month in September 1808,

---

31 'These and some irrecoverable words inked over at a later date', Douglas Hall, Tabley House Papers.

shortly after an occasion recorded by Farington. 'Calcott told me Turner while he was at Sir John Leicester's last Summer painted two pictures for Sir John, views of Tabley, of his 250 *guineas size*, yet Thomson who was there said that His time was occupied in *fishing* rather than painting.'[32] *Tabley: Windy day* (Pl. 39b) and *Tabley: Calm morning* were exhibited at the Academy of 1809 when one critic wrote that the subject, 'which in any other hands would be mere topography, touched by his magic pencil have assumed a highly poetical character'.[33] Their success brought Turner, among other commissions, an invitation from Lord Egremont to paint Petworth House.

Nothing comparable to Turner at Tabley, let alone at Petworth, happened at Stourhead. Nor for a moment was it probable that any artist addressed Colt with the free and easy intimacy which Leicester permitted. Not, we suspect, because he did not wish it, but because the barriers he had built round his emotions as a result of his early experiences discouraged them. Warmth was certainly the quality he sought in others. Hester possessed it, and we can judge how great a loss she was. Cunnington had it; and Colt's other intimate, Richard Fenton.

It was something of this openness to feeling which must have made Leicester respond to Turner. Colt admittedly had appreciated Turner's quality first, but in the topographical mode only. In the language of feeling he was inferior and followed where others led. He was, as Woodforde said, a shy man, withdrawing from displays of emotion to the coolness of the intellect. And he was conservative, not only because he was a Georgian born in the mid-eighteenth century, but because his introverted temperament made him 'steady in his attachments'. It is characteristic that his purchase from Turner in 1815 should be associated both with the classical past, and, sentimentally, with his own. At the same time, to buy something in the manner of *that* version of *The Lake of Avernus* might appear progressive in the year when Sir George Beaumont had castigated Turner's *Crossing the Brook* as 'weak and like the work of an old man who no longer saw or felt colour properly; it was all of a *pea-green* insipidity'.[34] The 1815 version of *Lake Avernus* (Pl. 29a) is a considerable advance over the earlier one. The transitions are more subtly contrived; the dark tree which thrusts up into the light gives a foretaste of later paintings in which the drama of light and dark is stated in its bare essentials.[35] Colt Hoare, in his note on the painting in *Modern Wiltshire*, refers only to his own topography. His patronage of Turner stopped there. That he had gone so far was probably due to the friend whose collection of British paintings so far outshone his own.

Colt thought highly of Thomson's paintings, and in addition to *Distress by Sea*, bought *Distress by Land* (Pl. 46), called *Peasants in a Storm—*

[32] Finberg, *Turner*, p. 151.   [33] Whitley, op. cit.
[34] Finberg, op. cit., p. 220.   [35] See *Coast Scene near Naples*, Tate Gallery 5527.

Salisbury Plain when it was exhibited in 1811. He thought this an admirable specimen of the modern school, speaking 'to the *eyes*, as to good colouring and composition, and to the feeling *heart*, as to the expressions and distressful situations of the unhappy sufferers'. The picture represents 'a lovely young female, overtaken by a storm of thunder, lightning and rain, upon the bleak and desert plains of Salisbury; the British Circle of Stones at Stonehenge indicates the scene; her hair, hat, and cloak, are agitated by the wind; she presses closer to her breast her infant child, and a boy of a more advanced age is seen sheltering himself under her cloak'.[36] The lines from James Thomson's *Winter*, which are attached to it, have been distorted, and the gender switched to suit the theme.

> —how sinks her soul!
> What black despair! What horror fills her heart!
> Far from the tracts, and blest abode of men. . . .[37]

originally referred to a youth lost in a snow-storm. The storm, the stones, the barrows, the vastness of the plain are now mere tokens of sublimity; symbols painted on a back-drop to the group whose sufferings we are required to share as we contemplate their faces. The year after this picture was exhibited Constable was to admire 'some beautiful fancy pictures by Thomson'. He himself attached lines by the painter's namesake to *Hadleigh Castle*. And Wordsworth had described in *The Prelude* the almost compulsive nature of the image of the vagrant woman and her babes,[38] as well as the strong effect Salisbury Plain[39] had on his imagination. At the end of the century the image was still potent in Thomas Hardy, who was a frequent visitor to Stourhead in later life. It is expecting too much that Colt should grasp the significance of what Turner and Constable were trying to do in touching the emotions through more direct means. There were less subtle causes of misunderstanding between artists and patrons; and, for that matter, among the artists themselves.

In 1805, the British Institution was founded by a group of wealthy men for the encouragement of British art. Their aim was to provide an alternative to the Royal Academy for the exhibition of paintings. The list of founder-members included a duke, five marquesses, fifteen earls, four ladies, and seven baronets, among them Sir John Leicester Fleming and Sir Richard Colt Hoare. The management was entirely in the hands of the subscribers, which was ultimately the reason for dissension, for no artist was included, and many opposed it from the start. The galleries were opened in February 1806 at what was formerly Boydell's Shakespeare Gallery in Pall Mall. There were three rooms covered with scarlet wallpaper giving a very splendid appearance, like a suite in a private mansion.

---

[36] Hoare, *Modern Wiltshire*.
[37] 'How sinks his soul! etc.' 'Winter', lines 288 ff., *Poetical Works* (Oxford 1965).
[38] Cf. *The Prelude*, Book 8, lines 551 ff.   [39] Ibid., Book 12, lines 312 ff.

Among the painters who exhibited were West, Turner, Opie, and Copley. After the exhibition the galleries were hung with paintings of old masters from private collections, and were opened to students and other artists for copying. At this time there was no public gallery where this could be done. Angerstein, the banker, who had just acquired Claude's *Marriage of Isaac and Rebecca* and *Embarkation of the Queen of Sheba*, had given Academicians access to his collection in 1803, and said that for part of the year it should be open to students in general. It was not until 1824 that the government made a grant for purchasing his pictures as the basis for a National Gallery. Until then the British Institution fulfilled a need, supplemented by the Desenfans collection when it was bequeathed to Dulwich College in 1811.[40]

Two of the most influential voices in the affairs of the British Institution, and indeed of the art world generally, were those of Sir George Beaumont and Richard Payne Knight. Beaumont pursued a campaign against the work of Turner and his followers which was, we may suspect, as much a defence of his own practice as a painter as loyalty to a principle. Turner was too firmly established to be much harmed by aspersions of this kind. Callcott, however, appeared to suffer. He told Farington in 1813 that his sales were affected and that 'at the last year's private view of the Exhibition Sir George manifestly declined any intercourse with him, and turned from him when addressed by him'.[41] Callcott suspected that Lord Brownlow would have taken his *Diana and Acteon*,[42] in the Academy exhibition of 1810, if he had not been put off by Beaumont's remarks. Colt bought it in 1811. It is possible that Callcott made some alterations to it, as he wrote saying that he would pay every attention to render it worthy of Stourhead. Colt already had one of his paintings, exhibited at the Academy in 1808 as *A Mill near Llangollen from a sketch by Sir R. Hoare Bart.*

Beaumont told Farington that personally he liked Callcott, but did not approve his manner of colouring, nor his imitation of Turner. He said there was no knowing the pictures of one from those of the other. This, we must remember, was Turner of 1809 to 1812. Callcott did not follow Turner in his later manner, nor to extremes of any kind; and it was he who, on the accession of Queen Victoria, received a knighthood.

In 1815, Colt bought two pictures from the British Institution: R. T. Bone's *A Colour Grinder's Shop*, described by Hazlitt as 'a spirited and faithful imitation of nature', and William Collins's *A Cottage Child at Breakfast*, 'a pleasing little picture but inferior to Mr. Collins's general performances'.[43] Collins was one of the younger generation of painters

[40] By Sir Francis Bourgeois, R.A.
[41] Finberg, op. cit., p. 194.
[42] This is the title of the painting now at Stourhead, with figures by William Owen, R.A. Farington refers to 'his large upright landscape', but they are presumably the same.
[43] William Hazlitt, 'Criticism of the British Institution, 1815', in *The Champion. Works*, vol. 18 (1933), p. 93.

who, like his friend David Wilkie, were becoming sought after by collectors. As a boy he had known George Morland, and his work was at first influenced by him. There are traces of that influence in *Disposal of a favourite lamb*, which won Collins praise in the Academy of 1813. He became an associate in 1814, but he took so long over his pictures that he told Farington in 1817 he did not earn more than £300 a year; he therefore proposed 'to paint portraits of children making a *subject* of each picture'. This kind of pathos was very much to Colt's taste and the year following *The Cottage Child* he bought Thomson's *Girl deploring the loss of a favourite pheasant*.

Besides their annual show of new pictures the directors of the British Institution offered premiums and held exhibitions of the work of selected masters. Both these practices were criticized by artists, who thought they should be the judges of talent and resented the influence of powerful and wealthy patrons. As Farington (quoting Callcott) said, '"They are not patrons of Artists, but breeders of Artists". He considered the British Institution to be a nursery for such purpose.'

In 1814 Turner entered a painting for the premium, and, in conformity with the requirements that 'in point of Subject and Manner' it should be a companion to a work of Claude or Poussin, he modelled it on Lord Egremont's *Jacob and Laban* and called it *Apullia in search of Apullus. Vide Ovid*. Hazlitt wrote in *The Morning Chronicle*: 'The beautiful arrangement is Claude's; the powerful execution is his own. . . . All the taste and imagination being borrowed, his powers of eye, hand, and memory, are equal to anything.'[44] The other competitors were William Collins, Thomas Hofland, and Joshua Shaw. Turner's picture was stigmatized as 'not an original composition' and the prize went to Hofland. Since Beaumont was one of the judges, and Turner had done his best to conform with his taste, it seemed that prejudice had won the day.

Dissension between the Academy and the British Institution reached a climax in 1815. That year the directors put on a show of Flemish and Dutch old masters, the third of special exhibitions of this kind, although the first two in 1813 and 1814 had been devoted to Reynolds and Hogarth, Wilson, Gainsborough and Zoffany. The reason for the dispute was ostensibly the fear among artists that an institution formed to encourage their work was in fact a society of connoisseurs and dilettanti whose activities could only foster the sales of old and foreign paintings. Some substance was given to this by the rumour that 4000 guineas had been offered for a Raphael. The directors argued that they were only trying to stimulate quality in British painting by offering the example of acknowledged masters. But it was well-known that men like Beaumont and Payne Knight were biassed in favour of the past, and could be said to have a vested interest in the value of their collections. Beaumont's dislike of

[44] Ibid., p. 14.

innovation was apparent in his attacks on Turner. It is an interesting side-light that Constable's *Lock on the Stour* was unsold at the Institution's 1814 exhibition, and Farington thought he did well to let James Carpenter, the bookseller, have it for £20 with books to a certain value.

Payne Knight's dictatorial behaviour was observed even by his friends. It came partly from intellectual arrogance for which he had some justification, as his *Analytical Inquiry into the Principles of Taste* (1805) had shown. In his thesis, that the appeal of painting through the sense of sight was solely by means of light and colour, and that the progress of the art was from exact and distinct imitation of details (what the mind knew to be) to a more truly visual imitation (what the eye saw), he anticipated the theory of impressionism. However, he attacked pretension in painters, who responded with their customary suspicion of the intellectual approach to their art. They thought, perhaps rightly, that he belittled them with such statements as, 'Works of taste are frivolous or at most only elegant pursuits of the mind';[45] or assertions, with which Beaumont also disagreed, that painting was merely an imitative art, and not capable of operating so as to produce any moral effect.[46] Like many clever men, Knight was apt to throw out ill-considered statements which did not reveal the underlying thought processes. Nor was his judgement always sound; when talking of Richard Wilson's painting he had said there were 'better painters now living, Turner and the younger Barker of Bath'; which caused Thomas Lawrence to exclaim, 'Oh! no—not Barker surely!'[47]

During the exhibition of Dutch and Flemish paintings an anonymous satirical publication appeared, called *A Catalogue Raisonné of the Pictures now exhibiting at the British Institution*. It was in fact a defence of Turner and an attack on the directors for a misuse of their power. Men who 'unblushingly proclaim their determination to deprive the first genius of the day of encouragement, and set up inferior works, to put him down', clearly referred to Beaumont; and those who laboriously 'collect a mass of heterogenous matter and term it analyzing',[48] to Payne Knight. Authorship was variously attributed to Thomas Phillips, who denied it; Walter Fawkes, friend and patron of Turner; Thomson and Callcott.

A second *Catalogue Raisonné* appeared in 1816 on the occasion of an exhibition of Italian and Spanish paintings. 'It is pretty well understood to be a declaration of the views of the Royal Academy,' wrote Hazlitt in *The Examiner*, '. . . a society of hucksters in the Fine Arts, who are more tenacious of their profits as chapmen and dealers, than the honour of the Art.'[49]

Colt, believing that reason could triumph over invective, joined issue with a long letter to *The Annals of the Fine Arts*.[50] He deplored sarcasm

[45] *Farington Diary*, 6 June 1816, VIII, p. 74.
[46] Ibid., 23 Oct. 1812, VII, p. 122.
[47] Ibid., 2 Feb. 1808, V, p. 14.
[48] Quoted by Finberg, *Turner*, pp. 222 f.
[49] Hazlitt, *Works*, vol. 18, p. 105.
[50] MS. version, W.A.S.

and malevolence; nothing was easier than to ridicule 'serious subjects' or 'worthy characters'. There followed a history and defence of the British Institution: £37,182 in sales between 1806 and 1817; £6888 spent by order of the directors on the purchase of paintings, only one by a foreign artist; £3340 awarded in premiums, not including £1500 for commissions to commemorate the Battle of Waterloo. And congratulations all round on the state of British Art, with a comprehensive list of names in the fields of History, Portraits, Small Life, Landscape, and Rustic. Constable's is absent. Callcott, whom Colt did not apparently suspect of being the author of the Catalogue, was congratulated 'on having resumed his own original style of colouring, from which he had at one time strayed'. Colt noted the progress of water-colour painting which, as we have seen, he attributed to the influence of Ducros, and thus indirectly to himself. He alluded to the drawing of architectural antiquities, especially the work of Turner and Nash; and under this category he lamented Girtin's death.

He did not, of course, omit to draw attention to the taste and benevolence of his friend Sir John Leicester, whom he now persuaded to issue a *Catalogue Raisonné* of his own collection. The task was given to William Carey, on Colt's recommendation. Carey had started life as a painter and engraver; he later turned to writing and dealing, and was one of the principal people Leicester had consulted when forming his gallery. Carey said he would do it for nothing, merely for the opportunity to disprove the imputation by foreigners that England had hitherto produced no paintings worthy of notice; except that, due to the hasty departure of some amateur friends to the continent without discharging their obligations, he had lost £1600.[51]

In November 1818, Colt wrote to Leicester saying that Carey would like the job as he was very zealous for modern art.

> Why do you not add one of Collins's landscapes to your fine modern collection? [he asked] He is more the *painter of nature* than any of them—you might exchange one of *Turners* with him. I continue tolerably well—and am only plagued by *cramp* in the morning on first awaking—so that, if I have nothing worse—I ought not to complain. . . . Music, turbot, and a quiet party are great temptations—but fear I must withstand them—being full of occupations and my deafness really makes me quite unfit for society. I am no longer a farmer—for my sale took place last week—and I have one care the less—and hope *more* profit—I find cattle rise in price—and country matters look a *little* better —but very *little*. We shall be ruined by poor rates for want of employment—I hope the Salt works begin again to revive.[52]

[51] William Carey to R.C.H., 11 Mar. 1818, Tabley House Papers, Cheshire County Record Office.
[52] R.C.H. to Sir John Leicester, 11 Nov. 1818, Tabley Pt. III, addl. 1, Cheshire County Record Office.

The Hill Street Gallery was opened to the public in 1818, on Thursday afternoons, when there was an attendance of upwards of 600 people each week. Admission was free; and servants were ordered not to take money. There were over seventy paintings, all by British artists, including six of Turner's major works. The *Descriptive Catalogue* by Carey had 'occasional remarks by Sir Richard Colt Hoare, Bart.' which were in fact confined to de Loutherbourg's *Avalanche* (Pl. 32b). Mr. Walter Fawkes followed Leicester's example by opening his collection of English water-colours, including many by Turner. A visitor to England at the time remarked that in Paris the poorest Frenchman could visit the Louvre, whereas in England the fine arts were enjoyed only by the well-to-do.

There were those who dissented from Colt's picture of the happy state of art in England. Hazlitt had pointed to the neglect of Hogarth and Wilson in their lifetime. 'Indeed, patronage, and works of art deserving patronage, rarely exist together', he declared. 'For it is only when the arts have attracted public esteem and reflect credit on the patron that they receive this flattering support, and then it generally proves fatal to them.'[53] This thesis was repeated with more virulence in *The Annals of the Fine Arts*, with a personal attack on Colt to boot. The writer, calling himself 'The Ghost of Barry', having depicted art in Greece and Italy as 'a matter of public utility and interest', concerned with 'historical facts, sublime expression and glorious design', and 'providing a mass of continued employment, the most steady, uninterrupted, extensive, and stimulating the world had ever known', continued: 'In fashionable language, this mass of employment is, as Sir Richard Colt Hoare expresses it, *patronage* . . . it is a term, with due deference to the worthy Baronet, the most impertinent and ill-applied that ever was used, as is abundantly evident in the history of art, where, unhappily, we too often find its vigour and growth stunted, and liable to blight, when the great, and *their patronage*, came unluckily to interfere and tamper with it.'[54]

Colt replied, mildly enough, that the patronage of 'historical painting' was beyond the means of private individuals.[55] He did not come forward again as a champion; nor during the last twenty years of his life did he buy any more pictures to hang on his walls.

Hazlitt included Stourhead in his account of the principal picture-galleries in England, published in 1824. It did not come up to his expectations. Having briefly mentioned Veronese, a Holbein, and a Wilson, the drawings by Canaletto and the copies after Guido Reni in Henry Hoare's saloon, only Reynolds and Northcote are acknowledged. 'The rest of this Collection is, for the most part, *trash*; either Italian pictures painted in the beginning of the last century, or English ones in the beginning of this.

[53] Hazlitt, 'The Fine Arts, whether they are promoted by Academies and Public Institutions', *The Champion*, 28 Aug. 1814. *Works*, vol. 18, p. 38.
[54] *Annals of the Fine Arts*, part VI, p. 301.   [55] Ibid., part VII, p. 484.

It gave us pain to see some of the latter; and we will willingly draw a veil over the humiliation of the art, in the age and country that we live in.'[56] Whatever we may think of some of Colt's purchases, this was rather less than fair, both to himself and his grandfather. Perhaps Hazlitt was so entranced with the landscape that he could see little else but 'the view of Salisbury Plain, whose undulating swells shew the earth in its primeval simplicity, bare, with naked breasts, and varied only by the shadows of the clouds that pass across it'. Or the descent into Stourton,

> by a sharp-winding declivity, almost like going under-ground, between high hedges of laurel trees, with an expanse of woods and water spread beneath. It is a sort of rural Herculaneum, a subterranean retreat. The inn is like a modernised guard-house; the village church stands on a lawn without any inclosure; a row of cottages facing it, with their white-washed walls and flaunting honeysuckles, are neatness itself. Everything has an air of elegance, and yet tells a tale of other times. It is a place that might be held sacred to stillness and solitary musing![57]

[56] Hazlitt, *Works*, vol. 10, p. 61.
[57] Ibid., p. 60.

Chapter 2

The Topographers[1]

Hazlitt was undoubtedly right in praising the landscape at Stourhead; but in the account of his visit he omitted to mention the library, which was Colt Hoare's most significant contribution to the culture of his time. As we have seen, Colt paid particular attention to this room, which epitomized his deep preoccupation with the place he had inherited. And it fulfilled one of his grandfather's wishes, expressed in the belief that without lessons in history the most envied height of fortune would not be enjoyed.[2] Between 1786 and 1790 he made an important collection of books on the history and topography of Italy, of which a catalogue was printed in 1812. He gave these to the British Museum in 1825. Meanwhile he had acquired almost every printed book relating to the history and topography of his own country, concerning the subject generally and each individual county besides. At least one purpose he had in mind was to provide the source material from which a history of Wiltshire could be written without having recourse to other libraries. He had no manuscripts to speak of (always excepting his own journals and the magnificent collection of topographical drawings which Buckler, Carter, and others were making for him); but the records which his books contained were themselves the result of two centuries of unprecedented English scholarship, to which he had modestly contributed in his translation of the twelfth-century chronicle of Gerald de Barri (Giraldus Cambrensis).

Gerald's impartial acceptance of fact and fable in his travels through Wales illustrates just the kind of mediaeval confusion from which the English past had to be disentangled. One way to do this was by a critical examination of original documents, a task made more difficult by the dissolution of the monasteries, 'the greatest blow to antiquities that ever ENGLAND had, by the destruction and spoil of many rare Manuscripts, and no small number of famous Monuments'.[3] The impressive story of the

---

[1] For the historical background in this section I am indebted to D. C. Douglas, *English Scholars 1660–1730* (rev. ed. 1951); T. D. Kendrick, *British Antiquity* (1950); and Joan Evans, *A History of the Society of Antiquaries* (Oxford, 1956). Information about the contents of Colt Hoare's library is from *Catalogue of the Hoare Library*, compiled by J. B. Nichols (1840).
[2] Cf. p. 42.
[3] William Dugdale, *Antiquities of Warwickshire* (1656), preface.

recovery of many of the records, their editing and publication, is told by Professor David Douglas in his *English Scholars*. It was, he says, a conscious attempt to impart a sense of continuity to a people in the throes of change, by men who were personally, sometimes tragically, involved in the issues of their time, so that it is often difficult to distinguish polemical, historical, or topographical intentions.

John Leland (1503–52) was engaged on behalf of his master, Henry VIII, 'to peruse and diligently to serche at the libraries of monasteries and collegies...to the intente that the monuments of auncient writers... mighte be broughte oute of deadly darkenes to lyvely lighte'.[4] But during his journeys he conceived the idea of a description of Britain, and by 1546 there was 'almost neither cape nor bay, haven, creek, or pier, river or confluence of rivers, breeches, washes, lakes, meres, fenny waters, mountains, valleys, moors, heaths, forests, woods, cities, burroughs, castles, principal manor places, monasteries and colleges',[5] but he had not seen them. Not only seen, but recorded, so that there are few county histories for which his *Itinerary* is not a source. Patriotic fervour also inspired the topography of William Camden (1551–1623) who set out more systematically than Leland to describe each county, 'its antient inhabitants, estymology of its name, its limits, soil, remarkable places both ancient and modern, and its dukes or earls from the Norman Conquest'.[6]

William Burton (1575–1645), who acquired Leland's MSS. and presented them to the Bodleian Library, set new standards with his *Description of Leicestershire* (1622). But his pupil, William Dugdale (1605–85), was an antiquary of another dimension. The life of a man without learning and the remembrance of things past, he said, was 'noe better to be accounted of than to be buryed alive'.[7] The *Monasticon Anglicanum*, which bears his name although the credit is also Roger Dodsworth's, was compiled during the Civil War and afterwards when, as a participant on the unsuccessful side, his estates were sequestered and his movements restricted. The first volume appeared in 1655. 'It demonstrated as had never before been possible', writes Professor Douglas, 'the historical importance of the English monasteries. It made known for the first time a whole range of documents whose true significance had hitherto been unappreciated, and by doing so it illustrated almost every phase of English social and economic history in the Middle Ages.'[8] Dugdale was employed at the College of Heralds, eventually as Garter King at Arms. His *Baronage of England*, it has been said, was elevated to the rank of legal evidence by scrupulous accuracy and stubborn integrity.

These books filled essential places on Colt Hoare's shelves. Prominent among others were the twenty volumes of the second edition of *Foedera*

---

[4] Quoted by Kendrick, op. cit., p. 47.
[5] Ibid., p. 47.   [6] Ibid., p. 145.
[7] Douglas, op. cit., p. 14.   [8] Ibid., p. 36.

(1727–35), transcripts of alliances and other transactions in which England was concerned with foreign powers, which Thomas Rymer (1641–1713) laboured in poverty to produce from public records in the Tower, the Rolls, the Exchequer, Houses of Parliament, and other places.

For future historians the method and example of Thomas Madox (1666–1727) were as important as the matter. 'In Ancient Charters we may discern much of the Genius of our Ancestors; and much concerning their Manners and Customs', he wrote in the introduction to *Formulare Anglicanum*. And of his *History and Antiquities of the Exchequer of the Kings of England*:

> My ambition was to form this History in such a manner that it may be a pattern for the Antiquaries to follow, if they please. . . .
> For I think it is to be wished that the Histories of a Countrey so well furnished with Records and Manuscripts as ours is should be grounded throughout as far as is practicable on proper Vouchers. And for my own part I cannot look upon the History of England to be compleatly written till it shall come to be written after that manner.[9]

The Stourhead collection of Thomas Hearne's editions of English chronicles, including Leland's *Itinerary*, and *Collectanea* from original manuscripts, was the most magnificent known, said Joseph Hunter.[10] A manuscript catalogue was there as a guide to the many volumes containing a great variety of matter. Other important books in this library, 'beautiful as a room but rich in its contents',[11] are too numerous to describe; but certain later additions to published records, which were essential to the writing of *The History of Modern Wiltshire*, should be noted. Chief among them was the first printed edition of *Domesday Book* (1783). Previously the copy at Westminster had been kept under three locks, to be consulted for a fee of 6*s*. 8*d*., with an additional fourpence for every line transcribed. The Parliamentary Commission on Public Records issued a report in 1800, which was followed by regular publications, so that between 1802 and 1818 considerably more source material became regularly available. This ranged from the twelfth to the sixteenth centuries and included such matters as: taxes on church livings; grants of offices, lands, and patents of the creation of peers; enquiries made when the grant of a market, fair, or other privilege was solicited; records of rents reserved, salaries payable, or services to be performed for the Crown; *inquisitiones post mortem*, records made by a jury on oath of lands in possession of any person on death; records of pleadings, petitions, and appeals; taxes levied, and rights belonging to the crown from time to time.

[9] Ibid., p. 241.
[10] The Rev. Joseph Hunter, F.S.A. (1783–1861), 'Notices of Contemporaries', B.M. Add. MSS. 36527.
[11] Hunter, op. cit.

It was inevitable in an economy based on land that county histories should be chiefly concerned with its ownership and descent.

'The same class which filled the Parliaments of the early Stuarts with men eager to vindicate the privileges of their order also took its full share in proving its historical importance', writes Professor Douglas. 'These men turned as if naturally to the history of the shires they ruled, to family pedigrees, and to the exploits of their ancestors, and in a similar fashion, they became familiar with the ancient laws of inheritance and entail which held their society together.'[12]

The genealogical bias which has been noted in the study of churches was contributed by heralds, such as Dugdale, whose visitations were the occasion of much topographical observation. Indeed his method, in *Warwickshire*, of documenting in each town, village, or hamlet, the manorial succession, the genealogy and history of leading families, the foundation and appropriations of parish churches, and so on, was the model for subsequent county histories. The immediate successors to Dugdale's *Warwickshire* (1656) were Thoroton's *Antiquities of Nottinghamshire* (1677) and Atkyns's *Ancient and present State of Gloucestershire* (1712). During the eighteenth century others followed, of varying scope and importance, including works on Cornwall (1754), Cumberland (1777, 1794), Dorset (1774), Durham (1785–94), Essex (1740, 1768), Kent (1719, 1778–99), Norfolk (1781), Northamptonshire (1791), Somerset (1791). In the first two decades of the nineteenth century there appeared works on Berkshire (1802), Cheshire (1819), Hertfordshire (1815–27), Leicestershire (1795–1815), Staffordshire (1798–1801), Surrey (1804–14), and West Sussex (1815–30). All these, together with many minor publications, were in Colt Hoare's library to serve as examples for his own projected work. He had the manuscript of Collinson's *History of Somerset*; but his immediate source of inspiration was John Nichols's *History and Antiquities of the County of Leicester*, not only because of its form and content, but because the firm of Nichols had succeeded Miller as his publisher and printer.

John Nichols (1745–1826) was a most interesting man. Son of a baker, he was apprenticed at the age of twelve to the printer, William Bowyer the younger, who in 1766 took Nichols into partnership. Under Bowyer Nichols received a fair classical education, later becoming a considerable author, a friend of Dr. Johnson and a Fellow of the Society of Antiquaries. He was editor of *The Gentleman's Magazine* from 1792 until his death, and contributed many articles to it. His most important books were *Literary Anecdotes of the Eighteenth Century* (1812–15), still an invaluable source of bibliographical and biographical information; and the *History of Leicestershire* (1791–1815) which he completed at a loss of £5000, having already lost £10,000 and his entire stock of books by a disastrous fire in 1808.

[12] Douglas, op. cit., pp. 30 f.

Colt certainly knew Nichols as a fellow antiquary, but from 1803 Nichols left the printing business to his son, John Bowyer Nichols, who took over from Miller the publication of the second volume of *The Ancient History of Wiltshire* (1819–21).

The History of Modern Wiltshire was not so much the sequel as a return to the previous intention from which Colt had been turned aside by the originality of Cunnington's researches. He had, in fact, been collecting material all along, and in an undated letter of about 1819 he wrote, 'I am getting forward with the hundreds of Mere & Heytesbury in Modern Wilts, as are my coadjutors with other hundreds.'[13] In October 1821 he wrote to Richard Gough,

> I am now deeply engaged in promoting a Modern History of Wilts, & *my* first hundred of Mere is gone to press—it will abound with interesting portraits & other illustrations & I hope will do me credit. I have been fortunate in having found so able & zealous a coadjutor as Sir Thos Phillipps who will undertake the Northern district of our county whilst I do the South. We purpose to visit Oxford in June. . . . We want to examine Tanner's MSS,[14] who as well as Aubrey were Men of Wilts.[15]

Phillipps, then about thirty, had published privately *Collections for Wiltshire* in 1819. He contributed genealogies for Colt Hoare's volumes, but never wrote the northern history. It was between 1820 and 1825 that he made a prolonged visit to the continent and began the large-scale purchases of manuscripts for which he became famous. It is perhaps for this reason that Colt's intended visit to Oxford was postponed until August 1825, when he went to stay with Phillipps at Middle Hill.

The Hundred of Mere was published in 1822, setting a typographical standard for what was to be the most handsome county history yet to be produced. As most of Colt's possessions were within its compass it was a subject near to his heart. He could now look back to prehistoric times and over the lordship of the Stourtons to his grandfather's and his own achievements. He addressed it

> To my fellow countrymen in Wilts.
> To rescue from total oblivion the relics of Ancient Britain;
> to illustrate the remaining vestiges of its conquerors, the Romans;
> to investigate the monastic and ecclesiastical history of our country;
> to trace the genealogy of distinguished families, and the descent of property;

[13] R.C.H. to Messrs. Lackington, Finsbury Square. Bodleian MS. Don. d. 88, fol. 108.
[14] Thomas Tanner (1630–82), author of *Notitia Monastica* (1695), had projected a History of Wiltshire.
[15] Bodleian MSS. 28692, G.A. Gen. top. 40141.

to record the monumental inscriptions, and the biography of
celebrated characters;
and, above all, to endeavour by this example, to excite the zeal
of my fellow countrymen in the same desirable cause, is the sole
purport of this my humble undertaking.[16]

The plan of the history, as with Dugdale's, was to follow the hundreds
along the course of the rivers, beginning with the Wylye and the Hundred
of Mere which, besides the parish of that name, contained those of Stourton and Maiden Bradley. The history of Stourton begins with an extract
from Domesday Book and a story by one William Turner of the submission
received by William the Conqueror, followed by Leland's description of
the place. It continues with the family of Stourton, its pedigree, the descent
of the manor and documents relating to rights and privileges attached to
it. The account of the church is cursory as Colt hastens to record family
memorials, his own descent, his pleasure garden, his picture collection, his
views on painting and on the planting of trees. 'I have been perhaps too
minute in the foregoing description of the Desmesnes and Mansion-house
at Stourhead,' he wrote, 'but it should be considered that I write not only
for the general information of the publick, but for the gratification of those
branches of my family now living as well as my successors.'[17] We may
suspect a veiled message here as it was always his wish that the streams
issuing from 'the Golden Bottle'[18] might be reunited with 'the waters of
the Stour'. His exclusion from the business, which he thought due to the
persuasion of his 'fat uncle', never ceased to rankle.[19] It is understandable
that he should expatiate on a subject he knew so well; regrettable that he
was not more accurate and comprehensive. There are no details of the
building of his house, nor even who was responsible for the additions he
made to it. There are no plans, or drawings of the various elevations at
various stages, although these were in his possession. The records of
estates his family acquired and the plantations which were made are not
included. The siting of the old Stourton Castle is described four times with
variations;[20] five, if we include an addition made in 1844 when Aubrey's
drawing was reproduced in another volume. Dates are frequently unreli-
able, suggesting poor proof-reading; Alfred's Tower, for instance, is said
to have been built in 1722.

Many interesting documents are quoted, such as the detailed roll of
accounts of Richard de Chuseldon, Steward of Mere in the reign of
Edward I; this is not in its place however, but among the thirty pages of
addenda, which also include the information on geology and antiquities,

[16] 'Hundred of Mere', *The History of Modern Wiltshire* (1822).
[17] Ibid., p. 85.
[18] The sign of Messrs. Hoare and Co., in Fleet Street.
[19] MS. volume of memoirs, FS.
[20] 'Hundred of Mere', pp. 42, 42 (footnote), 63, 70.

as though the book were too hastily assembled for the press. Nichols's *Leicestershire*, which Colt certainly consulted,[21] is far more systematic, with a mass of tabulated general information at the beginning of the history. This, however, is to criticize Colt Hoare according to the standards which he set himself. His difficulties should not be under-estimated. Penruddocke Wyndham had foreseen some of these in the introduction to *Wiltshire, extracted from Domesday Book* (1788). 'Few people can be expected to engage in an operation, the trouble and expences of which would be certain, and the termination of which would scarcely be hoped for during the existence of a single life. And where shall we find a man whose abilities and circumstances might enable him, singly, to persevere in so complicated an undertaking?' Not only this, but the work was likely to be met with indifference if not obstruction, for in other counties papers of the utmost consequence had been timidly withheld for fear the titles of the owners might be called in question.

Colt Hoare's great achievement was to collect a library which made the project possible; and to inspire a group of men to bring it to a conclusion. These came from a varied social background. John Offer first met Colt during the explorations on the plain. He then lived at Imber and worked 'in the laborious task of usherage by day, while in the evening he followed his favourite pursuits of antiquity, heraldry and biography'.[22] When removed 'from the drudgery of a school' he studied the deciphering of Old English manuscripts and the Saxon language and 'acquired all the requisites to form an able county historian'. In 1822 Colt and Phillipps made an agreement[23] with him to help them in their work, by which he was to get £200 p.a. and travelling expenses should they require him to consult libraries or collections in London, Oxford, or elsewhere. Offer died of typhus at Stourhead in the same year. Another of the historians of Wiltshire was Lord Arundell of Wardour, a Catholic aristocrat, 'of frank manners and a noble bearing'.[24] The Reverend John Skinner, who did not favour Catholic emancipation, found him liberal-minded and devoid of bigotry and thought it wrong that such men should be 'excluded from a participation of what the most worthless and irreligious actually do enjoy'.[25] Shortly after finishing the *Hundred of Dunworth* (1829) Arundell went to live in Rome, where he died in 1834.

Henry Wansey, a retired clothier, was already engaged on the history

---

[21] There is an MS. questionnaire among 'Notes relating to Modern Wiltshire', in the library of the Wiltshire Archaeological Society at Devizes, intended for soliciting information for the History. This closely resembles the one published by Nichols in 1800 at the beginning of his third volume.

[22] 'Hundred of Heytesbury', p. 266.

[23] Notes for *Modern Wiltshire*, Devizes.

[24] Joseph Hunter, 'The Topographical Gatherings at Stourhead', 1825–1833, *Memoirs of the History and Antiquities of Wiltshire* (1851).

[25] The Rev. John Skinner, *Journal*, ed. H. Coombs and A. N. Bax ('Journal of a Somerset Rector'), 1930.

of Warminster in 1818. He had visited America in 1796 and written his impressions; he was also concerned about the conditions in poorhouses, particularly in Salisbury where they were very bad. His friend Richard Harris of Dilton Marsh was also a clothier. When in 1818 Colt invited Harris to provide material for the *Hundred of Westbury* he had already collected copies of many documents relating to the Westbury district from the Tower records, the Inquisitiones, and the *Testa de Nevill*; and with his friend Mr. Phipps, a leather draper, he had dug for Roman and British remains.[26] The manuscript[27] which Harris sent to Colt included particulars of the cloth industry round Westbury, then in its decline, with a list of manufacturers and details of their factories. These Colt omitted when he edited the *Hundred of Westbury*, presumably because he thought them of no interest.

Among others whose names appear on the title pages of *Modern Wiltshire* were Robert Benson, deputy recorder of Salisbury; George Matcham, a lawyer; and Charles Bowles, brother of the poet. William Henry Black, an assistant keeper at the Public Record Office, collected the documents for the *Hundred of Damerham* and arranged them for publication. He was then in his twenties, and later corrected Rymer's *Foedera* and catalogued the MSS of the Ashmolean.

Another professional who visited Stourhead was John Caley, Keeper of the records in the Augmentation Office and Secretary to the Record Commission. From all accounts Caley was an unsatisfactory archivist. His offices were said to be dark and dirty, and his records in the utmost disorder. If it was necessary to consult them, application had to be made at his private house where he kept the only index which no one else was allowed to see. The document, often the wrong one, was brought there from his office by a footman, after a search which might last as long as two weeks. The charge was arbitrary. He supplied Colt with material for his history from time to time, but sparingly, as Hunter puts it,[28] for he had no sympathy with antiquarian zeal.

Most of these men, and others, met at Stourhead for Colt's topographical gatherings. They were accustomed to expect a summons for a week in September, from Monday to Saturday. Persons not concerned with the *History* were included, especially if they were sympathetic, or had some special knowledge which might assist the work. The library to which new books were added yearly, was thus made useful to his friends. And apart from this, Colt liked to bring together men of kindred spirits to learn from one another, and be encouraged and assisted in any undertaking of their own. Joseph Hunter spoke with warmth of the rational pleasure which ensued.

---

[26] Henry Wansey to R.C.H., 21 Sep. 1818. T(ST) 383.907.
[27] In the Wiltshire County Record Office, Trowbridge.
[28] 'Topographical Gatherings at Stourhead.'

> Sir Richard usually breakfasted in his own apartments, where he occasionally admitted one or two of his guests, when he was seen with his tables and the floor strewed with books, manuscripts, and loose papers, engravings, seals, charters, and all the other paraphernalia of the antiquarian student, with abundance of copy, and proof-sheets, and fragments of his own work, on which he wrought daily with great assiduity. At twelve o'clock he usually joined the party in the library where he remained about half an hour, and did not again make his appearance till the hour of dinner approached, which was commonly served at five o'clock. The evenings were passed in conversation and other amusements.[29]

Colt noticed people who showed a predilection for his own pursuits but he also seemed to give to everyone the attention they deserved and sought to draw into notice those who wanted so drawing out. To the more studious, and especially those who had not easy access to so rich a collection of books, the library was sufficient. For others there were the pictures, the gardens, and the beauty of the walks which were a perpetual relief to all. 'The studies of the party were not very intensely pursued. There was no want of holiday; for there was no restraint upon anyone. Whatever anyone could contribute of information or amusement was most graciously accepted. The days passed smoothly and pleasantly along and it was a matter of regret to everyone when the day of separation arrived.'[30]

The meetings were not always in the autumn, for John Skinner, Rector of Camerton, went there in January 1824, leaving home at midday, but going by way of Frome, instead of Mells and Nunney, because of the deep snow. On the way he met Mr. Champneys of Orchardleigh, who had hardly been able to reach Frome from Stourhead with four horses to his carriage. Beyond Maiden Bradley the snow, which had drifted to the top of the hedges, had not been so well cleared as in other parts. If it had not been for a track cut for the coal carts going to the pits Skinner would not have been able to proceed.

> I never remember to have experienced anything like the cold whilst driving from Maiden Bradley to Stourhead; our delays were such it was nearly six before we arrived. I say 'we' because I had taken my servant with me by desire of Sir Richard as his party was larger than usual. I found dinner was over; but the worthy owner of the mansion left the company to see proper care taken of me, and after a hearty meal on a smoking hot beef steak I joined the party in the dining-room, consisting of Lord Arundel of Wardour, Mr. Merick, Mr. Bowles, and Mr. Offley; Mr. Wansey had excused his attendance on account of the

[29] Ibid.   [30] Ibid.

weather. After coffee we had a rubber of whist, in which I came off a gainer of 7s.—much beyond my expectations, as I so seldom play, and my antagonists were experienced men. Sir Richard, being so deaf, finds a relaxation in having his evening rubber; he was my partner, Lord Arundel and Mr. Merick were opponents.[31]

Skinner was in the library a little after eight the following morning, and was soon joined by others.

These gentlemen, I find, are principally engaged in tracing the descents of the landowners in their different districts which they are enabled better to do by consulting the records and topographical accounts so admirably arranged in Sir Richard Hoare's collection. Indeed, I believe there is not a library in the kingdom so well supplied in these subjects as that at Stourhead, since not only all the public records of Domesday and the Tower, but every private collection is so admirably arranged that Sir Richard can put his hand on the minutest book at a moment's notice. I got to the folios of ancient times and made extracts from Seneca respecting the deification of Claudius, and Pliny respecting the distance of Camalodunum from Mona.[32]

After a morning spent thus, Skinner walked through the snow with Mr. Bowles and Lord Arundell to visit the Catholic priest at Bonham. When the manor was sold to Henry Hoare in 1785, Lord Stourton had retained a house and chapel to serve the Catholics in the neighbourhood. This was occasionally a cause of friction, since Catholic emancipation was a political issue until bills were passed in 1829. The priest at Bonham took pupils in his house; and were these not, asked Skinner, as likely to become as good citizens as 'the puritanical levelling Methodists and Presbyterians?'[33]

Since Colt and he had excavated the chambered long barrow at Stoney Littleton, Skinner had become obsessed with the idea that Camerton was the site of Camalodunum, one of the first Roman settlements in Britain, although all the evidence placed it at Colchester. He sought to prove this by stretching the slender facts and juggling with linguistics, so that Colt would say, 'Oh, Skinner, you will bring everything at last to Camalodunum; be content with what you have already discovered. If you fancy too much you will weaken the authority of real facts.'[34] But Skinner never gave up his contention. After Colt had publicly refuted it in print he offered to extend the argument by sending a series of twenty-four letters, 'either singly or several together in a parcel',[35] giving the topographical history

31 Skinner, *Journal*, 3/4 Jan. 1824, p. 75.
32 Ibid.   33 Ibid., p. 77.
34 Ibid., 21 Aug. 1824.
35 MS. letter, John Skinner to R.C.H., 28 Nov. 1827, Bath Reference Library.

of Camerton from the Phoenicians to King Alfred. Skinner was evidently a trying, even a pathetic man, and an easy prey for jokers, of whom Colt was never one. On one occasion Skinner had been invited to an antiquarian meeting at the Bishop's Palace at Wells when, as he wrote, 'I suffered a severe attack during our symposium from all the party (excepting the Bishop and Sir Richard Hoare) who, from not understanding, endeavoured to ridicule my system of etymology by asking me the derivation of several strange words in order to puzzle and perplex me.'[36] It was during this visit that he noted what he considered the inappropriate and eccentric behaviour of the poet Bowles who, while the Bishop, Colt, and others were playing cards, threw himself on a sofa close to them and snored most loudly.

The following day a storm split one of the largest and most beautiful tulip trees in the palace grounds; and the Bishop, in spite of his distress, showed a serenity of temper which Skinner wished he might attain. 'But I fear I never shall,' he wrote, 'and much doubt will ever be calmed excepting in the grave.'[37] In 1839, having quarrelled with his sons and daughter, he shot himself in a wood near his house.

[36] Skinner, *Journal*, 7 Aug. 1828.
[37] Ibid., 8 Aug. 1828.

Chapter 3

The Pitney Pavement

Skinner lived long enough to fill one of the places in Colt's life now increasingly left empty by the death of his old friends. Penruddocke Wyndham died in 1819; and Richard Fenton in 1821, both younger men than he. Fenton was the closer to him, his enthusiastic companion in many Welsh journeys and adventures into history and prehistory. Colt had encouraged the *Historical Tour through Pembrokeshire* (1811), for which he wrote an introduction and made illustrations. Fenton's house and pleasure grounds in the beautiful Gwan Valley, near Fishguard, were modest in comparison with Stourhead; so too were his resources, and he died in need of charity. Colt went to Wales for the last time in 1819; thereafter he settled for an annual visit to Devon and Weymouth, until infirmity finally overcame his inclination.

John Offer, who had for long been Colt's assistant, died in his patron's house in 1822. Leman was the next to go, in 1826; Leicester, now Lord de Tabley, in 1827 and Henry Wansey in the same year. On 19 June 1828 John Fisher wrote to Constable:

> Poor Cox...is no more. He died of old age, unable to contend with two helps of salmon & lobster sauce, washed down with large drafts of Perry. A dissentry ensued &...his long distended bowels were unable to contract.
>
> But while I smile at the poor man's foible 'strong in death', I must do him justice. A more *irreproachable* friendly man did not exist. He was always benevolently employed, & at his funeral the congregation disturbed the service with sobs. After a great dinner, he used to steal into his kitchen, and give his cook a guinea. His domestics never left him; a silent but strong compliment from human nature. He is the author of twenty four quarto vols: & has hardly been convicted of a mistake. He was quoted as an authority in his life time, an event of rare occurence, for the prevalent feeling of men is jealousy of one another.[1]

[1] John Fisher to John Constable, 19 June 1828, *John Constable's Correspondence*, R. B. Beckett ed., VI, 'The Fishers', S.R.S. (1968), p. 237.

Of Colt's fellow-pioneers in *Ancient Wiltshire* there remained Phillip Crocker, who had been Steward at Stourhead for nearly twenty years.

About this time two Somerset gentlemen, Samuel Hasell and William Stradling,[2] were investigating the sites of Roman settlements near Somerton. It was, and still is, a piece of country spectacular in scenic beauty and rich in associations with antiquity. To the south High Ham juts into King's Sedge Moor; while to the north the area is enclosed by a ridge of the Polden Hills, which curve in a south-westerly direction from Street towards Charlton Mackrell, the wooded escarpments contrasting dramatically with the flat marshland, out of which rises the iron age camp on Dundon Beacon. The River Cary divides the Poldens from the High Ham mass, winding through Somerton Moor to become the straight canal of Sedgemoor Drain. Alfred's Isle of Athelney lies a few miles to the west in what must have been a marshy lake in Roman times.

Hasell lived at Littleton, just north of Somerton, where he had found extensive evidence of Roman occupation covering, he said, thirty acres. Whether or not this was an exaggeration, he had certainly located the sites of at least two villas, and by the end of 1826 had uncovered a range of apartments, revealing two tessellated floors. Apart from the letters to his friend Stradling, and a few to Colt, we know little about him. He was a landowner in a small way, and at the time appears to have been engaged in farming. His plans and drawings[3] have a competent, almost professional air, and he seems to have known what he was about. His wit had a malicious twist. Hasell seems to have resented the interest the nobility and well-to-do took in his researches, although he was ambivalent about them. In any case he sent Colt an account of his discovery, and some plans and drawings. It was not long before Colt announced his intention of visiting the Littleton antiquities, which Hasell, knowing it was not prudent to oppose fate or the wishes of great men, said he was welcome to do. He did not anticipate Colt's request to have the ground laid open ready, nor the ample instructions on how to do it. Colt, it is clear, foresaw another Cunnington. But Hasell, a much younger man, was unwilling to accept that role, at least without protest.

Colt came three times to Littleton between May and August in 1827, always without notice. Skinner too came over and tired Hasell with his dissertations on the analysis of words. To cap this, Colt published an account of the Littleton Villa in *The Gentleman's Magazine*,[4] which did not please Hasell much. 'I fancy the Bart. is none of the wisest, and from the frequent intercourse I have of late had with him, and other honourable

[2] The correspondence between Hasell and Stradling, and Hoare's letters to Hasell are in the Somerset County Record Office at Taunton (S.R.O.). Hasell's letters to Hoare are among the 'Catsgore papers' in the library of the Somerset Archaeological Society at Taunton Museum (S.A.S.).
[3] Some original drawings are among the 'Catsgore papers', S.A.S.
[4] Vol. XCVII, 1827.

visitors, I am sometimes tempted to exclaim: if wealth and titles did but command common sense, how blest would be our nobles.'[5] Hasell persisted, however, encouraged by Colt, who sent him *Stonehenge Illustrated,* 'most exquisitely got up but the substance. . . . *Sir Richard all over*'.[6]

The following year Colt arranged to spend three days at Somerton, where he had found a tolerable inn, and asked to be shown the sixteen sites which had been identified; in order to astonish the world with the extent of his investigations,[7] said Hasell, who suspected he was about to be robbed of the credit. Colt called again in August, on his way back from Devon, sadly provoked to find there was nothing going on, and complaining that the Somerset gentry had no true *taste*. 'Of course I considered myself an exception', wrote Hasell. 'From what he hinted I think he is likely to stir us up by some moving paper in some magazine, or paragraph in a newspaper. The poor old man says he shall frequently call here and talks of bringing down his horses again next summer for investigating our hills and dales.'[8] Hasell's letters to Colt show no such lack of respect; and as they became more closely acquainted it was apparent that the charms of Stourhead were working once again. Colt on his side was not only attentive but complimentary. He was contributing to the cost of operations, which were now centred on uncovering the site of a large villa on the lower slopes of a ridge near Pitney, looking towards Dundon Beacon and Glastonbury. There was evidence of at least two mosaic floors; and as those at Littleton had been destroyed 'by the idle curiosity of the vulgar',[9] Colt urged Hasell to employ watchmen at his expense.

By 15 June the soil had been removed to within a few inches of the principal floors and temporary sheds erected over them. Even so, Hasell reported,

> the common people in the night come and break down the sheds and commit every species of injury which mischief can devise; indeed so far do they carry their resentments that I am obliged to keep two night watchmen upon the grounds. Serious as the effects of their displeasure is, the cause which moves it is truly ludicrous. These people cannot imagine that from mere curiosity I should expend so much time and money, confusing the Romans of old with the Roman Catholics of the present day, they believe the concessions made to the latter in point of religion is to be followed by the restoration of their former property and that I am employed by the *Pope* to discover where this is.[10]

[5] Samuel Hasell to William Stradling, 1 Aug. 1827, S.R.O.
[6] S.H. to W.S., 1 Feb. 1828, S.R.O.   [7] S.H. to W.S., 2 June 1828, S.R.O.
[8] S.H. to W.S., 29 Aug. 1828, S.R.O.
[9] R.C.H. to Mr. Urban, 30 July 1827. Baker, *Illustrations of Somerset*, vol. XII, p. 178, Bath Reference Library.
[10] S.H. to W.S., 15 June 1829, S.R.O.

The pavements survived, and on 29 June were formally uncovered. Colt, insisting that drawings should be made as soon as possible, brought Crocker to assist Hasell. He had given his opinion that no pavements such as these had ever been found. The smaller had four panels with figures representing the seasons; the larger showed a central figure seated surrounded by eight others. These, it was frivolously suggested, were the Minister, Churchwarden, Clerk, Sexton, and other official persons once in the parish of Pitney.[11] Colt seriously published his view that they represented the lord of the manor surrounded by his vassals employed in various occupations, such as mining or coining. Among them he identified the foreman of the works looking angrily at a female who was scattering coin from a canister in the next compartment; a guard or *custos loci*; and a female he thought might be a ledger keeper. Skinner was furious, because that was his explanation. Sir Richard might be a great man, he said, but he was one of the greatest poachers that ever lived.[12] In fact the figures were plainly mythological including Mercury, Neptune, and a Mithraic person in a Persian cap.

Skinner thought Hasell should publish his account of the Pitney Villa without patronage; but Hasell was in two minds. His neighbours showed little concern over antiquities and he was encouraged by Colt's interest, although he was irritated at the suggestion that the drawings should be made by a professional, when he had offered his own quite adequate lithographed copies. Nevertheless when the Society of Antiquaries declined to publish he was glad of Colt's offer to do so privately and was happy to bear some of the expense. *The Pitney Pavement* was printed by Crocker of Frome in 1831. Even though Hasell did not like parts of the letterpress, his own name appeared prominently on the title page; so did Colt's. We may think that the credit is not properly apportioned and that, as Hasell satirically put it, 'the world now knows, for the news have said it, that to Sir Richard they are indebted for the discovery, explanation and publication'.[13] On the other hand if he had not done so, the discoveries round Somerton would quite probably have gone unrecorded, for Hasell lost interest and moved to London.

The Pitney Pavement was destroyed in 1836. Hasell's sites had not been re-explored when the present edition of the *Victoria County History* appeared in 1906. At that time Haverfield, who wrote the section on Romano-British Somerset, questioned Hasell's competence and suggested that he was an enthusiast who saw foundations too easily. But his letters do not bear this out. At Hurcot,[14] when he could not get permission to excavate, he persuaded the tenant to dig a drain which revealed the extent

[11] S.H. to W.S., 26 July 1829, S.R.O.
[12] S.H. to W.S., 19 Feb. 1830, S.R.O.
[13] S.H. to W.S., 19 Feb. 1830, S.R.O.
[14] S.H. to R.C.H., 25 May 1831, S.A.S.

of the villa he suspected was there. Elsewhere he refers to ruins between Ilchester and Pitney not marked on his plan because he did not know if they were Roman.[15] And, in fact, no site is mentioned in *The Pitney Pavement* for which there is not at least some confirmatory evidence in the form of Roman bricks, tiles, hypocausts, coins, or other remains. Extensive finds of pottery and coins have since been made in the grounds of Littleton House where he once lived; but many of the thirty acres are occupied by farm buildings of a later date and cannot now be explored. Other sites were re-explored in 1950–1,[16] some yielding positive evidence and some not. About the same time a villa was discovered and excavated at Catsgore, near Ilchester. A villa not on Hoare's plan was excavated at High Ham in 1861; and at the time of writing Mr. Roger Leech is successfully excavating buildings and burials at site 16.[17]

The last word from Hasell on the subject of Colt Hoare is in a letter written to Stradling in 1832 after a visit to Stourhead. 'I stayed rather longer than I anticipated—but tis a delightful place to stay at and I enjoyed it greatly.'[18]

The Pitney Pavement was the last of Colt's field excursions. The entries in the journals for his last years become very sparse, and in 1832 he wrote, 'Still home-bound deaf and lame. At home till 2 July, a long confinement at Marlborough till 4 August.' Thereafter he hardly moved from Stourhead, except to go to Bath to find relief. Work on *Modern Wiltshire* continued, and histories of the Hundreds regularly appeared. After *Mere* (1822) and *Heytesbury* (1824), Colt himself was responsible for *Everley, Ambresbury and Underditch* (1826), and *Cawden* (1835). The rest appeared under other names besides his own: *Branch and Dole* with John Offer (1825); *Dunworth and Vale of Noddre* with Lord Arundell (1829); *Westbury* with Richard Harris (1830); *Warminster* with Henry Wansey (1831); *Chalk* by Charles Bowles (1833); *Downton* by George Matcham (1834); *South Damerham* with W. H. Black (1835); and *Alderbury* with J. G. Nichols (1837). In 1834 Colt asked Henry Hatcher to compile *The History of Salisbury*. Hatcher, the son of a small farmer, was a schoolmaster, and for a short time Postmaster of Salisbury. He had assisted Coxe in his research on Roman roads, and Colt with *Giraldus* and *Recollections Abroad*. He had previously declined to work on *Modern Wiltshire*, but now he accepted and was given the collections made by Robert Benson. *The History of Salisbury* did not appear till 1843, when an embittered dispute arose between Benson and Hatcher over the authorship. The only other part to be published after Colt's death was George Matcham's *Hundred of Frustfield* (1844). This also contains additions to the other hundreds, including Stourton with,

[15] S.H. to R.C.H., 19 July (no year), S.A.S.
[16] See *Proceedings of the Somerset Archaeological Society* (1951), XCVI.
[17] *Somerset and Dorset Notes and queries*, Sept. 1969.
[18] S.H. to W.S., 22 June 1832, S.R.O.

among other matters, a more complete pedigree of the Hoare family than had appeared in Colt's first volume.

Added to his infirmities Colt had to contemplate his son's wasted life. By 1827 Henry was living apart from his wife. He had never followed any occupation, nor even managed properly his own affairs, so that at forty-three, though still a handsome man, he was suffering from the consequences of an irregular existence. 'Stourhead will be a very different place when he is in possession', wrote Hunter.[19] Henry's daughter, Anne, was married in 1835;[20] soon after Henry sued Charlotte for divorce. 'Marriages, they say, are made in heaven', wrote Colt, 'but surely *his* was not, but it was made contrary to my inclination; it was *his own* choice, & alas he has suffered sadly from his precipitancy.'[21]

On 18 April 1836 Colt wrote in his diary: 'Spring day. Out after confinement of five months.'[22] It was a sad year for him. Henry died at Hastings on 18 September, and his body was brought to Stourhead four days later. All that remained was to discharge his very considerable debts.

His son's death altered the whole succession at Stourhead. Colt had always maintained that the estates could never support a large family 'with credit to themselves'.[23] It was for this reason, he said, that he had not married again. His heir was now his half-brother, Henry Hugh; so Fleet Street and Stourhead would once more be united. In this knowledge Colt died, in his eightieth year, at a quarter to six in the morning of 19 May 1838.

[19] 'Notices of Contemporaries.'
[20] MS. Memoirs, FS.
[21] To Sir George Mathew, F.S.
[22] Diaries, 1816–37, T(ST) 383.37.
[23] MS. Memoirs, FS.

Conclusion

Colt Hoare's last years coincided with the decline of a predominantly rural economy and the close of an era of British social history. The 1832 Reform Bill began to erode the political power of the landowners. 1833 marked parliamentary recognition of responsibility for popular education. The return of the Tolpuddle martyrs in 1834 was an event of significance for the Trade Union Movement. In 1837 Victoria came to the throne, with all that her name connotes. Certainly, with industrial and imperial expansion proceeding hand in hand, the energies of Englishmen were diffused and no longer concentrated on their little patch, its embellishment and history. Colt Hoare and his kind, although they had enjoyed the civilized towns of Italy, and life in Bath or Cheltenham, had turned their backs on Birmingham. The excavations on Salisbury Plain might be seen as symbolic of the future dereliction of the landscape.

At Stourhead succeeding Hoares completed what had been begun, added a little, conserved what had been created. Colt left the estates to his half-brother, Henry Hugh (the Hugh of Hester's letters), and to his descendants 'in tail male'. Hugh was seventy-six when he came to Stourhead and only lived there three years. During that short time he added a portico to the house, according to Campbell's original design; rebuilt the obelisk with Bath stone; and employed John Bowyer Nichols to prepare a detailed catalogue of the library. He and his son, Hugh Richard, saw to a conclusion *The History of Modern Wiltshire*, the last part of which, *The Hundred of Frustfield*, appeared in 1844. In the garden, buildings were extensively repaired; and from 1850 onwards a wide variety of conifers was introduced, which included species unknown to previous generations. The big Californian Redwoods, Western Red Cedar, Monterey and Lawson Cypress were to become prominent features and give interest to the winter scene.

Henry Hugh and Hugh Richard were both partners in the bank. But when the latter died in 1857, Stourhead passed to his nephew, Henry Ainslie Hoare, and the sources of the Golden Bottle and the Stour were again divided, never to be reunited. Ainslie Hoare, the 5th baronet, was an interesting man in many respects, but in the annals of Stourhead he is a villain, for he sold the Stourhead heirlooms in 1883. These included some of the better pictures which Henry and Colt Hoare had collected, including Poussin's *Rape of the Sabines*, the Canaletto drawings of Venice which hung in the library, the Richard Wilsons, and Turner's paintings, including *Aeneas and the Sibyl, Lake Avernus* (Pl. 29a), perhaps the most significant loss because of its associations. Far more damaging than the sale of pictures was the dissipation of Colt's library with its unique topographical drawings and comprehensive range of historical and topographical books which made it a collection of such interest and usefulness. The library is still a beautiful room, but it has been separated from its function, which is now to some extent fulfilled by the Wiltshire Archaeological Society's library and museum at Devizes. This not only houses the material results of Cunnington's excavations and the documentary record of his researches, but fragments have been collected of what was lost to Stourhead after 1883, including many of Crocker's original drawings for *Ancient Wiltshire*, and Buckler's great architectural series. Ironically John Britton was ultimately responsible, for in 1839 he started *The Wiltshire Topographical Society* which, as he tried to run it from London, foundered after ten years. In 1852, however, he wrote to Cunnington's grandson (also William) saying that he wished to dispose of his Wiltshire books and manuscripts to someone in the county. Cunnington called a meeting at Devizes which resulted in the purchase of Britton's collection for £150, and support for a place to house it. Thus was The Wiltshire Archaeological and Natural History Society inaugurated in 1853.

When Ainslie Hoare died without male issue in 1894, Stourhead went to his cousin, Henry Hugh Arthur Hoare, who became the 6th baronet. He was twenty-nine when he succeeded; he lived for another fifty-three years. Stourhead's preservation is due to him as much as anyone. After a fire which gutted the central part of the house in 1902, but spared Colt Hoare's library and picture gallery, he saw to it that the interior was carefully restored. The exceptions were the saloon and west front which were considerably altered. Perhaps the most interesting cultural association in his lifetime was with Thomas Hardy, whose sense of antiquity found many affinities at Stourhead, and who was, perhaps, the last great exponent of landscape in English literature.

When Sir Henry Hoare's son died of wounds in 1917 the succession which Colt Hoare had established came to an end; and in 1946 the house and gardens with 2300 acres were given to the National Trust. The remainder of the estate was left to his cousin, Henry Peregrine Rennie Hoare, a descendant of that Richard, brother of 'Good' Henry, whose business never prospered.

Stourhead is now best known for its garden, which must of necessity be constantly renewed. Even for Henry Hoare the concept was a changing one. Throughout the process of its creation, whether he was celebrating a pagan rite, representing a Classical idyll, making a picturesque scene, or demonstrating patriotic loyalty, a subtle interplay was taking place between the human psyche and the landscape. These associations are now largely irrelevant. Colt Hoare's rhododendrons have proliferated; others have been added. The popular response at times is overwhelming, but there are still seasons when Stourhead 'might be held sacred to stillness and solitary musing'.

Appendix I

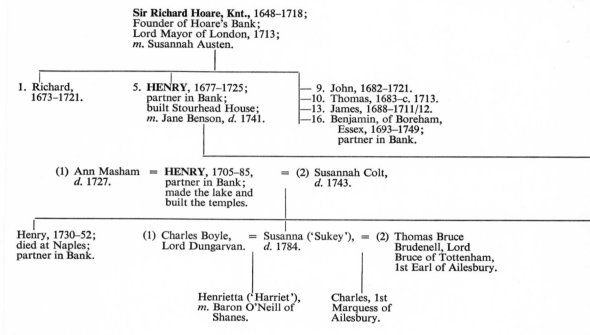

Sir Richard Hoare, Knt., 1648–1718;
Founder of Hoare's Bank;
Lord Mayor of London, 1713;
m. Susannah Austen.

1. Richard,
   1673–1721.

5. **HENRY**, 1677–1725;
   partner in Bank;
   built Stourhead House;
   m. Jane Benson, *d.* 1741.

— 9. John, 1682–1721.
—10. Thomas, 1683–c. 1713.
—13. James, 1688–1711/12.
—16. Benjamin, of Boreham,
       Essex, 1693–1749;
       partner in Bank.

(1) Ann Masham   =   **HENRY**, 1705–85,   =   (2) Susannah Colt,
    d. 1727.   partner in Bank;   *d.* 1743.
                         made the lake and
                         built the temples.

Henry, 1730–52;
died at Naples;
partner in Bank.

(1) Charles Boyle,   =   Susanna ('Sukey'),   =   (2) Thomas Bruce
    Lord Dungarvan.   *d.* 1784.   Brudenell, Lord
                                                         Bruce of Tottenham,
                                                         1st Earl of Ailesbury.

Henrietta ('Harriet'),
m. Baron O'Neill of
     Shanes.

Charles, 1st
Marquess of
Ailesbury.

OURHEAD

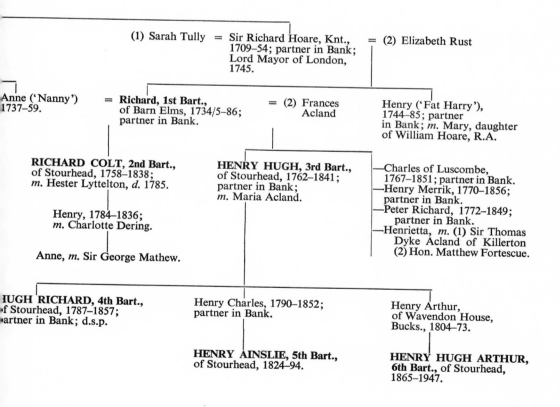

(1) Sarah Tully = Sir Richard Hoare, Knt., = (2) Elizabeth Rust
1709–54; partner in Bank;
Lord Mayor of London,
1745.

Anne ('Nanny') = **Richard, 1st Bart.,** = (2) Frances   Henry ('Fat Harry'),
1737–59.   of Barn Elms, 1734/5–86;   Acland   1744–85; partner
                    partner in Bank.   in Bank; *m.* Mary, daughter
                                                              of William Hoare, R.A.

RICHARD COLT, 2nd Bart.,   **HENRY HUGH, 3rd Bart.,**   —Charles of Luscombe,
of Stourhead, 1758–1838;   of Stourhead, 1762–1841;   1767–1851; partner in Bank.
m. Hester Lyttelton, *d.* 1785.   partner in Bank;   —Henry Merrik, 1770–1856;
                                m. Maria Acland.   partner in Bank.
                                                              —Peter Richard, 1772–1849;
Henry, 1784–1836;   partner in Bank.
m. Charlotte Dering.   —Henrietta, *m.* (1) Sir Thomas
                                                                Dyke Acland of Killerton
Anne, *m.* Sir George Mathew.   (2) Hon. Matthew Fortescue.

HUGH RICHARD, 4th Bart.,   Henry Charles, 1790–1852;   Henry Arthur,
f Stourhead, 1787–1857;   partner in Bank.   of Wavendon House,
artner in Bank; d.s.p.   Bucks., 1804–73.

                           HENRY AINSLIE, 5th Bart.,   **HENRY HUGH ARTHUR,**
                           of Stourhead, 1824–94.   **6th Bart.,** of Stourhead,
                                                           1865–1947.

Appendix II

Letter from William Cunnington to the
Reverend Mr. Richardson, of Woolverton, Somerset,
February, 1803

There are frequently found some flat circular Barrows from 20 to 50 feet in diameter, with no greater elevation than 12 to 14 inches; and these have frequently a small depression in the centre which indicates that the body was buried entire—I consider these as the most ancient tumuli; in one of them I found celts formed of stone etc. If you find any of this description on the apex of a hill, I would advise you by all means to open them; but recollect that in these as well as in any other barrows you may open, you must proportion the section to the size of the Barrow; if a large Barrow, the section of course must be large, otherwise you may miss finding the interment.

2. The next class of Barrows is numerous and are from five to 150 feet base diameter, and of different elevations—In the greater part of these cremation or burning has been practised; sometimes we find the burnt bones in an urn, but oftener in a cist or circular cavity cut in the Earth previous to the erection of the Barrow; sometimes the urn is inverted in a cist, sometimes on the earth, level with the adjoining ground, and the tumulus raised over it. When the interment is found in a cist, we sometimes find small urns near, & among the bones. Now as Somersetshire abounds with stone, it is probable you will find your skeletons, as also your urns, inclosed by stones set edgeways, and one or more over them to preserve them; therefore you have a much better chance of taking out your urns entire than we have in Wiltshire.

3. The next class of Barrows (which are few in number) are those in the form of an egg cut in two lengthways, and placed with the convex side upwards: under these you may find skeletons, & generally more than one.

4. The last are the oblong Barrows and these are of various sizes—we have one near us 377 feet in length—these have generally one end considerably wider than the other—Out of six oblong Barrows which I have opened, five produced skeletons: in the sixth cremation had been practiced.

GENERAL REMARKS

1. When you take off the turf, examine immediately under it, as on the top we have often met with urns, and generally the horns or pieces of the horns of Red Deer. As you proceed in your section, you will frequently meet with coarse pottery, animal bones, charred wood and ashes.

2. When you get within a foot or two feet of the bottom, shove a thick walking stick frequently into the earth as far as you can—this will often show the place of interment & save much trouble; for if there is a cist, the stick will slip in as if into ashes.—

3. If you come to a skeleton, learn as soon as you can the position in which it lies—N.B. I consider those with the head to the north as the most ancient.

4. Note down minutely the position in which you find the urns, skeletons etc. Observe, that you will rarely find the skeletons laying at length, but generally with the limbs drawn up, you will also find great evenness in the teeth.

Appendix III

Letter from William Cunnington to Thomas Leman

Heytesbury 1809

To the Revd. Mr. Leman.

Sir,

I should have answered your favor of November last (received with the Book) long ere this, but my health has been so very indifferent, that I have had very little inclination for writing.

I must first observe that I have ever had the highest respect for people who have had a liberal education like yourself; but I contend that the information to be gathered from the Roman & Greek Historians will afford little information as data for illustrating Abury, Stonehenge Marden etc. etc., the Works of an ancient people like the Celtic Britons.[1] The information to be gathered from Caesar and Tacitus relate to the Britons in their times—therefore all theories drawn from such sources in regard to our Celtic Britons are ever at war with facts.[2]

Of the truth of these remarks I am of opinion you would yourself bear testimony were you to favor Sir Richard Hoare with your company in the next Campaign.

1 ly. You say in your Letter that I do not appear to distinguish clearly as yet what have been the remains of a Villa or of a Station—In answer to this remark I have only to say that if I do not—then I deserve to be laughed at. But on the subject of the Roman Roads I confess my knowledge is limited, when compared to yours. However I have only asserted that the British Towns or dwellings were the basis of these Roads—the Roman Roads were therefore the lines of population—& as far as circumstances admitted, would of course be carried over the high lands.

2 ly. You conceive that the great Tumulus near Marden was an high Altar etc. If I were to reason from cases analogous to the discoveries made at Marden, I should draw different conclusions—but I will send my paper containing our discoveries, you will then judge for yourself.

3 ly. The Stones which compose the Temple at Stonehenge.—In this Note you quote Mr. Whitehurst's opinion of the Stones who supposed them Volcanic. At this period, when the science of Mineralogy is so much studied, this Gentleman's opinion has no weight—The Stones composing the outer Circle, the Trilithons, and the great Stones which mark the entrance are Sarsens—viz, a fine grained Sand-Stone. They were not taken from Quarries, but are found singly upon the Downs; & whether found upon the Downs, a foot, or two under the ground, their superfices are rounded by attrition.[3]

---

[1] Perhaps no more than the manners & customs of the Otaheitians.
[2] The Book which best illustrates British Antiquities is the Bible.
[3] Some of the Sarsens near Marlborough, & others ploughed up near Stonehenge appear to have been bored through by the Teredo.

The inner Circle & inner oval are Aggregates, chiefly varieties of Granite—two or three of Horn Stone etc.

4 ly. In the following page you say that the Stratum immediately following the Chalk[4] is Clay. But this is a mistake, as the stratum immediately following the Chalk is more generally Sand—of this Mr. Townsend of Pewsey will convince you—as next to my friend Wm. Smith, no person knows so much of the subject of Strata.[5]

5 ly. You say, why should it be thought remarkable that the chippings of the Stones of Stonehenge should be found in the Barrows near this Work? This fact is no otherwise remarkable, than that it helps to overturn the system of the Welch Antiquaries, who want to make Stonehenge a Work of the 5th Century—We have two or three more Barrows to open near the Temple & should we find similar Stones in them, it would completely prove the very high antiquity of Stonehenge, but I want no farther proof myself.

6 ly. In regard to the curious Stone found in the Barrow close to the Cursus which you suppose was used as a Hone, I have a higher opinion of its value among the Britons—& in this opinion I think the sober Borlase will support me. I have a vast variety of Whetstones etc. which once belonged to the Britons, but no Whetstone or Hone like the Stone in question, such were not easily procured—A few years ago we found in a barrow a curious Laminated Stone which was perforated, but from its nature could never have been used as a Whetstone.

7 ly. Old Winchester. In my account of this work you have several notes—You first object to my making yourself and Mr. Whitaker say, that the Britons had *raised* Roads. I now assure you that I so understood you—but have now erased the word *raised*, as I find I have been mistaken.

Mr. Whitaker is a writer with a vivid imagination, but soars too high into the regions of fancy, & frequently draws his conclusions from slender data. To what an extent has he not carried the Commerce of the Belgæ before the Roman invasion!

I have doubts whether the Phoenicians ever traded to this Country for Tin—but think they obtained it through the medium of the Gauls.[6] In the time of Diodorus Siculus this article was conveyed through Gaul to Italy, & I think that before the Roman invasion Gaul was the medium through which all the British commerce passed. On the early & continued intercourse between the Britons & Gauls, I argue from the following reasons. I consider this Island was first peopled from Gaul, of course the Britons & Gauls in religious manners & customs resembled each other—& from the two countries being contiguous, this intercourse would long continue. I learn also from Monfaucon, and some other french Writers which have accidently fallen in my way, that some Tumuli that have been opened in France have produced similar articles to what have been found in British Tumuli. And I learn that there are many Earthen Works which resemble ours, also Stone Monuments etc etc.

4 Viz—West & North West.

5 In the study of Antiquities, some knowledge of Strata & Mineralogy is necessary.

6 The period in which it is said the Phoenicians traded to Britain is very remote; surely the Voyage was too long if we take into consideration the state of Navigation & Commerce in this early period.

Since writing the above I have been favoured by Mr. Lambert with a sight of a large German folio, written by a Johann Chris[n.] Betmann & published at Berlin in 1751. This Writer treats on a variety of subjects, among which he treats of the Antiquities in his Country—In page 415 he gives two plates of Stone Hatchets, Brass Celts etc. the greater part of which were found in Tumuli in the March of Brandenbourgh. As similar articles to the above have been found in France & Italy—Should we err much in supposing that these articles once belonged to a primitive people who in some remote period inhabited the greater part of Europe & who were supplied with the Brass articles through the medium of the Gaulish Ports by the Phoenicians? Knowing nothing of the German language, I am indebted to Mr. Coxe for the above account.

19+L.A.

After peace is made between this Nation & France, I make no doubt but Sir Richard Hoare will take a Voyage to France for the sole purpose of exploring the Celtic Antiquities in that Country.

If the result should turn out as I anticipate viz. a similarity in the Earthen Works etc. & the Tumuli produce Brass Daggers, Glass & Amber Beads, articles in Ivory etc. these discoveries would sufficiently prove the connection between the two Countries, & also point out the most probable place or places from whence the Phoenicians *obtained* the British Tin—most probably from some of the Gaulish ports in the Mediteranean. Mr. Whitaker like Stukely makes the Britons a great Nation, but Mr. Whitaker is two Centuries too early. In our Antiquarian researches we discover nothing to prove to the contrary but that the Britons before the Roman invasion were a rude people.[7] Under the Roman Government Britons emerged from Barbarism[8]—it was during that period that agriculture & Commerce flourished;—to prove these assertions we have only to refer to our discoveries on the Wiltshire Downs.

Again, his asserting that the Britons first laid out the Watling & Ikenild Roads, I think is extremely improbable. The former, if Caesar is to be credited was to pass through a Country of Barbarians, for such the Britons in the interior were at that period. Yet these Britons according to Mr. Whitaker erected *Towns* upon the great Watling Road made by their *invaders the Belgae*! But the circumstance of the Watling & Ikenild[9] Roads retaining a British name in Bede, & in Richard's Itinerary, ought not to be deemed sufficient authority for forming such an hypothesis, viz, that these Roads were erected by the Britons. If erected as I conceive they were by the Romans, nothing can be more reasonable than to suppose that the Britons through whose Country these roads passed should give them a British name, & nothing more likely that these British names should finally prevail over the Roman.

On reading Mr. Whitaker's account of the Belgic Britons—of their forming such Works of enterprise as carrying Roads from Kent to the extremity of Wales for the purpose of trading with Ireland for Cattle etc.[10]—the great progress made by this people in Agriculture & Commerce etc., puts one in mind of Stukely who makes his Hero Hercules migrate from lower Egypt with 240,000 Men, & this only a *few* generations after the flood. Previous to the Roman invasion, the roads of the Britons I conceive were like the trackways of Savages in the present day—they were not in straight lines, nor yet made with Stone—therefore could bear no comparison with Roman Roads. In regard to the ridge or trackways of the Britons, such ways have been the Roads of all Nations from the Aborigines till the introduction of the turnpike Roads. It did not require superior intellect to learn that travelling upon a high ridge or dry plain was preferable to travelling through Vales which in early periods abounded with Wood, Swamps & probably with Wild Beasts. Yet I do not believe that these

---

[7] From Caesar, Mela & other ancient Writers we learn that the Druids were skilled in Geography, Astronomy etc etc, & among the moderns the respectable Mr. Wm. Owen has given me a paper upon their Mythology, which tends to prove them a *very* enlightened people. I confess I am at a loss to reconcile these things otherwise than by supposing that the Druids kept all the learning to themselves.

[8] Viz—when compared to the polished state they were in under the Romans.

[9] As we have two or three Ikenild Streets, are we sure that Dr. Stukely and Mr. Whitaker are right in the etymology of this word. Is it not straining a point too far when Mr. Whitaker makes his Derbyshire Ikenild Road run to the Iceni. Mr. Whitaker writes so *well*, who can help believing his Visions?

[10] Considering the state of society among the Britons & Gauls at this period, to me nothing appears so improbable as that the Gauls etc should want Cattle, & that these animals should be taken in such a round about way as from Ireland to Wales in Ships—and then through Wales & all England by land to be shipped again in Kent! I presume the Irish Vessels could not carry the Cattle to Gaul!

trackways, paths, or Roads of the Britons, had any connection with Tumuli, or the Tumuli with the Roads.[11]

You again object to my clearing the high lands in the Chalk Country of Wood—I have said "that the hills *were only slightly covered with Wood*, & of course easily cleared." That the Britons first occupied & cultivated the high lands, I have had the joint opinions of the late Mr. Davis of Horningsham, Mr. Wm. Smith and several intelligent Farmers—but on this subject we want no other evidence than what the high Chalk land presents us in the present day. We find little squares formed by [Lynchets] (the marks of ancient agriculture) all over the sides of our Hills.[12] Even our great ridge wood South of Heytesbury on which Sir Richard Hoare has discovered a Roman Road was also in tillage. It is now a common practice to dig in these [Lynchets] for flints, & when at this Work the Labourers have frequently met with Roman Coins, Fibulas, broken pottery (of Roman form) Brass pins etc etc. I have many articles of this kind, & I think the evidence is full proof that this ancient agriculture was the Work of the Romanized Britons.[13]

9 ly. You also say, and which I had before overlooked, that Old Winchester has no resemblance to a Saxon Camp. Being upon the subject of Camps, it is my duty here to acknowledge how much I am indebted to you for your little treatise on Camps, which has been of great assistance to me. But there is one part & only one part, if I remember right that I now see cause to object to, & that is, you have not discriminated between the Camps of the barbarous Saxons of the 5th, & the Camps of the more civilized Anglo Saxons of the tenth Century—If you trace the history of Camp-making from what you see in this Country—viz, beginning with the slight rude Works of the Celtic Britons, & ending at Badbury, erected by Edward the older, we must draw the following conclusions—viz, the height of the Vallum, the great depth of the Foss, & multiplicity of each was the perfection of the art of Castrametation among the Saxons—the latter people never formed a square Camp—But when the Saxons first invaded Britain & perhaps for a Century after, I conceive that the Saxons erected simple & rude Works, when compared to their Camps raised by this people in the 7th, 8th & 10th Centuries. By frequent observation the different gradations are easily discerned.

Old Winchester Camp is not unlike Quarly—yet I think there is hardly a doubt of the latter being a Saxon or Danish Work. But neither at Old Winchester or Quarly would the ground admit of any other form. But in regard to old Winchester having been a British City as you conceive—We have sufficient proof to the contrary from having examined the area in which there is not the least signs of its ever having been inhabited otherwise than as a temporary Post.

[11] The Roman Roads passed of course through the British Tumuli. The Tumuli were not raised with any reference to the British trackways or Roads—the Britons were guided in fixing on spots for interring their dead, from circumstances (in all probability) purely local, but which at this period we can only conjecture. If the Britons preferred interring near their Roads, why do we find so many Tumuli in Vales?—& again if on high lands, upon such situations as were quite unconnected with the Roads?—What connection have the Tumuli in the environs of Stonehenge, Brigmilston, Everly etc with the British trackways?
[12] What Mr. Stackhouse calls Terraces.
[13] At this period a Roman Writer says we employed (I think) 600 Vessels in carrying Grain to the Continent.

Bibliography

Manuscripts

1 WILTSHIRE COUNTY RECORD OFFICE, TROWBRIDGE

Stourhead Archive

383.4	1707–1807 1808–1838	Loose accounts, with some letters or agreements, relating mainly to pictures and books, but also to sculpture, some glass, china, porcelain, silver, furniture and garden statuary.
383.6	1749–1770	Volume of accounts, mainly household but including payments to John Cheere, Michael Rysbrack and Henry Flitcroft.
383.29–46	1740–1845	Rentals.
383.50	1783–1814	Rent totals.
383.57	1716–1797 1798–1838	Loose accounts (estate).
383.58	1717–1729	Accounts.
383.66	1792–1806	Account, mainly for building work on the house.
383.106	1829	'Terrae Hoareanae'; survey of the estate with maps.
383.108	1803	Particulars of woods and plantations.
383.250	c. 1833	List of lodges built at Stourhead by Richard Colt Hoare, endorsed with a table of trees planted, 1798–1833.
383.316	1722	Map of Stourhead.
383.716	1580–1714	Abstract of Title to the manors of Stourton and Stourton Caundle.
383.907	1736/37–1835	Correspondence; the earlier mainly to Henry Hoare II about pictures, sculpture, and architecture; the later mainly to Sir Richard Colt Hoare about matters of antiquarian interest.
383.909	1756	Narrative written and circulated by Margaret, Countess of Cork and Orrery, describing the circumstances of an estrangement between Henry Hoare II and the Earl of Cork and Orrery, following the marriage of Lord Dungarvan to Susanna Hoare, with quotations from private correspondence, annotated by Henry Hoare.

383.912	c. 1780	Eight quarto sheets written by Henry Hoare (1744–85), nephew to Henry Hoare II, describing the scene at Stourhead when his uncle revealed his unsuspected intention to settle Stourhead on his grandson, Richard Colt Hoare.
383.919	1785–91	Descriptions, some expenditure and memoranda, in a series of note-books relating to Richard Colt Hoare's tours on the continent; with a note-book containing lists of books, clothes to be taken abroad, general memoranda and an inventory of linen at St. James's Square.
383.924	1794–1816	Diaries. Brief notes only of visits, weather etc.
383.926	1796–1814	Journal. Summary of 924.
383.936	1815–1833	Journal. Summary.
383.937	1816–1837	Diaries (incomplete). As 924.

Savernake Archive
1761–1781   Letters from Henry Hoare II to Lord Bruce, Lady Bruce (Susanna, daughter), Harriet Boyle (grand-daughter).

2 MARQUESS OF AILESBURY, SAVERNAKE
1762–1781   Letters from Henry Hoare II as above; and from Richard Colt Hoare.
Reference numbers to correspondents in *Calendar of Documents*, compiled by Edith S. Scroggs (1948), 2 vols.

3 STOURHEAD
1701–1714   Volume of MS. letters from Sir Richard Hoare Knt. to his sons John, James, and Tom.

1792–1808   Summary of building accounts.

1797–1816   Ledger of Chippendale's accounts.

c. 1815   Small book of MS., memoirs, Sir Richard Colt Hoare.

1792–1855   Stourhead Annals, Vol. I. Mainly records of building, planting, game, etc.

4 HOARE AND CO., FLEET STREET, LONDON
1718–1785   Ledgers: Loans to customers; family accounts; Henry Hoare's personal ledgers 1752–78, 1778–83, 1770–85, 1732–49 (Wilberry).

1752–1836   Letters: Volume of family letters, Henry Hoare, Colt Hoare etc.; Tom Hoare to Sir Richard Hoare, 1708–1710; relating to Henry Hoare (1784–1836), son of Colt Hoare.

c. 1830   Book of MS., memoirs, Sir Richard Colt Hoare.

5 WILTSHIRE ARCHAEOLOGICAL SOCIETY, DEVIZES
1785–1838   MS. Journal of tour in Italy, 1785–87, Sir Richard Colt Hoare. Various note-books relating to tours and antiquities in Britain. Papers, collections, letters, and accounts relating to *Ancient Wiltshire* and *Modern Wiltshire*.

1796–1810   William Cunnington: Correspondence, 3 vols.; Papers relating to *Ancient Wiltshire*, I–XIII. (See notes on p. 283.)

6 BATH REFERENCE LIBRARY
   John Skinner, letters.

7 BODLEIAN
   MSS. 28692. G.A. Gen. Top. 40141. Letter R.C.H.

8 BRITISH MUSEUM
   28545 fol. 182–195. Letters R.C.H. to A. B. Lambert.
   28795. John Skinner letters to Camalodunum.
   Add. MSS. 36527. Biographical notes on contemporaries by Joseph Hunter, F.S.A.

9 CARDIFF CITY LIBRARY
   Journals of Tours, 1793–1810, Richard Colt Hoare, 3. 127.

10 TABLEY HOUSE, CHESHIRE
   Letters from R.C.H. and William Carey.

11 LINNEAN SOCIETY OF LONDON
   Smith correspondence.

12 R.I.B.A., LONDON
   MS. Journal of tour in Italy, Greece, and Egypt 1787–89, Willey Reveley.

13 SOCIETY OF ANTIQUARIES, LONDON
   Minutes.

14 SOMERSET ARCHAEOLOGICAL SOCIETY, TAUNTON
   Catsgore papers; letters S. Hasell to R.C.H.

15 SOMERSET COUNTY RECORD OFFICE, TAUNTON
   Letters: S. Hasell to W. Stradling; R.C.H. to S. Hasell.

16 NATIONAL LIBRARY OF WALES, ABERYSTWYTH
   Letters to Sir Richard Colt Hoare, 15257D.
   Letters in the Mysevin MSS. 13221E, 13222C, 13223C, 13224B.

Notes on the Source Material for Part III

Copies of all William Cunnington's records of his researches are in the library of the Wiltshire Archaeological and Natural History Society at Devizes (W.A.S.). They are in thirteen books, bound in three volumes, and are referred to in the notes as 'Papers' together with the book and page number. Copies of these are also in the archives of the Society of Antiquaries at Burlington House, London.

Letters to and from William Cunnington are bound in three volumes at Devizes. They are filed in alphabetical order of the correspondent. The letters are numbered, but some have no date. In the notes they are referred to as 'Letters', together with the number and, where possible, the date.

References to the Ancient History of Wiltshire are given as *A.W.*, I, or *A.W.*, II. The section on the Romans, which forms part of Volume II but has separate pagination, is referred to as *A.W.*, II (Rom.).

I am indebted to Mr. R. E. Sandell for access to the late Lt. Col. R. H. Cunnington's unpublished MS., 'From Antiquarian to Archaeologist'.

References to material in the Wiltshire County Record Office are indicated as before, T(ST) and the index number.

Chronological list of the printed works of Sir Richard Colt Hoare, abridged from the *Catalogue of the Hoare Library* (1840).

1800	Description of the House and Gardens at Stourhead (Salisbury).
1804	Giraldus Cambrensis, *Itinerarium Cambriae* (London).
1806	The Itinerary of Archbishop Baldwin through Wales, A.D. 1188, by Giraldus de Barri, translated into English, and illustrated with Views, Annotations and a Life of Giraldus, 2 Vols. (London).
1807	Journal of a Tour in Ireland (London).
1812–1821	The Ancient History of South Wiltshire (Preface dated 1810, London). The Ancient History of North Wiltshire (London, 1819). The Ancient History of Wiltshire, Roman Period (London, 1821).
1812	A Catalogue of Books relating to the History and Topography of Italy.
1814	A Tour through the Isle of Elba in 1789, illustrated with eight views by John Smith after sketches by the author. (Text repeated in *Recollections Abroad*.)
1815	A Journal of the Shrievalty of Richard Hoare Esq., in the years 1740–1. (Bath.)
	A Catalogue of books at Stourhead relating to the History and Topography of England, Wales, Scotland and Ireland (London).
	Hints to travellers in Italy (London).
1817	'An Account of the Stone Barrow in the parish of Wellow at Stoney Littleton, co. Somerset', *Archaeologia*, XIX.
	'On the Conduct of the Directors of the British Institution in regard to their present Patronage of British Artists; with some account of the present State of the Arts in England', *Annals of the Fine Arts*, II, 4.
1815–1818	Recollections Abroad: Journals of Tours on the Continent between the years 1785 and 1791, 4 vols. (Bath.)
1819	A Classical Tour through Italy and Sicily. (Abridged from *Recollections Abroad*.)
	Hints on the topography of Wiltshire. To which is appended Queries submitted to the Nobility, Gentry, and Clergy of the County of Wilts, with a view to promote a General History of the County (Salisbury).
	A Guide to Stourhead House and Demesnes (Bath).
	Pedigrees and Memoirs of the Families of Hoare (Bath).
1821	Monasticon Wiltunense: a list of the Religious Houses in North and South Wiltshire, compiled chiefly from Bishop Tanner's Notitia Monasticon (Shaftesbury).
	Repertorium Wiltunense. Printed with a view to facilitate Inquiry into the Topography and Biography of Wiltshire (Bath).
1823	Hungerfordania: or, Memoirs of the Family of Hungerford.
	'An Account of Antiquities found at Hamden Hill, with fragments of British Chariots', *Archaeologia*, XXI.
	'An Account of a Roman Bath found at Farley, Wilts.', *Gentleman's Magazine*, XCIII.
1824	Monastic Remains of the Religious Houses of Witham, Bruton, and Stavordale, com' Somerset.

1827	A short Treatise on the ancient Roman Town of Camalodunum, now Colchester, in Essex (Shaftesbury).
	'Observations upon Four Mosaic Pavements discovered in the County of Hants.', *Archaeologia*, XXII.
	'An Account of a Roman Villa at Littleton, co. Somerset', *Gentleman's Magazine*, XCVII.
	(With others) Registrum Wiltunense. Extracts from Records in the British Museum, from A.D. 892 to A.D. 1045.
1828	Antiquitates Wiltunenses; an Account of the Relics found in the Wiltshire Barrows.
1829	Tumuli Wiltunenses; A Guide to the Barrows on the Plains of Stonehenge (Shaftesbury).
1830	'An Account of the Roman Villa at Pitney, Somerset', *Gentleman's Magazine*, C.
	Chronicon Vilodunense. Extracted from the Cotton MSS by W. H. Black.
1831	The Roman Pavement at Pitney, co. Somerset (Frome).
1834	Course of the Wansdyke through Wiltshire and Somersetshire. Fol. foolscap sheet.
1822–1844	History of Modern Wiltshire (London).
1822	Hundred of Mere by R.C.H.
1824	Heytesbury by R.C.H.
1825	Branch and Dole by John Offer and R.C.H.
1826	Everley, Ambresbury, and Underditch by R.C.H.
1829	Dunworth and Vale of Noddre by James Everard, Baron Arundell, and R.C.H.
1830	Westbury by Richard Harris and R.C.H.
1831	Warminster by Henry Wansey and R.C.H.
1833	Chalk by Charles Bowles.
1834	Downton by George Matcham.
1835	South Damerham by W. H. Black and R.C.H.
	Cawden by R.C.H.
1837	Alderbury by R.C.H. and J. G. Nichols.
1843	Salisbury by R. Benson and H. Hatcher.
1844	Frustfield by George Matcham and R.C.H.

Other Sources

Acton, Harold M. M.	*The Bourbons of Naples 1734–1825* (1956).
Addison, Joseph	*The Spectator*, 1712.
Agassiz, D.	*A. L. Du Cros, Peintre et Graveur 1748–1810* (Lausanne, 1927).
Akenside, Mark	*The Pleasures of Imagination* (1744).
	Poetical Works (1855).
Annable, F. K. and Simpson, D. D. A.	*Guide Catalogue to the Neolithic and Bronze Age Collections in the Devizes Museum* (Devizes, 1964).
Annals of the Fine Arts	(1817–20).
Ashbee, P.	*The Bronze Age Round Barrow in Britain* (1960).

Atkinson, R. J. C. — *Stonehenge* (1960).

Baker, J. — *A Picturesque Guide through Wales and the Marches* (1794).

Beckett, R. B. ed. — *John Constable's Correspondence*, Suffolk Records Society. Vol. II, 'Early Friends and Maria Bicknell' (1964); Vol. VI, 'The Fishers' (1968).

Boase, T. S. R. — *English Art 1800–1870* (Oxford, 1959).

Britton, John — *The Beauties of Wiltshire* (1801).

—— ed. — *The Natural History of Wiltshire by John Aubrey, F.R.S.* (1847).

Brydone, P. — *A Tour through Sicily and Malta* (1773).

Burney, Frances — *Dairy, 1768–1778*, ed. Annie Raine Ellis (1913).

Campbell, Colen — *Vitruvius Britannicus* (1715–25).

Cardigan, Earl of — *The Wardens of Savernake Forest* (1949).

Clark, Sir George — *The Later Stuarts* (Oxford, 1961).

Clark, H. F. — *The English Landscape Garden* (1948).

Clark, Sir Kenneth — *The Gothic Revival* (1928, rev. 1950).

Clerk, Sir John — *Memoirs*, ed. John Gray (Edinburgh, 1892).

Colvin, H. M. — *A Biographical Dictionary of British Architects 1660–1840* (1954).

Constable, W. G. — *Richard Wilson* (1953).

Cooper, Anthony Ashley, 3rd Earl of Shaftesbury — *The Moralists: A Philosophical Rhapsody* (1709).

Coxe, William — *Sketches of the Natural, Civil, and Political State of Swisserland* (1789).

Cunnington, Lt. Col. R. H. — 'The Cunningtons of Wiltshire', *W.A.M.*, June, 1954.

—— — 'From Antiquarian to Archaeologist', MS. W.A.S. (Devizes).

Daniel, Glyn — *A Hundred Years of Archaeology* (1950).

Dodsley, R. — *A Description of the Leasowes* (1764).

Douglas, D. C. — *English Scholars 1660–1730* (1939 rev. ed. 1951).

Douglas, James — *Nenia Britannica: or a Sepulchral History of Great Britain* (1793).

Dugdale, William — *Antiquities of Warwickshire* (1656).

Evans, Joan — *A History of the Society of Antiquaries* (Oxford, 1956).

Farington, Joseph — *Diary*, ed. J. Grieg (1922–8).

Fenton, Richard ('A Barrister') — *A Tour in Quest of Genealogy through several parts of Wales, Somersetshire and Wiltshire* (1811).

Finberg, A. J. — *The Life of J. M. W. Turner, R.A.* (Oxford, 1939, 1961 ed.).

—— — *A Complete Inventory of Drawings in the Turner Bequest* (1909).

Fitz-Gerald, D. — 'Irish Gardens of the Eighteenth Century', *Apollo*, Sept. 1968.

Gage, John — 'Turner and the Picturesque', *Burlington Magazine*, Jan. and Feb., 1965.

Gentleman's Magazine	1788, 1789, 1817, 1818.
Gilpin, William	*Observations on the River Wye and Several Parts of South Wales* (1782).
Goethe, J. W.	*Italian Journey*, trans. W. H. Auden and Elizabeth Mayer (1962).
Goldwater, R. and Treves, M.	*Artists on Art* (1947).
Gore, St. John	'Prince of Georgian Collectors', *Country Life*, 30 Jan. 1964.
——	'A Worthy Hier to Greatness' *Country Life*, 4 Feb. 1964.
Gray, Thomas	*Poems* (1919, 1966 ed.).
Grinsell, L. V.	*The Ancient Burial Mounds of England* (1953).
——	*The Archaeology of Wessex* (1958).
Gunnis, Rupert	*A Dictionary of British Sculptors 1660–1851* (1953).
Hadfield, Miles	*Gardening in Britain* (1960).
Hall, Douglas	'The Tabley House Papers', *Walpole Society*, XXXVIII, 1960–2.
Hardie, Martin	*Water Colour Painting in Britain:* I. The Eighteenth Century (1966); II. The Romantic Period (1967).
Haskell, Francis	*Patrons and Painters* (1963).
Hazlitt, William	*Works*, 10 and 18 (1933).
Hipple, W. J., Jr.	*The Beautiful, The Sublime, and the Picturesque in Eighteenth Century British Aesthetic Theory* (Carbondale, 1957).
H.M. Stationery Office	*Complete Inventory of the Drawings of the Turner Bequest* (1909).
Hoare, H. P. R.	*Hoare's Bank, a Record 1672–1955* (1932, rev. ed. 1955).
Hogarth, William	*The Analysis of Beauty* (1753).
Honour, Hugh	*Neo-Classicism* (1968).
Hunter, Joseph	'The Topographical Gatherings at Stourhead', *Memoirs of the History and Antiquities of Wiltshire* (1851).
Hussey, Christopher	*The Picturesque* (1927, 1967 ed.).
——	*English Gardens and Landscapes 1700–1750* (1967).
——	'Wilbury Park', *Country Life*, CXXVI, 1959.
Ingersoll-Smouse, F.	*Joseph Vernet* (Paris, 1926).
Jones, Thomas	'Memoirs', *Walpole Society*, XXXII, 1951.
Kendrick, T. D.	*The Druids* (1927).
——	*British Antiquity* (1950).
Ketton-Cremer, R. W.	*Horace Walpole* (1940, 1964 ed.).
Knight, Richard Payne	*The Landscape* (1794).
——	*An Analytical Inquiry into the Principles of Taste* (1805).
King, Edward	*Munimenta Antiqua* (1799–1805).
Kurz, Otto	'Huius Nympha Loci', *Journal W.C.I.*, XVI, 1953.
Lees-Milne, J.	*Earls of Creation* (1962).
Leoni, Giacomo	*The Architecture of Palladio* (1721).

Leslie, C. R.	*Memoirs of the life of John Constable*, (1843, 1951 ed.).
Levey, M.	*Rococo to Revolution* (1966).
Lewis, Lesley	*Connoisseurs and Secret Agents* (1961).
Lovejoy, A. O.	*The Great Chain of Being* (New York, 1960).
Mack, Maynard	'The Shadowy Cave: some speculations in a Twicken-ham Grotto', *Restoration and Eighteenth Century Literature*, ed. C. Camden (Rice University, Texas, 1963).
Malins, Edward	*English Landscaping and Literature 1660–1840* (1966).
Manwaring, Elizabeth Wheeler	*Italian Landscape in Eighteenth Century England* (New York 1925, 1965 ed.).
Masson, Georgina	*Italian Gardens* (1961).
Milton, John	*Complete Poetry* (1964).
Moir, Esther	*The Discovery of Britain* (1964).
Monk, S. H.	*The Sublime*, Ann Arbor (1960).
Musgrave, Clifford	*Adam and Hepplewhite Furniture* (1966).
——	*Regency Furniture* (1961).
Nares, Gordon	'Painshill', *Country Life*, CXXIII, 1958.
Nichols, John	*History and Antiquities of the County of Leicester* (1795–1815).
Nichols, J. B.	*Catalogue of the Hoare Library at Stourhead* (1840).
Ovid	*The Metamorphoses*, trans. M. M. Innes (1955).
Owen, A. L.	*The Famous Druids*, Oxford (1962).
Pevsner, N.	'Genesis of the Picturesque', *Arch. Rev.*, May XCVI, Nov. 1944.
——	'Richard Payne Knight', *Art Bulletin*, XXXI, Dec. 1949.
Pevsner, N. and Lang, S.	'The Egyptian Revival', *Arch. Rev.*, May 1956.
Piggott, Stuart	*William Stukeley* (Oxford, 1950).
——	*Neolithic Cultures of the British Isles* (Cambridge, 1954).
——	*The Druids* (1968).
Pococke, Richard	*Travels through England*, ed. J. J. Cartwright (1889).
Pope, Alexander	*Correspondence*, ed. G. Sherburn (Oxford, 1956).
——	*Poetical Works* (1966).
Quarterly Review	1811.
Redgrave, R. and S.	*A Century of British Painters*, 1866 (Phaidon ed. 1947).
Reveley, Willey	Journal of a tour in Italy, Greece and Egypt, 1784–1789, MS. R.I.B.A., London.
Richards, R. D.	*The Early History of Banking* (1929).
Roethlisberger, M.	*Claude Lorrain* (1961).
Rousseau, J. J.	*Julie ou la Nouvelle Hélöise* (Paris, 1960 ed.).
Russell, Bertrand	*History of Western Philosophy* (1961), New York, 1945; London, 1948.
Sandell, R. E.	'Sir Richard Colt Hoare', *W.A.M.*, CCIX, 1961.
Shenstone, William	*Works* (1773).

——	*Letters*, ed. M. Williams (1939).
Siren, O.	*China and the Gardens of Europe in the Eighteenth Century* (New York, 1950).
Skinner, John	*Journal of a Somerset Rector*, Coombs, H. and Bax, A. N. ed. (1930).
Smith, J. E.	*A Sketch of a Tour on the Continent* (1807).
Somerset Archaeological Society	Proceedings of, XCVI, 1951.
Spence, Joseph	*Anecdotes*, ed. James M. Osborn (Oxford, 1966).
Stroud, Dorothy	*Capability Brown* (1950, rev. ed. 1957).
Stukeley, William	*Stonehenge* (1740).
Stukeley, William	*Abury* (1743).
——	*Itinerarium Curiosum* (1724).
Summerson, Sir John	*Architecture in Britain 1530–1830* (Harmondsworth, 1953, rev. eds. 1955 and 1963).
Sutton, Denys	'An Eighteenth Century Artist rediscovered', *Country Life*, June 1960.
Swinburne, Henry	*Travels in the Two Sicilies* (1785).
Thomson, James	*Poetical Works* (1908, 1956 ed.).
Virgil	*The Aeneid*, trans. W. F. Jackson Knight (Harmondsworth, 1958).
Walpole, Horace	'Visits to Country Seats', *Walpole Society*, XVI, 1927–8.
——	'On Modern Gardening', *Anecdotes of Painting* (1786).
Waterhouse, E. K.	*Painting in Britain 1530–1790* (1962).
——	'English Painting and France in the Eighteenth Century', *Journal W.C.I.*, XV, 1952.
Watson, Steven	*The Reign of George III* (Oxford, 1960).
Webb, M. I.	*Michael Rysbrack* (1954).
Wesley, John	*Journal*, ed. N. Curnock (1909).
Whately, Thomas	*Observations on Modern Gardening* (1770).
Whitley, W. T.	*Artists and their friends in England 1700–1799* (London and Boston, 1928).
——	*Art in England 1800–1820* (Cambridge, 1928).
Wigstead, Henry	*Tour to North and South Wales* (1800).
Willey, Basil	*The Seventeenth Century Background* (1962).
——	*The Eighteenth Century Background* (1962).
Williams, Basil	*The Whig Supremacy* (Oxford, 1962).
Williams, I. A.	*Early English Watercolours* (1952).
Willis, Peter	Charles Bridgeman: Royal Gardener. Unpublished Ph.D. thesis, Cambridge University, 1962.
Wittkower, Rudolf	*Architectural Principles in the Age of Humanism* (1949, 1952, ed.).
Woodbridge, K.	'Henry Hoare's Paradise', *Art Bulletin*, XLVII, Mar. 1965.
——	'The Sacred Landscape', *Apollo*, Sept. 1968.

Woodforde, D. H., ed.   *Woodforde Papers and Diaries* (1932).

Woodward, Sir Llewellyn   *The Age of Reform* (Oxford, 1962).

Wordsworth, William   *Works*, ed. Selincourt (Oxford, 1940–9).

Wraxall, Sir Nathaniel   *Historical Memoirs* (1815).

Young, Arthur   *Travels in France and Italy, during the years 1787, 1788 and 1789* (Bury St. Edmunds, 1792–4), (Everyman, 1906).

Ziff, Jerold   'J. M. W. Turner on Poetry and Painting', *Studies in Romanticism*, III, 4, 1964.

Index

In this index two groups of entries for related subjects have been brought together under the headings *Antiquities* and *Painters and Paintings*. Page numbers followed by the letter n refer to footnotes. An asterisk (*) preceding the title of a painting indicates that the painting was, and, in some cases, still is, at Stourhead.